YORK

EDITED BY ALEXANDRA F. JOHNSTON
AND MARGARET ROGERSON

Appendixes
Translations
End-notes
Glossaries
Indexes

MANCHESTER UNIVERSITY PRESS

© University of Toronto Press 1979
Toronto Buffalo London
Printed in Canada

Published in Great Britain by
Manchester University Press

Library of Congress Cataloging in Publication Data

Main entry under title:

York. 2

(Records of Early English Drama)
Bibliography: p.
Includes indexes.
1. Performing arts – England – York – History –
Sources. 2. English drama – England – York – History
and criticism – Sources. 3. York plays. 4. York, Eng. –
History – Sources. I. Johnston, Alexandra F., 1939-
II. Rogerson, Margaret. III. Series.
PN2596.Y6Y6   790.2'09428'43   78-14756

ISBN 0 – 7190 – 0767 – 4

The research and typesetting costs of Records of Early
English Drama have been underwritten by the Social
Sciences and Humanities Research Council of Canada.

RECORDS OF EARLY ENGLISH DRAMA

VOLUME 2

Records of Early English Drama

Contents

VOLUME 1

ACKNOWLEDGMENTS vii

INTRODUCTION
York and National Events ix
Civic Government x
Craft Guilds and Religious Guilds xiii
Principles of Selection xv
The Documents xvii
Editorial Procedures xlii

SELECT BIBLIOGRAPHY xlvii

THE RECORDS 1

VOLUME 2

FRONTISPIECE: Map of York 1610,
after Speed

APPENDIXES
I
Undated Ordinances from
A/Y Memorandum Book 617
II
Inventories of the Guilds of
Corpus Christi, 1416-1546 628

III
Pater Noster Guild Returns,
1388-9 645
IV
Alleged Letter from Henry VIII
concerning a St Thomas Play 649
V
Pageant Masters of the Mercers'
Guild, 1488-1590 651
VI
Pageants in the Corpus
Christi Play 657

TRANSLATIONS
The Records 687
Appendix I 841
Appendix II 851
Appendix III 863

END-NOTES 867

ABBREVIATIONS 888

GLOSSARIES 889
Latin 891
Anglo-Norman 907
English 911

INDEXES 929
Subject 930
Place & Name 946

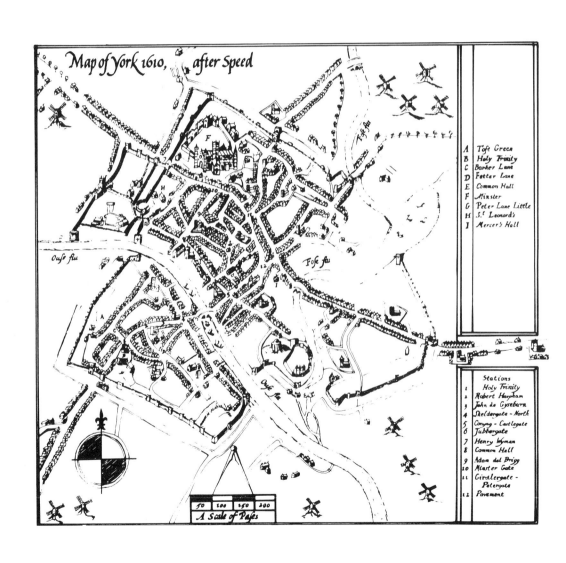

Map of York 1610, after Speed

A   Tofe Green
B   Holy Trinity
C   Barker Lane
D   Fetter Lane
E   Common Hall
F   Minster
G   Peter Lane Little
H   St Leonard's
I   Mercer's Hall

Ouse flu
Fofe flu
Tofe flu
Ouse flu

A Scale of Pafes

Stations
1   Holy Trinity
2   Robert Harpham
3   John de Gyseburn
4   Skeldergate - North
5   Coynng - Castlegate
6   Jubbergate
7   Henry Wyman
8   Common Hall
9   Adam del Brigg
10 Alaster Gate
11 Girdlergate -
    Petergate
12 Pavement

Undated Ordinances from A/Y Memorandum Book

f 10v

...

[Item ordeigné est & establi par commune assent des Pestours   5
Deuerwyk que nul de lour Artifice des ore en auaunt vende nul
roundel ne Escu de [⟨...⟩] payn demayn A nul Regratir de payn
pur mettre a vent sur peyne de demy marc A paier eut xl d. a la
Chaumbre et xl d. a la Pagyne des ditz Pestours de Corpore
Christi]   10

...

f 19   *Glovers*

Ordinaciones cerotecariorum

... En primes endroit del primer constitucion qil soit tenu en   15
ceste fourme cestassauoir que desorenauaunt chescun homme du
dit Artifice qui occupiera come mestre en lour mistre qil paiera
a son comencement iij s. iiij d al chaumbre du Mairaltee & al
sustentacion del lumer de corpore christi du dit Artifice v s.
Item que desorenauaunt nul Mestre du dit Artifice tiendra   20
ouerte sa shopp pur monstrer ne vendrer ceo qaffiert a son mistre
en les dymenches forspris en le fest du Pentecost / les comunes
foyrs et del fest de seint Pier Aduincula tantque al fest de seint
Michel donques prochein / sur peyne de xx d apaier a chescun
forfaiture al dite chaumbre du Mairaltee et al dit lumer de /   25
corpore christi xx d
Item que nul mestre du dit Artifice resceyuera ou mettera
ascun Apprentice / a ouuerer par task le prochein ann apres
son terme dapprentice soit passe deuaunt qil soit lowe par
vn an entier oue / ascun Mestre du dit Artifice & soit troue   30
sufficeant & able pur ouerer en lour mistre sur peyne de iij s.

iiij d appaier / al Chaumbre du Mairaltee suis⟨..⟩ & au dit lumer
de corpore chr*ist*i iij s. iiij d

f 20v

...   5

les ordinaunces des Chaundelers

...

Primerment q*ue* chescun mestre qi viendra pur occupier le dit
artifice qil soit approue sufficeant & sacheant p*ur* oue*r*er &
occupier en le dit artifice et qil paiera au comencement quant   10
il p*r*imes tendra shoppe & occupiera come mestra vj s viij d
Cestassauoir lune moite al oeps du dit artifice p*ur* mayntenir
lo*ur* dit pagyne & laut*r*e moite a la chaumbre du counseil al oeps
& p*r*ofit de la Co*mmu*nialtee de la Citee aua*u*ntdite
...   15

f 21

Escriueners de Text

...

Et q*ue* nul du dit artifice face au contraire de ceste ordina*u*nce en   20
ascun poyint suisdit il paiera xx s. des*t*erlinges cest assauoir x s. a
la Chaumb*r*e du counseil & x s. al oeps de lo*ur* pagyne & lumer
app*ar*tenance a lo*ur* dit artifice
...

                                                                               25

f 22

Pelt*e*res

...

·Skynners· Primerment q*ue* touz les forfaito*ur*es q*ui* sount duez en le dit
Artifice & sount auenirs soient leuez & lune moite dycelles paye   30
a la Chaumbre de counseil & lautre moite al dit artifice p*ur*
mayntener lo*ur* pagyne & lo*ur* lumer
...

It*e*m q*ue* touz Gentz Vphalders q*ui* vendont furure*r*s deinez ciu
dite cite ou les s*u*burbes soient contributo*ur*s appaier a lo*ur*   35
pagyne de corpore chr*ist*i

    It*e*m si aucun du dit artifice soit rebell ou ⌃'distourbe' medie
ou disobeie a lez Sercho*ur*s ou a lez Pagent Meistres de mesme
lartifice q*ui* serront po*ur* le temps faisantz duement lo*ur* office qil
paiera vj s viij d lune moite a la chambre & lautre al dit artifice   40
p*ur* maintenir lour pagyne & lo*ur* lumer ...

9 sacheant] *over erasure*   10 au] *over erasure*

f 22v

Adhuc de Bowers

...

Item que si ascun du dit artifice preigne apprentice en le dit art il
paiera a son primer entree al oeps de lour pagyne iij s iiij d   5

...

f 23

The Skynners Ordnance   10

In primis it is ordeynd that all þe fforfetes þat heraftre shall falle
and be due shalbe enployed þat oon half to þe Chaumbre and þat
oþer half to þe craft to þe supporting of þeier pageant and oþere
chargez   15

...

Item þat euery vphaldster þat sellis eny ffurrez within þis Citie
or þe suburbez of þe same shalbe contributory and pay unto þe
pagent of þe Skynners in þe playe of Corpus Cristi

...   20

f 26
les Ordinances des Couuereours Eadem in nouo registro

A lour honurable seignour Meir de la Citee Deuerwyk suppliount   25
humblement si pleser vous soit considre le poure estate del
artifice des Couuereours de la dite Citee coment ils sount chargez
ouesqez vne pagyne a tresgraundes costages & Importables qar ils
sount pluis pousez gentz & poures qils soleient estre auaunt ces
hures & soleient auoir autre suppoiale & eide pur sustiner lour   30
dit pagyne auaunt ces hures Cestassauoir de chescun apprentice
du dit artifice a son primer entree al dit artifice xij d et de
chescun seruant qi prist lower en le dit artifice chescun an iiij d
dount ils suppliont si pleiser vous soit qe desormes nul apprentice
soit pris en le dit artifice pur meyndre terme ne pur pluis long qe   35
pur vj annz & qil paiera en son entre en tout ij s. Cestassauoir
xij d al oeps de lour dite pagyne & xij d a la Chaumbre de Counseil
Et chescun seruant par an iiij d al oeps de lour dit pagyne come
soleit estre auaunt ces hures
    Item qe chescun mestre quaunt il soit enfraunchese & hauntera   40
lartifice primerment come mestre qil paiera al oeps du dite
pagyne xl d

...

f 26v*

Les ordinances des Coupers

A lour treshonurable & tresreuerent seignour Meir de la Citee
deuerwyk Suppliont treshumblement voz poures conciteinz les   5
Coupers deuerwyk qe come ils ount tresgraund charge a lours
poures estates pur sustiner & mateigner lour pagyne & Iue de y
ceste iour de copore christi desicome lour artifice & eux mesmes
sont trespoures gentz si bien destate come dauoir & dedeinz
brief lour est moult enpaire et auxint les Iunours qestoient   10
ouesqez eux pur sustiner la dit pagyne sont oustez de eux Qe
please a votre tresbountinouse seignourie en amendement de
lour dit artifice ordeigner & suffrer estre registre deuaunt vous qe
qiconqez qi desormes fait leuer nouelle shoppe & comence
doccupier come mestre en la dite Citee paia a son comencement   15
vj s ˹viij d˺ lune moite al Chaumbre du mairaltee & lautre
moite a lours sercheours du dit artifice pur sustiner lour pagyne
auauntdite & ceo en complisement de charitee
    Item ordeigne est par touz les Artificers del Coupercraft
suisdite qe chescun homme de mesme lartifice qi face ascun   20
oueraigne ou fait faire en mesme lartifice et le dit oueraigne soit
troue fausement oeuere par les Sercheours de mesme lartifice
qil forfetra les deniers qensuent cest assauoir pur vn Sea noun
duement fait xij d et de chescun Autre veseil de mesme le price
xij d. sil soit troue fauty en merisme ou en oueraigne celly qi   25
le fist ou fist faire paiera les xij d lun moite a la Chaumbre du
mairaltee sur le Pont de Ouse et lautre moite al supportacion de
lour pagyne du Corpore christi
    …

                                                                      30

f 29v*   *Barbers*
[Item que ceaux que sount aliens ou autres estraunges vsent fisyk
ou surgerie deinz la Citee & preignent auauntage pur lours
affaires qils soient contributours a sustener & mayntener lour
dite pagyne & lour lumer sur peyne de vj s viij d a paier en la   35
fourme suisdite
    Item si ascun rebel du dit artifice pur venir a lour assemble pur

[quia infra
folio lxxij^{do}]

ordeigner necessarie purueaunce pur lour pagine lumer ou autre
ordeignaunce lisible & honest affaire par couenable garnishment
sinon qil est resonable excusacion il paiera vne liuere de cire   40

8 copore] *for* corpore

a lo*ur* lumer]

...

f 30

   Ceux sount les ordeigna*u*nces des Capmakers Deu*er*wyk   5

...

Item q*ue* celui ou ceux es queux maynes tiele man*er*e de faux
oeure soit trouee chescun foithe soit am*er*cie a iij s dount ij s
s*er*ront leuez al oeps [d⟨....⟩] ˹de˺ *commu*nialte de la dite Citee
& xij d al oeps del pagyne des Capmakers aua*u*ntditz ...   10

f 30v

       Cardemakers

As hon*u*rable Seigno*ur*s & sages Meir & Aldermans de la Citee 15
Deu*er*wyk monstrent si pleiser vous soit les voz simples veisynes
de la *Commu*nialtee de la Citee aua*u*ntdite Ioh*a*n Baker Ioh*a*n
de Burton Willi*a*m Orgoner Thomas Iuno*ur* Willi*a*m de Bredon
Rob*er*t de Houeden Hen*re* del Chirche Cardmakers & les autres
Mestres del Artifice des Cardmakers de la dite Citee p*ur commu*ne 20
p*ro*fit en relief & eide de lo*ur* dite Artifice qest en poynt dep*er*ir
p*ar* malueis gentz qount fuez & se retretz hors de la dite Citee
ouesq*ez* biens & chateux des autr*es* loialx gentz dount p*ar*
vost*re* sage auys & counseil due remedy poet estre mys celle
p*ar*tie p*ur* temps auenir si pleiser vous soit 25
  Cestassauoir q*ue* nul tiel estra*u*nge q*ui* soit fuy ˄ ˹ou venu˺ des
foreins lieux soit mys p*ur* oue*r*er en le dit Artifice vltre deux
io*ur*s saunz ces qil eit sufficeant recorde p*ur* lui p*ar* *let*tr*es* de
south seal autentik de sa conu*er*sacion & de ˹sa˺ bone fame ou
qil p*ur*ra trouer sufficeantz plegges a maynep*re*ner p*ur* lui & p*ur* 30
ses faitz *sur* peyne de vj s viij d appaier a la chaumbre & autres
vj s viij d al pagyne de lo*ur* dite Artifice: p*ar* celui q*ui* s*er*ra troue
faisaunt a cont*r*arie de ceste ordeigna*u*nce

...

                35
f 31*

    The ordenaunce of the crafte of Cardemakers

In p*ri*mis that na straunger that ys fled or co*m*myn fra straunge
places be set in Werk in the cardemakercrafte ouer twa days bot 40
yf that he hafe sufficeant recorde for hym be letters vnder sele
auctentyke of hys conu*er*sacion and of hys gud*e* fame / or ellys

that he may fynde sufficiant plegges to vndertake for hym and
for hys dedys of payne of vj. s viij. d to be payde to the chambre
and other vj s. viij d. to the pageant of thair crafte be hym that
sall be funden doyng the contrary of this ordenaunce / ... Item
that he that sall make any fals Werk and vncouenable in the   5
sayde / crafte sall pay at ylk a tyme that he makes any slyke
defaute xl d. vnto / the Chambre and xl d. to the pageant ...

f 32

[Tannours Gaunters Parchemyners   10

...

Par ont ordeigne est que chescuny des ditz Artificers que
desormes atchate ascun peaux laynuz as ditz Bouchers sinoun qils
eient lours orailles chiefs et leyns a y celles entierement afferauntz
qil paia pur chescun forfaitour dont est attentz iij s. iiij d. al   15
Chaumbre du meiraltee et autres iij s. iiij d. al sustentacion du
lumer de corpore Christi del artifice de celui en quy default serra
trouez]

...

                    20

                    f 33v
Pynnercraft   En primes ordeigne est & assentu que nul mestre del artifice de
Pynnercraft desormes receyue ne teigne nul homme estraunge du
dit Artifice pur ouer⟨..⟩ ouesqez luy sinoun qil soit mys al dit
artifice pur seruir en manere dapprentice come affiert dauncien   25
vsage & custume & sicome est vse en la Citee de loundres des
vagarauntz & vacabundes & en autres Citees du roialme sur peyne
de forfaitoure de xl d a la Chaumbre de counseil & xl d a la
sustenance de lour pagyne del artifice auntdit ...

                    30

f 34

Sellarij

... Primerment si nul debat de chose tochaunt lour Artifice y soit
entre Ascun del Artifice auauntdit / celui qui se sentera greuee ou   35
molestee monstera sa greuence as mesters du dit Artifice & iles
ordeigneront dument redresse solunc ceo que les semblera mieult
de bone foi & reson & celui qui serra troue rebel ou a contrary

29 auntdit] for auauntdit

celle partie paiera as Sersours & Gouernours du dit Artifice ∧ 'pur
supportteller la pagyne de corpore christi' x s et v s al commun
Chaumbre du Mair & communialtee de la citee Deuerwyk ...

ff 45-5v   *Dyers*   5
[Item que chescun que desore comence primerment destre
Meistre en la dite Arte a son comencement paye a les Meistres du
pagyne du dite Arte al oeps del pagyne et a la Chaumbre du Meir
de la Citee xx s par owels porciouns | Item que chescun apprentice
que serra fait & resceu au dite Arte desore en auaunt paie a son   10
entree al dite Arte al oeps del pagyne & a la Chaumbre xx s
...
Item acorde & ordeigne est par toutz les Meistres suisditz que
celui / que freynt ou face forfaiture en ascuns des Articles
suisnomez & de ceo soit atteynt par quatre Meistres de la dite   15
Arte serra tenuz de paier maytenant a les ditz Meistres de lour
dite pagyne que serrount pur le temps ⌐&¬ a la Chaumbre
auauntdite xx s]
...
                                                                           20
f 51v

Cuttellers

... A chescun foitz que ensy soit conuict il paiera xl d lun moite
A le Chaumber du counseill du meiraltee & lautre moite Al   25
supportacion de lour pagyne de corpore christi ...

f 58v

Potters
...   30
En primes si ascun seruant du dite artifice soit troue oue larcyn a
la valu de vj d ou oultre que adonques nulle Meistre du dite
artifice lui dorra nul oueraigne pur oeuere sur peyne de xx s
appaiers al Chaumbre du Meiralte al oeps des communes & al
sustentacion del pagent de corpore christi du dite Artifice par   35
owels porcions
...

2 corpore] *in similar hand but different ink*

f 64

Peyntourz Stanours Goldbetours

...

In primis ordeigne est & purueu que touz les Meisters & Artificers
suisditez par lour commune assent assemblent en la demaigne   5
prochein apres le fest du Pasque chescun an pur eslier lours
Sercheours pur lan auenir & ordeigne pur lour pagent de corpore
christi & autres choises affaire busoignable pur la gouernaunce
ᴧ ʹdu dit pagentʹ et que nul se absentera celle temps sauns
resonable cause sur la peyn de vj s viij d appaierz lun moite a la   10
Chaumbre & lautre a lour Artifice pur la supportacion de lours
dit pagent

...

Item que si ascun homme dautre Artifice occupie & vse a oeuerer
en les Artifices suisditz oue pensel pur fylour ou ascunes maneres   15
des colours sil soit fraunchise qil paie al pagaunt des ditz Artificers
et sil ne soit fraunchise que lui fraunchise et paie a mesme le
pagaunt sur la auauntdite peyn chescune foith qil soit atteynte.

f 76   *Cordwainers*   20

...

Et eciam pro eo quod artifices predicti annuatim portant graues
expensas & onera magna pagine sue & multorum ludencium in
eadem necnon torchearum magne pulcritudinis in processione
diei corporis ac in monasterio beati petri Ebor' ac aliarum   25
expensarum plus quam certi alij diuersorum artificiorum . Ideo
petunt & humiliter supplicant quod eis concedatur & ordinari
possit in releuamen grauium onerum & expensarum suorum sicut
Tapitarij huius ciuitatis habent ex recordo & irrotulamento hic in
camera videlicet quod quilibet Scotus & alius alienigena qui natus   30
non erat in regno & terra anglie ad istam ciuitatem veniens &
occupauerit vt magister in arte predicta Cordewanariorum quod
in prima occupacione sua soluat quadraginta ᴧ ʹsolidosʹ vsui
communitatis huius ciuitatis & alios xl s arti de les Cordewaners
predicte applicandos   35

...

f 77v   *Cordwainers*

...

Item quod si aliquis artis predicte electus fuerit ad aliquod   40

---

8 busoignable ... gouernaunce] *over erasure*   25 corporis] Christi *omitted*

officium in arte illa siue fuerit scrutatoris aut magistri fraternitatis
aut alicuius quatuor magistrorum occupancium pro pagina &
lumine corporis christi aut pro occupacione aliquarum aliarum
materiarum pertinencium virtute alicuius officij ad bonum
regimen & regulam artis predicte et recusauerit aut contradixerit   5
vel restiterit illud super se assumere & perficere quod tunc perdet
& soluet in forma predicta x s sterlingorum

...

f 90*   10

Ordinaciones Barbitonsorum

In primis ordinatum est de vnanimi consensu & plena voluntate
omnium magistrorum artificij barbitonsorum huius ciuitatis
Ebor' quod nullus eorum occupet nec operetur rem aliquam vel   15
aliquod opus arti sue pertinentia aliquo die dominico nisi tantum
fleubotamando homines in infirmitatibus constitutos. seu alias
curas & medicinas infirmis faciendo / & si aliquis presumpserit
contrarium facere huius constitucionis pro vice qualibet soluet
vj s viij .d. vsui & proficuo communitatis & supportacioni pagine   20
& onerum predicti artificij equis porcionibus applicandos
    Item quod omnes alienigene & extranei quicumque fuerint
exercentes phisicam vel artem sirurgie infra ciuitatem istam qui
mercedem aliquam pro facto suo recipient sint annuatim
contributorij ad sustinendum & manutenendum predictam   25
paginam barbitonsorum lumenque suum & alia onera eorumdem
sub pena vj s viij d modo quo premittitur applicandorum
    Item si aliquis artificij predicti rebellis fuerit & venire
recusauerit ad congregaciones suas faciendas pro necessaria
ordinacione & prouisione pagine sue & luminis sui vel alterius   30
ordinacionis cuiuscumque artis sue lictis & honestis cum fuerit
competenter premunitus nisi racionabilem excusacionem
ostenderit perdet & solvet ad sustentacionem luminis dicti
Artificij iij s. iiij d. tociens quociens culpabilis fuerit in hoc ⟨...⟩
Camere et arti soluendos   35

...

f 90v

...

Item quod Scrutatores & magistri pagine dicte Artis eligentur   40

34 ⟨...⟩] dictis

quo*libet* anno die lune pro*ximo* post festu*m* Natiuitatis S*an*cti
Ioh*ann*is Bapt*iste* et eode*m* die lune Scrutatores Anni pre*cedentis*
compotu*m* suu*m* mag*is*tris artis pre*dicte* tu*n*c ib*ide*m presentibus
de om*n*ibus rebus illo anno pre*c*edenti contingentibus sub pena
iij s. iiij d p*r*out sup*er*ius specificat*ur* de illis qui non veniu*n*t cu*m*   5
pre*muniti* fu*er*int forisfaciend*orum* dict*is* Art*i* et Cam*ere*

...

ff 128v-9*

...   10

Ordinac*i*o de piscib*us* vendendis infra ciuitatem Ebor'

ffyshemong*ers* | In p*r*imis it ys ordaynd be the assent of the mair*e* Shirefs Aldermen
and C*om*mons of the Citee of York*es* þ*a*t na man na woman
occupie or dele wyth the Craft*e* of ffysshmangers bot thay   15
alleanly þ*a*t deles wyth na nother crafts that ys to say nouther
Cardemakers Taillo*ur*s Cordewaners Sadelers ne none other
maner*e* of crafty man of what condicion so eu*er* he be bot if he
com*m*e and com*m*one wyth the Sersours of the fysshemang*er*
craft þ*a*t are or*e* sall be for the tyme so þ*a*t he may be knawen   20
for honest bathe [bithe] to þe citee and to the crafte be forsayd
And þ*a*t he pay at hys entre xx s. þ*a*t is to say xiij s iiij d. to the
chaumbre and vj s and viij. d to the crafte and ⸢do⸣ all other
custumes and dewtees þ*a*t p*er*tiens to the same crafte | the whilk
vj s viij d. so to the crafte to be payd / sall be keped to the vse   25
and rep*er*acion of thayr*e* pagent and to vpholde and releve ∧⸢of⸣
a lyght to be borne befor*e* goddys body on corpus cristy day

...
Ista pe*n*a xx s moderata est in t*em*po*r*e Will*elm*i Bowes maioris
ad vj s. viij d camere & xl d. arti penes illos q*ui* non su*n*t tene*n*tes   30
commu*n*itat*is* apud ponte*m* fosse / ad volu*n*tatem maioris, &
q*u*oad tene*n*tes com*mu*nitat*is* ⟨...⟩ pro nobis xl d. camere sint in
grac*i*a maior*is* & q*u*od contentent arte*m* de xl d†

f 283   35
Cuuryours plus inde in alio libro sup*er* xxj fol*io* cu*m* fol*io*
sup*er*filat*o*

Reuerendo domino suo Maiori huius Ciuitatis Ebor'. Om*n*es

---

1 post] *MS* post post   4 illo] *over erasure*
5 illis] *over erasure*

® iste
ordinaciones de
novo
corriguntur alij
ordinaciones
novas istis
apponuntur
tempore Edw
ffawcett
maioris

magistri de la Curyour craft istius ciuitatis eorum pauperem
statum considerare & qualiter annuatim onerantur cum pagina in
ludo Corporis christi & alijs oneribus eis quasi importabilibus &
eis graciose concedere quod nullus artificij predicti capiat aliquem
Apprenticium in arte predicta pro minore termino quam sex   5
annorum sub pena vj s. viij d. camere consilij ciuitatis & arti
predicte ad sustentacionem pagine sue equis porcionibus
soluendorum per magistrum qui contrarium fecerit & sub pena
forisfacture Apprenticij contra formam istius ordinacionis
capiende Et quod quilibet magister artis predicte statim cum   10
aliquem apprenticium acceperit soluat pro illo in primo introitu
suo .xij d. camere predicte & alios xij d arti predicte

Item quod quilibet seruiens in arte predicta conducendus &
mercedem vel salarium recipiens soluat annuatim iiij d magistris
pagine predicte si fuerit apprenticius ad artem illam in Ciuitate   15
predicta et si non fuerit apprenticius soluat annuatim ad paginam
predictam .viij. d.

Item quod quilibet / seruiens qui bene & fideliter seruiuit
magistro suo in arte predicta per sex annos vel amplius secundum
terminum inter eos concordatum soluat / in prima leuacione   20
shoppe sue iij s. iiij d pro sustentacione pagine predicte Et / si
aliquis extraneus venerit / ad Ciuitatem ad occupandum artem
predictam & non fuit apprenticius in arte predicta in ciuitate
predicta quod soluat / vj s. viij d. camere consilij predicti & vj s.
viij d. ad sustentacionem pagine sue ad primam leuacionem   25
shoppe

...

Inventories of the Guilds of Corpus Christi, 1416-1546

The properties belonging to the Guild which were used in the Corpus Christi procession and in the Creed Play have been included in the main body of the text. The possessions of the Guild were inventoried from time to time and provide a fuller picture of the wealth of the Guild and the relation of the procession and play properties to the rest of the property. The five inventories range from an early list (1416) to the description of the shrine made by the royal commissioners in 1546. They are here reproduced in their entirety.

1416   Y : C99:1

mb 1d

Ornamenta & vtensilia fraternitatis.

Item ijdem Custodes respondent de decem torcheis pertinentibus dicte fraternitati ob reuerenciam Corporis christi

Summa torchearum .x.

Signa

Et de Sex signis depictis cum calicibus ponendis super sex torcheas coram defunctis

Summa signorum vj.

Castella.

Et de decem Castellis depictis. cum decem paruis pokettis de Cannevas pro eisdem cooperiendis

Summa Castellorum .x.

Vexilla.

Et de xl. vexillis depictis. cum j poket de Canuas pro eisdem includend*is* cu*m* papiris

Sum*m*a vexillor*um* .xl.

Sanapp*e*   Et de x. Sanapp*is* de Canuas p*ro* portaci*one* dictor*um* dece*m*   5
torch*earum* in processione Corp*or*is christ*i*

Sum*m*a sanap*parum* .x.

Roundelet*tes*   Et de iij. duodenis instrumentis ligneis s*cilice*t Roundelet*es* p*ur*   10
le Reuet*tes* sup*er*ponend*is*

Su*m*ma Roundelet*tes* xxx. vj.

Reuet*tes.*   Et de xl. Reuet*tes* recept*is* de p*re*decessorib*us*   15
Et de xl. Reuet*tes* nouis emptis

Ciphi.   Et de lx. & viij. Ciphis ligneis inueteratis debilib*us* & liquore*m*
no*n* continentib*us*
Et de [xx]iiij. ciphis nouis empt*is*.   20

Su*m*ma ciphor*um* nouor*um* [xx]iiij.

Mappe.   Et de j. mappa mensali linea cont*inente* in longitud*ine* xiiij vl*n*as.
Et de ij. mapp*is* mensal*ibus* quar*um* vtraque cont*in*et in   25
long*itudine* xiij. vl*n*as
Et de ij. mapp*is* mensal*ibus* quar*um* vtraque cont*in*et in
long*itudine* x. vl*n*as
Et de j. mappa mensal*i* de op*e*re Twill cont*inente* in long*itudine*
(blank) ex dono d*om*ini Will*el*mi de Neuton   30
Towell.   Et de j. Towell listed de op*e*re Twill. cont*inente* in long*itudine*
xiiij vl*n*as ex dono Ioh*anni*s lee & vx*o*ris eius

Su*m*ma mappar*um* vj.

     35
Naprons.   Et de vj. naprons panni linei pro principalib*us*

Su*m*ma naprons .vj.

Cacabus.   Et de j. magno Cacabo dat*o* p*er* Oliuam de Cotyngham   40

Su*m*ma Cacab*orum* .j.

Olle eree

Et de j. magna olla erea . data per Aliciam de Welton .
Et de j. magna olla erea data per dominum Iohannem Crome
nuper vicarium in choro ecclesie Ebor'
Et de j. olla erea data per Margaretam Sowreby non recipitur quia
vt supra

    Summa ollarum erearum .iij.

Vasa stannea

Et de vj. duodenis vasorum ⌜stanneorum⌝ garnest. & .j. disco .&.
ij. chariours
Et de dimidio duodeni vasorum stanneorum ex legato Beatricis
lathom

    Summa vasorum stanneorum .vj. duodeni
    & di. garnest .j. discus
    & ij. chariours.

Salers

Et de xviij. salers pro sale de pultro

    Summa salars .xviij.

Sanappe purgative

Et de ij Canuas Sanappis pro mundacione vasorum

    Summa .ij.

Chaplettes

Et de vj. Chaplettes cum .vj. alijs Scripturis paruis . cum
racionibus pro eleccione principalium

    Summa Chaplettes vj.

libri ordinacionum

Et de ij. libris. vno de veteri ordinacione. & alio de noua cum
nominibus inscriptis

    Summa librorum ij.

Lettere indulgenciarum

Et de ij letteris indulgenciarum vna de Archiepiscopo Ebor' & alia
de Episcopo Karliel

    Summa letterarum ij.

Arche.

Et de ij. archis & seris pro vtensilibus inde conseruandis

    Summa archarum ij.

Pecia argenti   Et de j. pecia argenti ex dono domini Ricardi Arowis quondam
vicario ecclesie sancte Marie Super Bischophill

Summa peciarum j.

Ciphi murre   Et de j. cipho murre argento ornato ex dono Agnetis Wyman.

Summa j.

Coclearia   Et de ij. coclearibus argenteis Receptis de domino Thoma Tanfeld   10
vicario pro introitu suo.

Summa .ij.

1449-51 Y: C99:3   15

mb 1

...

Vnde compotant dicti Custodes & petunt allocacionem Et primo
de expensis & solucionibus factis super feretrum argenteum cum   20
pertinencijs videlicet de vno Iocali argenteo & deaurato vocato le
broche in sumitate campaniles posito Item in tectura &
cooperacione iiij^or parcium eiusdem feretri vocatarum Ilez siue
roves cum argento deaurato vna cum ornatura & venustacione
lateris borientis eiusdem feretri cum monilibus & anulis aureis &   25
argenteis Item de vno cooperturio argento deaurato pro magno
berillo siue cristallo vocato mustrance ordinato & per Iohannem
Stultyng operato prout simul patent in pondere auri & argenti
deaurationi iiij lib. vj vnc. iij quart. & di. debity precium le vnc.
v. s. summa xiij li. ix s. iiij d ob. Et pro melioracione cuiusdem   30
Iocalis continentis reliquias sanctorum scilicet cum vno pede
rotundo argenti & deaurati pondere vnius vnc. & di. precium vij s.
vj d cum vno lapide cristallino in medio iocali posito precium iij s
iiij d Et de vno Iocali argenteo deaurato pro le Bedall in signum
fraternitatis ordinato & per eundem I. Stultyng operato ad   35
formam duorum angelorum genuflectancium in tabernaculo &
supportancium calicem cum hostia ad honorem corporis christi
quasi in presencia patris & filij & spiritus sancti .prout patet in
pondere viij vnc. & l quart. precium le vnc. v s. summa xli s. iij d
Et de ij Imaginibus maioribus scilicet Petri & Pauli de argento   40
deauratis cum xxiiij alijs Imaginibus argenteis & anameld .

22 campaniles] *for* campanilis

op*eratis* p*er* Georgium Wylardby pro*ut* patent sim*ul* in pond*er*e
viij vnc. iij qu*art*. & di. p*re*cium le vnc. xxx d *summ*a xxij s. ij d
It*e*m sol. eid*e*m Georgio p*ro* cuiuslibet Imag*inis* op*e*racio*n*e xvj d
*summ*a xxxiiij s. viij d Et de vno tabernac*ul*o aur*e*o prius recept*o*
de stauro & hic ad feretru*m* posit*o* p*re*cium xv s. Et de vno anulo
aur*e*o cu*m* saphiro ib*ide*m affixo p*re*cium xx s. Et de vno al*io*
anulo aur*e*o cu*m* j perll ib*ide*m affixo p*re*cium iiij s. Et de vno
monile aur*e*o quond*am* ex dono dompni I. Castell p*re*cium v s.
Et de j monile aur*e*o ex leg*atione* Ioh*ann*e Nalton p*re*cium xj s.
iiij d Et de vno monile arg*e*nt*e*o deaur*ato* ib*ide*m fixo p*re*cium
ij s. vj d Et de j lapide p*re*cioso voc*ato* adamond ib*ide*m fixo
p*re*cium x s Et de j serkelett arg*e*nt*e*o sumpt*o* de stauro &
feret*ro* fixo p*re*cium vj s. viij d Et de viij torch*e*is hoc anno de
nouo fact*is* p*re*cium xxviij s vj d Et de iij lib. cere in cereis
ardent*ibus* circa feretru*m* in f*e*sto corp*ori*s christi & mo*d*o in
capella S*an*cti Will*e*lmi in obit*ibus* gen*er*alibus p*er* annu*m*
p*re*cium ij s. Et de j torch*e*a p*ri*us recept*a* ad stauru*m* posita
p*re*cium iij s iiij d Et de v duss*ans* ciphis nouis hoc anno empt*is*
p*re*cium iij s. iiij d Et de vasis de pultro hoc anno ordinat*is* &
renouat*is* vid*e*lic*et* iij duss*ans* dublers iiij duss*ans* dissches
ij duss*ans* saucers cu*m* xx^ti salt salerz p*re*cium xvij s. Et de vna
cista noua p*ro* feretro in secret*o* deferend*o* & securo custodiend*o*
p*re*cium vij s. ij d Et de vno Instrumento q*u*adrato de Wayscot
ordinat*o* p*ro* feretro s*er*uando ab vmectate & pluuia vna cu*m* iiij
lanciol*is* & al*ijs* p*er*tin*e*nc*ijs* p*re*cium v s. viij d vna cu*m* batelment*es*
sup*er* le bere & xiiij al*ijs* lanciol*is* p*ro* vexill*is* Et p*ro* pictura &
coloracio*n*e eoru*m*dem xvj d Et p*ro* iiij valencez de bucasyn
color*is* blod*ij* depict*is* cu*m* calicibus aur*e*is & stell*is* aur*e*is
int*er*posit*is* cu*m* lez frengez de filis diu*er*sorum colorum p*re*cium
iiij s. viij d Et de iij vlnis de bukasyn blod*ij* color*is* pro
circumforinc*ijs* & ligatur*is* xvij vexillor*um* magnor*um* p*re*cium
xviij d Et de j panno largo & quadrato depicto cu*m* imag*in*e
S*an*cte Trinitat*is* p*ro* feretro sane defendendo p*re*cium iij s. iiij d
Et de vj garland*is* hoc anno f*a*ct*is* p*re*cium viij d Et de iij libris
cu*m* al*ijs* cedul*is* p*ro* capellan*is* in p*ro*cessione cantant*ibus* ordinat*is*
p*re*cium xij d Et de ij angel*is* depict*is* tenent*ibus* cereos p*re*dictos
in capella S*an*cti Will*e*lmi xij d Et de xx d sol. Rob*er*to Dewe p*ro*
ligatur*a* ciste p*re*dicte & clauibus ⸢iiij⸣ & ser*is* iiij^or cu*m* al*ijs*
nec*e*ssar*ijs* Et de xv vln*is* panni depict*i* cu*m* calicib*us* & script*is*.
p*re*cium iij s. vj d Et de vno alio panno depicto cu*m* Imagine

5

10

15

20

25

30

35

40

12 Et de] *MS* Et de Et de

Sancti Gregorij missam celebrantis coram Imagine christi precium
iiij s vj d Et de xxiiij reuettes de nouo emptis precium iij s. vj d
Et de vno libro anglicano prius recepto & modo ad staurum
posito cum xvij vexillis aptis & alijs viij vexillis secundarijs cum
alijs ornamentis & parcellis pro le Crede Playe ordinatis precium   5
viij ˈli.ˈ .ij.ˈs .x.ˈd Et pro ij pecys de nattez ordinatis pro
stannis tegendis in aula predicta pro honestis ibidem sedentibus
precium ix d. Item sol. cuidem femine pro factura xxvj napkyns
& pro le hemmyng pannorum predictorum iiij d Item sol. cuidam
Sissori pro fincione & le borderyng vexillorum predictorum vj d.   10

Summa xxxv li. x s. x d ob.

1465 BL: Lansdowne MS 403

15
ff 2-5v
Statutum enim extat & prouisum sano Confratrum istius Gilde
consilio vt vnusquisque nuper magister ffraternitatis & eiusdem
Custodes circa diem compoti sui liberent & committant Magistri
& custodum Successorum suorum cure ac custodie thesaurum   20
& iocalia cum ceteris bonis quibuscumque dicte Gilde
pertinentibus que subsecuntur in hunc modum. In primis
vicesimo secundo die Mensis Octobris Anno domini millesimo
CCCCmo sexagesimo quinto Dominus Willelmus Caber Rector
ecclesie sancte Helene Ebor' nuper Magister dicte Gilde simul &   25
nuper custodes eiusdem liberauerunt domino Thome Oureum
Rector ecclesie parochialis in Northstrat Ebor' tunc Magistro
dicte fraternitatis & eiusdem pro tunc custodibus iocalia
subscripta

   In primis liberatum fuit prefato domino Thome Oureum &   30
custodibus fferetrum ex argento deauratum dedicatum in honore
adorandissimi corporis christi per sacrosancte recordacionis
dominum Thomam Spoford nuper Episcopum herfordensem
vndecimo die Mensis Iinij videlicet die sancti Barnabe apostoli
Anno domini Millesimo CCCCmo quadragesimo nono. Qui   35
quidem venerabilis episcopus & pius varia iocalia & munera non
pauca vt retroactis compotis patet euidenter ad dicti sancti
fferetri edificacionem gratuite obtulit & deuote

17 Statutum … Gilde] *in display script*   30-1 In … custodibus] *in display script*
34 Iinij] *for* Iunij

Idem autem *sa*nctum fferetru*m* digne appre*c*iatur   cclvj li
Item j cristallus magna & concauata vocat*a* Mustraunce cum
duob*us* angeleis argenteis appre*c*iatur   x li vj s viij d
Item j ymago *sa*ncte Trinitat*is* in capite feretri appre*c*iatur *(blank)*
Item j tabernacu*lu*m de auro & de perle cu*m* ymagine beate marie   5
virginis ex dono d*ic*ti d*o*m*i*ni Thome ep*iscop*i herfordens*is*
appre*c*iatur   *(blank)*
Ite*m* j Magnu*m* monile deauratu*m* cu*m* lapid*ibus* blod*ij* coloris
appre*c*iatur   v s
Item aliud monile paruu*m* cu*m* quatuor folijs circa mediu*m*   10
feretri   xvj d
Item aliud monile p*a*ruu*m* cu*m* quadam scriptura
appre*c*iatur   xviij d
Item j tabernaculum de auro & de Margarita vocat*a* perle cu*m*
ymagine b*e*ate marie magdalene & cu*m* tribus anulis aureis*(blank)*   15
Ite*m* j anulus de berillo appre*c*iatur   *(blank)*
Ite*m* j agnus dei de argento deauratus cu*m* nomi*n*e iesu Item
ymago *sa*n*c*ti laurencij de arge*n*to deaurato cu*m* vno diademate
circumcepto cum margaric*is*   xvj s vj d
Item vnu*m* cocliar de argento deauratu*m* in su*m*mitate feretri   20
appre*c*ia*t*ur   iij s vj d
Item aliud cocliar de argento deauratu*m* in su*m*mitate feretri
appre*c*ia*t*ur   *(blank)*
Item vna zona circumfixa ad fundamentu*m* feretri
appre*c*iatur   *(blank)*   25
Item j pixis argenteus deauratus p*ro* spe*c*ie*bus* aromatibus
ordinat*us* appre*c*iatur   xxvj s viij d
Item j Anulus insculptus cu*m* ista scriptura In god is all
Appre*c*iatur   xl s
Ite*m* j zona argentea & plenarie stipata appre*c*iatur   xxx s iiij d   30
Item j monile aureu*m* cu*m* vno dyama*n*s appre*c*iatur   xx s
Item j tabernaculu*m* argent*e*um deauratu*m* cu*m* ymagine b*e*ate
marie in ip*s*o i*n*clusa appre*c*iatur   xij s iiij d
Item j anul*us* aureus appre*c*iatur   iiij s ij d
Item j anul*us* deauratu*s* habe*n*s lapide*m* pre*c*iosu*m*   35
appre*c*ia*t*ur   iij s
Item j Murenula aurea cu*m* cruce aurea pe*r* ea*m* dependente
appre*c*ia*t*ur   *(blank)*
Item j tabernaculu*m* argenti deauratu*m* cu*m* ymagine b*e*ate marie
virginis in ip*s*o inclusa ex auro   *(blank)*   40
Item j stake de currallo ex dono ₍^'de'₎ Robe*r*ti Wystow   *(blank)*
Item j anul*us* aureus ex dono m*a*rgare*te* Balzay   *(blank)* |

Item iij Stalkis de corallo pendent*es* sim*ul* sup*er* vn*um* ligame*n*   ij s
Item ij magni crucifixi de argento deaurat*i* c*um* ij alijs crucifixis
deaurat*is* minorib*us* insim*ul* pendent*ibus* sup*er* vn*um* ligame*n* &
c*um* ij monilib*us* de argento c*um* j bede de berillo   *(blank)*
Item j nowch parat' c*um* perle & c*um* ij cordib*us* q*uorum* vn*um*   5
plan*um* alter*um* anameld & c*um* ij anulis aureis quor*um* vn*um*
est anamelde & j crux de auro c*um* ymagine chr*isti* crucifixi &
ymagi*ne* b*eate* marie vi*r*ginis sim*ul* app*re*ciatur   *(blank)*
Item j agnus dei de argento deaurat*us* de dono Agne*tis*
Kylborn   v s   10
Item j crucifixus ex argento deaurat*us* app*re*ciatur   xvj d
Item xlix berilli in quod*am* sacculo   *(blank)*
Item j zona c*um* rosis de argento deaurat*a* appre*ciatur*   *(blank)*
Item j cor de auro c*um* j dyademaunt app*re*ciatur   *(blank)*
Item j stalk de corallo in fine deaurat' app*re*ciatur   xx d   15
Item j p*aruus* crucifixus argent*eus* app*re*ciatur   viij d
Item j tabelett de auro c*um* ymagine s*an*c*te* Trinitat*is* chr*isto*fere
& s*an*c*te* Barbare   xxij s
Item j iocale vocat*um* Moder de Perele in eo sculpt*a* Natiuitat*em*
d*om*ini n*ost*ri [chr*ist*i] iesu chr*ist*i & posit*um* in argento   20
circum*aur*ato app*re*ciatur   xl s
Item j knopp magn*um* de perell p*re*ciatur   iij s iiij d
Item j crucifixus de argento c*um* ij ymaginibus app*re*ciatur   xx d
Item j cocliar de argento deaurat*um* feretro afix*um* p*re*ciatur   iiij s
Item j tab*er*nacul*um* de auro ex dono d*om*i*ne* Iohan*ne* Ingylby   25
p*re*ciatur   liiij s iiij d
Item j monile de auro vocat*um* hart of golde ex dono d*om*i*ne*
Alicie Constabyll filie eiusd*em* p*re*ciatur   xx s
Item j singul*um* [vn] nigr*um* ex dono d*om*i*ne* Margar*e*te Clarevas
p*re*ciatur   xx s   30
Item j ⟨..⟩ux de auro cum parte quadam crucis dominica in ea
inclusa ex dono eiusd*em* Margar*e*te p*re*ciatur   xxx s
Item j anul*us* aure*us* c*um* j monil*i* vocato hart de argento   *(blank)*
Item j monile vocat*um* hart de auro ex dono Kat*er*ine
Styllynton   *(blank)*   35
Item j monile de cupro deaur*atum* ex legat*o* Ioha*nn*is Belamy
p*re*ciatur   *(blank)*
Item j anul*us* aure*us* ex legat*o* Kat*er*ine Burgh p*re*ciatur   *(blank)*
Item j anul*us* argent*eus* deaurat*us* ex dono Elene Benyng
p*re*ciatur   *(blank)*   40

31 ⟨..⟩ux] crux

Item j monile vocatum agnus dei aureum & j anulus aureus ex
dono agnetis Shrewodd preciantur   (blank)
Item j anulus argenteus preciatur   (blank)
Item j pila Aurea vocata Musce ball ex dono Elene Gare quondam
vxoris Thome gare junior preciatur   l s   5
Item j cor Aureum ex dono Agnetis Sherwod preciatur   iiij s
Item j par precularum ex dono vxoris Thome Wansforth
preciatur   xxvj s
Item j Cocler argent preciatur   iij s
Item Crucifixus ex dono Agnetis Burlay preciatur   v s | 10
In primis vnum par precularum de argento deauratum
continentium septuaginta quinque beedes cum duobus magnis
knoppis de perle cum vno crucifixo & ij monilibus cum vno anulo
argenteo deaurato appreciatur   xl s
Item aliud par magnum precularum de corallo continentium   15
complete psalterium de domina cum xvij gaudijs deauratis & j
monile cum scriptura iesu christi & cum vno anulo de auro
appreciatur   xlviij s x d
Item aliud par precularum de corallo cum quatuordecim gaudijs
de argento deauratis continentium complete psalterium de   20
domina cum j crucifixo duplici de argento deaurato cum vnum
knopp de perle appreciatur   v s
Item aliud par precularum de corallo cum vij gaudijs de argento
deaurato cum j stalk de corallo appreciatur   ij s iiij d
Item aliud par precularum de corallo cum vndecim gaudijs de   25
argento deaurato   ij s iiij d
Item aliud par precularum cum quibusdam bedis de argento &
quibusdam de corallo cum ij anulis argenteis & j bruche   vj s viij d
Item aliud par precularum cum bedis de argento deauratis cum j
crucifixo duplici deaurato appreciatur   (blank) 30
Item j paruum par precularum cum quibusdam bedes de argento
& quibusdam de corallo cum j crucifixo de argento deaurato   iiij s
Item j par precularum de argento ex dono Margarete danby
preciatur   vj s viij d
[Item j presur ex dono Iohannis Lynton   ix s ix d]   35
Item j cocliar de argento deauratum ex dono domini Thome
Clyff capellani preciatur   iiij s vj d
Item j cocliar de argento deauratum datum pro introitu Agnetis
Marshall preciatur   iiij s

4-6] *added in the same hand*   21 vnum] *for* vno

Item j par precularum de corallo cum [quadraginta] 'lix' gaudijs
de argento & quibusdam de eis deauratis ex dono Iohanne filij
Ricardi watson preciatur   x s
Item j cocliar deauratum ex dono Batildis Wakefelde
preciatur   (blank) | 5
In primis vnus calix argenteus appreciatur xl s Et vnum iocale
argenteum cum lapide cristallino continente reliquias preciosas
videlicet partem dominice crucis partem vestimenti sancti Thome
Cantuariensis Archiepiscopi & partem de hibitu sancti francisci
partem gloriosi ducus loncastrie & duos lapidos preciosos de   10
turnulo sancte katerine eductos Summa totalis iocalium xx s
Et aliud iocale de argento deaurato in signum & noticiam Gilde
super pectus bedelli populo publice demonstrandum appreciatur
lj s iiij d Et sigillei commune fraternitatis de argento appreciantur
xij s Et sigillum priuatum de argento appreciatur iij s iiij d Et   15
vnus ciphus magnus de muirro cum ligatura plana ex argento
deaurata qui vero ciphus indulgencialis digno nomine censetur
& hac de causa Beate quidem memorie dominus Ricardus Scrop
quondam archiepiscopus Ebor' vere penitentibus & confessis qui
si de hoc cipho sobrie tamen cum moderamine & non excessiue   20
nec ad voluntatem . mente pura potauerint quadraginta dies
indulgencie contulit graciose Eadem enim murra appreciatur xl s
Quam quidem ◦ murra seu ciphum Agnes Wyman olim vxor
Henrici Wyman quondam maioris ◦ Ciuitatis Ebor' ffraternitati
corporis christi obtulit quam deuote . cuius anima pace requiescat   25
perpetua amen Et j ciphus de murro cum ligatura de argento
deaurato appreciatur xxxvj s vj d Item j cista bene ligata sub
quinque clauibus pro stauro & euidencijs ac sigillo communi
conseruandis ordinata appreciatur xxvj s viij d |
    In primis vnum Missale receptum tempore domini Iohannis   30
ffox Magistri gilde v marcis Item j vestimentum de blodio &
orforay de verede & powderd cum stellis de auro preciatur vij s
Item ⌃'j' corporax de panno linio & j case de blodio preciatur
(blank) Item j corporax de panno linio & j case burdealexander
viride preciatur (blank) Item ij Cruettes de pewder appreciantur   35
viij d ⌃ꞌque omnia fueruntꞌ ex dono & legato domini Iohannis
3ork primi nuper capellani fraternitatis siue gilde Corporis christi
cuius anime propicietur deus amen
    Item vestimenta de blodio serico vocata vellowett ordinata pro
presbitero diacono & subdiacono cum iij capis sericis eiusdem   40

23-4 murra ... maioris] *written at bottom of folio in later hand*

secte appreciantur xxxiiij li Et j vestimentum album de bustiane
pro presbitero missam celebrante appreciatur xiiij s Et aliud
vestimentum de bustiane preciatur vj s viij d Et iij parui panni
de passione christi appreciantur xvj d. Et pannus depictus cum
ymagine beati Gregorij pape celebrantis missam coram ymagine   5
saluatoris appreciatur iiij s vij d Et vij stole de nouo facte eam
ad intencionem ordinate vt super humeros Magistri & sex
custodum fraternitatis in solempni processione corporis christi
valeant congrue deportari appreciantur xlvij s vij d Et j
vestimentum de rede burdalexander appreciatur viij s   10

    In primis lettere patentes domini Regis de noua fundacione &
creacione fraternitatis corporis christi appreciantur x li Et alie
littere fundacionis Gilde appreciantur vj li Et vnus quaternus de
pergameno in quo scribuntur copie litterarum patencium domini
regis & litterarum fundacionis fraternitatis appreciatur iiij s Et   15
vnus liber continens statuta & ordinaciones antiquas & in quo
libro registrata sunt nomina fratrum & sororum gilde appreciatur
xx s Et vnum monimentum sub sigillo communitatis ciuitatis
Ebor' appreciatur vj s viij d Et tres bulle de summa curia educte
cum duobus transsumptis appreciantur xx s Et quatuor littere de   20
indulgencijs Episcoporum appreciantur x s Et alie littere
indulgenciarum quas dominus Thomas Spoforde nuper episcopus
herfordensis presbiteris quibuscumque concessit qui missarum
celebracione deuote dixerint istam colectam

    Omnipotens sempiterne deus salus & vita credencium &c. cum   25
secreta & postcommune quas quidam collectam secretam &
postcommunem ipsemet episcopus fabricauit & statuit vt
fidelium mentes pro fratribus & sororibus istius Gilde alliceret
exorare Et eedem littere indulgenciarum appreciantur x s Et
nouem scripta instrumentorum & euidenciarum de mortuarijs   30
presbiterorum ciuitatis Ebor' non soluendis appreciantur vj li.
Et si quis aliquod istorum scriptorum graciose & pie indultorum
alienare consenserit se dei digno iudicio nouerit
excommunicacionis sentencia irretiri Et duo spirpta de anno
redditu habendo in Skeldergate Ebor' appreciantur x s Et vnum   35
portiferum continens xliij pecias de pergameno appreciatur xl s
Et parua tabula de gracijs dicendis appreciatur xij d Et xxij
rotule quibus antecessorum Compoti inseruntur appreciantur
xxij s |

    In primis vna capsula lignea supra summum altare in capella   40

34 spirpta] *for* scripta

sancti will*elm*i supra pontem vse app*re*ciatur iij li. Et vnu*m*
baiualatoriu*m* pictu*m* deaurat*um* pro dicto feretro in processione
ferendo vj s viij d Et octo puluinaria albi coloris p*ro* portantiu*m*
feretru*m* humeris ordinata app*re*ciantur ij s ij d Et iiij*or*
ymagines euangelistar*um* & xvj ang*e*li cum scutis & rotulis nup*er*   5
depict*i* si*mu*l calicib*us* duob*us* de cupro deaurat*is* ∧ᴿcum ij
cristyls' p*ro* dicto baiulatorio & feretro supportand*o* xxxviij s
Et ij panni parui de bukysyn depict*i* cu*m* calicib*us* deaurat*is* p*ro*
dicto baiulatorio cu*m* vna celatura lignea quadrata & cu*m* quatuor
lanceolis app*re*ciantur iiij s Et pann*us* pictus cu*m* ymagine   10
su*m*me trinitat*is* app*re*ciatur iij s Et quatuor pecie de valauncez
bold*ij* coloris cu*m* calicib*us* & stellis deaurat*is* app*re*ciantur v s.
Et iiij sacculi linei p*ro* iiij pelles d*ic*t*i* baiulatorij honeste
co*n*seruand*o* app*re*ciantur vj d Et vn∧ᴿa᷎ cista breuis ligat*a* cu*m*
ferro p*ro* feretro tute custodiend*o* app*re*ciatur viij s viij d   15
    In primis liber vocatus Originale continens Artic*u*los fidei
catholice in lingua anglicana nup*er* script*us* app*re*ciatur x li*b*ri
Et alius liber i*n*uet*er*atus de eode*m* ludo C s Et alius liber de
eode*m* anglice vocat*us* Credeplay co*n*tine*n*s xxiij quat*er*nos. Et
xvij vexilla magna app*re*ciantur iiij li. & iiij vexilla minora de   20
serico rubeo p*re*ciantur vj s viij d Et noue*m* alia vexilla vocat*a*
pennons de nouo factis cu*m* scutis fidei & calicib*us* depictis
app*re*ciantur xj s vj d Et xxiiij*or* instrumenta ferrea vocata
sokkett*es* ordinat*a* p*ro* extensione vexillor*um* app*re*ciantur iiij s
vj d Et vna mitra pap*a*lis app*re*ciatur x d Et vna corona regis   25
cu*m* ceptro & yn cirotheca app*re*ciatur vj d Et xij rotule nup*er*
scripte cu*m* articu*lis* fidei catholice |app*re*ciantur iij s iiij d Et
vna cistula quadrata cu*m* vna sera & claue p*ro* dictis vexillis
seruand*is* app*re*ciatur ij s Et ij mitre e*pisco*porum app*re*ciantur
xij d Et vna clauis p*ro* s*ancto* petro cu*m* ij pecijs vnius tunice   30
depicte app*re*ciatur xij d Et iiij alia vexilla vocat*a* pennons iij s
iiij d Et x diademata p*ro* chr*ist*o & ap*ost*olis cu*m* vna larua &
alijs nouem cheuerons vj s
    In primis quatuordecem torchie app*re*ciantur (*blank*) Et iij
Iudassez veter*es* app*re*ciantur xiiij d Et xij castella picta cu*m*   35
calicib*us* aureis & laminis de ferro eiusd*em* castellis p*er*tinentib*us*
app*re*ciantur iiij s Et xxxiiij vexilla picta p*ro* torcheis ordinat*a*
app*re*ciatur xx s |
    In primis octo mappe cu*m* ij alijs mappis secundarijs
app*re*ciantur vj s viij d. Et qui*n*q*ue* alie mappe de nouo facte   40

12 bold*ij*] *for* blodij

continentes lxxiij vlnas appreciantur xxiiij s vij d. Et vnum
manutergium appreciatur ij s Et ij alia manutergia minora
appreciantur ij s iiij d Et xxiiij napkyns appreciantur xij d Et vj
napeones appreciantur ij s Et ix dossans de ciphis appreciantur
v s Et xxᵗⁱ salina de peltro appreciantur iiij s Et lx roundels pro   5
reuettes appreciantur xvj d Et vnus paruus lineus pro tabula vbi
ciphi sunt situandi appreciantur viij d Et lxiiij olle terree vocate
reuettes appreciantur ix s Et vna cista longa cum iij seris & iij
clauibus pro dictis pannis lineis conseruandis appreciatur xvj s Et
alia cista breuis sine coopertolio in boetria appreciatur xij d Et   10
alia longa cista cum vna claue pro dictis reuettes custodiendis
iij s iiij d Et alia parua cista appreciatur (blank). Et vna mappa
de twill continens viij vlnas appreciatur vj s viij d

   In primis vna olla magna enea cum iij longis pedibus appreciatur
vj s viij d Et alia olla enea minor appreciatur vj s viij d Et alia   15
olla enea appreciatur iij s viij d Et viij dossans & x doblers &
xv dossans discorum & ij disci cum x dossans & vno de salsarijs
appreciantur v li. xiij s iiij d Et duo intrumenta vocata
markyngirens appreciantur viij d Et vnum hausorium de auricalco
preciatur viij d & aliud laddell de ligno preciatur j d Et j fustinula   20
vocata fleschcroke appreciatur vj d Et par follium appreciatur
iij d Et vnus cultellus rubiginosus parui valoris appreciatur
quarta Et duo pecie j doubeler fract'

Late fifteenth century   BL: Lansdowne MS 403   25

ff 7-8v*
      Memorandum þat thes er þe personelles off Iowelles þat
            standeth vpon þe Schryne off corporis christi

                                                                                 30
In Primis a pair bedes siluer and gylt with one Crucifix gylt one
      Agnus a bruche a Byrall with I Ryng and a stone þerin
Item a pare Bedez Siluer & Gylt with one crucifix of þe same
      bedez Gylt
Item a pair Bedez le Small Corall with one hert of golde   35
Item a pare Bedez le corall þe gaudez siluer & Gylt with one
      Stalke le corall
Item a pare bedez le Corall with gawdes siluer & gylt a crucifix
      and iiij Gemmes with one Grete knop sett with perle
Item a pare bedes off corall þe gaudesse siluer & gilted with one   40

4 napeones] for naprons   31 and] MS and and

cricifix siluer & gilt and I bruche le siluer & gilt

Item a pare siluer bedes with Gaudez Gilted a pair gemmows
    and one Rose of siluer

nota Item a pare bedez off grete Corall þe gaudes le gold

Item vij Rynges off golde With one Ryng off birall   5

Item iij cruciffixesse le siluer and Gilted

Item a crosse off golde With iij perlez

Item ij hertez off golde

Item a Bruche of golde

Item ij owchesse off golde sett with preciouse stones & perlesse   10

Item iij Bruches of siluer with stones in them

Item iij Bruchesse off siluer & gilt one with precius stones

Item a Crucifix siluer & gylt

Item ij agnus siluer & Gilt / Item a gemmoy of siluer

Item V stalkez of Corall typped with siluer & gylt | 15

Item I birall closed with siluer

Item a Skalep of Siluer

Item a table off Golde with ij leyffz set with perle

Item xj siluer spones gilted

Item a girdell þe corse blew þe pennaunt & þe Buccle gilt with   20
    xxxj Barrez gylt /

nota Item a blak gyrdill þe pennaunt & þe buccle golde with vij
    Stuthes

Item a rede Girdill buccle and þe pennaunt gilted harnest thorow
    owte with Sternez gylted   25

Item a Girdill þe corse le gold þe pennaunte & þe buccle siluer &
    gilt

Item a Smalle girdill þe corse blew harnest thorowowte & gilted

Item a rede girdill þe pennaunt siluer & gilt harnest thrugh owte
    with roses & straburez   30

Item a blew girdill pennaunt & þe bocle siluer & gilt with xxxij
    Stothez

Item a pare bedez of siluer þe Gaudez gilted

Item a hart of gold

Item a table off þe moder of perle with roses enameled   35

Item a hart of Siluer

Item ij Tabylesse of Gold

Item a Tabernakyll of oure lady siluer & gylt

Item a Crucyfix off Siluer

Item vij gold Ryngez   40

4 Item] MS Item Item

Item a pare Corall Bedez þe gaudez siluer with a siluer ryng
Item a pair Bedz of Siluer & Corall with ij gold ryngez
Item a pair bedez of Corall þe gaudes siluer & gilted with a
    ryng off gold
Item a paire Siluer bedez þe gaudesse siluer & gylted with ij   5
    Crucifixesse gylted with a stawke of corall
Item a pare bedez off golde with I gold ryng
Item a pare Siluer bedez of x with a grete gold ryng
Item a paire bedez of Corall þe gaudz siluer & gylt with one
    Birall & a stalk off Corall closed in Siluer þe one gylted | 10
Item a pare Corall bedez þe gaudez siluer & gilt with one gold
    ryng
Item a pair bedez one halffe siluer þe oder halffe Corall
Item a pair smal corall bedez þe Gaudez siluer & gilt with one
    owche of gold and viij grete perlesse   15
Item a pare bedez le Coral þe gaudes siluer & gylt with a bruche
    of golde with preciouse Stones
Item a pare bedez of grete corall þe gaudes siluer
Item a pare of bedez of siluer & corall þe gaudz siluer & gilt
Item a Skalep harnest with siluer   20
Item a Crosse of gold with a chyne of gold
Item a hart of gold
Item a Crosse of gold
Item a Stalke le corrall
Item j golde Ryngez   25
Item a Spice box le siluer & gilt
Item a Bruche siluer & gilt with stonesse þerin
Item a pece le siluer gylted with þe Coueryng
Item a Muste ball of gold with one precius stone in þe End

    30

1546 PRO: E117/10/1

The Shryne
called Corpus
christi Shryne
in yorke.
An Inuentory of the Iuelles therunto belongyng surveyed &   35
exteamyd by the right Reuerend ffather in god Robert
archebisshop of yorke & other the kynges maiesties Commissioners
the xijth of May Anno regni Henri⟨.⟩ Octaui dei gracie Anglie
ffrancie & hibernie Regis fidei defensoris & in terra Ecclesie
Anglicane & hibernae supremi Cepitis xxxviijno   40

Thatistosey

ffirst the said Shryne is all Gilte havyng vj
ymages gylded with an ymage of the birthe of
our lord of mother of perle syluer & gylt &
xxxiij small ymages ennamyled stondyng
aboute same and a Tablett of golde / ij Golde   5
Rynges one with a Safure & the other with a
perle / & viij other litle ymages and a great
Tablett of golde havyng in yt the ymage of our   Cxx li.
lady of mother of perle Whiche Shryne   & aboue
conteyneth in lenght iij^e quarters of a yard &   10
a nayle / and in brede a quarter di. & more /
And in height di. yerd ouer & besides the
Steple stondyng vpon the same / Extemyng
the same Shryne besides the said Steple
tobe Worthe | 15

The said Steple havyng a Whether Cokke
theruppon all Gylte / & a Ryall of Golde /
iiij^{or} olde nobles / ij gylted Grootes hangyng
vpon the said Steple / also beyng within the   20
same Steple a Berall wheryn the sacrament is
[all] Gylte   borne havyng in the said Berall ij ymages or   xl li. xiiij s vj d
angelles of syluer & gylt beryng vp the said
sacrament / The ffoote & Coueryng of whiche
said Berall is syluer & gylte / Weying togeder   25
with the Golde & Berall besides the said Shryne
Ciiij^{xx} I owz at iiij s vj d the oz summa

A Syluer Bell hangyng in the said steple
waying iij owz & di. at iij s iiij d the oz   xj s viij d   30

A peyer of Beades with xiiij Crucifixes weying
x oz iij^e quarters / a peper box weyng vj oz
iij^e quarters / ix Rynges with Counterfett
Stones in iij^e of them / iij^e Bukcles with a   35
cheyne / a Treangle / a harte / a Tache / a
litle Ryng a litle Tablett of seynt Michell
weyng togeder iiij^{or} oz iij^e quarters / ij peaces
of Corall weyng I oz iij^e quarters / ij Cristalles
a bygger . & a lesse beyng closed with syluer   40
weyng iij^e oz / viij peyer of Corall beades with   xxx li.
their Gaudies & a Crucifix weying xxxvj oz [lxxv]   xvj s vj d

xvij sylu*er* Spones of seu*er*all Sort*es* weyng
xx oz / lxxv bead*es* rounde weyng vij oz / vj
Corse Gyrdell*es* beyng Typped havyng bukcles
weyng xxix oz / viij Tablett*es* of seu*er*all facions
havyng in some of them Count*er*fett Stones   5
weyng vj oz iij^e qu*arter*s / iij^e bukcles & ij of
them havyng count*er*fett stones in them weyng
iiij^or oz & a q*uarter* in all C´iiij˥ xxxvij oz at
iiij s vj d the oz *sum*ma
                                                              10

A pomaunder of gold / a litle Tablett of gold &
*with*in the same an ymage of seynt kat*er*yne of
mother of perle / v Ryng*es* of gold *with* a litle
Golde.   harte / a Tablett of gold / ij fflowers of perle /   x li. vj d
iij^e bukcles / a harte of gold *with* a Dyamond &   15
a litle Crosse weyng all togeder v owz iij^e
qu*arter*s & di. oz at xxxiij s iiij d the oz

Ten peyer of Corall Bead*es* *with* their Gaudies
parcell Gylte.   weyng xx^ti oz / a pep*er* Box weyng iiij^or oz in   lx s   20
all xxiiij oz at ij s vj d the oz *sum*ma

V peac*es* of Corall typped *with* sylu*er* weyng
iij^e oz a qu*arter* iiij^or peyer of bead*es* all sylu*er*
with the knoppes havyng the Gaudies gylte   25
wayng xvj oz / X Corall bead*es* *with* ij sylu*er*
Syluer.   gaudies / iiij^or Cristall Stones / a pomaunder   Cxv s
enclosyd in sylu*er* / a Crucifix / ij seynt Iames
shell*es* a Cristall Ryng & a litle ymage weyng togeder
ix oz di. in all xxviij oz iij^e qu*arter*s at iiij s the oz   30

Whereof	
The Shryne by estymacion	Cxx li.
The Steple *with* the wed*er*cok	xl li. xiij s vj d
The sylu*er* bell *with*in ye steple	xj s viij d
Iuell*es* of Golde	x li. vj d
Iuell*es* all Gylte	xxx li. xvj s vj d
Iuell*es* p*ar*cell Gylte	lx s
Iuell*es* of Sylu*er*	Cxv s

*Sum*ma To*talli*s of the value
belongyng to the said Shryne   CCx li. xviij s ij d.

III Pater Noster Guild Returns, 1388-9

Ebor'

Audita proclamacione facta ex parte domini regis in Ciuitate   5
Ebor' vt certificetur & notificetur illustri domino nostro Regi &
venerabilissimo consilio suo de omnibus & singulis ordinacionibus
fundacionibus & honeribus fraternitatum seu gildarum infra
comitatum Ebor'. Hinc est quod custodes fraternitatis oracionis
dominice in Ciuitate Ebor' fundate de omnibus & singulis   10
fundacioni seu gubernacioni dicte fraternitatis pertinentibus
dicto domino nostro Regi & excellentissimo consilio suo notificant
& certificant sub hac forma. Primo quo ad causam fundacionis
dicte fraternitatis: sciendum est quod postquam quidam ludus
de vtilitate oracionis dominice compositus in quo ludo quam   15
plura vicia & peccata reprobantur & virtutes commendantur in
ciuitate Ebor' lusus fuit: talem ac tantum saporem habuit: vt
quam plures dixerunt, Vtinam iste ludus in Ciuitate ista
gubernaretur in salutem animarum & in consolacionem Ciuium
& vicinorum. Vnde pro illo ludo futuris temporibus in salutem & 20
emendacionem animarum tam gubernancium quam audiencium
illius ludi gubernaturo: fuit plena & integra causa fundacionis &
associacionis confratrum fraternitatis eiusdem. et ideo onus
principale dicte fraternitatis est: pro illo ludo gubernaturo in
maiorem laudem dei dicte oracionis opificis. & pro peccatis &   25
vicijs reprobandis. Et quia in peccatis continuantes inhabiles sunt
vocare deum patrem suum: ideo primo dicti confratres tenentur
euitare societates & occupaciones inhonestas ac bonis & honestis
occupacionibus adherere. Item tenentur in maioribus deuocionibus
suis pro confratribus & consororibus dicte fraternitatis viuis & 30
defunctis specialiter orare. vt viui confraternitatem suam sic

custodire valeant? vt paternitatem diuinam lucrari mereantur. &
vt mortui cicius eorum precibus a cruciatibus relaxentur. Item
tenentur adesse in exequijs & sepulturis defunctorum confratrum
seu consororum suorum dicte fraternitatis. Et si aliquis confrater
nichil habuerit proprium pro expensis circa propriam sepulturam   5
suam faciendis? quod ceteri confratres sui sumptibus suis propriis
caritatiue ipsum faciant sepeliri. Et si longe a ciuitate aliquem
confratrem dicte fraternitatis mori contigerit & sepeliri quod
ceteri confratres sui obitum suum infra ciuitatem Ebor' facient
celebrari. Item inhibetur cuilibet confratri fraternitatis predicte   10
ne causa confidencie in aliquo auxilio confratrum suorum sit
audacior litigandi vel pugnandi vel aliquam causam iniustam
aliqualiter manutenendi. sub pena amissionis totius auxilij &
amicitie seu releuaminis fraternitatis antedicti Et quia vana est
fidelium congregatio absque aliquo opere caritatiuo gubernaturo?   15
ideo dicti confratres constituerunt istam clausulam. quod si forte
contingat aliquem ipsorum confratrum depredari seu bona vel
catalla sua casualiter cremari vel aliqua causa iniusta incarcerari
seu visitacione diuina ad statum paupertatis deuenire? quod
ceteri confratres sui se adiuuent secundum suam egestatem   20
caritatiue iuxta disposicionem custodum dicte fraternitatis? ne
forte auxilij pereat in defectu. Item tenentur inuenire vnam
candelam de septem luminaribus in honore septem peticionum
in oracione dominica in ecclesia cathedrali Ebor' pendentem ad
laudem & honoram omnipotentis dei eiusdem oracionis factoris.   25
sancti petri. gloriosi confessoris sancti Willelmi & omnium
sanctorum diebus dominicis & festiuis comburendam Item
tenentur gubernare & quotienscumque necesse fuerit renouare
quamdam tabulam de toto processu vtilitatis oracionis dominice
factam pendentem super vnam columpnam in ecclesia cathedrali   30
predicta prope candelam predictam. Item tenentur
quotienscumque ludus dicte oracionis dominice in forma ludi in
Ciuitate Ebor' monstratur cum lusoribus eiusdem per certas
principales stratas ciuitatis Ebor' equitare & pro meliori ornatu
in sua equitacione habendo in vna secta indui. & pro dicto ludo   35
pacifice gubernando aliqui eorum tenentur equitare seu ire cum
illis lusoribus quousque dictus ludus totaliter finiatur. & semel in
anno commestionem simul facere & nouos custodes pro dicta
fraternitate custodienda quolibet anno de nouo eligere & eisdem
custodibus de nouo electis de toto quod fecerint temporibus   40
elapsis ad opus dicte fraternitatis fidelem compotum reddere.
Item ordinatum est quod nullus recipiatur in confratrem

fraternitatis eiusdem antequam examinetur per custodes dicte
fraternitatis si sit in voluntate honeste viuendi & faciendi
fraternitati predicte pro gubernacione eiusdem prout poterit
cum dictis custodibus concordare. Et quia fundatores dicte
fraternitatis cognouerunt se ipsos indiscretos pro talibus   5
ordinacionibus disponendis: ideo in fine omnium dictarum
ordinacionum: addiderunt talem clausulam. Quandocumque &
quotienscumque forte contigerit nos vel successores nostros
custodes & confratres dicte fraternitatis esse sapientiores; quod
nullus nostrum seu successorum nostrorum sit rebellis vel resistens   10
contra disposiciones nostras seu ᷑'ipsorum' successorum
nostrorum si forte constitucionem aliquam ad maiorem laudem
dei seu dicte fraternitatis releuamen de nouo fecerimus seu
fecerint in futurum. Virtute cuius clausule ceteri custodes dicte
fraternitatis in maiorem laudem dei addiderunt quod quidam   15
capellanus diuina celebraturus annuatim per dictos confratres
teneatur & conducatur pro confratribus & consororibus dicte
fraternitatis viuis & defunctis & omnibus benefactoribus
eorundem Solent eciam ijdem confratres communiter ad finem
singularum sex septimanarum annuatim simul congregare & pro   20
salubri statu domini Regis & bono regimine regni anglie & pro
cunctis confratribus & consororibus dicte fraternitatis presentibus
& absentibus viuis & defunctis & omnibus dicte fraternitatis
seu dictorum confratrum benefactoribus specialiter orare. Ac
eciam semel in anno pro confratribus & consororibus dicte   25
fraternitatis defunctis vnum obitum generalem facere. Nec
pertinent ad dictam fraternitatem terre redditus nec tenementa
vel aliqua alia catalla, excepto solummodo apparatu pro dicto
ludo disposito. qui quidem apparatus ad aliquem alium vsum nisi
tantum ad dictum ludum: modicum vel nichil potest proficere   30
Et habetur vna cista lignea pertinens ad dictam fraternitatem pro
dicto apparatu inponendo In quorum omnium & singulorum
testimonium quia sigilla custodum dicte fraternitatis pluribus
sunt incognita: sigillum in spiritualibus vicarij generalis venerabilis
in christo patris & domini Thome Ebor' archiepiscopi anglie   35
primatis & apostolice sedis legati ᷑'nos' dicti custodes
procurauimus hijs apponi: Et nos Ricardus de Thoren Canonicus
residenciarius ecclesie Ebor' ac prefati venerabilis patris in
spiritualibus vicarius generalis sigillum quo in hujusmodi nostro
officio vtimur ad instanciam dicte fraternitatis presentibus   40

35 domini] MS domini domini

apposuim*us* in fidem & testi*m*oniu*m* o*m*niu*m* pre*m*issor*um*.
Dat*um* Ebor' xxj° die mens*is* Ianuarij . anno d*om*ini mill*e*si*m*o .
ccc^{m o} . lxxx^{m o} . octauo.

Alleged Letter from Henry VIII concerning a St Thomas Play

The following letter is printed by James Orchard Halliwell, *Letters of the Kings of England* I (London, 1848), 354. It is said to be from Henry VIII to an unknown Justice of the Peace in York. It is accompanied by the following note:

> MS collection of York Documents, Rawlinson's Collection in the Bodleian Library. This is here translated from the Latin; and, although without date, it is extremely curious and interesting, as it clearly shows that the monks made their miracle-plays a vehicle for spreading particular religious and political opinions. An early play on the subject of St Thomas is still preserved.

A search in the Bodleian Rawlinson manuscripts for the original has been unsuccessful. Although the manuscript of the Corpus Christi Play was unknown in 1846, the single copy of the Scriveners' Pageant of Doubting Thomas was known to have survived.

> Trusty and well-beloved, we greet you well. And whereas we understand by certain report the late evil and seditious rising in our ancient city of York, at the acting of a religious interlude of St. Thomas the Apostle, made in the said city on the 23rd of August now past; and whereas we have been credibly informed that the said rising was owing to the seditious conduct of certain papists who took part in preparing for the said interlude, we will and require you that from henceforward ye do your utmost to prevent and hinder any such commotion in future, and for this ye have my warrant for apprehending and putting in prison any papists who shall, in performing

interludes which are founded on any portions of the Old or New Testament, say or make use of any language which may tend to excite those who are beholding the same to any breach of the peace.

Given, etc.

V Pageant Masters of the Mercers' Guild

CHARTULARY AND MINUTE BOOK D19

		...			...
f 11v*	1488	William Russell Robertum Thorne Iohn Thomson William middlyton		1495	Iohn Spenser Edmund Warwyk Richard Newtour William Malson
		...			...
	1489	Thomas Tailliour William Staveley Richard Cuilsby Roberto Cook	f 156	1499	Thomas Staveley Robertus Sharp Thomas ffissher Iohannes Iohnson
		...			...
f 12	1490	Myghell Quharton Iohn Gell Robert Persson	f 156v	1500	Thomas Staveley Thomas ffissher Robertus Sherp Iohannes Iohnson
		...			...
f 9v	1492	Alanus Staveley Robertus Persson Thomas Catlynson Iohannes Tawnte	f 157v	1501	Iohannes Gylliat Iunior Edwardus Hunter Iohannes Rasyn Iohannes Benson
		...			...
f 10v	1494	William Gylde Richard Marshall Iameys Manhoue George Nicholson	f 158	1502-3	Iohannes Kent Giles Clarvas Iohannes Sherman Robertus wild

...

f 159v	1504-5	Iohannes Kent
		Robertus Wilde
		Egidius Clarvax
		Iohannes Norman

...

f 161	1512-13	Radulphus Langley
		Robertus Elwolde
		Robertus Bekynghm
		Iohannes Thomson

...

f 161v	1513-14	Willelmus Iameson
		Ricardus Plompton
		Iacobus Thorn
		Robertus Makblith

...

f 162	1514-15	Willelmus Kirke
		Iohannes Marshall
		Iohannes Ellys
		Robertus Iamys

...

162v	1515-16	Iohannes Wedderall
		Willelmus Barker
		Thomas Burton
		Iohannes Iameson

...

f 163	1517-18	Willelmus Nawton
		Petrus Robynson
		Iohannes Shawe
		Iohannes Wath

...

f 163v	1519-20	Iohannes Wath
		Iohannes Shawe
		Ricardus Bossall
		Iohannes Metcalf

...

f 164	1521	Iohannes Aldercorn
		Ricardus Glewe
		Cristoferus Kydd
		Robertus Hall

...

JOURNAL BOOK A D14

°The Names of all the Pageant Master synce Anno 1526°

...

f 65	1526	Henry wood
		Barth yorke
		Georg norman
		...
	1527	Iohn mald
		Myles Iackson
		Iohn Iackson
		Myles Hodgson
		...
	1528	Iohn Iohnson
		George atkirke,
		Thomas rasyng
		Thomas Thornton
		...
	1529	Georg Dawson
		Myles Cooke
		Henry Shawe
		Henry wood
		...
	1530	Anthony Atkirk
		Thomas Apleyard
		Myles Bell
		William Beckwyth
		Percyvall Metcalf
		...
	1531	Bartho Dawson
		William Vale
		Ralf Tenant
		Henry Dyckonson
		...
	1532	Iames Iackson
		Ralf Hall
		Iames Garth
		Robert Paycock

...

1533	Georg Pullen	1541	Iohn Peghan
	Thomas Smyth		Edward gilping
	Peter Shaw		Georg Hall
	Robert Mamond		Iohn Darling

1533 Georg Pullen
Thomas Smyth
Peter Shaw
Robert Mamond
...
1534 Oswyn Edwyn
Iames Harryngton
william watson
william mayson
...
1535 William Lullay
Richard plasket
...
1536 Iohn Bachelar
Iames Atkinson
Robert Smyth
Peter Iackson
...
1537 Iohn Bacheler
Iames Atkinson
Robert Smyth
Peter Iackson
...
1538 Wylliam Penyngton
Thomas Atkinson
Thomas Symson
Iohn Townend
...
f 65v 1539 Anthony Eden
Iohn Thornell
Iohn Hewytson
William Cowper
...
1540 Thomas Bankhows
Henry wood
Hewgh Graues
Iohn wharye

...
1541 Iohn Peghan
Edward gilping
Georg Hall
Iohn Darling
...
1542 Iohn Harryson
Richard North
Ralf Baker
Robert Stanburne
...
1543 Oswald Chambers
Adame Bynkes
Bryand Thomson
Thomas Coattes
...
1544 Henry Race
Edward Ranecock
Gilbert Heckleton
Wylliam Elden
...
1545 William Sauadge
Anthoney Pulley
Gregory Paycok
Richard Pease
...
1546 Leonard Temple
Christofer stockdal
Robert willye
William Iackson
...
1547 Cuthbert Nendyke
Wilfride Nelstron
Iohn Remyngton
Thomas Hyll
...
1548 Robert wylly
Ralf Tenant
william Iackson
Wylliam Gylmyng

		...			...
	1549	Nicholas Ardington		1558	Andrew Trew
		Thomas stanelay			Iames Hall
		Thomas Hutchinson			Iohn chambers
		Peter Pullen			Richard Morton
		...			...
	1550	Iames Sauadge		1559	Andrew Trew
		Thomas Hewytt			Richard Morton
		christofer Herbert			Iohn Chambers
		Richard marshall			William ffuster
		...			...
	1551	Iames Savadg		1560	Andrew Trew
		Thomas Blanchyrd			Richard morton
		christofer Herbert			Iohn Chambers
		Richard marshall			William ffuster
		...			...
	1552	Anthony Lowther	℞ this year 5 dyd refuse & paid 13s (.) 4d a man.	1561	Iohn Goodyeare
		Iohn wood			Wylliam pacock
		Iohn Ledall			Georg Davyll
		Robert Clark			Georg Turton
		...			...
	1553	(blank)		1562	Richard blythe
		...			William outhwhate
f 66	1554	Iohn Eyre			Iames Ellwycke
		William Allan			Georg Cowpland
		Ralf Mycklethwate			...
		Iohn Granger		1563	Hewgh Allan
		...			Lawrance Robinson
	1555	Henry Dobson			Iames Lepington
		Thomas Ellerd			Anthony Owsherby
		Symon Amplefrith			...
		Ralf Graves	℞ peter hall dyd pay 13s 4d for refusyng	1564	Georg Gilmyng
		...			ffabyan ffarlay
	1556	William watson			Martyn marshall
		Thomas Dunyngton			ffrances Bayne
		Iohn Collinson			...
		Iohn Eshe		1565	Georg Gilmyng
		...			ffabyan ffarlay
	1557	Robert Brooke			Martyn marshall
		Leonard willand			ffrances Bayne
		Robert Allan			...
		Wylliam farlay		1566	(blank)

...

	1567	ffrances Bayne		1576	Iohn metcalf yonger
		Wylliam Ledall			Iames williamson
		Wylliam Howson			Henry Hall
		Anthony Pulley			Peter Smyth

...   ...

f 66v	1568	Robert Paycock		1577	William ffrysbe
		Robert Mawd			Iames Crosse
		Iohn metcalf			Ralf Hart
		Richard noble			Marmaduke sotheby

...   ...

1569.
Robert Pacock
Robert mawd
Iohn metcalf
Richard noble

1578
William Lullay
Wylliam Burton
Robert Myers
Iohn fysher

...

1570.
Percyvall Brook
Edward exilbe
christofer Bekwith
christofer Iackson

1579
Thomas Herbert
Wylliam Robinson
Iohn Aske
Iohn mawd

...

1571.   (blank)

1580
William wood
Bryand byrkhead
Iohn Graves
Henry Banyster

...

1572   (blank)

...

1573.
Iames Bekwyth
Ralf Richardson
Georg Aslaby
Iohn Iackson

1581
Iames Bland
Robert Harryson
Thomas Copley
Anthony Calton

...

1574
Leonard Beckwyth
christofer Consytt
william Skotte
william Skotte

f 67   1582
Iohn Smythies
Iohn watson
Iohn North
Thomas moxand

...

1575
Richard Hutton
Iohn Herbert
Henry Nevyll
Thomas Mosley

1583
christofer Hewycke
Thomas Maskewe
Robert Dawson
Wilfrd Brand

...

1584   Anthony Sandwith
       Peter Hodgson
       wyll*ia*m watson
       wyll*ia*m w*illia*mson

...

1585   Thomas Barker
       Rob*er*t Hudson
       Georg Dunyng
       Wyll*ia*m Hancock

...

1586   Ioh̄n farmery
       Richard Herbert
       Henry Mudd
       Lawrans edward*es*

...

1587   Leonard Grenbury
       ffranc*es* Wayd
       Georg Rose
       Iohn Wadsworth

...

1588   Wyll*ia*m Marshall
       Gilbert Coldwell
       Wyll*ia*m Ienkinson
       Iohn Granger

...

1589   Iohn Gowland
       Th*om*as Peghan
       chr*is*tofer Hutton
       Henry Thomson

...

1590   Rob*er*t Burnytt
       Richard hawkeshyrsh
       Wyll*ia*m wooller
       Lawrans wade

...

Pageants in the Corpus Christi Play

The following list of crafts and pageants is based on the second list of pageants in the 'Ordo gathering' (pp 25-6). Only the references contained in the records concerned with the ownership and financing of particular pageants are tabulated here. Other incidental references and the evidence of pageant houses are not included. For such supplementary references consult the general index. The craft name is given in modern spelling. Where a single craft is referred to by more than one name, the second name is given in parentheses. The last entry under each episode gives the folio number of the beginning of each pageant as it appears in the manuscript of the plays themselves (BL MS Add 35290), the name of the craft ascribed there to each episode and any changes that have been made. We have not tabulated changes made by later hands in the text of the cycle, but only the information relevant to craft ownership.

Pageant 1   Owners: Tanners (Barkers)
The Creation of Heaven and Earth

1476   E20 f 281v   p 111
Fines: half to go to craft for pageant costs and other general expenses.

E20 f 282   p 111
Pageant money: 'foreigners' buying or selling red leather in York to pay 4d a year.

1574   E22 f 155v   p 375
Pageant money: 'foreigners' selling leather to pay 6d a year.

1608   E22 f 136v   p 527
As 1574, 'pageant money' referred to as 'custom money'.

   f 4 'The Barkers'

Pageant 2   Owners: Plasterers
The Work of Five Days

1390   E20 f 46   p 7
Fines: half to go to craft for pageant costs.

1411-12   E20 f 21v   p 16
Fines: as 1390

1419-20 or 1433-4   E20 f 57v   p 33
Plasterers building stone walls or foundations or otherwise infringing on Masons' craft to contribute to Masons' pageant; see below, Pageant 52 (before 1431-2) and Pageant 16 (after 1431-2).

1422-3   E20 f 258   p 39
Plasterers and Tilers (owners of Pageant 14) join to finance the pageants of both crafts. Fines: half to go to crafts for pageant costs.

1474-5   E20A f 142   p 104
Plasterers and Tilers: masters of both crafts to answer for pageant money of their 'foreign' workmen.

1572   E20A f 230   p 370-1 (Collated with E22 f 144v and B25 ff32-3v)
Plasterers, Tilers and Bricklayers. Ordinances common to these three building crafts. Pageant money: anyone working in the crafts to pay 4d a year.

   f 7v 'Playsterers'

Pageant 3   Owners: Cardmakers
The Creation of Adam and Eve

Undated   E20 ff 30v-1   p 621
Pageant money: 'foreigners' setting up as masters to pay 6s 8d. Fines: half to go to craft for pageant costs.

1485   B2-4 f 163   p 136
Cardmakers, Tapiters (owners of Pageant 34) and Linenweavers (owners of Pageant 53) join to finance and present the pageants of Cardmakers and Tapiters.

1529   B11 f 55   pp 249-50
Cardmakers' and Fullers' pageants made into a single dramatic unit. Crafts to pay

equal amounts to pageant fund. Fullers (owners of Pageant 4).

f 9v 'Cardmakers'. f 12 'Cardemakers' (this episode is entered twice).

Pageant 4   Owners: Fullers (Walkers)
The Prohibition of the Tree of Knowledge

1529   B11 f 55   pp 249-50
See above, Pageant 3.

1559   CC5(1) f 73   p 330
Payment to John Clerk for entering the Fullers' pageant in the register.

f 13 'The ffullers pagyant', 'Adam and eve this is the place'. f 13v 'The regynall of the ffullers pagyant Deus /'. This episode is written entirely in a sixteenth-century hand.

Pageant 5   Owners: Coopers
Fall of Man

Undated   E20 f 26v   p 620
Pageant money: new masters to pay 3s 4d. Fines: half to go to craft for pageant costs.

1471   E20 f 27   pp 102-3
Pageant money: hired men to pay 4d a year if apprenticed in York, 6d a year if apprenticed elsewhere.

f 15v 'The Coupers'

Pageant 6   Owners: Furbishers (of armour) ie, Armourers
Expulsion from the Garden

1444   E20A f 121v   pp 62-3
Copy of letter to mayor asking for help to finance their pageant.

1475   E20A f 140   pp 104-5
Ordinances. Pageant masters to make reckoning second Sunday after Corpus Christi. New masters to be chosen then. All masters of craft to go with pageant masters and

pageant through city.

1575   E22 ff 80v-1   pp 378-9
New ordinances repeat sense of 1475 ones.

    f 19v 'The Origenall Perteynyng to þe Crafte of Armourers'

Pageant 7   Owners: Glovers
Cain killing Abel

1475   E20A f 140v   p 105
Pageant money: all sellers of gloves, purses or key bands to pay 2d if a York citizen,
4d if 'foreign'. Exemption was given to Mercers and those who sold 'London ware'.

    f 22 'The Origenall perteynyng to the Craft of gloueres / Sacrificum Cayme &
    Abell'

Pageant 8   Owners: Shipwrights
The Building of Noah's ark

No information

    f 24v 'The Shipwrites'

Pageant 9   Owners: Fishmongers and Mariners
Noah's ark during the Flood

Undated   E20 ff 128v-9   p 626
Fishmongers. Pageant money: masters setting up in craft to pay 6s 8d towards
pageant and Corpus Christi torches. Fines: half to go to craft for pageant and
torches.

1419-20 or 1433-4   E20 f 64v   pp 33-4
Mariners and Fishmongers. Dispute about the pageant. Council offered Mariners
a choice: (i) Mariners to pay 6s 8d a year to Fishmongers who then would become
wholly responsible for pageant; (ii) Fishmongers to pay 1s a year and present one-
third of the pageant. Mariners chose (ii).

1425   E20 f 279v   p 42
Fishmongers. Pageant money: annulment of former ordinance that Cooks who

sold fish should contribute to the Fishmongers.

1478   E20 f 304v   p 118
Mariners. Pageant money: masters to pay 2d a year to pageant and Corpus Christi torches, ordinary sailors to pay 1d a year. Fines: half to go to craft for pageant and torches.

1561   B23 f 23   pp 333-4
Fishmongers. Pageant money: poor people selling fresh-water fish no longer to contribute.

1585   B29 ff 81-2   pp 415-16
Mariners and Fishmongers. Pageant money: if pageant performed, members were to pay an equal sum per head.

   f 27 'The ffysheres and Maryners Noye'

Pageant 10   Owners: Parchmentmakers
The Sacrifice of Isaac by Abraham

1422-3   E20 f 258v   p 36
Fines: half to go to craft for pageant costs and other general expenses.

   f 32 'The Parchmynes and bokebynder / Abraham'

Pageant 11   Owners: Hosiers
Pharaoh with Moses and the Children of Israel

1403   E20 f 148v   pp 13-14
Disagreement between Drapers and Hosiers. Council ruled that the Hosiers, including those who sold 'drape de leyne', were to be responsible for the Moses pageant. Lucy T. Smith, *York Plays,* p xx, note 3, has suggested that in 1403 the Drapers and Hosiers presented this pageant together. In view of later ordinances instructing Hosiers who infringed on the Drapers' craft to contribute to the Drapers' pageant (see under Pageants 51 and 53), it seems possible that the 1403 disagreement was concerned with Hosiers who practised in the Drapers' craft. The entry need not imply that the Drapers were connected with Pageant 11.

   f 38 'The Hoseers Rex pharao'

Pageant 12   Owners: Spicers
The Annunciation to Mary by Gabriel

1433   E20A f 120   pp 53-4
Pageant money: sellers of sweet wine to contribute.

   f 44 'The spicers'

Pageant 13   Owners: Founders
Joseph wishing to send her away secretly

No information

   f 48 'The Pewteres and ffoundours'

Pageant 14   Owners: Tile-thatchers
Bethlehem with the birth of the boy

1419-20 or 1433-4   E20 f 57v   p 33
Tilers who infringe on Masons' craft to contribute to Masons; see above, Pageant
2 (Plasterers).

1422-3   E20 f 258   p 39
See above, Pageant 2.

1425   E20 f 284v   pp 41-2
Some Tilers to contribute to Carpenters' pageant (Pageant 46).

1474-5   E20A f 142v   p 104
See above, Pageant 2.

1527   B11 f 23   p 242
Pageant money: William Lawrence, a tilemaker to contribute to Tilers' pageant.

1572   E20A f 230   p 370 (Collated with E22 f 144v and B25 ff 32-3v)
See above, Pageant 2.

   f 51 'The Tille thekers Joseph'

Pageant 15   Owners: Chandlers
The Offering of the Shepherds

Undated   E20 f 20v   p 618
Fines: half to go to craft for pageant costs.

1417-18   E20 f 60v   pp 30-2
Chandlers making 'Paris candles' to contribute to Saucemakers (owners of Pageant 37).

1518   B9 f 96v   p 217
Whitchandlers and Saucemakers to contribute to Girdlers (owners of Pageant 20); had previously contributed to Millers' pageant (Pageant 41).

1563   B23 f 99   p 342
Pageant money: 4s from Innholders' pageant money to go to Chandlers.

1569   B24 f 133   p 356
Pageant money: half of Innholders' pageant money to go to Chandlers.

   f 56 'The Chandelers'

Pageant 16   Owners: Goldsmiths (before 1431-2); Masons (1431-2 to 1561);
   Minstrels (after 1561)
Herod questioning the Three Kings

1431-2   E20 f 257v   pp 47-8
Masons give up *Fergus* (Pageant 53) and take over one of the Herod pageants from the Goldsmiths.

1561   B23 f 40   p 334
Minstrels stated as having responsibility for pageant.

E20A ff 222-3v   pp 334-8
Minstrels have responsibility for pageant in ordinances.

1578   E22 f 143v   pp 385-9
Copy of 1561 ordinance.

   f 59v 'The Masons' (in hand of major scribe); 'Mynstralls' (in a sixteenth-century hand).

Pageant 17   Owners: Goldsmiths
The Offering of the Three Kings

1420   E20A f 42   p 35
Indenture concerning Goldsmiths' pageant house on Toft Green.

1561   E20A f 221v   p 334
Ordinances concerning the renting of play properties and costumes.

  f 64 'Golde Smyths /'

Pageant 18   Owners: Community of St Leonard's Hospital (before 1477);
   Masons (after 1477)
The Presentation of Christ in the Temple

1477   E20 f 291v   pp 112-13; CC1A f 114v   p 115
Masons take up responsibility for pageant. Pageant money: 13s 4d from Labourers.

1537   B13 f 96   p 263
An order between Masons and Labourers about pageant (unspecified).

1567   B24 f 82   p 351
Council orders Purification pageant to be registered.

  f 70 in sixteenth-century hand 'Hatmakers Masons and Laborers purificac*ionis*
  Marie the Laborers is assigned to bryng furth this pagyant. It is entryd in the
  Latter end of this booke / next aftir the Sledmen or palmers / and it begynnyth
  by the preest All myghty god in heaven so hye /'. f 212v in sixteenth-century
  hand (as is the episode) 'Hatmakers Masons & laborers'.

Pageant 19   Owners: Marshals
Flight into Egypt

1428   E20 f 287v   pp 45-6
Pageant money: disagreement between Marshals and Smiths about collection.

1442   E20 f 288   pp 59-60
Marshals and Smiths to present their two pageants and share the costs.

1480   B2-4 f 201   pp 123-4
Marshals, (Black)smiths and Bladesmiths combined to form a single craft presenting

the Marshals' pageant and the Smiths' pageant (Pageant 24).

f 71 'The Marchallis'

Pageant 20   Owners: Girdlers
The Slaughter of the Innocents

1446   BI: Prob. Reg. 2 f 138v   p 68
A gilded crown and gilded and enamelled belt left to guild as play properties by William Revetour.

1475-6   E20 f 74v   p 107
Pageant money: non-members practising as Girdlers to contribute; 'makers' 4d a year, and 'sellers' 2d a year. Exemption given to Mercers.

1485   E20 f 74v   p 136; B2-4 f 163   pp 136-7
Pageant money: non-members practising as Girdlers to contribute twice as much as members.

1518   B9 f 96v   p 217
Pageant money: Whitchandlers and Saucemakers to contribute 5s a year (previously paid to the Millers); see above, Pageant 15.

1554   B21 f 46v   p 312
Girdlers fined for delaying Corpus Christi play for an hour.

CC4(2) p 69   p 314
Fine payment recorded.

1569   B24 f 131v   p 355
Pageant money: Girdlers claiming contribution from Ironmongers. Searchers sent for by Council to defend claim.

f 76 'The Gyrdillers and naylers /'

Pageant 21   Owners: Spurriers and Lorimers
The Discovery of Christ in the Temple among the Doctors

1401   E20 f 42   p 13
Spurriers and Lorimers. Fines: half to go to craft for pageant costs.

1468 or 1481 E20 f 42 p 13
Hatmakers to be contributory.

1494 B7 f 109v p 176
Spurriers and Lorimers to walk with pageant along route. Pageant money: 'foreigners' to pay 4d a year.

1538 CC3(3) f 14 p 264
Record of fine for non-payment of pageant money.

1554 B21 f 45 p 311
Pageant money: Saddlers who sold spurs, buts or stirrups to contribute.

1569 B24 f 134v p 356
Pageant money: Bottlers to contribute.

   f 82 'The Sporiers and lorimers'

Pageant 22 Owners: Barbers
The Baptism of Christ by John

Undated E20 f 29v pp 620-1; E20 f 90v pp 625-6
Pageant money: 'foreigners' to contribute.

   f 84 'The Barbours'

Pageant 23 Owners: Taverners (Vintners)
The Marriage in Cana

1433 E20A f 119v pp 53-4
Vintners and sellers of sweet wines petition mayor. Vintners sometimes contribute to Mercers' pageant (Pageant 56). Ask for pageant money from all who sell sweet wine.

1481-2 E20 f 363 p 125
Pageant money: all sellers of sweet wines to contribute.

1483 B2-4 f 91v p 129
One John Harper allowed to sell wine without paying pageant money.

1526   B11 f 8v   pp 239-40
As 1481-2.

1551   B20, bound in end papers   pp 296-7
Pageant money: all admitted to craft to contribute.

1554   B21 f 46v   p 311
Pageant money: all Vintners to pay an equal amount.

1566   B24 f 82   p 351
Council orders that Vintners' pageant to be registered.

> MS order reverses Pageants 23 and 24 according to scripture and the first Ordo
> list. Vintners' pageant missing. f 92v in sixteenth-century hand, 'The vinteners',
> 'Leo this is a yoyfull day / Arch declyne / for me' and ff 92v-5v left blank.

Pageant 24   Owners: Smiths
The Temptation of Christ in the Desert

1428   E20 f 287v   pp 45-6
See above, Pageant 19.

1442   E20 f 288   pp 59-60
See above, Pageant 19.

1480   B2-4 f 201   pp 123-4
Marshals, (Black)smiths and Bladesmiths a single craft presenting the Marshals'
pageant (Pageant 19) and the Smiths' pageant.

1493   B7 f 100v pp 174-5 (Collated with E22 f 149v); E20 f 340   pp 175-6
Pageant money: Bladesmiths no longer to contribute. Blacksmiths making axes to
pay 16d to Bladesmiths' pageant (Pageant 30) besides money to their own pageant.

1530   B11 f 89   p 252
Locksmiths and Blacksmiths to agree to bring out pageant together.

1537   B13 f 96   p 263
Mayor to arbitrate between Locksmiths and Blacksmiths about pageant.

1553   B21 f 16   p 308
Pageant money: Blacksmiths and Bladesmiths to collect pageant money of both

crafts and then to make an equal division.

    f 90 'The Smythis Loke' added in a later hand.

Pageant 25 Owners: Curriers
The Transfiguration of Christ

Undated E20 f 26 p 619
Pageant money: everyone entering apprenticeship in the craft to pay 1s; every journeyman to pay 4d a year; every master setting up in craft to pay 3s 4d.

1424 E20 f 283 p 40
Fines: half to go to craft for pageant costs and other general expenses. Pageant money: every journeyman apprenticed in York to pay 4d a year, 8d if apprenticed elsewhere; every master apprenticed in York to pay 3s 4d on setting up in the craft, 'foreigners' to pay 6s 8d.

    f 96 'The Couriours'

Pageant 26 Owners: Ironmongers
Simon the Leper

1420 E20 f 80v pp 34-5
Fines: half to go to craft for pageant and other general costs. Pageant money: all sellers of iron ware to contribute, anyone setting up shop to pay 13s 4d to pageant.

1487 B6 f 92v p 153
Widow of ironmonger pays half a mark not to be pageant master.

1561 B23 f 50 p 340
John Granger, merchant, to act as pageant master for Ironmongers.

1566 B24 f 82 p 351
Council orders pageant to be registered.

1569 B24 f 131v p 355
Girdlers (owners of Pageant 20) claiming pageant money from them.

B24 f 157v p 357
Leonard Temple claiming he had spent 43s over two years to present the Iron-

mongers' pageant. 20s came from the city treasury and the rest of the money from those who bought and sold nails.

f 100v 'The Ironmongers'. Text missing. ff 100v-1v left blank.

Pageant 27   Owners: Plumbers
The Woman taken in Adultery

No information.

Episode combined with Pageant 28. No mention of Plumbers in MS.

Pageant 28   Owners: Capmakers
The Raising of Lazarus

Undated   E20 f 30   p 621
Fines: half to go to craft for pageant costs.

1494   E20 ff 371v-2   pp 176-7
Pageant money: anyone setting up as a master to pay 1s 8d to pageant if a York citizen, 'foreigners' to pay 10s. All 'foreigners' to pay 4d a year.

1553   B21 f H   p 307
Pageant money: Sledmen to contribute (see Pageant 48).

1567   B24 f 82   p 351
Cappers mentioned in order to register pageants possibly because of connection with Purification pageant.

1569   B24 f 134v   p 356
Pageant money: Hatters and Cappers to pay equal amounts.

1591   E20 f 371v   p 176
Hatters and Cappers made a single craft.

f 102 'The Cappemakers &c' in hand of major scribe and 'hatmakers' in sixteenth-century hand.

Pageant 29   Owners: Skinners
Jerusalem, with citizens and boys

Undated   E20 ff 22, 23   pp 618, 619
Fines: half to go to craft for pageant and other general costs. Pageant money: all fur-sellers to contribute.

1500   E20A ff 171A-1   pp 184-5
As Undated, above.

1517   B9 f 91v   p 214
Pageant money: Vestmentmakers to pay half of costs of Skinners' pageant.

B9 f 93v   p 215
Pageant money: every master vestmentmaker to pay 8d and every journeyman 4d a year to chamberlains, who turned it over to the Skinners.

1582   B28 ff 70-1v   pp 400-1
Pageant money: all gatherers of rabbit skins to contribute. All merchants buying or selling skins to pay 6d a year. Master vestmentmakers to pay 8d a year and journeymen 4d if the pageant was played.

   f 106v 'The Skynners'

Pageant 30   Owners: Cutlers
The Conspiracy

Undated   E20 f 51v   p 623
Fines: half to go to craft for pageant costs.

1445   E20 f 53   p 64
Pageant money: Thomas Vsclyf, merchant, to pay 10d a year to pageant and Corpus Christi torches of Cutlers, Bladesmiths and Sheathers.

1479-80   E20 f 52   p 123
As Undated, above.

1483   E20 f 52v   p 131
Pageant money: masters to answer for pageant money of their 'foreign' workers, not more than 6d a year per worker.

1493   B7 f 96v   p 169
Pageant money: Cutlers received 5s a year from Linenweavers via city chamberlains.

1500   E20A f 201v   p 185 (Collated with B8 f 80v)
Pageant money: Horners to contribute.

1518   B9 f 94v   pp 215-16
Pageant money: Linenweavers and Woollenweavers to be separate crafts. Linenweavers to pay 5s a year to Cutlers.

   f 113 'The Cuttlerers'

Pageant 31   Owners: Bakers
The Last Supper

Undated   E20 f 10v   p 617
Fines: half to go to craft for pageant costs.

1411-12   E20 f 65v, 68   p 16
Anyone selling bread must pay pageant money to Bakers.

1503   B9 ff 3v-4   pp 191-3
Pageant money: disagreement between Bakers and Cooks (owners of Pageant 36)
about the storage of Cooks' wagon in Bakers' pageant house and the right to Watercarters' and Sandcarters' pageant money. Cooks to pay Bakers 3s 4d a year and to
be allowed to store wagon in their pageant house and collect Watercarters' and Sandcarters' money. See also Bakers' Accounts 1544-1609.

1554   CC4(2) p 59   p 315
Two Bakers fined for not attending the pageant.

   f 120v 'The Baxsteres'

Pageant 32   Owners: Waterleaders (Watercarters)
The Washing of the Apostles' Feet

See above, Pageant 31.

   MS of Pageant 31 includes this episode. See below Pageant 37.

Pageant 33   Owners: Cordwainers
The Agony and Betrayal

Undated   E20 ff 76-7v   pp 624-5
Pageant money: 'foreigners' setting up as masters to pay 40s to pageant and other general costs.

1417, 1427 or 1442   E20 ff 75v, 78   p 30
Masters not to acquire any servants from another master before noon on St Stephen's day or pay half a mark to the pageant. Twelve men of the craft to walk with the pageant.

1522   B10 f 37v   p 227
Pageant money: William Hay, girdler, had set up as a cordwainer without payment of any sort. Ordered to pay pageant money each year.

1580   QQ80/4/1 ff 1v, 3   pp 395-6 (f 1v collated with QQ80/4/2 f 1v)
Pageant money to be paid without grumbling. If pageant played company to walk with pageant.

   f 125 'The Cordewaneres'

Pageant 34   Owners: Bowers and Fletchers
Trial before Caiaphas

Undated   E20 f 22v   p 619
Pageant money: anyone entering apprenticeship to pay 3s 4d to pageant.

1388   E20 f 44   p 6
Fletchers (associated with Bowers). Fines: half to go to craft for pageant costs.

1395   E20 f 20v   p 8
Fines: half to go to craft for pageant costs.

   f 132 'The Bowers and fflechers'

Pageant 35   Owners: Tapiters
First Trial before Pilate

1419   E20 f 43v   pp 32-3
Fines: half to go to craft for pageant and other general costs. Pageant money:

'foreigners' setting up as masters to pay 26s 8d to pageant and other general costs.

1475-6 E20 ff 295v-6 pp 107-8
Pageant money: Linenweavers previously paid 6s a year to Tapiters, now released from obligation. Tapiters who set up linen looms no longer to pay pageant money to Linenweavers. Dyers to pay 3s 4d a year; every coverlet-seller to pay 2d a year.

1476 B1 f 20v p 110
Pageant money: Linenweavers no longer to pay Tapiters.

1478 E20 f 296v pp 118-19
Cancelled ordinances reaffirming pageant support.

1485 B2-4 f 163 p 136
See above, Pageant 3.

1490 E20 f 302 pp 160-1
Pageant money: Tapiters who dye yarn, cloth or wool to contribute to Dyers.

1551 E20 f 292v pp 300-1
Fines: one-third to go to craft for pageant costs.

B20 f 70v p 300
Pageant money: all working with coloured yarn to contribute.

    f 134v 'The Tapiters and Couchers'

Pageant 36 Owners: Dyers (Litsters)
The Presentation of Christ before Herod

Undated E20 f 45v p 623
Pageant money: masters setting up in craft to pay 10s; anyone entering apprentice-ship to pay 10s.

1477 B1 f 67v pp 111-12
Fines: half to go to craft for pageant costs.

    f 152 'The lysteres'

Pageant 37   Owners: Cooks
The Remorse of Judas

1503   B9 ff 3v-4   pp 191-3
See above, Pageant 31.

1529   B11 ff 59v-67   pp 250-1
Pageant money: poultry-sellers to contribute 6d a year; they had previously paid Butchers (owners of Pageant 44).

   f 160v 'The Cokis and watirlederes'

Pageant 38   Owners: Saucemakers
The Hanging of Judas

1417-18   E20 f 60v   pp 30-2
Pageant money: all making Paris candles, except Butchers, to contribute one-third of pageant costs. (1417-18) New rule: all except Butchers to pay 2d a year. Non-members of craft who sell sauces to pay as much as members.

1421-2   E20 f 283v   pp 48-50
Four pageants combined into one dramatic unit to be called the Condemnation of Christ - those of Saucemakers (Pageant 38), Tilemakers (Pageant 39), Turners, Hayresters and Bollers (Pageant 40), and Millers (Pageant 42). Saucemakers and Tilemakers to be responsible for new pageant. Millers to contribute 10s a year, Hayresters 5s. Repairs: Millers to contribute one-third, Hayresters one-sixth; one man from Millers, one from Hayresters, and the pageant masters to supervise repairs. (1432) New rule: Tilemakers to present pageant, Saucemakers to pay 5s a year and 1d each when repairs needed. Repairs to be supervised by two men from each craft.

1515   B9 f 81   p 212
Millers take over pageant from Tilemakers.

1518   B9 f 96v   p 217
Pageant money: Millers no longer to have Saucemakers' and Whitchandlers' money, which is to go to the Girdlers (owners of Pageant 20). Millers to have Tilemakers' ·money.

   f 167 contains amalgamated episodes. 'The Tyllemakers' in hand of original scribe cancelled and 'Mylners' written in sixteenth-century hand.

Pageant 39   Owners: Tilemakers
The Condemnation of Christ by Pilate

See above, Pageant 38.

1420, 1421, 1427   Tileworks Accounts: VC Box XII and Vq 1x   pp 36, 37, 44
Vicars' Choral involved in pageant.

Pageant 40   Owners: Turners and Bowlmakers
The Scourging and Crowning with Thorns

See above, Pageant 38.

1482   E55A ff 9-9v   p 129
Pageant money: all Carpenters, Joiners and Carvers who do any turning to contribute to the Turners and Ropers. This decision modified, and all who turn bowls,
dishes, wheels or chairs to pay.

1487   B6 f 92   pp 152-3
Hayresters paying pageant silver to Ropers.

1551-2   B20 f 64v   p 300; B20 f 126   p 304
1482 and 1487 orders confirmed.

1554   B21 f 45   p 311; B21 f 57   pp 312-13
Pageant money: all Carpenters, Joiners and Carvers who do any turning to contribute to the Turners and Ropers. This decision modified, and all who turn bowls,
dishes, wheels or chairs to pay.

Pageant 41   Owners: Shearers
The Road to Calvary

1405   E20 ff 42v-3   pp 14-15
Fines: half to go to craft for pageant costs. Pageant money: masters taking apprentices to pay 12d.

1425   E20 f 279   p 41
Pageant money: Fullers to contribute to the Shearers.

1517   B9 f 91v   p 214
Pageant money: common Carters to contribute.

f 175 'The Shermen'

Pageant 42   Owners: Millers
The Parting of Christ's Garments

See above, Pageant 38.

Pageant 43   Owners: Painters
The Stretching out and Nailing of Christ

Undated   E20 f 64   p 624
Pageant money: Goldbeaters (associated with Goldsmiths, owners of Pageants 16 and 17) to contribute.

1422   E20 f 247v   pp 37-8
Painters' and Stainers' pageant to be removed. Material combined with that of Pinners' and Latteners' pageant (Pageant 44). Painters and Stainers to contribute to Pinners and Latteners 5s a year, to be paid to the pageant masters of the Pinners and Latteners on the vigil of Corpus Christi.

1482   E20 f 379   p 128
Pageant money: 'foreign' Pinners to pay 2d a year. Pinners and Wiredrawers to be one craft, all to contribute.

1521   B10 f 18v   p 223
Pageant money: Painters to receive Pinners' pageant money.

1561   B23 f 13   p 332
Pageant money: Painters complain that they pay more than Pinners. Both to pay same amount.

1562   B23 f 50   p 340
Christopher Grason, pinner, to bring forth Painters' pageant.

1564   B23 f 163   p 344
Pageant money: Tinklers and makers of fish-hooks to pay 4d a year. 'Foreign' Pinners to contribute.

  MS contains combined episodes. f 181 'The Pynners' in hand of original scribe 'and paynters' added in a sixteenth-century hand. 'Crucifixio Chr*ist*i'

Pageant 44   Owners: Latteners
The Raising of Christ on the Mountain

Undated   E20 f 33v   p 622
Fines: half to go to craft for pageant costs.

Undated   E20 f 64   p 624
Pageant money: Painters, Stainers and Goldbeaters all to contribute.

See also above, Pageant 43.

Pageant 45   Owners: Butchers
The Death of Christ on Calvary

1431   E20 f 21v   p 47
Pageant money: 'foreigners' to pay 4d a year. Fines: half to go to craft for pageant costs.

1522   B10 f 37v   p 227
Pageant money: Hew Howlley, haberdasher, set up as a butcher without payment to craft. Ordered to pay pageant money.

1529   B11 f 59v   pp 250-1
Pageant money: Poulterers no longer to contribute (see above, Pageant 37).

1550   B20 f 14   p 294
Pageant money: 'foreign' Butchers not to pay this year because of plague.

 f 184 'The Bocheres Mortificacio Christi'

Pageant 46   Owners: Saddlers
The Harrowing of Hell

Undated   E20 f 34   p 622
Fines: half to go to craft for pageant costs. Pageant money: masters to pay 12d for each apprentice.

1398   E20 f 34v   p 10
Fines: half to go to the craft for pageant costs.

1551 B20 f 56 pp 297-8
Pageant money: Glasiers to pay one-third of pageant costs or else the Saddlers and Glasiers each to pay the same amount.

   f 194v 'The Sadillers'

Pageant 47 Owners: Carpenters (Wrights)
The Resurrection of Christ

1425 E20 f 284v pp 41-2
Pageant money: Tilers making louvers to contribute.

1462 E20 f 293v pp 92-3
Pageant money: 'foreigners' to contribute.

1482 E20 ff 367-8 pp 126-7 (Collated with E55A f 4)
Pageant money: Carpenters, Carvers, Joiners and Cartwrights to pay equal amounts. Masters to pay 4d a year for each journeyman, servant or apprentice.

1485 B2-4 f 160 p 136
Disagreement between Carpenters and Sawyers about presentation of Fergus pageant (see below, Pageant 54).

1500 B8 f 101v pp 182-4
Pageant money: Cartwrights. Every master previously paid 4d a year for each apprentice, now to pay 6d a year no matter how many apprentices he has. Every journeyman to pay 4d. The Cartwrights to make four new wheels for the wagon and to be released from paying for pageant repairs from then on.

1507 B9 f 37 pp 204-5
Pageant money: Cartwrights to contribute.

1554 B21 f 45 p 311; B21 f 57 p 312
See above, Pageant 40.

1563 E20A ff 227-7v p 342
Anyone dealing commercially with boards or 'lattes' to contribute to Carpenters' pageant.

1575 B26 f 60 p 380
Ordinance of 1563 revoked except in case of 'foreigners'.

f 200 'The Carpenteres'

Pageant 48   Owners: Winedrawers
The Appearance of Christ to Mary Magdalene

No information.

> f 205v No ascription in hand of major scribe. Centred over episode and cancelled
> in sixteenth-century hand 'Wevers assyned in anno domini in Cliijth William
> Cowplande then maier'. 'Sledmen' written in left-hand margin; 'palmers' in right.
> Running heading for most of episode 'The wynedrawers' in hand of major scribe.

Pageant 49   Owners: Wool-packers
Travellers to Emmaus

1428   E20 f 285   p 46
Pageant money: all wool-sellers to contribute.

1553   B21 f H   p 307
By 1535 the Sledmen had become owners of this pageant as they had a pageant
fund of 2s 8d in that year [CC3(2), pp 52, 154 pp 258, 261]. Woollenweavers
take over from Sledmen. Sledmen to contribute to Cappers (owners of Pageant 28).

1555   B21 f 90   p 321
All who profit from guests and guests' horses and have no sign to contribute.

> f 209 'The wyndraweres' in hand of major scribe cancelled and 'Sledmen'
> written above in the hand that wrote 'Sledmen' on f 205v (see above). Running
> heading on 'wyndraweres' corrected to 'Sledmen' by a sixteenth-century hand.

Pageant 50   Owners: Scriveners
The Appearance of Christ to the apostle Thomas and others

Undated   E20 f 21   p 618
Fines of 10s to go to pageant and ceremonial torches.

1486-7   E20A f 149   p 152
Pageant money: Textwriters, Luminers, Turners and Flourishers: 'foreigners' to
pay 4d a year.

1554   B21 f 46v   p 312
Pageant money: Corn-merchants to contribute.

CC4(2) p 69   p 314
John Meltynby, scrivener, paid by chamberlains from fine money because there was
no one else to share charges.

   f 218 'The Escreueneres' in hand of major scribe cancelled and 'Escreveners'
   written in by later hand (?).

Pageant 51   Owners: Tailors
The Ascension of Christ into Heaven

1386-7   E20 f 38   p 4
Pageant money to be collected. Searchers to account the third Sunday after Corpus
Christi. Searchers to spend only 4s for collecting and Corpus Christi expenses.

1492   B7 f 77   p 166
Pageant money: 'Kendale men' bringing cloth to York to sell to contribute to
Drapers and Tailors.

1505   B9 f 25   p 201
Drapers request contribution from Tailors for their pageant (Pageant 53).

B9 f 26   p 201
Pageant money: Tailors ask respite to consider contributions to Drapers by those
Tailors and Hosiers selling cloth.

1508   B9 f 42   p 205
Pageant money: Tailors and anyone else selling broad southern cloth to pay 1s a
year to Drapers' pageant (Pageant 53).

1529   B11 f 54   p 249
Pageant money: all Tailors selling broad southern cloth to pay 2s a year to Drapers.

1551   B20 f 52v   p 297
Pageant no longer played, Tailors' pageant money to be used as lord mayor decrees.

B20 ff 63-3v   p 299
Ordinance concerning Kendal men reconfirmed (see 1492).

   f 221 'The Tailoures' in hand of major scribe. 'Potters' in a later hand cancelled.

Pageant 52   Owners: Potters
Pentecost

Undated   E20 f 58v   p 623
Fines: half to go to craft for pageant costs.

   f 226 'The Potteres'

Pageant 53   Owners: Drapers
The Death of the Blessed Mary

1492   B7 f 77   p 166
See above, Pageant 51.

1505   B9 f 25   p 201
Pageant money: Mayor William Holbeck and Council decreed that all Tailors and
Hosiers who sold broad southern cloth should contribute to Drapers.

B9 f 26   p 201
See above, Pageant 51.

1508   B9 f 42   p 205
See above, Pageant 51.

1522   B10 f 43   p 227
Pageant money: all who sell broad southern cloth to contribute.

1523   B10 f 63Bv   pp 230-1
List of pageant money and money for pageant repairs.

1529   B11 f 54   p 249
See above, Pageant 51.

1548   B19 f 16v   pp 291-2
Corpus Christi Play to be played without Death of Virgin.

1549   B19 f 69v   p 293
As 1548.

1551   B20 f 56   p 297
Drapers no longer to perform pageant. Ordered to pay 13s 4d to be used for other
pageants as lord mayor decrees.

1554 B21 f 63 p 313
Four drapers refuse to pay pageant money.

1561 B23 f 10 pp 331-2
As 1548.

  f 231 'The Draperes'

Pageant 54 Owners: Masons (before 1431-2); Linenweavers (1477-85);
  see also Pageants 3, 16 and 18
The Carrying of the Body of Mary (Fergus)

1431-2 E20 f 257v pp 48-9
Masons give up *Fergus;* see above, Pageant 16.

1475-6 E20 ff 295v-6 pp 107-8
Linenweavers no longer to pay Tapiters (owners of Pageant 35).

1476 B1 f 20v p 110
Linenweavers to present *Fergus,* no longer to pay Tapiters. Pageant money: all
owners of linen looms to pay 3d a year. Masters setting up in the craft to pay 8d to
pageant.

1479 B1 f 21 p 123
Linenweavers' fines: half to go to craft for pageant costs. 'Foreigners' to pay 4d a
year. Journeymen to pay 1d a year.

1485 B2-4 f 160 p 136
Disagreement between Sawyers and Carpenters about presentation of *Fergus,* see
above, Pageant 47.

B2-4 f 163 p 136
Linenweavers no longer to present *Fergus,* to assist Tapiters and Cardmakers
(Pageant 3).

1486 C4:1 mb 1 p 143
Linenweavers fined for not playing *Fergus.*

1493 B7 f 96v p 169
Linenweavers to contribute 5s to Cutlers (owners of Pageant 30).

1518   B9 f 94v   pp 215-17
As 1493 above. Woollenweavers not to assist in this contribution unless the Linen-weavers present *Fergus.* Linenweavers not to take pageant money from 'foreigners'.

Not in MS.

Pageant 55   Owners: Woollenweavers
The Assumption of the Virgin

1486   C4:1 mb 4d   p 145
Pageant used in royal entry.

1518   B9 f 94v   pp 215-17
See above, Pageant 54.

1528   B11 f 35   p 245
Linenweavers to pay 4d each to Woollenweavers (owners of Pageant 55).

1540   B9 f 102v   pp 268-9
Linenweavers to contribute to Woollenweavers, masters 2d per loom, journeymen 1d a year.

1548   B19 f 16v   pp 291-2
Corpus Christi Play to be played without Assumption of Mary.

1549   B19 f 69v   p 293
As 1548.

1553   B21 f H   p 307
Woollenweavers having lost pageant, take over Sledmen's pageant (Pageant 49).

1555   B21 f 90   p 321
See above, Pageant 49.

1561   B23 f 10   pp 331-2
As 1548.

1584-1607
Collection of pageant money; see p 426 and note.

   f 234 'the wefferes Thomas ap*ostolus*'. This episode ascribed to the weavers is

not the Assumption of the Virgin but the appearance of the Virgin to Thomas
with music.

Pageant 56   Owners: Mayor, etc; Innholders (by 1468-9)
The Coronation of the Virgin

1477   E20A f 195A   p 114 (Collated with B1 f 68)
Fines: half to go to craft for pageant costs.

1484   B5 f 24   pp 133-4
Civic subsidy of 2s. Records of subsidy in Chamberlains' accounts (1468-1554),
pp 101-315.

1528   E20A ff 195v-6   pp 245-6
Fines: half to go to craft for pageant costs and other general expenses. Reckoning
to be made Sunday after Corpus Christi.

1548   B19 f 16v   pp 291-2
Corpus Christi Play to be played without Coronation of Virgin.

1549   B19 f 69v   p 293
As 1548.

1551   B20 f 52v   p 297
No longer to present pageant; pageant money to be used as lord mayor decrees.

1561   B23 f 10   pp 331-2
As 1548.

1563   B23 f 99   p 342
To pay 4s to Chandlers (owners of Pageant 15).

1564   B23 f 166   p 343
Fines as 1528 above. Pageant money: if Corpus Christi Play not performed, Innholders not to pay any more than other crafts to the city treasury.

1569   B24 f 133   p 356
Pageant money: half to go to Chandlers.

1585   CC6(1) f 70v   p 419
Pageant apparently used in Midsummer Show.

f 242 'The Osteleres' in hand of original scribe. 'Als Inholders' in sixteenth-century hand. This episode is the Assumption of the Virgin. f 252 'The Inholders' is a fragment of a Coronation pageant.

Pageant 57   Owners: Mercers
The Last Judgment

1433   E20A f 119v   p 53
Pageant money: Mercers claim pageant money from Vintners (owners of Pageant 23).

1541   B15 f 20   p 270
Pageant used in royal entry.

See also Mercers' documents (1433-1590).

f 246 'The merceres'

Translations: The Records

The Latin and Anglo-Norman documents have been translated as
literally as possible. Our intention has been to aid the reader in
understanding what the documents say. Ambiguities in the
original have, therefore, been left ambiguous. We have made no
attempt to condense or otherwise gloss over awkwardness in
style, especially in formulae. The arrangement of the translations
parallels that of the text. Repetitive entries have been translated
once and then cross-referenced. No indication is given of the
documents in English surrounding those in Latin or Anglo-
Norman. Place names and Christian names have been normalized
but not surnames. Capitalization and punctuation are in accordance with modern practice. As in the text, diamond brackets
indicate obliterations, square brackets cancellations and ° °
additions in later or different hands. No indication is given of
interlineations in the text. Round brackets enclose words not
in the original language but needed for grammatical sense in
English. Formulaic Latin headings for English entries have not
been translated. English headings for Latin entries do not
appear in translations.

1220-5
Statute Book YM: M1/1/b

f 7v

...

Item, one will contrive stars with all things pertaining to them
except the rushes which the boy bishop of future (times will
acquire): one on Christmas night for the shepherds and two on
Epiphany night if the presentation of the three kings be done.

...

1325
Miscellaneous Register   YM: M2/4/g

f 28v   *(16 August)*

...

Feast of
Corpus Christi

They also decided to the honour of God that the feast of Corpus
Christi be celebrated with a double office in the choir and at the
altar henceforth.

...

1343
Constitution of Archbishop de Zouche   BI: Reg. 10

f 264*   *(12 February)*

... Desiring nevertheless ... to enlarge the praise and glory of
omnipotent God and of the same Lord, our Jesus Christ, as far
as we are able ... we proclaim, establish, ordain, and determine ...
that that most distinguished day, viz, (the day) of Friday which
is called the day of preparation before Easter ... be praised,
glorified, honoured, and sanctified truly and worthily by each
and every one of you subject to us in our city and diocese and
in the individual churches of the same ... on pontifical authority.
... And so, let this be a festive day and a double feast henceforth
... let unseemly conversations and illicit discussions cease, let the
regular judiciary order pause and all irregular noises be still on
that day. ... Let all abstain from plays, spectacles, markets, trade
and commerce, and from all rural work, craft work, and equally
from all servile labour, uncleanness, and sin ...

1366
Will of Thomas de Bukton, rector of Rudby   YM: L/2/4

f 44   *(29 November; probated 2 January)*
... Item, I leave to the solemnity of Corpus Christi celebrated
each year in the city of York 100 shillings ...

1370
St Leonard's Hospital Accounts   YM: M2/6/c

f 29*

Gratuities

And to the minstrels on the feast of St Leonard, 3s 4d ... And
given to various men for a certain interlude (played) before

the master at Christmas, 2s. ...

1371
York Minster Chamberlains' Rolls   YM: E1/1 *MP*

mb 2*

Various expenses   ... And to the minstrels on the feast of the Translation of St William, 3s 4d. And to the same for the four days of Pentecost, 13s 4d. ...

YM: E1/2 *PM*

Minor and
various expenses

mb 2
... And to the minstrels on the feast of St William, 3s 4d. ...

1374
York Minster Chamberlains' Rolls   YM: E1/3 *MP*

mb 2
(*as E1/1 above 1371*)

1375
St Leonard's Hospital Accounts   YM: M2/6/c

(...)

f 44v*
... ⟨Item, given⟩ to the minstrels on the feast of St Leonard 3s 4d. ...

York Minster Chamberlains' Rolls   YM: E1/4 *MP*

mb 2
(*as E1/1 above 1371*)

1376
A/Y Memorandum Book   Y: E20

f 3*
Rents of Ouse Bridge to be levied by their wardens.

f 4v
For one building in which three Corpus Christi pageants are housed per annum   2s

York Minster Chamberlains' Rolls   YM: E1/5 *PM*

mb 3
(as E1/2 above 1371)

Will of William de Thorp, clerk   YM: Reg. Wills I L2/4

Will of William
de Thorp, clerk

f 63   *(21 November; probated 24 November)*
... Item, to Sir Richard de Yhedyngham, my books of plays if
he wants to have them, and a cabinet if he wants to have (it),
and if he doesn't (so) wish, I leave that cabinet to the church
of the blessed Mary ad Valvas to put things in. ...

1378
St Leonard's Hospital Accounts   YM: M2/6/c

Gratuities

f 71
Item, given to the minstrels on the feast of St Leonard as a
gratuity, 2s. ... Item, given to one minstrel at the same feast at
the command of the warden, 6d. ...

1382
York Minster Chamberlains' Rolls   YM: E1/7 *PM*

mb 2
(as E1/2 above 1371)

1385
St Leonard's Hospital Accounts   YM: M2/6/c

Gratuities

f 74
In gratuities made to the minstrels on the feast of St Leonard,
6s 8d. ... Item, given to two minstrels on the feast of the Purification of the Virgin Mary in the presence of the warden and the
brothers, 4d. ...

1386-7
A/Y Memorandum Book   Y: E20

f 38   *Tailors*

...
Item, the said four searchers will collect each year within the city

® That (there be) the proper amount from each man of the said guild for the
an account of support of their pageant of Corpus Christi and will make all the
expenses on expenditures to sustain and maintain the said pageant and will
pain of 10s give account each year the third Sunday next after the said feast
of Corpus Christi without any more delay, on pain of 10s to
pay, one half to the four searchers aforesaid and the other half
to the Council Chamber on Ouse Bridge in York.

...

f 40 *Tailors*
Item, that no searchers who will be designated to guard and
search the aforementioned guild will spend in the collection of
the money for their pageant and for their expenses on the day
of Corpus Christi 4s in coin and for all other small expenses
for all year 2s 8d, no more, and if it be proved that any searcher
act contrary to this, he will forfeit 20s for the use of the
commonalty and for the support of the light aforesaid in equal
portion.

...

1387
A/Y Memorandum Book Y : E 20

f 163v

Duffeld, Catton Memorandum that although a certain dispute recently had been
and Robert de moved between Robert de Waghen, carpenter, on the one hand,
Halton and and John de Duffeld, skinner, John de Catton, baker, and Robert
Waghen de Halton, dyer, and men of their own three crafts, on the other
hand, about the building and repair of a certain house on the
Tofts for housing their Corpus Christi pageants, nevertheless
they came to an agreement under this form, viz, that the said
Robert de Waghen will undertake competently to build and
repair the said house for housing the three said pageants within
the same, under the supervision of the mayor and the honourable men of the city from around the feast of Pentecost in the
tenth year of King Richard to the election of the said mayor
who was (mayor) at the time. And the said Robert de Waghen, to
keep and fulfill this well and faithfully, chose John de Ruddeston,
barker of York, as surety and guarantor, John, who indeed
bound himself and his executors to building the said house if
the said Robert has failed because he was away in the building
and repair of the said house.

York Minster Chamberlains' Rolls   Y M : E 1/8 *MP*

mb 2

And to the minstrels on the Translation of St William, 3s 4d, and
to the same for four days at Pentecost, 13s 4d. ...

1388
A/Y Memorandum Book   Y : E 20

f 164

Memorandum that William de Seleby, then mayor of York, gave
to Stephen de Yolton of Tollerton 100s which Master Thomas de
Bukton gave under a set form for acquiring the four torches
burning in the procession around the body of Christ on the same
feast of Corpus Christi, on the eighth day of May in the eleventh
year of the reign of King Richard the second after the conquest
of England. And the said Stephen will pay 6s 8d toward the
work of the said light till the next (feast of the) Purification, and
the aforesaid William de Seleby is the guarantor for the aforesaid
money.

f 44   *(13 December)*

fletchers

...

First, that no fletcher of this city will work henceforth any
Sunday at any work belonging to their said guild, nor put any
arrows, bolts, nor other of their darts in front to show for sale on
any Sunday on pain of 40d to pay, one half to the Chamber and
the other to their pageant of Corpus Christi, and this each time
that they or any of them shall be convicted, except for putting
the heads on the shafts when need be, the aforesaid ordinances
not withstanding.

...

York Minster Chamberlains' Rolls   Y M : E 1/9 *MP*

mb 4*
(as E1/1 above 1371)

1388-9
Pater Noster Guild   PRO: C47/46/454*

(21 January)
... First, as to the cause of the founding of said fraternity, it
should be known that after a certain play on the usefulness of
the Lord's Prayer was composed, in which play, indeed, many
vices and sins are reproved and virtues commended, and was
played in the city of York, it had such and so great an appeal
that very many said: 'Would that this play were established in
this city for the salvation of souls and the solace of the citizens
and neighbours.' Wherefore, the whole and complete cause of
the foundation and association of the brothers of the same
fraternity was that that play be managed at future times for the
health and reformation of the souls, both of those in charge of
that play and of those hearing it. And thus, the principal work
of the said fraternity is that the play should be managed to the
greater glory of God, the deviser of the said prayer, and for the
reproving of sins and vices ... Item, they are bound, whenever
the play of the said Lord's Prayer is shown in the form of a play
in the city of York, to ride with the players of the same through
certain principal streets of the city of York and to be dressed
in one livery, to give greater ornament to their riding. And some
of them are bound to go or ride with those players until the
said play be completely finished for the peaceful managing of
the said play. ... Nor do any rents or land, or holdings, or any
other chattels, excepting only the apparatus intended for the use
of the said play, belong to the said fraternity, which apparatus,
indeed, cannot in the least serve any other purpose except only
the said play. And there is one wooden chest belonging to the
said fraternity to hold the said apparatus. ...

1389
York Minster Chamberlains' Rolls   YM: E1/11 *MP*

mb 2
(as E1/1 above 1371)

YM: E1/14 *PM*

Minor and various expenses   mb 2*
... And to the minstrels on the feast of the Translation of St

William, 3s 4d. ...

1390
A/Y Memorandum Book   Y : E 20

f 46*

Plasterers

® These
ordinances are
cancelled and
other new ones
are made which
are written in
the new register

...

[Item, that none of the guild take apprentice for a shorter term
than for seven years on pain of a half mark to pay, 40d to the
Chamber and 40d for the use of their pageant of Corpus Christi.]

...

York Minster Chamberlains' Rolls   Y M : E 1 / 12 / 1 *MP*

mb 2
(as E1/1 above 1371)

Y M : E 1/15 *PM*

mb 2
(as E1/2 above 1371)

1391
York Minster Chamberlains' Rolls   Y M : E 1/17 *MP*

mb 2*
(as E1/1 above 1371)

1394
A/Y Memorandum Book   Y : E 20

f 17v*   *(28 April)*

Concerning
the Corpus
Christi Play

More in the
second folio
following

...

On the same day it was agreed that all the pageants of Corpus
Christi shall play in the places appointed from ancient times and
not elsewhere, but just as they shall be prearranged by the
mayor, the bailiffs, and their officers, so that if any pageant does
otherwise, the members of the craft of the said pageant shall pay
6s 8d in the chamber of the mayor for the use of the commons.

...

York Minster Chamberlains' Rolls   YM: E1/19 *MP*

mb 1
(as E1/1 above 1371)

1395
A/Y Memorandum Book   Y: E20

f 20v   *(30 December)   Bowers*

...

Which forfeiture will be raised and paid by those who act contrary to the said ordinances as many times as they are found in default, that is, one half of the said forfeitures for the use of the commonalty of the city of York in the Council Chamber and the other half for the maintenance of the pageant of their aforementioned guild.

...

York Minster Chamberlains' Rolls   YM: E1/22 *PM*

mb 2
(as E1/2 above 1371)

1396
City Chamberlains' Rolls   Y: C1:1

mb 1
...

Expenses on the feast of Corpus Christi together with gifts to the minstrels of the lords for the whole year, 11s 6d

Item, it is reckoned for the staining of 4 pieces of cloth for the fabric of the pageant, 4s. And for the carrying (and) re-carrying of timber for the railings before the king, 2s 1d. And for 8 porters guiding and moving a pageant, 5s 4d. And for a new banner and apparatus, 12s 2d. And for the players, 15s 4d. And for bread, beer, wine, and meat, and faggots for the mayor and the honourable men during the day at the play, 18s 8d. And to the door-keeper of Holy Trinity for housing the pageant, 4d. And to the minstrels on the feast of Corpus Christi, 13s 4d. And for iron nails for repairing the pageant, 5d. And for 20 fir spars for the aforesaid railings before the king, 5s 10d. And to Robert Paton for pageant building in carpentry work for two days, 12d. And for the painting for the pageants, 2s. And for 19 saplings bought from John de

Craven for the aforesaid railings, 6s 8d. And to William de Warneby, carpenter, for his work at the same place, 4s 4d.

Total £4 11s 6d

And to the visiting minstrels of the lord king and of the other lords, £7 7s 4d.

Total *(blank)*

Total £7 7s 4d

...

Minor expenses And for 2 membranes of parchment at the time of the billets of Corpus Christ, 6d.

...

York Minster Chamberlains' Rolls YM: E1/23 *MP*

mb 2
(as E1/1 above 1371)

YM: E1/24 *PM*

mb 3
(as E1/2 above 1371)

1397
York Minster Chamberlains' Rolls YM: E1/10 *MP*

mb 2

Minor and various expenses ... And to the minstrels on the feast of the Translation of St William, 3s 4d. ... And to the minstrels on the feast of St William, 6s 8d. And to the same for the four days of Pentecost, 26s 8d. ...

1398
A/Y Memorandum Book Y: E20

f 34v *Saddlers*
... And that henceforth a half of all said fines of their guild and ordinance, as is mentioned above, be paid to the searchers and governors [of their said guild] of their said guild to support their pageant of Corpus Christi and in other such needs as will seem best to them. ...

York Minster Chamberlains' Rolls YM: E1/27 MP

mb 2*

Minor and
various expenses

... And to the minstrels on the feast of the Translation of St
William, 6s 8d. And to the same for the four days of Pentecost,
26s 8d. And to the same from the gratuity (fund) of the chapter
on the same occasion, ⟨.....⟩ 13s 4d. ...

1399
A/Y Memorandum Book Y: E20

f 19v

°Concerning the ordinance of the Corpus Christi Play in the
twenty-second year of the reign of King Richard the second, and
more about the same matter in the second folio preceding, and
about the torches of the honourable citizens in the fourth folio
preceding, and about the Bucklermakers and Sheathers in the
eighth folio preceding, and about the pageant of Moses and
Pharaoh in the one hundred and twelfth folio following, and
the order of the pageants at the end of this book. °†

To the honourable men, the mayor and aldermen of the city of
York, the commons of the same city beg that, inasmuch as they
incur great expense and costs in connection with the pageants
and plays of Corpus Christi day, the which cannot be played or
performed on the same day as they ought to be, because the
aforesaid pageants are played in so many places at considerable
hardship and deprivation to the said commons and strangers who
have travelled to the said city on the same day for the same
purpose, that it please you to consider that the said pageants
are maintained and supported by the commons and the craftsmen of the same city in honour and reverence of our Lord Jesus
Christ and for the glory and benefit of the same city, that you
decree that the aforesaid pageants be played in the places to
which they were limited and assigned by you and by the aforesaid
commons previously, the which places are annexed to this bill
in a schedule, or in other places from year to year according
to the disposition and will of the mayor and the council of the
Chamber, and that anyone who acts in contravention of the
aforesaid ordinances and regulations shall incur a fine of 40s to
be paid to the Council Chamber of the said city, and that if any
of the aforesaid pageants be delayed or held back through fault

or negligence on the part of the players, that they shall incur a
penalty of 6s 8d to the same Chamber. And they (the commons)
beg that these aforesaid matters be performed, or otherwise the
said play shall not be played by the aforesaid commons. And
they (the commons) ask these things for the sake of God and as
a work of charity for the benefit of the said commons and of
the strangers who have travelled to the said city for the honour
⟨of⟩ God and the promotion of charity among the same commons.

Places where the play of Corpus Christi will have been played:
first at the gates of Holy Trinity in Micklegate; second at Robert
Harpham's door; third at John de Gyseburne's door; fourth at
Skeldergate and North Street; fifth at the end of Coney Street
opposite the Castlegate; sixth at the end of Jubbergate; seventh
⟨at⟩ Henry Wyman's door in Coney Street; eighth at the end of
Coney Street next to the Common Hall; ninth at Adam del
Brigg's door; tenth at the gates of the Minster of blessed Peter;
eleventh at the end of Girdlergate in Petergate; twelfth on the
Pavement.

And it has been ordained that the banners of the play with the
arms of the city be delivered by the mayor ⚬on the eve of Corpus
Christi,⚬ to be set in the places where the play of the pageants
will be, and that each year on the day after Corpus Christi,
the banners be returned to the Chamber to the hands of the
mayor and chamberlains of the city and kept there for the entire
year following, under penalty of 6s 8d to be paid to the needs
of the commons by anyone who shall have kept the banners
beyond the next day and shall not have given them up in the
manner which is stated.

f 16v *(27 April)*

...

Concerning the
ordinance of the
torches of the
honourable men
who have city
livery

Memorandum that on the twenty-seventh day of April in the
twenty-second year of the reign of King Richard the second
after the conquest of England, it ⟨was⟩ ordained and agreed in
the Guildhall in the presence of the mayor, sheriffs, and aldermen
of the city of York with the consent of the whole commons then
assembled in the same place, that all those who have and will
have from now on summer livery after the fashion of the summer
livery of the honourable men of the aforesaid city, that each of
them should go with the mayor and honourable men in the
procession on the feast of Corpus Christi as far as the church of
St Peter and the hospital of St Leonard, and that each of them
should have his torch carried and lighted in front of the said

procession every year on the aforesaid feast. And whoever may have defaulted in this regard will pay 6s 8d to the use of the commons.

York Minster Chamberlains' Rolls   YM: E1/29 MP

mb 2
(as E1/27 above 1398)

Pater Noster Guild Account Roll

Lucy Toulmin Smith, ed., *York Plays,* xxix*
... but the said John says he had spent on various expenses about the play of Sloth on behalf of Richard Walker 2s 1d, therefore he seeks to receive allowance of the aforesaid ...

1401
A/Y Memorandum Book   Y: E20

f 42*   *(7 July)   Spurriers and Lorimers*
[... No spurrier or harnessmaker of the said city or the suburbs of it is to fashion himself or to have fashioned by ⟨his⟩ servant in another guild, but only in the Spurriers, that which belongs to his trade, on pain of 13s 4d to be paid by him who acts contrary to this ordinance, that is, one half to the mayor and commonalty of the said city and the other half for the use of the pageant of the guilds and crafts aforesaid. ...]
°Memorandum that on the twelfth day of May in the time of Richard York, mayor, it was added that the Hatmakers of this city be contributors to the pageant of the aforesaid craft and they pay without contradiction, under pain of 40d from each one.°

1402
York Minster Chamberlains' Rolls   YM: E1/34 MP

mb 2
(as E1/1 above 1371; sums doubled)

YM: E1/36 PM

mb 1
(as E1/2 above 1371; sums doubled)

1403
A/Y Memorandum Book   Y : E 20

f 148v   *(8 May)*

Of the pageant
of Moses and
Pharaoh etc,
Hosiers

Let it be remembered that the eighth day of May, the year of
the reign of our lord the King Henry the fourth, since the conquest of England the fourth, it is accorded and assented before
the mayor of the city of York, the chamberlains, and other good
people of the same city in the Council Chamber on Ouse Bridge
in York between the people of drapercraft and the people of
hosiercraft of York, that all hosiers who sell stockings or make
stockings to sell with the upholders who sell cloth of wool

More on the
seventeenth
folio in the
present book

henceforth will have the charge of the pageant of Moses and
Pharaoh, etc, in the play of Corpus Christi, except the Dubbers
and those who are assigned to them.

York Minster Chamberlains' Rolls   Y M : E 1/3 7 *MP*

mb 2*

Minor and
various expenses

... And to the minstrels in the feast of the Translation of St
William, 6s 8d. And to the same for the four days of Pentecost,
20s. And to the same on the feast of St William the sixth weekday of Pentecost, 6s 8d. ...

1405
A/Y Memorandum Book   Y : E 20

ff 42v-3

...

Tondours

These are the constitutions and ordinances ordained by all the
masters of the guild of Shearers of the city of York on the feast
of the Purification in the seventh year of King Henry the fourth
since the conquest of England.

First, because great damages and losses have constantly befallen
the same guild because of cloths which are not properly made,
it is ordained and agreed by the assent and consent of all the
masters of the said guild, that henceforth the searchers of the
said guild will present to the mayor of the said city the faults
found and approved by the said searchers and two other competent masters of the same guild elected to judge the alleged
fault and that, wherever a fault is found, he who is found at
fault will pay 3s 4d, one half to the Council Chamber and the

other half to their pageant of Corpus Christi, if it be that those who have received something damaged complain and bring forward the damaged goods.

...

And also, that each master who takes an apprentice in the same guild will pay for each apprentice on his entry for the use of their pageant, 12d. And he who is found rebellious and does not wish to pay the said 12d will pay 3s 4d in the aforementioned manner.

And also, that in each year that the mayor shall send the billet of their pageant of Corpus Christi to the men of the said guild as is the custom of the city, all the masters of the said guild shall assemble in a certain place at the assigned time, and there they shall take order for their pageant and their light, and for properties and equipment of the same, and whoever is found rebellious towards the assembly as mentioned above and toward the said ordinances will pay 3s 4d as mentioned before.

...

York Minster Chamberlains' Rolls   YM: E1/38 *PM*

Minor and various expenses

mb 2
... And to the minstrels on the feast of St William, 13s 4d. ...

1408
Corpus Christi Guild Register   BL: Lansdowne MS 403

f 17v*
First constitution. We ordain that on the feast of Corpus Christi all chaplains walk in the procession in surplices in a decent manner, processionally in the age-old order, unless they can reasonably be excused. And in order that the worship of God may be increased more reverently, in order that the priesthood may be thought of more worthily, and that the people may more suitably be incited to devotion by these things, we ordain that the six masters, or at least two of them, who must manage others in processions of this kind, shall carry white rods, during their terms in every general procession to distinguish them from others, considering that such a firm and devout pace may be due, ordered and proper to the praise of God, the respectability of the priesthood, the edification and good example of all Christian people, but most of all for the honour of God and of the city of York.

f 19
Seven. We order that ten great torches be borne before the
sacrament in the procession of Corpus Christi, and that only six
processionally before the body of a deceased brother. And that
each brother and sister pay at least two pence each year to the
support of the said lights during the quarter just before the
feast of Corpus Christi.
...

1411-12
A/Y Memorandum Book Y : E 20

ff 65v, 68* *Bakers*
... Therefore, so that the aforesaid | abuse might be removed
henceforth, it was ordered and firmly established that no baker
of the city or any agent of his should carry or cause to be carried
outside his (specified) place any type of bread available for
sale, to the houses, windows, or dwellings of any regrater within
this city or the suburbs of the same, under penalty of 3s 4d, for
the use of the commons and for the craft of Bakers for the
support of their pageant and of their other burdens, to be applied
in equal proportions as often as anyone presumes to go against
this ordinance. ...

f 21v *Plasterers*
...
Item, that no member of the guild take an apprentice for a
shorter term than seven years ⟨on pain of 6s 8d⟩ to pay 40d to
the Chamber and 40d for the use of their pageant of Corpus
Christi.
...

1415
A/Y Memorandum Book Y : E 20

ff 252v-5*
The order of the pageants of the play of Corpus Christi at the
time of William Alne, mayor, in the third year of the reign of
King Henry the fifth after the conquest of England. °Compiled
in the year of our Lord 1415 by Roger Burton, common clerk,
(who) had it registered. °

°The billets of pageants must be delivered in succession in the subscribed form to the craftsmen by six sergeants-at-arms of the mayor in the first or second week of Lent, yearly, (and) are to be written by the common clerk. °†

Tanners	God, the almighty Father, creating and forming the heavens, the angels and archangels, Lucifer and the angels who fell with him into hell
Plasterers	God the Father in his (own) substance creating the earth and all things which are in it in the space of five days
Cardmakers	God the Father forming Adam from the mud of the earth and making Eve from Adam's rib and breathing into them with the breath of life
Fullers	God forbidding Adam and Eve to eat from the tree of life
Coopers	Adam and Eve and the tree between them, the serpent deceiving them with fruits, God speaking to them and cursing the serpent, and the angel with a sword casting them from Paradise
°Armourers°	Adam and Eve, the angel with a shovel and distaff assigning work to them
°Glovers° Gaunters	Abel and Cain offering sacrifices
Shipwrights	God warning Noah to make an ark from smoothed boards.
°Fishmongers° Pessoners & Mariners	Noah in the ark and his wife, Noah's three sons with their wives with various animals

Parchmenters Bookbinders	Abraham offering °Isaac, ° his son, upon the altar, the servant with wood, and the angel
Hosiers	Moses raising up the serpent in ⟨the desert⟩, king ⟨Pharaoh⟩, eight Jews wondering ⟨and waiting⟩
Spicers	°A learned man declaring the sayings of the prophets concerning the future birth of Christ, ° °Mary, ° the angel greeting her, Mary greeting Elizabeth
°Pewterers Founders	°Mary, ° Joseph wishing ⟨to send⟩ her ⟨away⟩, ⟨an angel speaking to them⟩ that they might go to Bethlehem °
°Pewterers Founders	Mary, Joseph wishing⟨to send her away⟩ secretly, the angel speaking to them so that they go to Bethlehem ° ǀ
Tilers	Mary, [with ⟨... ....⟩] Joseph, the mid-wife, the new-born boy °lying in a manger° between the cow and the ass, the angel speaking °to the shepherds° and the players in the following pageant
Chandlers	Shepherds speaking to one another, °the star in the East, ° the angel announcing °the joy over the new-born boy to the shepherds°
°Goldsmiths° Orfevers °Masons° Goldbeaters Moneymakers	The three kings coming from the East, Herod asking them about the boy Jesus, °and the son of Herod, ° and two counci°llors and a messenger, ° Mary with the boy and the star above and the three kings offering gifts

°formerly° the House of St Leonard °now Masons°	Mary with the boy, Joseph, Anna, the midwife with the young doves, Simeon receiving the child into his arms, and the two sons of Simeon
Marshals	Mary with the boy and Joseph fleeing into Egypt, with the angel announcing it (to Joseph)
Girdlers Nailers °Sawyers°	Herod order⟨ing that the children be killed, four⟩ soldiers with spears, two ⟨councillors of the king, and⟩ four women weeping ⟨at the killing of their children⟩
Spurriers Lorimers	Jesus, °the learned men, the boy° sitting ⟨in the temple in the midst⟩ of them, asking them and answering ⟨them, four Jews, Mary and Joseph⟩ seeking him and fin⟨ding him in the temple⟩
Barbers	Jesus, John ⟨the Baptist baptizing him, and two⟩ angels ⟨assisting⟩
°Vintners°	Jesus, Mary ⟨the bridegroom with the bride, the ste⟩ward with his ser⟨vant with six jars of water when the water⟩ was turned ⟨into wine⟩
°Smiths° Fevers	Jesus ⟨on the pinnacle of the temple, and the devil⟩ tempting him ⟨with stones, and two angels ministering, etc⟩
Curriers	Peter, James, and John, Jesus ascending the mount and transfiguring ⟨himself before them, Moses and Elijah⟩ appearing, and ⟨the voice speaking in a cloud⟩

Ironmongers	°Jesus,° Simon ⟨the leper asking Jesus to eat with him,⟩ two disciples, Mary Magdalene ⟨washing the feet of Jesus⟩ with ⟨her⟩ tears ⟨and wiping ⟨them⟩ with her hair⟩
Plumbers Pattenmakers	Jesus, ⟨two apostles,⟩ the woman taken in adultery, four Jews accusing her ǀ
Pouchmakers Bottlemakers Capmakers	[Jesus, four apostles,] Lazarus in the tomb, Mary Magdalene and Martha, and two Jews wondering
°Skinners° °Vestmentmakers°	Jesus on the ass with her colt, the twelve two apostles following Jesus, six rich men and six poor men, eight boys with palm branches singing *Benedictus*, etc and Zacheus climbing the sycamore treee
Cutlers Bladesmiths Sheathers Scalers Bucklermakers °Horners°	Pilate, Caiaphas, two soldiers, °three Jews,° °and° Judas selling Jesus
Bakers °Waterleaders°	The paschal lamb, the Lord's supper, the twelve apostles, Jesus girded with a linen cloth washing their feet, [the paschal lamb,] the institution of the sacrament of the body of Christ in the new law, the communion of the apostles
Cordwainers	Pilate, Caiaphas, Annas, fourteen armed soldiers, Malchus, Peter, James, John. °Jesus,° and Judas ⟨kiss⟩ing Jesus and betraying him
Bowers Fletchers	⟨Jesus, An⟩nas, Caiaphas, and four Jews striking [and] buf⟨fet⟩ing °Jesus, Peter, the woman accusing Peter, and Malchus°

⟨Tapiters⟩
⟨Couchers⟩

⟨Jesus,⟩ Pilate, Annas, Caiaphas, two councillors, and four Jews accusing Jesus

⟨Litsters⟩

⟨Herod,⟩ two councillors, four soldiers, Jesus, and three Jews

⟨Cooks⟩
Waterleaders

⟨Pilate,⟩ Annas, Caiaphas, two Jews, and Judas ⟨return⟩ing to them thirty (pieces of) silver

⟨Tilemakers⟩
Millers
°Ropers°
°Servers°

°Jesus,° ⟨Pilat⟩e, Caiaphas, Annas, six soldiers holding poles with banners and four others leading Jesus from Herod, seeking for Barabas to be released and Jesus to be crucified, and in the same place binding and whipping him, and putting a crown of thorns on his head, three soldiers casting lots upon the clothing of Jesus

⟨Turners⟩
⟨Hayresters⟩
⟨Bollers⟩
⟨Shearmen⟩
⟨Toundours⟩

J⟨esus⟩ covered with blood carrying the cross to Calvary, Simon of Cyrene, the Jews const⟨rain⟩ing him to carry the cross, Mary the mother of Jesus, then John the apostle first relating the condemnation and journey of her son °to Calvary,° Veronica wiping blood and sweat from the face of Jesus with a veil on which is imprinted the face of Jesus, and other women lamenting Jesus |

Pinners
Latteners
Painters

°The cross,° Jesus stretched out on it on the ground, four Jews beating (him) and dragging him with cords, and afterwards raising the cross and the body of Jesus nailed to the cross upon the mount of Calvary

Butchers Poulters	The cross, two thieves crucified, Jesus hung on the cross between them, Mary the mother of Jesus, John, Mary (the mother) of James, and Salome, Longinus with a spear, a slave with a sponge, Pilate, Annas, Caiaphas, the centurion, Joseph °of Arimathea° and Nicodemus taking °him° down and putting [him] in the tomb
°Saddlers° Sellers °Glaziers° Verrours Fusters	Jesus harrowing hell, twelve good and six evil spirits
Carpenters °Joiners Cartwrights Carvers Sawyers°	°The centurion testifying to Pilate, Caiaphas and Annas °with other Jews,° the signs accompanying the death of Jesus, °Jesus rising from the tomb, four armed soldiers and the three Marys sorrowing, Pilate, Caiaphas and Annas,° a youth clad in white sitting at the tomb, talking to the women°
Winedrawers	Jesus, Mary Magdalene with spices
Brokers Woolpackers °Wadmen°	Jesus, °Luke and Cleophas dressed as pilgrims°
Scriveners Illuminators °Pardoners° Questors Dubbers	Jesus, Peter, John, ⟨James,⟩ Phillip, and the other apostles with a piece of broiled fish and ⟨a honey⟩comb, and Thomas the apostle touching the wounds of Christ
°Tail⟨ors⟩° Talliaunders	Mary, John the evangelist, eleven apostles, two angels, Jesus ascending above them, and four angels bearing a cloud

Potters	Mary, two angels, eleven apostles, and the Holy ⟨Spirit⟩ descending upon them, and four Jews wondering
Drapers	Jesus, Mary, Gabriel with two angels, two virgins and three Jews ⟨of Mary's family,⟩ eight apostles, and two devils
°Linenweavers°	Four apostles ⟨carrying the bier of Mary,⟩ and Fergus hanging upon the bier ⟨with two oth⟩er Jews °and one angel°
°Woolweavers°	Mary ascending with a crowd of angels, eight apostles, and Thomas, the apostle of India, preaching in the desert
°Ostlers°	°Mary,° Jesus crowning her ⟨and⟩ singing ⟨with a crowd of ang⟩els |
Mercers	Jesus, Mary, twelve apostles, four angels with trumpets and four with a crown, a spear, and two whips, four good spirits and four evil spirits, and six devils

® Look further on the following folio

Porters	8 torches	Chaloners	4 torches
Coblers	4 torches	Fullers	4 torches
Cordwainers	14 torches	Girdlers	torches
Cutlers	2 torches	Tailors	torches
°Weavers'° servants	4 torches	And 58 citizens of the city had torches as well on Corpus	
Carpenters	6 torches	Christi Day	

It was ordered that the Porters ⟨and⟩ Cobblers go before first, and then the Weavers' servants and the Cordwainers from the right. And from the other side, the Fullers, Cutlers, Girdlers, Chaloners, Carpenters, ⟨and⟩ Tailors. And then the honourable citizens, and afterwards the Twenty-four, the Twelve, the mayor, and the four torches of Master Thomas de Bukton.

...

Barkers	The creation of heaven and earth
Plasterers	The work of the five days
Cardmakers	The formation of Adam and Eve
Walkers	The prohibition of the tree of knowledge
Coopers	The deceit of the devil in (the form of) a serpent
Furbers	The assigning of work to Adam
Glovers	Cain killing Abel
Shipwrights	The building of Noah's ark
Fishmongers and Mariners	Noah's ark during the flood
Parchmenters	The sacrifice of Isaac by Abraham
Hosiers	Pharaoh with Moses and the children of Israel
Spicers	The annuncition to Mary by Gabriel
Founders	Joseph wishing to send her away secretly
Tilers	Bethlehem with the new-born boy
Chandlers	The offering of the shepherds
°Masons	Herod questioning the three kings°
Goldsmiths	The offering of the three kings
St Leonard's °now the Masons°	The presentation of Christ in the temple
Marshals	How Christ fled into Egypt
Girdlers	Slaughter of the innocents in place of Christ
Spurriers	The discovery of Christ in the temple among the learned men
Barbers	The baptism of Christ by John
Taverners	The marriage in Cana of Galilee
Smiths	The temptation of Christ in the desert
Curriers	The transfiguration of Christ
Ironmongers	The feast in Simon's house
Plumbers	The woman taken in adultery
Hartshorners	The raising of Lazarus
Skinners	Jerusalem, with citizens and children
Cutlers	The selling of Christ by Judas
Bakers	The supper of Christ with the disciples
Waterleaders	Washing of the ap⟨ostles'⟩ feet
Cordwainers	The capture of Christ praying on ⟨the Mount⟩
Bowers	The mocking of Christ before Ca⟨iaphas⟩
Tapiters	The accusation of Christ before Pilate
Litsters	The presentation of Christ before Herod
Cooks	The contrition of Judas before the Jews

Saucemakers	The hanging of Judas
Tilemakers	The condemnation of Christ by Pilate
Turners, Bollers	The scourging and crowning with thorns
Shearmen	The leading of Christ and the manifestation to Veronica
Millers	The division of the vestments of Christ
Painters	The stretching out and nailing of Christ
Latteners	The raising of Christ on the Mount
Butchers	The death of Christ on Calvary
Saddlers	The harrowing of hell
Wrights	The resurrection of Christ
Winedrawers	The appearance of Christ to Mary Magdal(ene)
Woolpackers	The appearance of Christ to the pilgrims
Scriveners	The appearance of Christ to the apostle Thomas and to others
Tailors	The ascension of Christ to heaven
Potters	The descent of the Holy Spirit
Drapers	The death of the blessed Mary
Masons	The carrying of the body of Mary
°Ostlers° Weavers	The assumption of the blessed Mary
® °Ostlers° Mayor, etc	Her crowning
Mercers	The last judgment

°Burton had it registered°

Potters	8 torches
Glovers	4 torches
Smiths	4 torches
°Weavers°	8 torches
Corpus Christi	10 torches
William Selby for the soul of Master Thomas Bukton	4 torches
Fishers	2 torches

1416

Corpus Christi Account Rolls Y: C99:1

mb 1*

...

Money for torches

And of 10s received from sir Thomas Bolton
And of 8s 6d received from sir Henry Wresill
And of 5s 2d received from sir Robert Burdon
And of 8s 4d received from sir John Helperby

And of 10s received from sir William Brigge
And of 6s 10d received from sir Walter Buttirwyk

Total 48s 10d

...

Greater expenses Concerning which the same wardens reckon in the first place,
for the renovation of 2 torches, viz, for 18 pounds of wax 9s
And for the manufacture and the wick of the same 2s
Item, paid to 10 men carrying 10 torches on the feast of Corpus
Christi for the procession, 4d to each one 3s 4d
Item, paid to the same men for the carrying of the said torches
from the Hospital of the Holy Trinity to the Monastery of the
Holy Trinity 3d
Item, paid to them for drinking money on the feast of Corpus
Christi 4d

...

mb 1d

...

Ornaments and tools of the fraternity Item, the same wardens give an account of the 10 torches belonging to the said fraternity for the veneration of the body of Christ,
Total of torches, 10

Standards And of 6 standards embroidered with chalices to be set about the 6 torches before the dead,
Total of standards, 6

'Castles' And of 10 painted 'castles' with 10 small canvas bags to cover them,
Total of 'castles', 10

Banners And of 40 embroidered banners, together with 1 canvas bag to put them in, together with papers,
Total of banners, 40

(Protective) Cloths And of 10 (protective) cloths of canvas for carrying of the said 10 torches in the Corpus Christi procession,
Total of cloths, 10

Roundelets And of 3 dozen wooden devices, ie, roundelets, for placing atop the revets,
Total of roundelets, 36

Revets

And of 40 revets received from their predecessors
And of 40 revets bought new,

...

1417

A/Y Memorandum Book Y : E 20

ff 187v-8* *(7 June)*

...

Concerning the
organization of
the Corpus
Christi Play

All these, together with a multitude of other citizens, were
gathered in the Common Hall on the seventh day of June, in
the year of our Lord 1417, and in the fifth year of the reign of
King Henry the fifth after the conquest of England, and although
it may be contained in a certain ancient constitution or ordinance
made at the time of Robert Talkan, formerly mayor of York, in
the twenty-second year of the reign of King Richard the second,
and although (it was) read through there concerning the play to
be maintained on Corpus Christi in the city of York, viz, that all
the pageants of the play called Corpus Christi Play be maintained
and brought forth in their order by the crafts of the said city for
the benefit of the citizens of the same city and of all strangers
coming there on the aforesaid feast, especially for the honour
and reverence of our Lord Jesus Christ and for the profit of the
said citizens. And that the play of the individual pageants
themselves shall be: first at the gates of Holy Trinity Priory in
Micklegate; second before Robert Harpham's door; third before
the late John Gyseburn's door; fourth at the intersection of
Skeldergate and North Street; fifth at the end of Coney Street
opposite Castlegate; sixth at the end of Jubbergate; seventh
before the late Henry Wyman's door in Coney Street; eighth
before the Common Hall at the end of Coney Street; ninth at
the late Adam del Bryg's door in Stonegate; tenth at the end of
Stonegate at the gate of the Minster of the blessed Peter; eleventh
at the end of Girdlergate in Petergate; twelfth and last on the
Pavement as is ⟨more fully⟩ contained in that ancient constitution
and ordinance written in this register facing the beginning.
Nevertheless, the mayor, the honourable men, and the whole
said commons, by their unanimous consent and assent, order
⟨that⟩ all those who receive money for scaffolds which they may
build in the aforesaid places before their doors on public property
at the aforesaid sites from those sitting on them shall pay the
third penny of the money so received to the chamberlains of the

city to be applied to the use of the same commons. | And if they have refused to pay or agree upon a third penny of this kind or other (monies) with the chamber decently, that then the play be transferred to other places at the will and disposition of the mayor holding office at the time and of the council of the Chamber of the city. No one spoke against this kind of ordinance except only a few holders of scaffolds in Micklegate. And furthermore, it was ordained by common consent that the embroidered banners of the Corpus Christi Play, with the arms of the city, be delivered yearly on the night before Corpus Christi to be placed in the places where the play of the pageants will be on the following day, and that each year these banners must be brought back without delay to the Chamber of the council of the city on the day after the said feast of Corpus Christi, to the hands of the mayor and chamberlains of the city, and they must be kept there for the entire next following year, under penalty of 6s 8d to be applied to the work of the commons by each and all who have kept these banners beyond that next day and have not given them up in the manner which is stated.

And indeed, because of the closeness of the said feast of Corpus Christi and the shortness of time, the said matter was not able to be committed to the aforesaid execution fully. Therefore, those assembled in the Chamber of the council on the twelfth day of June in the abovesaid year of the lord and the king, considering that it would be improper and not to the profit of the commons that the said play be performed in the same certain places and in no other yearly, since everyone bear his charge towards the upholding of this play according to his estate, it was therefore unanimously ordained that for the benefit of the commons the places for the performance of the aforesaid play would be changed unless those before whose places the play used to be performed have paid whatever was enjoined yearly to the commons for having this, his individual profit, thus. And it was ordained that in all the years following while this play is played, it must be played before the doors and holdings of those who have paid better and more generously to the Chamber and who have been willing to do more for the benefit of the whole commons for having this play there, not giving favour to anyone for his individual benefit, but rather that the public utility of the whole of the commons of York ought to be considered. And the abovesaid reverend gentleman

John Moreton, in the matter of his buildings, submitted himself
completely to the disposition and ruling of the mayor and the
council of the Chamber (as to) how much (he should pay)
towards the abovesaid play for (having) the play before the gate
of his house in the quarter of Micklegate and at other buildings
of his in the city.

...

f 75v* *Cordwainers*

...

Item, that no master of the Cordwainers shall receive, conduct,
or procure personally or through another in his name, any
servant from the service of another master of the said craft or
set him at work before the feast of St Stephen after noon, at
which time all servants of the said craft make an agreement to
stay with their masters by custom. And if any master has done
differently, he will pay a half mark for the support of his pageant
and 40d to be applied to the use of the commons of York.

...

f 78* *Cordwainers*

Item, it was ordered that twelve honourable men of the aforesaid
craft go yearly on the feast of Corpus Christi with their pageant
as they shall be assigned by the four masters of the same craft,
and if anyone has been chosen and refused to go, he will pay 10s,
to be fulfilled in the way stated above, so that he who goes in
one year will not go again until the third year next following,
and so that those who will go, will have 40d on the aforesaid
feast for their expenses from the aforesaid craft.

...

1417-18
A/Y Memorandum Book   Y : E 20

f 60v

...

There follows the agreement of the Saucemakers and sellers of
Paris candles

And because a serious complaint had been made here in the
Council Chamber by the Saucemakers, craftsmen of the city,
namely, by those whom we commonly call Salsemakers, that
although by the hitherto usual custom the members of the

Saucemakers' craft, as well as all candlemakers outside the Flesh
Shambles who used to sell Paris candles in their houses and
windows, have sustained that pageant in the feast & play of
Corpus Christi in this city both in its costs and its expenses, in
which it is shown that Judas Iscariot hung himself and cried out
in the midst; further, although the Skinners and other craftsmen
of this city of York in great number, who are not Saucemakers,
make and presume to sell, through themselves and their wives,
Paris candles in their homes and windows, nevertheless, they,
having been asked, refuse to be contributors to the support of
the said pageant. And unless a remedy be quite speedily imposed
so that from now on they be contributors of this kind with the
Saucemakers, the Saucemakers themselves will be unable to
support that pageant any longer. Wherefore, in the year of our
Lord 1417 and in the fifth year of the reign of King Henry the
sixth after the conquest of England, it was decided by the mayor,
William Bowes, and the council of the Chamber that each and
every craftsman of the city, of whatever kind they be who are
not butchers or wives of butchers and who, through themselves
or through their wives, sell Paris candles by retail within the city
of York and the suburbs of the same, shall from now on contribute
every third penny along with the Saucemakers of this city to
maintaining the aforesaid pageant in the feast and play of Corpus
Christi. Afterwards, when John Moreton was mayor, the aforesaid ordinance notwithstanding, it was agreed between the
Saucemakers and the makers of Paris candles that anyone making
or selling such Paris candles would pay 2d per annum for the
presentations of the aforesaid play and no more, with the exception of butchers or their wives, as mentioned previously. And it
was further ordained that if any persons from other crafts who
are not Saucemakers should sell mustard or other sauces, it was
ordained that such (persons) would pay just as (much as) the
other Saucemakers of the city do towards the upkeep of the
aforesaid pageant. And that henceforward no member of the
craft of Saucemakers of this city would take any apprentice
in that craft for a lesser term than for the term of seven years
together under penalty of 6s 8d to be given in equal proportions
to the commons of the city and to the craft of Saucemakers.
And that if (there be) any foreigner or, perchance, some apprentice who has not completed his term and the years of his apprenticeship fully in the craft of Saucemakers, and who has set up
shop and occupied (it) here as a master, he shall pay at the first

Saucemakers
and sellers of
Paris candles

setting up or at his occupation of this kind 13s 4d, to be applied
in the manner and for the uses aforesaid, unless by chance an
apprentice of this sort, is the son of some master craftsman of
the Saucemakers of the aforesaid city born and an apprentice
in that craft in this city before the aforesaid ordinance (was
established). And that anyone who has completed the term of
his apprenticeship well and honourably would pay, when he has
set up as a master for the first (time), 40d to be given in equal
portions to the commons of the city and to the aforesaid craft.
And the other Saucemakers' ordinance is found in the red book
past the middle among other constitutions of the city.

1419
A/Y Memorandum Book   Y : E 20

f 43v*

Of the Tapiters   ...

              Addition to the ordinances of the Tapiters

      ...

Other
constitutions are
contained in the
eighth folio
preceding

And that no master of the aforesaid craft of the aforesaid city
should take anyone as his apprentice to be instructed in the
aforesaid craft unless that apprentice be English-born and a
freeman, under penalty of 26s 8d for the Chamber and 13s 4d
to the upkeep of the pageant and other burdens of the aforesaid
craft.

    Item, if there were any foreigner born outside the land and
kingdom of England, of any nation whatsoever who wished
from now on to set up as a master in the craft of the aforesaid
Tapiters within the liberty of the aforesaid city of York, it has
been ordered by all the masters of the aforesaid craft of the
aforesaid city that any such person at his first setting-up as a
master should pay to the Chamber of the aforesaid city 53s 4d,
and to the support of the pageant of the aforesaid craft in the
play of Corpus Christi and (to the support) of the other burdens
of the same craft, 26s 8d, sterling.

f 201   *(16 June)*

   ...

They were met in the Council Chamber of this city of York,
upon Ouse Bridge, on the day after the feast of Corpus Christi
in the year of our Lord 1419, touching the seventh year, indeed,
of the reign of King Henry the fifth, where various craftsmen of

the Skinners' craft came and lodged the serious complaint that various craftsmen of the Carpenters and Cordwainers of the aforesaid city on the feast of Corpus Christi in the aforesaid years broke the burning torches as they were carried in the procession of the said feast before the body of Christ there present, and then dragged them down with their staves and Carlisle axes which they brought there, and committed other enormities, to the grave disturbance of the king's peace and to the hindrance of the play and procession of Corpus Christi. Indeed, Simon Calton and Benedict Williamson, carpenters, and Thomas Durem, cordwainer, were arrested and imprisoned upon that complaint. And the aforesaid Simon and Benedict, coming before the mayor and the council of the city here in the Chamber after the aforesaid offence had been charged against them, acknowledged that they had committed the aforesaid deeds and placed themselves upon the mercy, grace, and order of the mayor and council of the Chamber of the city, and in order to do this, the aforesaid Simon and Benedict, John Mosse, John Bolron, William Kyrkeby, Richard Ferrour, William Cunsby, John Haxeby, Thomas Cunnysburgh, and John Shathelok, wrights and citizens of York, were obligated through their written pledge for £100 sterling, as is more fully contained in the same.

...

f 57v*

...

In the name of God, amen. Since, during the times of many mayors, there was a certain dispute moved and pending among the men of the craft of Masons of this city of York for one part, and the men of the Tilers and Plasterers of the same city for the other part, concerning and over the exaction and payment of money for the pageants of the same three aforesaid crafts for the feast and play of Corpus Christi customary each year in the aforesaid city, finally, for the re-establishment of peace among the aforesaid parties, it was judged by Thomas Gare, mayor of this city, and the chamberlains, and other honourable men of the said city present at that time, that all Tilers and Plasterers of this city of York who build stone walls or stone foundations of houses or any other work pertaining to the craft of Masons would be contributors for those works to the craft of Masons of this city, from then on, just as they used to be of old. And

<aside>◦Concerning Masons, Plasterers, and Tilers of houses◦</aside>

that those Tilers and Plasterers, who from then on were able to excuse themselves because they do not perform any work or anything else proper to the craft of Masons, ought to be excused and pay nothing to those Masons, but be entirely quit of obligation.

f 64v*

...

Memorandum that since a dispute has been moved and is pending among the Sailors and the Fishmongers having boats in Ousegate concerning the means of paying towards the pageant of Noah's ark, to which each party has been each year and is now a contributor, it was finally ordered upon the advice of Thomas Gare, mayor of York, and put to a vote of the aforesaid Sailors, whether from then on they wished to pay 6s 8d each year to the Fishmongers of Ousegate for the play of the aforesaid pageant of Noah, and then the men of Ousegate themselves would produce the aforesaid pageant for themselves and the Sailors, or whether the Fishmongers of Ousegate themselves would pay 12d each year to the aforesaid Sailors to their profit, and thus the Fishmongers would produce one-third of the play of the aforesaid pageant, so that the Chamber of the city council might be no longer disturbed in this regard with the Fishmongers of Ouse Bridge. And then the aforesaid Sailors chose to receive 12d yearly from the aforesaid Fishmongers of Ousegate.

Agreement
between the
Sailors and the
Fishmongers
of Ousegate

1420
A/Y Memorandum Book Y : E 20

f 80 *(5 February)*

Ironmongers

To the reverence, praise, and honour of almighty God, and for the advantage and convenience of the citizens of the city of York, and of all the people of the lord king, by the unanimous agreement and peaceful will of John Aldestanemore, John Brounflete, Robert Feriby, John Radclyf, Simon del Style, John Buttercram, Hugo Gardiner, John Preston, John Skyrmer, Henry Skyrmer, William Preston, William Ouresby, and Robert Bedford, ironmongers of the aforesaid city, through the advice and consent of Thomas Gare, mayor of York, and the council of the Chamber of the same, it was confirmed and ordered on the fifth day of February in the year of our Lord 1419 that no person of the aforesaid craft, man or woman, shall hereafter within the aforesaid city open his shops to place or show for sale anything proper to his craft on any Sunday, set aside to the glory and praise of God, under a penalty of 20s, to be applied in equal portions to the aforesaid Chamber for the use of the commons and to the aforesaid craft toward the future upkeep of the pageant and other burdens of the same by him or her who at any time in the future shall have acted contrary to this constitution.

Item, since it is the case that the craftsmen of the aforesaid craft yearly sustain a great burden in supporting their play and pageant on the feast of Corpus Christi, and that although there are many engaging in the said craft, yet few are paying for the annual burdens of the same, therefore, it was ordered that if any henceforth shall have sold anything called in English ironware and shall not have made the thing himself, ironware imported from overseas excepted, he must pay with the aforesaid craftsmen yearly to the support of the play, the pageant, and their other burdens.

...

f 80v

...

Item, since the pageant of the Ironmongers is very expensive and requires yearly repair, and they are few who contribute and pay to this pageant and the burdens of their play, it was therefore ordered that any man or woman who henceforth shall have put up, or set up or joined a shop in the craft of ironmongery within the liberty of the city, unless he was previously an apprentice in the said craft and of good reputation, must pay at his beginning 13s 4d, that is, one half to the Chamber and the other half to the aforesaid craft in support of the pageant, the play, and their other burdens. Thus always, that if the person putting up, setting up, or joining the shop has been able, let him pay the said sum in the manner stated above; if, however, he is unable and has been less adequate, then let the sum be reduced to a lesser sum according to the discretion and will of the mayor at the time, and of the Ironmongers of the city, similarly existing at the time.

...

B/Y Memorandum Book Y : E 20 A

f 42

® Concerning one plot of land on the Tofts leased to the Goldsmiths of York for a term of eighty years for 8d per annum

This indenture bears witness that we, the mayor and the commons of the citizens of the city of York, have leased to Alan de Bedale and Henry Forester, citizens and Goldsmiths of York and searchers of the same craft, a certain plot of land on the Tofts in the said city as it lies there along the side of the wall of the Friars Preacher (Dominicans) of York, and it contains four royal ells in width and five and three-quarters royal ells in length, for building a house there for sheltering and having the pageant of the Goldsmiths of the said city in it, and the aforesaid plot of land with the house which is to be built there, together with free access and exit to it, is to be held by the said Alan and Henry and their successors as searchers of the said craft in the said city, from us and our successors, freely, well, and peacefully, from the feast of St Martin in the winter in the year of our Lord 1420 to the end of the next eighty fully complete years following from them. They are to pay yearly to us and our successors, or to those who shall be masters of Ouse Bridge at the time, 8d sterling on the two term-days of the year, viz, on the feasts of Pentecost and of St Martin in the winter, in equal portions. And if it happens that the said yearly rent of 8d be in arrears at any term-day on which it should be paid, (and) shall not have been paid in part or in full within eight days, then it shall indeed be permitted to us and our successors, or to those who shall be masters of Ouse Bridge at the time, to reseize and repossess the said plot of land, together with the house which is to be built there, into our own hands, the present lease notwithstanding in any way, without dispute, hindrance, or demand of the said searchers or of their successors or of anyone else. And the said Alan and Henry and their successors, searchers of the said craft, will repair and keep up the said house at their own costs and expenses in all respects throughout the entire abovesaid term. At the end of the same term, they will surrender the said house competently repaired. And we, the mayor and commons of the said city, and our successors will warrant and defend against all people the said plot of land, together with the house to be built upon it as said above and with free access and free exit to it to the said Alan and Henry and their successors, searchers of the said craft, for the said rent while the said form lasts on the stated terms. In testimony of which, the seal of the office of mayor of the said city

and the seals of the said Alan and Henry have been affixed in
turn by the parties to this indenture. Given at York on the
third day of November in the abovesaid year of the Lord and the
eighth year of the reign of King Henry the fifth after the conquest
of England.
...

Vicars Choral Accounts   YM: Tileworks Accounts, VC Box XII*

... And in the week in which the feast of St Barnabas falls ... And
paid to Heron for our play, 2s 2d. And paid to the labourer of
the said Heron, 2d. ...

1421
Vicars Choral Accounts   YM: Tileworks Accounts, Vq 1x*

... And in the week in which the feast of the Ascension falls ...
And paid to Robert Scrueton, 3s 3d. ...

1422
A/Y Memorandum Book   Y: E20

ff 247-7v   *(31 January)*
Painters and Stainers

He who is ignorant of nothing knows, and the whole people
lament, that the play on the day of Corpus Christi in this city,
the institution of which was made of old for the important
cause of devotion and for the extirpation of vice and the reformation of customs, alas, is impeded more than usual because of
the multitude of pageants, and unless a better and more speedy
device be provided, it is to be feared that it will be impeded
much further in a very brief passage of time. And the craftsmen
of the Painters, Stainers, Pinners, and Latteners of the aforesaid
city, formerly appointed separately to two pageants which must
be performed in the aforesaid play, viz, one on the stretching
out and nailing of Christ on the cross, and the other, indeed, on
the raising up of the Crucified upon the Mount, knowing that the
matter of both pageants could be shown together in one pageant
for the shortening of the play rather profitably for the people
hearing the holy words of the players, consented for themselves
and their other colleagues in the future that one of their pageants

should be left out from now on and the other maintained following what the mayor and the council of the Chamber wished to arrange. And upon this business the searchers and craftsmen of the aforesaid crafts came before Richard Russell, the mayor of York, the aldermen and other honourable men in the Council Chamber situated here on Ouse Bridge on the last day of January in the ninth year of the reign of King Henry the fifth after the conquest of England and presented to them their desire and intention as stated above, viz, William Drax, John Multon, John Cave, John Potell, John Bryg, Thomas Midilton, William Couper, John Scragge, Adam Lutton, Robert Leche, William Crofte, Robert Kyrkeby, Richard Lambert, John Midylham, Thomas Steresacre, pinners; David Payntour, William Morlay, John Gerard, and William Clyfton, painters; and Thomas Cuke, Thomas Hirste, Thomas Hendechild, John Wyman, Walter Multon, and Richard Marche, stainers. Wherefore, the aforesaid mayor, aldermen, and honourable men, receiving this kindly and commending the aforesaid craftsmen for their laudable proposal, ordered and ordained, on their own counsel and that of all the aforesaid craftsmen, that from this day forward the pageant of the Painters and Stainers should be thoroughly removed from the aforesaid play, and that the craftsmen of the Pinners and Latteners should take upon themselves the burden of performing in their pageant the matter of the speeches which were previously performed in their pageant and in the pageant of the Painters and Stainers, and that the Painters and Stainers each year should collect among themselves from the men of their craft 5s sterling yearly and pay them yearly to those who are the masters of the pageant of the Pinners and Latteners ⟨at the time⟩, yearly on the eve of Corpus Christi. And if at any time they default in this payment, then they wish and agree that they and all their successors be distrained and strictly compelled in their homes and places of habitation or elsewhere, where they can be better and ⟨more easily⟩ distrained by the mayor and those who are chamberlains of this city at the time, to pay 40s of good English money to those who were masters of the pageant of the Pinners and Latteners at the time, on the next Sunday following the said feast without further delay. And that the punishments levied in this case shall remain in their power until satisfaction has been made fully to the aforesaid ⟨pageant⟩ masters concerning the aforesaid 40s together with the costs and expenses borne in their recovery, thus always, so that he who

is mayor at the time may receive and have one half of the aforesaid 40s for the use of the commons and those who shall have
been pageant masters of the Pinners and Latteners at the time
shall have the other half for the use and maintenance of their
said pageant. For making which payments well and faithfully,
indeed, in the manner and form written above, and | for holding
to and fulfilling the present ordinance in everything, the aforesaid David Payntour, William Morley, John Gerard, William
Clyfton, Thomas Hirst, Thomas Hendechild, John Wyman,
Walter Multon, and Richard Marche for their part pledge themselves and their successors of their crafts, provided only that the
said craftsmen of the Painters and Stainers do not meddle in
the pageant of the Pinners or in their accounts hereafter in any
way.

> Burton having been formally requested to do so,
> (had it registered).

1422-3
A/Y Memorandum Book   Y : E 20

ff 258-8v

Plasterers and Tilers of houses

...

First, it has been ordered that any plasterer working and making
plastering and tiling be a contributor in paying to each pageant
of those crafts, and also that any tiler doing tiling and plastering
be a contributor in a payment to each of the aforesaid pageants
under penalty of 3s 4d, to be applied to the use of the commons,
and 3s 4d to the aforesaid pageants.

Item, that any tiler who does only tiling should pay yearly to
both pageants aforesaid, 3d and no more. And that four masters
should be chosen equally each year to oversee both pageants of
the aforesaid crafts.

...

Item, that no master of the aforesaid crafts should put any
apprentice or assistant of his, of whatever sort he might be, to
work at plastering or tiling outside the presence of his master,
unless it be true that the apprentice or assistant has been examined
previously by the aforementioned searchers and approved by
them, and allowed because they know their craft and because
they be considered good workers. And if any master acts contrary, he shall incur a penalty of 3s 4d for the use of the Chamber

and of the aforesaid pageants as often as he has been found guilty.

Item, that craftsmen of the aforesaid crafts should go with their aforesaid pageants and should produce them all throughout the city as though (they were) the same men. |

...

Parchmenters

By the advice and consent of all the master craftsmen of the craft of the Parchmenters of this city of York, it was agreed and ordered in the time of Thomas Esyngwald, mayor, that those who are searchers of that craft at the time be able to inspect freely in that craft as often as they think it opportune, and that if any one of the aforesaid craft shall have rebelled against them executing their office properly, that he then should pay to the Chamber of the council for the work of the commons and the support of the pageant and of other burdens of the aforesaid craft 40d, to be divided into equal portions.

...

1424
A/Y Memorandum Book Y: E20

f 283* *(7 February)* Curriers

...

Item, on the seventh day of February in the second year of the reign of King Henry the sixth, it was agreed by all the masters of the aforesaid craft that on the next Sunday after the feast of the Purification of blessed Mary, they would choose their new searchers for the coming year, and that on the next Sunday after the feast of Corpus Christi, they would choose their pageant masters, and that their former pageant masters then would render up an account of their tenure in the past year and will give up all their properties belonging to the pageant and play into the care and hands of the searchers under penalty of 6s 8d.

...

Bridgemasters' Account Rolls Y: C82:2

mb 1*

⟨M⟩ickle⟨gate without and with⟩in ⟨Ra⟩ton Row a⟨nd To⟩fts

...

And from the Skinners and Dyers of York for the pageant house in the same place at the stated times: this year   2s

...

And from the Tanners of York for land on the Tofts at the stated
times: this year   12d
And from the Mercers of York for land in the same place at the
stated times: this year   12d
And from the Tapiters of York for land in the same place at the
stated times: this year   12d
And from the Carpenters and Cordwainers of York for land in
the same place at the stated times: this year   2s
And from the Bakers of York for land in the same place at the
stated times: this year   12d
And from the Goldsmiths of York for land in the same place at
the stated times: this year   8d
...

1425
A/Y Memorandum Book Y: E20

f 279* (5 January) Decision of Council

® About Fullers
and Shearers

... and they agreed and ordered among other things that the
Fullers of this city of York should hold their inspection of cloth
fulled by foreign fullers in such a way that they show them no
hate or malice in inspecting, and that all Fullers of this city be

® More on the
21st folio
following about
the same persons

able to shear freely, if they wished, all the cloth which they
themselves fulled, if they had the knowledge of shearing, without
giving anything to the Shearers of this city; but that, if these
Fullers took it upon themselves customarily to shear any (pieces
of) cloth large or small which were not of their own fulling, they
should then be contributors with the Shearers to their pageant
and to their other burdens ...

f 284v* (1 June)

Ordinance for Tilers and Wrights about louvers
... were met here in the Chamber and there came before them
John Bolron, William Kyrkeby, John Hexham, John Mosse, and
William Warter, carpenters, on their own behalf and that of all
the men of their craft of this city of York, and John Ase, William
Coupeland, John Kyrkham, John Symond, and Richard Watson,
tilers of houses, on their own behalf and that of all the men of
the craft of Tilers of the same city. And they submitted themselves to the judgement of the mayor and the council of the
Chamber concerning the commercial production of new louvers,
which are called draught louvers. The mayor and councillors
decided that all the men of both of the aforesaid crafts should be

good friends to one another, and that in token of the friendship to be forged among them, those craftsmen here present should exchange a kiss, and so it was done. And because they found that the chief manufacture of the louvers which are called draught louvers belonged and belongs principally to the Carpenters, they therefore decided that all Tilers both present and future of this city making and selling such louvers should be contributors yearly to the Carpenters' pageant of one penny from the first payment term, beginning with the feast of Corpus Christi this year. Further, (they decided) that tilers of houses should hereafter place louvers, whether they be of their own manufacture or of the manufacture of the Carpenters, upon all houses without murmur or contradiction. So that louvers of this kind shall be inspected by the searchers of the Carpenters before they be placed on houses, and that the best louver shall be sold henceforth for 10d and no more, but a second louver of a smaller size for 8d, and another louver of a third size for 6d, whether they be made by the men of the one craft or of the other. And that all distraints upon the Tilers taken and held by the Carpenters before this time for a payment to the pageant of the Carpenters shall be paid back to the Tilers without anything to be paid thence to the Carpenters. And if anyone has been unwilling to obey, that he should be imprisoned at the pleasure of him who is mayor at the time and of the council of the Chamber, and pay 40s to the work of the commons. And that from now on, they should repair and install old louvers upon houses as they have been accustomed to do, upon the abovesaid penalty.

Burton had it registered

f 279v (11 September)
Constitutions of the Cooks

...

And since in ancient times when the common cooks of this city were accustomed to buy fish fresh from the sea and sell the same retail as they pleased, they were then contributors to the pageant of the Fishmongers, but because lately they have been forbidden to sell any fish fresh from the sea, henceforth except those which they have cooked, broiled, or baked as belongs to their craft, therefore, it is ordered that they no longer be contributors to the pageant of the Fishmongers, but that they be quit of that forever.

...

1426
A/Y Memorandum Book   Y: E20

f 278-8v*   *(6 June)*

...

In the name of God, Amen. In accordance with a certain custom
followed for many years and times, all the craftsmen of the city
of York at their own expense have caused a certain sumptuous
play of the Old and New Testaments compiled in different
pageants to be performed every year, and put on at diverse sites
of the aforesaid city on the feast of Corpus Christi; likewise,
making a certain solemn procession then for reverence of the
sacrament of the body of Christ, by beginning at the great doors
of the Priory of the Holy Trinity of York and so going processionally to the cathedral church of York and thence to the
Hospital of St Leonard at York, the aforesaid sacrament having
been left there, with the light of many torches and a great multitude of priests dressed in surplices preceding, and the mayor and
citizens of York with a great abundance of other people flowing in

® About the
feast of Corpus
Christi

following. On this matter, a certain very religious man, Brother
William Melton of the order of Friars Minor, a professor of
scripture and a most famous preacher of the word of God, coming
to this city, has commended the said play to the people in several
of his sermons, by affirming that it was good in itself and most
laudable; nevertheless, he used to say that the citizens of the
aforesaid city and the other foreigners coming in to it during the
said festival, attend not only to the play on the same feast, but
also greatly to feastings, drunkenness, clamours, gossipings, and
other wantonness, engaging the least in the divine service of the
office of that day and that, alas, for that cause, they lose the
indulgences granted to them in that matter by Pope Urban IV of
happy memory. That is, (he granted) to the faithful of Christ
who shall attend the morning office of the same feast in the
church in which that feast is being celebrated, (an indulgence of)
one hundred days; to the faithful who shall attend the mass, the
same; to the faithful who shall attend the first vespers of this
feast, likewise a hundred days; to those at second (vespers), the
same; to those who shall attend prime, terce, sext, none, and the
office of compline, forty days for each of those hours; to those
who shall attend the morning and evening (offices), mass, and the
offices of the aforementioned hours throughout the octave of
this feast, one hundred days for each day of the octave, as is

more fully contained in the holy canons proclaimed by him. Therefore, it seemed good to this Brother William that this play should take place on one day and the procession on the other, so that the people could come together in the churches on the aforesaid feast and attend divine service for the consequent indulgences, and he persuaded the people of the city to this. Wherefore, Peter |Bukcy, mayor of this city of York; Richard Russell, lately head of the Staple at Calesia; John Northeby, William Bowes Sr, John Moreton, Thomas Gare Sr, Henry Preston, Thomas Esynwald, Thomas Bracebryg, William Ormesheued, John Aldestanemore, aldermen; Richard Louthe, John Dodyngton, sheriffs; John Hewyk, Thomas Doncastre, John Usburn, Thomas More, Robert Yarom, Robert Midelton, Godfrey Sauvage, Thomas Snawdon, John Loftehouse, John Bolton, John Lyllyng, John Gascoigne, William Craven, Thomas Aton, Thomas Davy, John Baynbrig, Thomas Kyrkham, William Bedale, William Gaytesheued, John Louthe, and John Warde, out of the Twenty-four, met here in the Council Chamber of this city on the sixth day of June in the year of grace 1426 in the fourth year of the reign of King Henry the sixth after the conquest of England. They were moved more readily by the words, exhortations, and healthful warnings of the aforesaid Brother William, and considering very correctly that it is not a transgression nor does it offend God if good be changed to better. Therefore, after a careful discussion among themselves of the matter already mentioned, they gave their unanimous and express consent that this matter should first be made public to the commons in the Common Hall and, after the common consent has been obtained, that the past observances should be changed for the better. About which, after the aforesaid mayor and the commons of this city had gathered together in the same Common Hall on the tenth day of the aforesaid month of June in the aforesaid year, and after the solemn publication had been made there, it was ordered by common agreement that that solemn play which, as is said above, used to be played on the very feast of Corpus Christi from now on should be presented each year on the Wednesday which is the eve of the same feast, and that the procession should always be made solemnly on the day of the feast itself, so that the whole people then staying in the aforesaid city would be able (to be free) for matins, mass, vespers, and the other hours of the same feast religiously, and to partake in the indulgences quite graciously conceded by the said Roman pontiff, Pope Urban IV,

How the play on the feast of Corpus Christi is changed to the vigil so that it might occur during the feast itself

in that regard.

Burton had it registered

...

1427
York Minster Chamberlains' Rolls   YM: E1/39 MP

mb 2

Various expenses and repairs
... And given to the minstrels on the feast of the Translation of St William and for the four days of Pentecost, 26s 8d. ...

Vicars Choral Accounts   YM: Tileworks Accounts, VC Box XII

... Item, paid to Master Robert Skurueton for the interlude of Corpus Christi on the term-day of sir Thomas Tanfeld, 16d. Item, paid for the same interlude of Corpus Christi the same year, 3s 8d. Item, paid in drink with the masters of the play, 4d. ...

1428
A/Y Memorandum Book   Y: E20

f 285   *(2 July)*

Ordinance of the Wool Brokers

... and beyond this, a proclamation was made and the wool brokers John Sylton, John Marche, and Robert Appilby were selected and sworn in and, (it was ordered) that they would take for their labour 2d from the consignment from the buyer. And that all who maintained houses in the liberty of the city, for keeping their wools there would be contributors each year to the pageant of the Brokers in the Corpus Christi Play.

Burton having been formally requested to do so, had it registered

Bridgemasters' Account Rolls   Y: C82:3

mb 1

Micklegate without and within Raton Row and Tofts
...

And from the Skinners and Dyers of York for the pageant house in the same place at the stated times, this year   2s

...

And from the Tanners of York for their pageant house at the
stated times, this year   12d
And from the Carpenters and Cordwainers of York for land in
the same place on the Tofts at the stated times, this year   2s
And from the Mercers of York for their pageant house at the
stated times, this year   12d
And from the Bakers of York for their pageant house at the
stated times, this year   12d
And from the Goldsmiths of York for their pageant house at
the stated times, this year   8d
And from the Tapiters of York for their pageant house at the
stated times, this year   12d
...

1430
York Minster Chamberlains' Rolls   YM: E1/39a MP

mb 3
(as E1/39 above 1427)

1431
A/Y Memorandum Book   Y: E20

f 21v*   *(1 February)*   *Butchers*
...
And likewise, on the eve of the Purification of the blessed Virgin
Mary in the ninth year of the reign of King Henry the sixth, it
was ordered by Richard Russell, then mayor, and the council
of the Chamber of this city, that any butcher coming to that
city from outside with meat for sale ought to pay 4d yearly to
the masters of the pageant of the Butchers of this city for the
production of their play on the feast of Corpus Christi.
...
Item, if any stranger or another who has been an apprentice or
servant in the aforesaid craft and ⟨...⟩ for the purpose of working
as a master in the aforesaid craft and his work be found faulty
he shall make reparation properly for the said work to the one
who has been injured in this way, and also he shall pay to the
Chamber and to the use of their said pageant 13s 4d in the
manner stated below.

1431-2
A/Y Memorandum Book Y: E20

ff 257-7v

Goldsmith

In the name of the Lord, Amen. It ought not to be passed over,
but rather remembered that the Goldsmiths of this city of York
in years past have borne heavy burden and excessive expenses
for their two pageants in the play of Corpus Christi. And now
times have changed for them and they have been made poorer
in goods than usual, and by ways and means stated above have
made frequent suit to mayors and to the council of the Chamber
for having aid either as relief of their unsupportable burdens or
else that they be relieved of one of their pageants, since, as
costs which grow daily on this account explain, they have not
been able to sustain the burden of both of their pageants any
longer undue hardship. On the other hand, indeed, the Masons
of this city have been accustomed to murmur among themselves
about their pageant in the Corpus Christi Play in which Fergus
was beaten because the subject of this pageant is not contained
in the sacred scripture and used to produce more noise and
laughter than devotion. And whenever quarrels, disagreements,
and fights used to arise among the people from this, they have
rarely or never been able to produce their pageant and to play
in daylight as the preceding pageants do. Therefore, these
Masons have been striving with great need to be relieved from
this pageant of theirs and assigned to another which is in harmony
with sacred scripture, and which they will be able to produce and
play in daylight. And for fulfilling their desires of this kind, both
aforesaid parties have importuned and begged in the presence of
the mayor and council of the Chamber to have their good consent
and gracious will in this matter. Wherefore Thomas Snauden,
mayor, the aldermen, and the council of the Chamber of this
city, willing and receiving kindly the wishes of the men of the
aforesaid crafts, and judging them consonant with probity,
decided that the aforesaid Goldsmiths, for the lessening of their
heavy burdens, be freed of one I of their pageants, ie, that of
Herod, and similarly, that the aforesaid Masons be freed and quit
of the pageant of Fergus, and that those Masons have for themselves and their craft the aforesaid pageant of Herod which
the Goldsmiths had to produce formerly and play at their own
expense in the Corpus Christi Play, in the more lavish manner

which is seemly for the praise of the city, every time the aforesaid play shall be played in the aforesaid city.

...

1432
A/Y Memorandum Book   Y: E20

f 283v*   (1 September)

In the name of the Lord, Amen. Since recently, in the time of
Henry Preston, mayor, upon the advice of the council of the
Chamber, the pageant of the Saucemakers in the Corpus Christi
Play, in which Judas used to hang himself and burst in the
middle, and the pageant of the Tilemakers, in which Pilate has
condemned Jesus to death, and the pageant of the Turners,
Hayresters, and Bollers, in which Jesus had been bound to the
pillar and flogged, and the pageant of the Millers, in which
Pilate and other soldiers used to play at dice for the clothing of
Jesus and to cast lots for them and to divide them among themselves, were combined together in one pageant, after the other
aforesaid pageants were stopped forever, which pageant indeed
will be called the pageant of the Condemnation of Jesus Christ;
after this, the craftsmen of the aforesaid crafts used to disagree
among themselves about this, the manner of payment to the
said pageant. But finally, nevertheless, upon the good mediating
advice of Thomas Bracebrig, mayor, all the aforesaid craftsmen
put themselves under the judgment of William Scoreburgh,
John Staynburn, draper, Robert Bolton, combsmith, and Richard
Neuland, as being disinterested parties, and they, taking the
responsibility upon themselves, reconciled these crafts as follows:
that is, that the Saucemakers and the Tilemakers would bear,
from then on, the burden and expenses of the aforesaid pageant
and would produce it to be played yearly in a good and fitting
way, so that they would be willing to answer before him who
was mayor at the time when they were forewarned of it, and
that the Millers will pay and hand over each year forever on the
eve of Corpus Christi to the Saucemakers and Tilemakers, that
is, into the hands of the masters of the aforesaid pageant, 10s
sterling in aid of the expenses of this pageant under penalty of
13s 4d, to be equally divided between the Chamber of this
city and the repair of the aforesaid pageant, and that one or two
millers would go with the pageant on the day of the same play
and collect refreshments of food and drink with the Saucemakers

On the pageant
of the
Condemnation
of Christ of
the Saucemakers
and the Tile-
makers (.... ....)

and Tilemakers. And that the Hayresters and those who formerly
have paid yearly to them will pay on the eve of Corpus Christi to
the wardens of the aforesaid pageant 5s in aid of the expenses
of the same pageant, under penalty of 10s to be paid in the
manner stated above, and that one of them would go about with
the play and the aforesaid pageant and have refreshments with
the masters of the same (pageant) and with them if he wishes.
And if at any time the pageant should need repair, that the
Millers should be contributors of (every) third penny of the costs
and the Hayresters, of half of the sum to be paid by the abovesaid Millers, and that one miller and one hayrester should oversee
the costs concerning the repair of the aforesaid pageant with
those who are the masters of the same at the time. And that
none of the aforesaid four crafts may place any signs, arms or
insignia upon the aforesaid pageant, except only the arms of this
honourable city. And that no member of the aforesaid four
crafts shall litigate or make any quarrel with any (member) of
the same crafts about any particular of the aforesaid pageant
under penalty of 3s 4d to be applied to the use of the work of
Foss Bridge (to be paid) by whoever has done the contrary in
this regard, as often as he has been convicted of this on sufficient
evidence in the future.

To this agreement it has been added and ordered on the first
of September in the eleventh year of the reign of King Henry VI
in the time of Thomas Snaudon, mayor, by the deliberation and
decision of the aforesaid John Staynburn, Robert Bolton, Richard
Neuland, and of John Man, as disinterested parties chosen by
all the craftsmen of the aforesaid Saucemakers and Tilemakers,
that annually on the eve of Corpus Christi the Saucemakers
should pay to the Tilemakers 5s in money for their share of the
aforesaid pageant forever under penalty of 10s to be paid equally
to the Chamber and to the use of the aforesaid pageant. And
that, as often as the said pageant needs repair, then the Saucemakers shall pay one penny just as the Tilemakers will pay
yearly, and that this repair shall be overseen by two men from
one craft and two from the other, and that the two or three
Saucemakers (who) shall go around with the aforesaid pageant
on the day and during the Corpus Christi Play may have their
refreshments at the same time if they wish.

Burton having been formally requested to do so,
had it registered

Agreement between City and Corpus Christi Guild   Y : A15*

In the name of the holy and undivided Trinity, amen. Indeed,
if we are ordered to worship and praise the Lord in his saints,
how much more fitting, right, and healthful it seems to us and
to any Catholic that we should give the thanks of festive worship
and praise to him, in memory of the body, by which he daily
restores us spiritually, of him whose kindness to us was so
copious that he, wishing to show his rich love for us by special
generosity, has shown his own self to us, and transcending
every fullness of giving, and exceeding every means of loving,
gives himself as food. Behold how singular and admirable is his
generosity when the giver comes as the gift and the same is given
thoroughly with the giver, and how great and prodigious is the
giving when he gives who gives himself. Indeed, in consideration
of these things, certain persons of both sexes of the city of York,
called as a group the brothers and sisters of the fraternity in
honour of, and in common speech (simply), Corpus Christi, in
the same city from and throughout a time of whose contrary
there is no human memory, more readily than usual aroused by
the consent and will of John Bolton, mayor, and of the commons
of the citizens of the said city of the same fraternity, as indeed
this whole city was (and) is of the brotherhood, offer at their
own expense a certain shrine of sumptuous work, lately both
carved and moreover painted with gold, which henceforth (is)
to be enriched and ornamented more preciously with the purest
silver and gold with the Lord's help, which they wish also to be
carried each year in the hands of priests on the feast of Corpus
Christi itself if good weather permits, or on some other feast
day following when it can be done more conveniently through
set streets and squares of the said city with a solemn public
procession, with the sacrament of the body of Christ enclosed
in it and in crystal or beryl or some other thing open to the
sight of men more suitably for the sacrament, always preceded
by the light of the torches of the good citizens of the aforesaid
fraternity, so that from this, faith and devotion may be increased
among the present people. And now the mayor and citizens,
mindful of the things written above, exulting for joy and desiring
to bring to the best end the things which were well begun to the
memory and praise of the abovesaid vivifying sacrament, wish
and grant inviolably and with most firm faith on behalf of themselves and their successors by the present document one special

place, for the honour of the most sacred sacrament, to the aforesaid shrine in the well-known chapel in the honour and to the
renown of the most holy confessor, William, once archbishop
of York, established on Ouse Bridge in the aforesaid city, so that
it may honourably reside there every year. And indeed, the said
mayor and commons of the aforesaid city of York have granted
that those who are the six chaplains, the wardens of the abovesaid fraternity at the time, should have the freedom of the aforesaid shrine and power to go to the aforesaid shrine each year as
often as there is occasion and specially on the aforesaid feast of
Corpus Christi, and take it and carry it or cause it to be carried
outside the said chapel without any impediment of the aforesaid
mayor and citizens, and to make a procession with it for the
memory and festive worship of the aforesaid sacrament in the
aforesaid way. When the procession is well and peacefully
ended, the aforesaid six wardens may reverently replace the
aforesaid shrine in the aforesaid chapel of St William at the said
place at their own will, as is said above. Moreover, it is agreed
among the mayor and citizens and the aforesaid wardens that the
wardens of the aforesaid shrine should have and guard the keys
of the closing of the abovesaid little box. In addition, (it is
agreed) that one key of the outer covering and veil of the aforesaid shrine should always remain in the Council Chamber of the
said city, under the control of the mayor of the same, for him
alone, so that that mayor, whoever he be, without question or
delay for the other keys, may cause that shrine to be shown
when he wishes to any honourable persons, lords or ladies, or
others of noble birth wishing to see the same uncovered, so that
their devotion may grow from this and the honour of the said
city increase, and most especially that the praise or honour of
the beholders may redound to the Lord. And thus, by the
grace of God, perhaps through certain men devoted to God, the
improvement of the aforesaid shrine may truly come from that.
In faith and witness of all and each of which (agreements), both
the common seal of the aforesaid city and the seals of the present
wardens of the aforesaid fraternity, viz, of sir John Bernyngham,
sir Roger Bubwyth, sir John de Grymesby, sir John Crauen, sir
John de Sutton, and sir William Bryg, chaplains, have been
affixed one after another to the parts of this indenture. Given
at York on the sixteenth of January, AD 1431, in the tenth year
of the reign of King Henry the sixth after the conquest of England.
 Burton having been formally requested to do so,
 had it registered

Will of Nicholas Blackburn the elder, merchant and mayor
BI: Prob. Reg. 2

f 605   *(20 February; probated 10 April)*
... and (I leave) four torches yearly to the fraternity of Corpus
Christi in York, to be burned at the procession on the feast of
the same Corpus Christi as long as they last ...

1433
B/Y Memorandum Book   Y: E20A

f 120
Of selling sweet (wine) at retail here within the liberty of the
same city and that all those who sell sweet wines within the
same liberty ought to be yearly contributors along with the
Vintners of this city and pay to the pageant of the same Vintners
proportionally as they encroach more or less and sell sweet
wines of this kind.

City Chamberlains' Rolls   Y: C1:2

mb 1
...

Expenses on the feast of Corpus Christi

And to the players in the pageant of the Coronation of blessed
Mary on the feast of Corpus Christi 20s. And to the minstrels
on the same day according to custom 20s. And for the repair
of the aforesaid pageant 19s 1d. And for the rent of the
Chamber of the mayor and of the honourable men on the same
day 6s 8d. And on the presentations of bread, wine, and fruits
on the aforesaid day £3 14d.

...

For the winter livery of the waits of the city

And for the winter livery of three city minstrels, bought from the
same William Gyllyngton 27s 10d.

Heralds, messengers, and minstrels of lords £3 7s

And paid to heralds, messengers, and minstrels in this year £3 7s.

...

1435
Bridgemasters' Account Rolls   Y: C82:5

mb 1

Micklegate without and within Raton Row and Tofts

...

And from the Skinners and Dyers of York for the house of their pageants at the stated times of this year   2s

...

And from the Mercers of York for their pageant house on the
Tofts at the stated times, this year   12d
And from the Bakers of York for their pageant house in the
same place at the stated times, this year   12d
And from the Tanners of York for their pageant house in the
same place at the stated times, this year   12d
And from the Tapiters of York for their pageant house in the
same place at the stated times, this year   12d
And from the Carpenters and Cordwainers of York for their
pageant house in the same place at the stated times, this year   2s
And from the Goldsmiths of York for their pageant house at
the stated times, this year   8d

...

1436
Bridgemasters' Account Rolls   Y: C82:7

mb 1

...

Micklegate
without and
within Raton
Row, Tofts

And from the Skinners and Dyers of York for the house of their
pageants at the stated times, this ⟨year⟩   ⟨2s⟩

...

And from the Mercers of York for their pageant house on the
Tofts at the stated times, this year   ⟨12d⟩

...

And from the Bakers of York for their pageant house in the
same place at the stated times of this year   ⟨12d⟩
And from the Tanners of York for their pageant house in the
same place at the stated times, this year   ⟨12d⟩
And from the Tapiters of York for their pageant house in the
same place at the stated times, this year   ⟨12d⟩
And from the Carpenters and Cordwainers of York for the house
of their pageants at the stated times, ⟨this year⟩   ⟨2s⟩
And from the Goldsmiths of York for their pageant house at
the stated times, this year   ⟨8d⟩

...

1437
Bridgemasters' Account Rolls Y : C82:8

mb 1

...

Micklegate without and within Raton Row, Tofts

And from the Skinners and Dyers of York for the house of their pageants at the stated times, this year   2s

...

And from the Mercers of York for their pageant house on the Tofts at the stated times, this year   12d

And from the Bakers of York for their pageant house in the same place at the stated times of this year   12d

And from the Tanners of York for their pageant house in the same place at the stated times, this year   12d

And from the Tapiters of York for their pageant house in the same place at the stated times, this year   12d

And from the Carpenters and Cordwainers of York for the house of their pageants at the stated times, this year   2s

And from the Goldsmiths of York for their pageant house at the stated times, this year   8d

...

1438
Will of John Preston, Chaplain of Bubwith BI : Prob. Reg. 3

f 546 *(25 September; probated 11 October)*
... Item, I leave to John Robynson all my books of pricknote. Item, I leave to Richard Raby three books, viz, one portable breviary in two volumes, and a third called a song book. ...

1440
Bridgemasters' Account Rolls Y : C82:10

mb 1

...

Micklegate without within Raton Row and Tofts

And from the Skinners and Dyers of York for the house of their pageants at the stated times, this year   2s

...

And from the Mercers of York for their pageant house on the Tofts at the stated times, this year   12d

And from the Bakers and Tanners of York for their pageant house in the same place at the stated times, this year, viz, for

each party 12d   2s
And from the Tapiters of York for their pageant house in the
same place at the stated times, this year   12d
And from the Carpenters and Cordwainers of York for the house
of their pageants at the stated times, this year   2s
And from the Goldsmiths of York for their pageant house at
the stated times, this year   8d
...

1442
City Chamberlains' Rolls   Y : C 1 : 3

mb 2
...

Summer and winter clothing	And for 78 (lengths of) striped cloth bought and given to 3 waits, 17s; together with 6 ells of light blue given to the aforesaid waits for Christmas, 12s	29s
Heralds and minstrels	And to the heralds, messengers, and minstrels of the king, the dukes, the barons, the knights, and other honourable persons in this year Total 119s 4d	119s 4d
Expenses on the feast of Corpus Christi	And on various presentations of pain-demaine, of wines, (and) of fruits made to the honourable persons here present for the praise and honour of the city, together with other expenses of the mayor, of the aldermen, and of other honourable men, and for the play of the Vineyard, in this year 20d	61s 4½d

...

Bridgemasters' Account Rolls   Y : C82 : 11

mb 1*
...

And from the Carpenters ⟨...⟩
And from the Goldsmiths ⟨...⟩

...

1444
Bridgemasters' Account Rolls   Y : C 8 2 : 1 2

mb 1

...

Micklegate
without and
within Raton
Row and
Tofts

And from the Skinners and Dyers of York for the house of their
pageants at the stated times, this year   2s

...

And from the Mercers of York for their pageant house on the
Tofts at the stated times, this year   12d
And from the Bakers of York for their pageant house in the same
place at the stated times, this year   12d
And from the Tanners of York for their pageant house in the
same place at the above stated times of this year   12d
And from the Tapiters of York for their pageant house in the
same place at the stated times   12d
And from the Carpenters and Cordwainers for the house of
their pageants at the stated times   2s
And from the Goldsmiths of York for their pageant house at
the above stated times of this year   8d

...

1445
A/Y Memorandum Book   Y : E 2 0

f 53   *(3 June)*

...

Memorandum that on the third day of June in the twenty-third
year of the reign of King Henry the sixth after the conquest of
England, in the Council Chamber in the presence of Thomas
Crathorn, mayor of the city of York, it was ordered and most
firmly agreed by the unanimous consent and assent of all the
crafts of the Cutlers of the aforesaid city on the one hand and
by Thomas Usclyff, chapman of York, on the other, that the
aforesaid Thomas shall pay 10d yearly to the upkeep of the
pageant and light of the aforesaid craft on the feast of Corpus
Christi. And that the same Thomas Usclyff henceforth shall
not be elected (to the office of) master of that pageant nor to
any other office pertaining to the same craft, but that he shall be
entirely free from every office and burden pertaining to the
same craft, excepting entirely the annual payment of the said
10d.

And because it was the custom from of old that all those citizens and foreigners who may have sold knives or daggers within the liberty of the aforesaid city, either retail or wholesale, have paid toward the upkeep of the pageant of Corpus Christi and the light of the crafts of the Cutlers, Bladesmiths, and Sheathers, and now there are some who refuse to pay henceforth toward the said pageant and light as has been stated; therefore, it was ordered on the day and year aforesaid that foreigners and all citizens of whatever sort displaying knives and daggers in stalls, laying them out, and selling them, and drawing them from sheaths for the purpose of selling them within the liberty of the same city, or placing knives and daggers of whatever sort upon their points or their ends for selling either retail or wholesale, with the complete exception of the Merchants and Mercers of this city, be contributors with the aforesaid crafts to the upkeep of the aforesaid pageant and light as was the custom before these times, and further, that the searchers of the aforesaid crafts then following must make their inspection of the foreigners as well as of the citizens of the city of each and every trade which belongs to their crafts, and all faults to be found in the same they will present to him who is the mayor at the time to be corrected, punished, and remedied at his discretion etc.

City Chamberlains' Rolls   Y : C 2 : 2

mb 2

...

Summer and winter clothing	And on 78 (lengths of) striped cloth bought for the minstrels for the summer livery	17s 8d
	...	
	And for 6 ells of red motley bought and given to the aforesaid minstrels for the second part of their livery for Christmas	13s 4d
	...	
H(eralds, messen)gers, and minstrels	And to the heralds, messengers, and minstrels of the king, of the dukes, of the barons, of the knights, and of the other honourable persons in this year	109s 10d

Total 109s 10d

Expenses on
the feast of
Corpus Christi

And on various presentations of pain-demaine,
wines and fruits made to the honourable persons
here present for the praise and honour of the city,　　　50s 1d
together with other expenses of the mayor,
aldermen and other honourable men
Total 50s 1d

...

1446
City Chamberlains' Books　Y : CC1

p 26*
...

Expenses on the feast of Corpus Christi

Expenses on the feast of Corpus Christi incurred
by the mayor, the aldermen, and others, foreigners,　　52s 10d
for the honour and glory of the city

...

pp 31-3
Heralds and minstrels

Given as a gratuity to a certain minstrel of Ralph Puddeszay	6d
Given as a gratuity to 4 players of the city	6d
...	
Given as a gratuity to 2 minstrels of John Sauage, knight	12d
As a gratuity to John Bull, waferer	6d
Given as a gratuity to John Waferer	8d
Given as a gratuity to Hugo Loyter, minstrel of the bishop of Durham	12d
Given as a gratuity to a certain minstrel of Thomas Lumley, knight	4d
Given as a gratuity to Joan Piper of York	2d
Given as a gratuity to Christopher Harpour	12d
Item, to 2 minstrels of the earl of Westmorland	16d
Item, to 1 minstrel of Robert Roos, knight	4d
Item, to 1 minstrel of Lord de Clyfford	8d
...	
Item, to 2 minstrels of the duke of Norfolk	20d
Item, to a certain minstrel of the Baron de Graystok	8d
Item, to a certain minstrel of York	8d

Item, to John Waferer and Robert Waferer on the third Sunday
in Lent   20d
Item, to the city minstrels on Easter   3s 4d
Item, to 2 minstrels of the lord of Cambridge   20d
Item, to 1 waferer of the lord of Salisbury   6d
Item, to 1 minstrel of William Fitz William   6d
Item, to 1 minstrel of the lord of Wells   8d
Item, to 1 player   6d
Item, to 2 minstrels of Robert Oghtred, knight   12d
Item, to 1 minstrel of the baron de Graystok   8d
Item, to 3 minstrels of Durham   8d
Item, to 1 minstrel of William Lumley, knight   6d
Item, to 1 other minstrel   4d
Item, to 4 minstrels of the duke of York on the sixth day of
May   6s 8d
Item, to 3 minstrels of Newcastle upon Tyne   20d
Item, to 2 minstrels of France   8d |
Item, to 4 minstrels of the lord of Salisbury on the tenth
day of May   3s 4d
Item, to 1 minstrel of Thomas Metham, knight   8d
Item, to 4 minstrels of the lord of Exeter on the fourteenth day
of May   6s 8d
Item, to 1 waferer from the south country on the nineteenth day
of May   6d
Item, to 1 fool of the lord of Westmorland on the twenty-third
day of May   4d
Item, to 2 minstrels from Lincoln, 16d, with 1 minstrel of Ralph
Pudesay, 6d   22d
Item, to 1 minstrel of Hugh de Wilowby   6d
Item, to the players on the Sunday next after the feast of the
Ascension of the Lord   12d
Item, to 1 blind minstrel   4d
Item, to the city minstrels on the vigil of the Nativity of St John
the Baptist   20d
Item, to a certain minstrel of Richard Musgrefe, knight   6d
Item, to the minstrels on the feast of Corpus Christi   20d
Item, to 1 minstrel on the thirteenth day of August   4d
Item, to 6 minstrels of the lord of Gloucester on the seventh day
of September   10s
Item, to 4 minstrels of the lord king on the third day of
October   20s
Item, to 2 minstrels of the earl of Northumberland and of

Thomas Percy, knight, on the fourth day of October	20d
Item, to 1 minstrel in Baggergate	4d
Item, to 1 minstrel	1d
Item, to Whetlay the minstrel on the tenth day of October	8d
Item, to 1 player on the eleventh day of October	7d
Item, to 1 minstrel on the twelfth day of October	8d
Item, to 1 minstrel of William Bowes, knight	8d
Item, to 3 minstrels of John Penyngton, knight	12d
Item, to 4 minstrels of the duke of Buckingham on the second day of November	6s 8d
Item, to a minstrel of the earl of Northumberland on the eighth day of November	8d
Item, to John Wafferer on the seventeenth day of November and to 1 fool, 1d	9d
Item, to 2 minstrels of the Lord de Clifford and 1 minstrel from Allerton	18d
Item, to 5 minstrels from the marches of Dorchester on the twenty-fifth day of November	5s
Item, to 2 minstrels of William Maleuerer, gentleman, on the fourth day of December	12d
Item, to 1 minstrel of Lord Lescrope de Bolton	12d
Item, to Simon Harpour and to 1 other minstrel on the seventeenth day of December	6d

£4 10s 9d |

Item, to the city minstrels on Christmas	3s 4d
Item, to the players on the same feast	8d
Item, 1 trumpet	8d
Item, 1 fiddler in the same week	4d
Item, to players on the feast of the Circumcision	12d
Item, to 1 minstrel	4d

...

Item, to 1 minstrel from Knaresborough	12d
Item, to 3 players from Donnington	12d
Item, to 1 player from Wakefield	6d

...

Item, to the city minstrels on the feast of St William	20d
Item, to Robert Wafferer on the same feast	12d
Item, to 2 minstrels of the Lady de Dancourt	16d
Item, to Simon Harpour on the same day	4d
Item, to 5 trumpeters of the lord of Salisbury on the nineteenth day of January	6s 8d

Item, to 1 minstrel of Lord William Plompton   8d
Item, to 1 minstrel of Robert Ogle, knight, on the twenty-sixth
    day of January   6d
                Total £7 9s 7d

Codicil of the Will of William Revetour, deputy civic clerk
BI: Prob. Reg. 2

f 138v *(Will: 2 August; Codicil: 11 August;*
    probated 3 September)
... Item, I leave to the fraternity of Corpus Christi in York a
certain book called the Creed Play, together with the books and
banners belonging to it. And to the guild of St Christopher a
certain play concerning St James the apostle compiled in six
pageants. ... Item, I leave to the Girdlers of the city of York for
their play on the feast of Corpus Christi one gilded brazen crown
and one girdle with gilded and enamelled bosses. ...

1447
City Chamberlains' Books   Y : CC 1

p 67
Expenses on the feast of Corpus Christi   43s 4d

pp 70-1
            Heralds, messengers, (and) minstrels
First, to 2 minstrels of the Lord de Dacre   12d
And to 1 minstrel with the hart   4d
And to 1 minstrel of the Lord de Clyfford   8d
And to 1 minstrel of John Haryngton   6d
...
And to 3 minstrels of the Lord Fitzhugh   2s
And to 3 minstrels from Beverley and to another called
    Wetelay   2s
And to Simon Harpour with 2 minstrels of the Lord de
    Graystok   2s
And to John Wafferer on the Sunday next before the beginning
    of Lent   8d
...
And to Robert Wafferer and John Wafferer on the Monday in
    the first week of Lent   9d
And to John Waferer on the twenty-third day of March   12d

® (before) the
feast of
St Valentine

And to the city minstrels on the vigil of Easter   3s 4d

And to 2 minstrels on the sixteenth day of April   6d

And to Hugo Luter with the bishop of Durham on the eighteenth
day of April   12d

...

And to 2 minstrels of the Lord de Clifford on the twentieth
day of April   4d

And to 1 minstrel of John Haryngton on the same day   6d

And to 4 minstrels of the duke of Exeter on the twenty-seventh
day of April   4s

And to 1 minstrel of Thomas Cheworth, knight   8d

And to 4 minstrels from the town of Leicester   2s

And to 2 minstrels from the town of Newcastle upon Tyne   12d

And to 1 minstrel of Henry Brounflete, knight   6d

And to 4 minstrels of the earl of Erandale on the twenty-second
day of May   3s 4d

And to 1 minstrel of Walter Tailbois, esquire   8d

And to 4 minstrels of the earl of Salisbury on the twenty-third
day of May   3s 4d

And to 1 minstrel of Thomas Neuyll, knight   6d

And to 3 minstrels of the earl of Northumberland, viz, to
Christopher on the penultimate day of May   2d

And to 3 minstrels from Pocklington on the last day of May   8d

And to 3 minstrels from London on the first day of June   12d

And to 4 players from London on the Sunday next after the
feast of Corpus Christi   6s 8d

And to the minstrels on the feast of Corpus Christi   16s

And to 1 minstrel on the Sunday next after the feast of Corpus
Christi   6d

And to 1 jester of Robert Waterton, knight, on the thirteenth
day of June   2d

And to 2 minstrels of Lord de Gray   12d

And to 3 city minstrels on the vigil of the Nativity of St John
the Baptist   20d

And to John Wafferer on the penultimate day of June   4d

And to 2 minstrels on the fourth day of July   8d

And to 2 minstrels of the lord of Suffolk, Richard Tunstall and
Thomas Herryngton   12d

And to 1 minstrel called 1 tregitour   4d

And to 6 minstrels of the lord king on the twenty-sixth day of
July   20s

And to 4 minstrels of the duke of York on the aforesaid day of

July	6s 8d
And to 2 minstrels of William Maulyuerer	6d
And to 2 minstrels of the Lord de Welughby	16d
And to 1 blind minstrel from the southern parts	4d
And to 1 waferer	2d
And to 1 minstrel of Henry Percy, Lord de Poyning	8d
And to 2 waferers of the earl of Salisbury and ⟨...⟩	12d
And to 1 minstrel on the twenty-seventh day of September	4d
And to 3 minstrels of William ⟨...⟩, knight, and Ralph Pudsay	8d
And to 5 minstrels of the earl of Suffolk	5s
And to 4 minstrels of the duke of Buckingham	⟨...⟩
And to 2 minstrels of Thomas Pudsay, knight	6d

...

And to 1 minstrel of the earl of Northumberland	8d
And to 2 minstrels of Lord Liscrop' de Bolton and of Walter Tailboys	12d
And to Jack Trumpet and to 1 minstrel of Henry Percy, knight	12d
And to 1 player with Joly Wat and Malkyn	⟨...⟩
And to 1 blind minstrel called the minstrel of God	6d
And to 2 minstrels of the earl of ⟨...⟩ on the eighteenth day of November	12d
And to 1 minstrel of the Lord de Haryngton, 12d, and to another lutanist, 2d	14d
And to 1 blind minstrel	2d
And to the city minstrels on Christmas	3s
And to various players on various days in the aforesaid feast	2s 10d
And to 9 minstrels of the lord of Salisbury 6s 8d, to the city minstrels 20d, to Robert Wafferer 2s, and to Simon Harpour 12d on the feast of St William and to Master William Pursevant	12s 8d
And to Robert Wafferer on Tuesday and after the feast of St William	9d
And to a certain minstrel of the duke of Exeter	8d
And to a certain minstrel Wafferer	4d

1448
City Chamberlains' Books Y : CC1

p 130

...

Expenses on the feast of Corpus Christi	43s 8d

pp 133-5

⟨...⟩

First, to John Wafferer	8d
And to Robert Wafferer on the same day, that is to say on the third day of March	8d
And to John Wafferer on the fourth day of March	8d
And to Robert Waferer on the same day	8d
And to a certain waferer of the earl of Salisbury on the eighth day of March	6d
And to 3 of the city minstrels of York at Easter	3s 4d
And to a certain minstrel of the Baron de Graystok on the same feast	6d
And to a certain juggler of John Neuyll	2d
And to 4 minstrels of the earl of Salisbury	4s
And to 2 minstrels of the Lord Fitzhugh	16d
And to a certain minstrel of John Nevill, knight	8d
And to 3 minstrels of the town of Beverley	18d
And to 3 minstrels of the Lord de Beaumond, 1 minstrel of Henry Percy, knight	4s
And to 3 minstrels of William Eueres, knight	12d
And to Christopher Harpour on the twelfth day of April	12d
And to 1 minstrel of the Lord de Clyfford on the same day, called Somersete	8d
And to 1 minstrel of the Lord de Bolton	6d
And to 2 minstrels of the Lord de Haryngton	12d
And to 2 minstrels of Robert Ogill, knight	8d
And to 1 minstrel of the duke of Norfolk	12d
And to Simon Harpour	8d
And to 2 minstrels of Richard de Middilton	8d
And to Hugo Luter	12d
And to 1 minstrel of Henry Brounflete	4d
And to 3 minstrels of the earl of Salisbury	3s 4d
And to 2 minstrels of the duke of Exeter	8d
And to 1 minstrel of William Maulyuerere, knight	4d
And to 1 minstrel of John Haryngeton, esquire	4d
And to 1 minstrel of Ralph Puddeszay, esquire	4d
And to 1 minstrel of Christopher Conyers	4d
And to 2 minstrels of the earl of Westmorland	12d

⟨...⟩

And to 2 players at the same time	12d
And to Joan Vnderwod on the same day	6d
And to 2 players (with) Joly Wat and Malkyn	2d

Total 36s 6d examined |

® 31s 1d

Item, paid to 2 minstrels of Thomas Harrington, knight   12d
Item, to minstrels on the feast of Corpus Christi   20d
Item, to Adam with the bells   4d
Item, to 1 waferer of the earl of Westmorland   6d
Item, to 1 minstrel of Lord John Sauage, knight   4d
Item, to 1 minstrel called Master William Spede   12d
And to 3 minstrels of John Percy de Cleueland   7d
And to 2 minstrels of the lord of Suffolk   10d
And to 2 minstrels of the lord king on the vigil of the Nativity
    of St John the Baptist   13s 4d
And to the city minstrels on the same day   20d
And to Thomas Buxnell   8d
And to 2 minstrels of the Lord de Wiloghby on the twenty-
    fourth day of July   16d
And to 1 minstrel called Nicholas Clerke   8d
And to 1 minstrel of the earl of Northumberland and to 1
    minstrel of the Lord de Dacre   16d
And to 1 waferer of the earl of Salisbury on the last day of
    September   4d
And to 3 minstrels of the lord duke of York   13s 4d
And to 1 minstrel of the Lord de Say   2s
And to 1 tibuvnell of Thomas Percy, gentleman   4d
And to 1 tibuvner of the lord of Wells   12d
And to 4 minstrels of the lord of Suffolk   6s 8d
And to 4 minstrels another time   10d
And to 3 waits of Nottingham on the twenty-third day of
    October   2s
And to 1 junior minstrel of the Viscount Beaumont called
    Bull   4d
And to 1 waferer of the Lord le Souche on the feast of All
    Saints   6d

...

And to 1 minstrel from the north country   4d
And to 1 minstrel in the month of December   2d
And to 1 minstrel of William Plumpton   6d
And to players on the feast of Epiphany   18d

Total 70s 1d examined |

And to the city minstrels on Christmas   3s 4d
And to 1 minstrel of Lord Thomas Percy   8d
And to the players on the aforesaid feast   8d

It ought to be paid by the commons from money to be raised

And to 8 minstrels of the earl of Salisbury on the feast of
  St William   8s

And to 4 minstrels of Lord Fitzhugh and to Thomas Buxnell
  on the same day   3s 4d

And to the city minstrels on the same day   20d

...

And to Robert Wafferer on the same day   12d

And to the same on the Tuesday then next following   12d

...

21s 4d   And to 2 minstrels of John Heryngton   8d

And to 1 minstrel of the duke of York   8d

And to 1 minstrel of Nicholas Radclyff   4d

                 Total £6 4s 11d

Henry VI Received in the Minster   Bodleian: MS Bodley 857

f 1v*
  This book belongs to William Marschall, chaplain of Peasholme

In the fourth year after one thousand, four hundred, as many tens, and one four, Henry the sixth was a pilgrim (at the shrine) of William on the vigil of Matthew during the canonical hours. While the choir glorified (God), he, with the metropolitans, gave praise to Peter.

When he had seen the shrines of Durham, Ripon, Bridlington, Beverley, and the flood-tides of Hull, he (again) honoured the (cathedral) close of York. Considering (this) a treasure-house worthy of him, he gave this praiseworthy sign as an honour to the church: dressed as a king he followed certain royal prerogatives; he celebrated the annual feast of the translation of Edward in a special way. Five prelates were present in their pontifical mitres, and there the order of rank was observed.

Then, leaving, the ruler of two kingdoms went south; the voice of the people blessed him as he, kindly, departed. May the heavenly prince who gives refreshment to his own defend him (the king) from treacherous enemies, I pray. Amen.

Bishop of Durham	Abbot of St Mary's
Bishop of Salisbury	
Bishop of Hereford	Abbot of Selby

1449
City Chamberlains' Rolls Y : C 2 : 5

mb 2-2d
...

Summer and winter clothing	On 18 ells of blue motley bought for the clothing of the said 6 servants for Christmas, and (that) of the city minstrels	36s

...

Herald and minstrels	And to the herald, messengers, and minstrels of the king, of the dukes, of the barons, of the knights, and of the other venerable persons in this year	£6 3s 5d

Total £6 3s 5d |

Expenses on the feast of Corpus Christi	On various presentations, as on pain-demaine, fruits and wine given to various venerable persons (and) gentlemen present in the city on the feast of Corpus Christi, for the praise and honour of the city, and on the expenses of the mayor and the aldermen of the same city, being together on the same feast	49s 9½d

Total 49s 9½d

...

City Chamberlains' Books Y : CC1A

f 28
And to Robert, clerk, for the play of the Coronation of the
blessed Virgin Mary on behalf of the mayor   8s

ff 29-9v*
Heralds, messengers, and minstrels

First, to John Wafferer on the fifth day of January   6d
And to 2 minstrels of Walter Tailboys on the same (day)   12d
And to 1 lutanist of the lord of Westmorland on the same (day)   6d
And to Simon Harpour on the ninth day of February   6d
And to 1 minstrel of William Plumpton and to another of
   Geoffrey Middilton   12d
And to Christopher Harpour on the sixteenth day of February   8d
And to 1 waferer of the earl of Salisbury   6d

And to 2 minstrels of William Malyuerer and of John
    Harryngton   12d

And to 2 minstrels of the lady of Norfolk and Viscount
    Beaumond   16d

And to Robert Wafferer   6d

And to 1 minstrel of William Puddesay   4d

And to 1 minstrel with the servant of William Fitz William   4d

And to 1 minstrel of John Butler, gentleman   4d

And to Richard Luter with the Baron de Graystok   8d

And to 1 boy called a jester   2d

And to 2 minstrels of the lord of Durham, Hugh Luter and
    his companion   20d

And to John Wafferer   6d

And to 2 waferers on a Sunday in the middle of Lent   2s

And to 2 minstrels of Lord Lescrop on the same day   20d

And to the minstrels of the city of York on Easter   3s 4d

And to 2 minstrels of William Plomipton   6d

And to 3 minstrels of the lord of Salisbury   3s 4d

And to 2 minstrels of Lord Fitz Hugh   16d

And to 2 minstrels of the Lord de Darcy, 4d, and to Alexander
    Neuell, 4d   8d

And to 2 minstrels of Thomas Neuyll, knight, and of the Lord
    de Clyfforde   12d

And to 1 minstrel of Lord Fitz Hugh   8d

And to Robert, a minstrel of Durham, with Hardyng of
    Newcastle   6d

And to 1 minstrel from London, called Luter   6d

And to 2 minstrels of Thomas Cheworth and Thomas Ramston,
    knight   12d

And to 3 minstrels of John Sauage, knight   20d

And to 1 minstrel of the Lord de Clyfford, called Somersete 8d

And to 1 minstrel of Lord Poynynges with 2 boys   12d

               Total 31s 4d |

And to 1 minstrel of William Rowes, knight   8d

And to 2 minstrels of Henry, Lord de Poynynges   4d

And to 1 minstrel, a story-teller   1d

And to 1 waferer of Thomas Haryngton, knight   4d

And to 1 waferer of the lord, the earl of Northumberland   6d

And to 1 minstrel of Thomas de Middilton of Kendale   4d

And to the city minstrels on the feast of the Nativity of St
    John the Baptist   20d

And to Robert Wafferer on the aforesaid feast	10d
And to 1 juggler on the twenty-eighth day of June	6d
And to the minstrels on the feast of Corpus Christi	20s
And to 1 minstrel called Tart	2d
And to 1 minstrel of Edward de Bethom, knight	4d
And to 2 minstrels of the earl of Deynshire	12d
And to 2 minstrels of the Lord de Beaumont	16d
And to 7 minstrels of the lord king on the fifth day of August	23s 4d
And to 1 luter from Beverley on the fifteenth day of the aforesaid month	4d
And to 1 minstrel of the duke of Suffolk	8d
And to 1·minstrel of Lord Thomas Rampston	6d
And to 1 minstrel of John Talbot and to 3 minstrels of Beverley	12d
And to 1 minstrel of Walter Tailboys, earl of Kyme	4d
And to 2 minstrels of the Lord de Harryngton	12d
And to 1 minstrel of the earl of Northumberland	8d
And to Christopher Harpour on the second Sunday of October	12d
And to John Fouldes, with the bishop of Durham on the same (day)	8d
And to 3 minstrels of Beverley on the twentieth day of October	18d
And to John Wafferer	6d
And to 1 minstrel	4d
And to 1 blind minstrel on the third day of December	6d
And to John Waferer and to Robert Wafferer on the fourth day of the aforesaid month	12d
And to the players on Monday on the feast of the Conception of blessed Mary	4d
And to 1 blind minstrel	4d
And to 1 minstrel of the earl of Westmorland	6d

Total 67s 5d

f 30

...

And to the city minstrels of Christmas	3s 4d
And to the city minstrels on the feast of St William	20d
And to 7 minstrels of the lord of Salisbury on the same feast,	
And to Christopher Harpour and John Somersete with the Lord de Clyfford	13s 4d

And to the minstrels of the lord Baron de Egremont	12d
And to 4 players at Christmas	8d
And to Henry Stirop' and his fellow-players	4d
And to 4 ⟨...⟩ players at the same time	4d
And to 2 players of the parish of St Denys	4d
And to 1 minstrel of William Gascoigne	6d
And to 2 minstrels of John Saynell, knight	12d
And to 1 jester at the same time	2d
And to John Tarte, player	4d

£6 3s 5d
® 24s 8d

...

Bridgemasters' Account Rolls   Y : C 8 3 : 2

mb 1

...

Micklegate within and without Raton Row with the Tofts

And from the rent of the house of the pageants of the Dyers and Skinners in the same place at the same times   12d 12d
...
And from the rent of the pageant house of the Mercers on the Tofts at the same times   6d 6d
And from the rent of the pageant house of the Bakers in the same place at the same times   6d 6d
And from the rent of the pageant house of the Tanners in the same place at the same times   6d 6d
And from the rent of the pageant house of the Tapiters in the same place at the same times   6d 6d
And from the rent of the pageant house of the Goldsmiths in the same place at the same times   4d 4d

...

1449-51
Corpus Christi Account Rolls   Y : C99 : 3

mb 1-2   *(Receipts)*
... And of 1 English book containing *(blank)* pages of instruction and information about the Christian faith, commonly called Creed Play, given by sir William Revetour, price £3 6s 8d. Item, from the gift of the same William, 17 praiseworthy and sumptuous banners, price £4. Item, 4 red silk banners laudably worked with gold, price 4s. Item, 4 embroidered banners called pennons, price 26d. Item, 13 diadems with 1 gilded mask, with wigs, and with the ornaments of the aforesaid play which have been furnished, price 6s 8d, and of one wooden vessel furnished

for the keeping of the same banners, price 3s 3d. Likewise given from the gift of sir William Revetour on such condition as is noted on the back of this roll. ...

... And of 1 English book received earlier and now put in store with 17 suitable banners and 8 other accessory banners, and other ornaments furnished in detail for the Creed Play, price £8 2s 10d. Item, paid to a certain tailor for the affixing and the bordering of the aforesaid banners, 6d.

Total £35 10s 10½d ⌐

Item, the said wardens seek an allowance for expenses incurred on the Corpus Christi supper. And first, on leavened bread, 8s 8d. Item, on light bread called simnel and pastil, 7s 10d. Item, on joined bread for the mayor and his companions, 9d, and on trencher bread, 3d. And of 19s paid for 13 dozen (pots) of better beer. And of 6d for second-best beer for the use of the kitchen and the servants for the time of their hire. And of 16s 4d paid for 18½ lambs. And of 3s 6d paid for beef, mutton, and veal meat, bought both for the aforesaid servants and for the few at the time of the feast. And of 2s 6d for 4 capons bought for the mayor and his companions. And of 17s ½d for 7 rabbits for the same. And of 8(d) for cinnamon powder and ginger for the same mayor and his companions. And of 23s 6d paid for 16 dozen pullets. And of spices bought for the kitchen, viz, on pepper, 3d; on cloves, 3d; on mace, 3d; on raisins, 3d; on coconut (?), 6d; and on sanders. 2d; total 20d. And for 1 pottle of vinegar, 3d; for honey, 2d; for eggs, 3d; for butter, 4d; for oatmeal, ½d; for salt for the kitchen, 2½d; for salt for the table for the cellars, 1d; for Ousewater, 2d; for skeps of coal, 2s. And for faggots and astelwood, 6d; total 4s. Item, paid to Robert Pottowe and John Gannton, cooks, with their servants, 4s to be divided among themselves. Item, paid to John Daystern for his duty there as a servant, 12s. Item, of 13d paid to 13 paupers for turning the spit. Item, paid to John Misterton who cleans the revets, cups, and vessels in the kitchen, 5d. Item, to Henry Sterop for bearing tables, benches, and trestles and carrying them to their proper places, 2d. And for 3 wanyons of barley for the feeding of the aforesaid pullets, 6d. And for green herbs to strew on the bench around the hall and in the area of the same, 3d.

Total £4 18s ½d

Item, the said wardens seek to be allowed for small expenses ... Item, paid to 4 deacons carrying the baudekin, 12d. Item, paid to a certain clerk carrying the cross before the procession on Corpus Christi day for 2 years, 4d. Item, paid to the overseer going through the city and exhorting the priests to be in the procession to the honour of Corpus Christi, 8d. Item, paid for the carrying of 10 torches before the aforesaid procession for 2 years, 6s 2d. Item, paid for the carrying of the new chest with the shrine inside and for the bier and trestles (to be carried) to the Priory of the Holy Trinity, thence to the Minster of St Peter and afterwards to the proper places, 8d. ... Item, paid to Thomas Scauceby, merchant, for the rent of the hall, the buttery, the kitchen, and for other accommodations for 2 years, 6s 8d. ...

mb 2d*
... And of 17 banners laudably and fittingly wrought, (having) cleverly on them the signs and mysteries of a certain play commonly called Creed Play, with 4 other silk banners embroidered and gilded with angels and maxims of the faith. Item, 4 pennons likewise embroidered. Item, 13 diadems with the wigs and other ornaments belonging to the same play. Item, 1 parchment book called original, written in the English tongue and containing (blank) pages from the gift of our estimable ⟨...⟩ brother, sir William Revetour, on whose soul may God have mercy, upon the condition ⟨...⟩ that within (every) 12 years at the most, if it can be fittingly (done) openly and publicly through the city of York in various ⟨places⟩, both to the praise of God and particularly to the educating of the people ⟨...⟩, indeed, so that the Creed may be brought a little to the good of the ignorant of the city ⟨...⟩ and the honour and great merit of the present fraternity, so long as ⟨...⟩ it is possible for us by ⟨...⟩, amen.

1450
City Chamberlains' Books Y : CC1A

f 60v

The feast of Corpus Christi

And for the expenses of the mayor and the aldermen and other honourable persons on the feast of Corpus Christi   55s 1½d
Total shows 55s 1½d

f 65v

Heralds and minstrels

First, to the city minstrels at Easter   3s 4d

...

And to the city minstrels on the vigil of the Nativity of St John
the Baptist   20d
And to 3 minstrels of the king on the sixth day of July   10s

...

And to the city minstrels at Christmas   3s 4d
And to the same minstrels on the feast of St William   20d

...

1451

City Chamberlains' Books   Y : CC1A

f 90v

Heralds and
messengers

Item, paid to the city minstrels at Easter   3s 4d

...

Item, to the city minstrels on the vigil of the Nativity of St
John the Baptist   20d
Item, to 5 minstrels of the king on the fifteenth day
of July   16s 8d
Item, to the city minstrels at Christmas   3s 4d
Item, to the same minstrels on the feast of St William   20d
Expenses on the feast of Corpus Christi   46s 1½d

Bridgemasters' Account Rolls   Y : C83:3

mb 1

...

Micklegate
without and
within Raton
Row with
the Tofts

And from the rent of the house of the pageant of the Skinners
and Dyers in the same place at the same times   12d 12d

...

And from the rent of the pageant house of the Mercers on the
Tofts at the same times   6d 6d
And from the rent of the pageant house of the Bakers in the
same place at the same times   6d 6d
And from the rent of the pageant house of the Tanners in the
same place at the same times   6d 6d
And from the rent of the pageant house of the Tapiters in the
same place at the same times   6d 6d
And from the rent of the house of the pageants of the Carpenters

and Cordwainers in the same place at the same times   12d 12d
And from the rent of the house of the Goldsmiths of York at
the same times   ⟨4d 4d⟩
...

1452
City Chamberlains' Books   Y: CC1A

ff 113-13v

Heralds and messengers

First, paid to the city minstrels at Easter   3s 4d
And to the same on the feast of Corpus Christi   20d
And to the same on the feast of the vigil of the Nativity of
St John the Baptist   20d
And to 6 minstrels of the king on the holy exultation of the
Holy Cross   20s
And to the city minstrels at Christmas   3s 4d
And to the same on the feast of the Translation of
St William   20d
Total 38s 4d

And for expenses incurred by the mayor and the council of
the Chamber on the feast of Corpus Christi   46s 3½d |

Winter and summer clothing

...
For 4 ells of blue motley cloth bought and given to the
minstrels   6s 8d
For 52 lengths of striped cloth bought and given to the same
minstrels   *(blank)*
...

1453
City Chamberlains' Rolls   Y: C3:1

mb 2

...

Summer and
winter clothing
And on 78 (lengths of) striped cloth bought for the city minstrels
for the same feast   13s 4d
And on 12 ells of poor light blue (cloth) bought for the same
minstrels for the second part of the said livery of the said six
servants of the commons   24s

And on 6 ells of worse blue (cloth) bought for the said minstrels
by the aforesaid mayor   8s

...

Heralds,
messengers,
and minstrels

And to the city minstrels on Easter, 3s 4d; on the
vigil of the Nativity of St John the Baptist, 20d;
on Christmas, 3s 4d, on the feast of St William in   11s 8d
the winter, 20d; and on the feast of Corpus Christi, 20d

And to 6 minstrels of the lord king here present in this year,
20s ...

mb 2d

Expenses on
the feast of
Corpus Christi

And on various presentations as on pain-demaine, fruits, and
wine, given to divers venerable persons and gentlemen present
in the city on the feast of Corpus Christi for the praise and
honour of the city, and for the expenses of the mayor and
aldermen of the same city being together on the same day.
                          Total 45s 4d

...

City Chamberlains' Books   Y: CC1A

ff 132v-3
Expenses on the feast of Corpus Christi   45s 4d
For 1 half-gallon of white wine bought from James Kexby   12d |

                Heralds, messengers, and minstrels
To the city minstrels at Easter   3s 4d
And to the same on the feast of Corpus Christi   20d
And to the same on the vigil of the Nativity of St John the
Baptist   20d
And to 6 minstrels of the lord king on the fifth day of
September   20s
...
And to the city minstrels at Christmas   3s 4d
And to the city minstrels on the feast of St William   20d

Bridgemasters' Account Rolls   Y: C83:4

mb 1*
...

And from the rent of the house of the pageants of the Skinners

Micklegate without and within with the Tofts and Raton Row

and Dyers of York in the same place at the same times   12d 12d

...

And from the rent of the pageant house of the Mercers of York in the same place at the same times   6d 6d
And from the rent of the pageant house of the Bakers in the same place at the same times   6d 6d
And from the rent of the pageant house of the Tanners in the same place at the same times   6d 6d
And from the rent of the pageant house of the Tapiters in the same place at the same times   6d 6d
And from the rent of the house of the pageants of the Carpenters and Cordwainers in the same place at the same times   12d 12d
And from the rent of the building or of the pageant house of the Goldsmiths in the same place at the same times   4d 4d

...

1454
City Chamberlains' Rolls   Y: C3:2

mb 2

...

And of the money received from Nicholas Blakburn, William Bouland, and others for holding a licence for the playing of the Corpus Christi plays   10s
before the building on their holding next to the gate of the Holy Trinity in Micklegate this year

b. And from James Kexby, 2s; from John Helme, 6s 8d; from the wife of John Pannall, 5s 8d; from William Gayte, 5s; from *(blank)* Barbour, for   19s 4d
plays of this kind to be held before their building in Micklegate

a. And from Thomas Sauceby and from others for the aforesaid play to be held before their building   20s
in Micklegate in the second station

Cash received at various places for holding a licence for the playing of the Corpus Christi Play

And from the abbot of Fountains, 8s; and from the churchwardens of the church of St John at the bridge for the same play to be held before the building and   11s 4d
churchyard of the aforesaid St John's by Mr Thomas Tubbar, one of the aforesaid wardens, 3s 4d

And from Henry Watson for playing this kind of play at the east
end of Ouse Bridge   13s 4d
And from John Henrison and from William Knolles for this kind
of play to be held at the Stalege   13s 4d
And from Randolph Babthorp, 5s; from John Swath, 2s 6d; and
from Thomas Bynglay, 2s 6d; for the same play to be held at the
end of Jowbritgate this year   10s
And from the building of William Gascoigne, knight, (and) from
Phillip Carvour, 12d; and from others for the play to be held
before the doors of the building of the same William   12d
And from the hospital of St Leonard, 6s; from the Augustine
Friars, 2s; and from Thomas Brignall, 2s; for the play to be held
at Stonegate landing   10s
And from Richard Cay for the play to be held before the doors
of his building in Stonegate this year   6s 8d
And from John Catryk, alderman, for the play to be held before
his building in the market this year   3s 4d
And from Nicholas Holgate, Thomas Curteys, and others for
this kind of play to be held before their buildings on the
Pavement   4s
                              Total £6 2s 4d

mb 3
...

Heralds,
messengers,
and minstrels

And to the city minstrels of the feast of Easter,
3s 4d; on the feast of Corpus Christi, 20d; on
the vigil of the Nativity of St John the Baptist,   11s 8d
20d; on Christmas, 3s 4d; and on the feast of
St William in this year, 20d

...

And to the minstrels of the duke of York on the arrival of the
same duke at York in this year   13s 4d

mb 3d
...

(Winter and
summer)
clothing

And for 1 length of broad cloth of murrey stripes bought from
John Marshall for the aforesaid 6 servants for Christmas as in
this year, 40s. And on 18 ells of light blue bought for the other
part of the same livery, (and) for 3 city minstrels, 20s. And for
the dyeing of the said 18 ells, 4s 4d. And for the shearing of
the same 18 ells along with the said striped broad cloth and the
shearing of 78 (lengths of) striped cloth bought for the minstrels,

2s 4d. And for the aforesaid 78 ⟨lengths of cloth of ray⟩ bought from the aforesaid John Marsshall, 16s 3d. ...

Expenses on the feast of Corpus Christi	And on the expenses of the mayor and the aldermen of the aforesaid city on the feast of Corpus Christi and on various presentations, such as on pain-demaine, fruits, and wine, given to various venerable persons present in the city of York on the same day	49s 11d

And to William Dernwater for the playing of the play of the Coronation of the blessed Mary on the same day   10s

Total 59s 11d

...

Bridgemasters' Account Rolls   Y : C 8 3 : 5

mb 1
...

Micklegate without and within with the Tofts and Raton Row	And from the house of the pageants of the Skinners and Dyers in the same place at the same times	12d 12d
	...	
	And from the pageant house of the Mercers in the same place at the same times	6d 6d
	And from the pageant house of the Bakers in the same place at the same times	6d 6d
	And from the pageant house of the Tanners in the same place at the same times	6d 6d
	And from the pageant house of the Tapiters in the same place at the same times	6d 6d
	And from the pageant house of the Carpenters and Cordwainers in the same place at the same times	12d 12d
	And from the pageant house of the Goldsmiths in the same place at the same times	4d 4d
	...	

Mercers' Pageant Documents   M A : D 6 3

(*27 February*)
By the present ⟨letters⟩ let everyone understand that we, Robert

Hewyk, parish clerk of Leeds in the county of York, Thomas
Fitt, tapiter, and Henry Clayton, weaver of York, are firmly
bound and held to the governor and wardens of the guild of
Merchants of the city of York, in the amount of £10 sterling to
be paid to the same governor and wardens, or their successors,
or their accredited attorney, on the next feast of Corpus Christi
after the date of the present (letters), without any further delay.
Indeed to the payment of the said sum as stated above, we bind
ourselves, our heirs, and our executors, and all our goods, and
each one of us personally for the whole amount in its entirety,
by the present (letters), sealed with our seals. Given on 27 February in the thirty-second year of the reign of King Henry the
sixth after the conquest of England.

   The condition of this obligation is that if the aforesaid Robert,
Thomas, and Henry keep and fulfil on their part each and every
agreement and condition contained in certain indentures made
between the abovesaid governor and wardens on the one hand
and the aforesaid Robert, Thomas, and Henry on the other,
about and concerning the production of a Corpus Christi play, to
wit, of the pageant called Doomsday, according to the meaning,
form, and effect of the aforementioned indentures, that thenceforth this obligation is to be considered annulled. Otherwise let
it stand in its strength and power.

Shirwod

1455
House Books Y : B 7

f 137   *(12 September)*

...

Memorandum to the brothers and sisters of the guild of Corpus
Christi of York present and future, that in the time indeed of
John Foxe, John Evenwod, Christopher Doblay, Robert Stokton,
Thomas Flesshner, and William Salisbery, chaplains of York and
wardens of the said fraternity in the year, namely, from the
incarnation of our Lord one thousand four hundred and fifty-
five, this book was begun newly made, and freshly written, and
compiled at the request of John Foxe, executor of William
Revetour, in accordance with the old and worn copy which
William Revetour, late chaplain in St William's Chapel on Ouse
Bridge, gave and willed to the aforesaid fraternity in his will.
And however, on this condition, that this incomparable play

shall be proclaimed in public every ten years in the future in various places of the said city of York for a suitable audience for the sake of their spiritual health. Accordingly, the inhabitants at these places must pay and worthily provide sufficient for the charges and expenses of the play.

Will of Robert Lasingby of the Parish of St Denys
BI: Prob. Reg. 2

f 342Av *(4 August; probated 28 February 1456)*
... Item, I leave to the fabric of my said church one twill cloth and the original (copy of the) play of St Dennis, that my burial be accomplished in the said church. ...

1457
Bridgemasters' Account Rolls   Y: C83:6

mb 1
...

Without Micklegate and within with Raton Row and the Tofts

And from the house of the pageants of the Skinners and Dyers at the same times   12d 12d
...
And from the pageant house of the Mercers in the same place for the same times   6d 6d
And from the pageant house of the Bakers in the same place at the same times   6d 6d
And from the pageant house of the Tanners at the same times   6d 6d
And from the pageant house of the Tapiters at the same times   6d 6d
And from the pageant house of the Carpenters at the same times   12d 12d
And from the pageant house of the Goldsmiths of York at the same times   4d 4d
...

Will of Isabella Kerr   YM: M2/6/e

f 34v *(5 September)*
... Item, I leave to John Candell my Corpus Christi torch. ...

1458
Bridgemasters' Account Rolls   Y : C83 : 7

mb 1

...

Without Micklegate and within with Raton Row and the Tofts

And from the house of the pageants of the Skinners and Dyers in the same place at the same times   12d 12d

...

And from the pageant house of the Mercers in the same place   6d 6d
And from the pageant house of the Bakers in the same place at the same times   6d 6d
And from the pageant house of the Tanners in the same place at the same times   6d 6d
And from the pageant house of the Tapiters in the same place at the same times   6d 6d
And from the houses of the pageants of the Carpenters and Cordwainers in the same place at the same times   12d 12d
And from the pageant house of the Goldsmiths in the same place at the same times   4d 4d

...

Will of John Tidman, chaplain   BI : Prob. Reg. 2

f 371v *(4 August; probated 26 August)*
... And I leave to Robert Haxby one gown of motley colour, one pair of clavichords, and one book called a ballad book. ...

1459
Bridgemasters' Account Rolls   Y : C83 : 8

mb 1

...

Without Micklegate and within with Raton Row and the Tofts

⟨And from⟩ the house of the pageants of the Skinners and Dyers in the same place at the same times   12d 12d

...

And from the pageant house of the Mercers in the same place this year at the same times   6d 6d
And from the pageant house of the Bakers at the same times   6d 6d
And from the pageant house of the Tanners: this year   6d 6d
And from the pageant house of the Tapiters at the same

times   6d 6d

And from the pageant house of the Carpenters and Cordwainers
at the same times   12d 12d

...

And from the pageant house of the Goldsmiths at the same
times   4d 4d

...

Mercers' Account Rolls MA: D53K

mb 1

...

External receipt   And of 3s 4d received from the fraternity of Corpus Christi for
their payment for accommodation in the hall of this fraternity
at the time of its general meeting this year

...

External and necessary expenses   And they paid for the carrying of the 6 torches of the said
fraternity in the procession on the feast of Corpus Christ this
year   2s

...

1460
Mercers' Account Rolls MA: D53L

mb 1

...

External receipt   And of 3s 4d received from the fraternity of Corpus Christi for
a certain payment for accommodation in the hall of the same
fraternity this year ...

External and necessary expenses   And they paid for the carrying of the 6 torches of the said
fraternity in the procession on the feast of Corpus Christi this
year, as in past years   2s

...

1461
Mercers' Account Rolls MA: D53M

mb 1

...

External receipt   And of 3s 4d from the fraternity of Corpus Christi for their
payment for accommodation in the hall of this fraternity at the
time of its general meeting this year

...

External and
necessary
expenses

And they paid for the carrying of the 6 torches of the said
fraternity in the Corpus Christi procession on the feast of the
same this year   2s
And they paid to Thomas Nandyke and his companions, the
pageant masters of the said fraternity, both for the repair of the
same pageant and for the hire of players in the Corpus Christi
Play, beyond all that which was collected among the craftsmen
contributing to the said play   30s 4½d
And for 8 dozen (pieces) of wax bought from Thomas Beverlay
himself for the new manufacture of the said 6 torches at the
price of 5s 4d the dozen   42s
And for the manufacture of the said 6 torches this year anew
by an agreement to buy wholesale   2s 10d

...

St Leonard's Hospital Accounts   YM: M2/6/d

f 22v

...

Gratuities

In gratuities made to the minstrels, 3s 4d; to John Wafferer,
12d; and to his associates present within the hospital on the
feast of St Leonard this year, 12d   4s 4d

...

1462
City Chamberlains' Rolls   Y: C3:3

mb 1*

...

Receipts for the
Corpus Christi
plays to be
held this year
at established
stations

And of 13s 4d from Nicholas Haliday and Adam Hudson for
licence of the Corpus Christi plays to be held opposite the
building on the holding at the gate of Holy Trinity in Micklegate
this year
And of 6s 8d from Thomas Scauceby, lord Thomas Wright,
Thomas Kilburn, and others for the second station
And of 11s from John Foulford and others for the third station
this year
And of 13s 8d from John Beese, Richard Sawer, Thomas Barbour,
and others opposite the church of St John the Baptist, viz, for
the fourth station
And of 10s from Laurence Marsshall, John Wathe, and others in

Coney Street for the fifth station
And of 7s from Robert Butler, Thomas Hojeson, and others for
the sixth station in Coney Street
And of 10s from John Shirwod and Robert Walker and others
for the seventh station
And of 6s 6d from Richard Key and others in Stonegate for the
eighth station
And of 2s 4d from Peter Parot, John Stalby, and others in the
market for the ninth station
And of 2s from Thomas Wrangwyssh and others on the Pavement,
for the tenth station

Total £4 2s 6d

...

mb 2

...

Rents resolute   And paid to Robert Leche for the playing of the pageant of the
Coronation of the blessed Virgin Mary this year   2s

...

Heralds, messengers, and minstrels   And paid to 3 city minstrels on Easter, 3s 4d;
on Corpus Christi, 20d; on the Nativity of St John
the Baptist, 20d; on Christmas, 3s 4d; and on   11s 8d
(the feast of) St William in the winter according
to custom, 20d

...

And to 5 minstrels of the lord king who were here in the month
of July this year   16s 8d
And to 5 other minstrels of the same lord king who were here in
the month of November   8s 4d
And to 2 footmen of the said lord king, 3s 4d; and to one
taborer of the same in the aforesaid month, 12d   4s 4d

...

And to 1 minstrel of the lord king leading 1 marmoset of the
same lord king   2s 4d

...

mb 3

...

Winter and summer clothing   And paid to William Chymnay for 12 ells of
musterdevillers cloth bought for 3 city minstrels   26s
at the said feast (Christmas)

...

Expenses of the mayor and the aldermen and others on the feast of Corpus Christi

And on the expenses of the mayor, aldermen, and other fellow-citizens of the city on the feast of Corpus Christi, together with various presentations, such as on pain-demaine, fruits, and wines given and presented to various lords and ladies, knights, prelates, and other gentlemen then present in the city, such as the countess (of) Warwick and others

45s 6½d

Total 45s 6½d

...

1465
Corpus Christi Register   BL: Lansdowne MS 403

ff 4v-5 *(22 October)*
First, one wooden box upon the high altar in the chapel of St William on Ouse Bridge, valued at £3. And 1 painted gilt bier for bearing the said shrine in the procession, 6s 8d. And 8 white cushions furnished for the shoulders of those carrying the shrine, valued at 2s 2d. And 4 images of the evangelists and 16 angels newly painted with shields and rolls, together with 2 copper chalices, gilded, and 2 crystals, for supporting the said bier and shrine, 38s. And 2 small pieces of buckram cloth embroidered with gilt chalices for the said bier, and 1 square wooden canopy and 4 poles, valued at 4s. And a piece of cloth embroidered with the image of the most high Trinity, valued at 3s. And 4 pieces of blue drapery with chalices and gilt stars, valued at 5s. And 4 linen sacks for keeping 4 hides of the said bier suitably, valued at 6d. And 1 short wooden chest bound with iron for keeping the shrine securely, valued at 8s 8d.

First, the book called original containing the articles of the Catholic faith recently written in the English tongue, valued at £10. And another old book of the same play, 100s. And another book of the same called in English the Creed Play, containing twenty-three quires. And 17 large banners, valued at £4. And 4 smaller banners of red silk, priced at 6s 8d. And 9 other banners called pennons with newly-made shields of the faith and embroidered chalices, valued at 11s 6d. And 24 iron devices called sockets furnished for the extension of the banners, valued at 4s 6d. And 1 papal mitre, valued at 10d. And 1 royal crown with a sceptre and 1 glove, valued at 6d. And 12 rolls recently

written with the articles of the Catholic faith, I valued at 3s 4d.
And 1 small square chest with 1 lock and key for keeping the
said banners, valued at 2s. And 2 episcopal mitres, valued at 12d.
And 1 key for St Peter and 2 pieces of 1 embroidered tunic,
valued at 12d. And 4 other banners called pennons, 3s 4d. And
10 diadems for Christ and the apostles with 1 mask and 9 other
wigs, 6s.

First, 14 torches, valued at *(blank)*. And 3 old judases, valued
at 14d. And 12 painted castles and golden chalices and plates
of iron belonging to the same castles, valued at 4s. And 34
painted banners furnished for the torches, valued at 20s.

Codicil of the Will of William Downham, chaplain
BI: Prob. Reg. 2

f 488 *(Will: 28 May; Codicil and Probate: 13 Janury 1466)*
... Item, I leave to William Ball all my books of the Pater Noster
Play. ...

1466
Bridgemasters' Account Rolls Y: C84:1

mb 1
...

Micklegate without and within with the Tofts and Raton Row

And from the pageant house of the Skinners and Dyers in the
same place at the same times   12d 12d
...
And from the pageant house of the Mercers in the same place
at the same times   6d 6d
And from the pageant house of the Bakers in the same place
at the same times   6d 6d
And from the pageant house of the Tanners in the same place
at the same times   6d 6d
And from the pageant house of the Tapiters in the same place
at the same times   6d 6d
And from the pageant house of the Carpenters and Cordwainers
at the same times   12d 12d
And from the pageant house of the Goldsmiths in the same place
at the same times   4d 4d
...

1468
City Chamberlains' Rolls Y : C 3 : 4

mb 1

...

Receipt of
money for
stations let for
plays on the
feast of
Corpus Christi

And of 10s from Nicholas Haliday and Adam Hudson for a
licence to hold plays before their doors at the gate of Holy
Trinity
And of 14s from Thomas Scauceby, Thomas Kilburn, and others
from the second station
And of 17s 9d from the widow of John Toller and others for
the third station in Micklegate
And of 16s from Thomas Barbour, Christopher Thomlynson,
Richard Croklyn, Richard Sawer, and others for the fourth
station at the end of North Street
And of 6s 8d from Richard Russell, John Smyth, and others
at the end of Coney Street for the fifth station
And of 8s from Alexander Menerous, from Nicholas Saunderson,
8s; and from the holding of the commons opposite, 3s 4d, for
the sixth station
And of 13s 4d from Thomas Aylde and others for the seventh
station in the middle of Coney Street
And of 9s from the master of the fraternity of St Christopher
at York, the tenants of St Leonard's, and others for the eighth
station at the end of Stonegate
And of 8s from William Gilmyn and from others for the ninth
station in the middle of Stonegate
And of 5s 8d from John Wilkynson and others for the tenth
station at the gates of the Minster
And of 3s from John Scalby, Peter Parot, and others for the
eleventh station in the Market
And of *(blank)* from *(blank)*

Total 111s 5d

mb 2

...

Rents resolute

And to the searchers of the Ostlers of the city for
the production of the pageant of the Coronation   2s
of blessed Virgin Mary on the feast of Corpus Christi

...

mb 2d

Heralds, messengers, and minstrels

And to three city minstrels of York on Easter, 3s 4d; on Corpus Christi, 20d; on the Nativity of St John the Baptist, 20d; on Christmas and (on the feast of) St William in the winter, 3s 4d   40s 8d

And to 7 minstrels of the lord king who were here in the city in the month of October   20s

...

Winter and summer clothing

And paid for 12 ells of blue motley bought for 3 city minstrels at the same time   24s

...

Expenses of the mayor and aldermen on the feast of Corpus Christi

And on the expenses of the mayor and aldermen and other persons on the feast of Corpus Christi, together with various presentations, such as pain-demaine, fruits, and wines, bought and given to various lords and gentlemen then in the aforesaid city; with 3s 4d given as a gratuity to a certain Augustinian friar preaching on the day after the said feast in the chapel of the cathedral church of blessed Peter in York, and (with) 6s 8d for the rent of the Chamber   63s 6d

Total 63s 6d

...

Bridgemasters' Account Rolls   Y: C84:2

mb 1

...

Micklegate without and within with the Tofts and Raton Row

And from the house of the pageants of the Skinners and Dyers of York this year at the same times   12d 12d

...

And from the pageant house of the Mercers in the same place this (year) at the same times   6d 6d

And from the pageant house of the Bakers in the same place at the same times   6d 6d

And from the pageant house of the Tanners in the same place at the same times   6d 6d

And from the pageant house of the Tapiters of York in the same place at the same times   6d 6d

And from the pageant house of the Carpenters and Cordwainers

of York at the same times 12d 12d
And from the pageant house of the Goldsmiths in the same place
at the same times 4d 4d
...

1472
Mercers' Account Rolls MA: D53Q

mb 1
... And received from the master and fraternity of Corpus Christi
occupying our hall, per annum, 3s 4d. ...

mb 2
...

Repairs for the
pageant house

Item, they reckon for the repairs made for the repair on the
pageant house on the Tofts, viz, they paid to 2 carpenters working
there for three days, 3s. And they paid for 2 (pieces) of wood
for the solings and the bars for the doors, 14d. And they paid for
boards for the doors, 12d. And for a stone and a half of iron
with the working of the same for the bands and crooks, 3s 4d.
And for 1 small door with crooks, 8d. And for 1 lock with a
key, price 4d. And they paid for 200 double and single spikings,
7d. And they paid for the cleaning of the house, 2d.
Total 9s 4d
...

York Minster Chamberlains' Rolls YM: E1/44 MP

mb 1

Gratuities

... And as a gratuity, given at the command of the lords of the
chapter to the players present at the feast of the Translation
of St William, 6s 8d; and for 4 days in the week of Pentecost,
13s 4d, just as has been the custom in former years, 26s 8d.
And to 4 deacons carrying the cloth above the head of St William,
viz, on the Translation, 12d, Deposition of the same, 12d, and
for the 4 days in the week of Pentecost, 2s. ...

1474
Mercers' Account Rolls MA: D54T

mb 1

Receipts for
ships

...
Item, the said master and constables reckon, viz, from the

fraternity of Corpus Christi for the occupation of the Great Hall, per annum 3s 4d ...

Waxes and rosin put to the making of the 6 torches made anew, the price of 1 pound 3-3/4d

Total 36s 7d

...

1475
City Chamberlains' Rolls   Y: C3:6

mb 2

...

And of 10s received from Adam Hudson for the first station at the gate of Holy Trinity

And of 12s received from William Scauceby and from Thomas Kilburn for the second station

And of 14s 8d received from the wife of John Tollerer for the third station

And of 14s received from William Plomer and Richard Wels, textwriter, for the fourth station

And of 6s 8d received from John Smyth, cordwainer, and from Nicholas Bille for the fifth station

The Corpus
Christi Play

And of 6s received from Robert Butteller and from John Wildyng for the sixth station

And of 12s received from John Bawde, saddler, and John Gylde for the seventh station

And of 8s received from Nicholas Bewik for the eighth station

And of 7s 5d received from John Barbour in Stonegate for the ninth station

And of 5s received from John Wilkynson and John Tirry for the tenth station

And of 3s 4d received from John Scalby and William Hogeson for the eleventh station

And of 12d received from the mayoress for the twelfth station on the Pavement

Total 100s 1d

...

mb 3

...

Heralds,
messengers,
and minstrels

And paid to the city minstrels of York for the period of Easter 3s 4d. And paid to the same minstrels on the vigil of the Nativity of St John the Baptist, 20d. And paid to the same minstrels on the feast of Corpus Christi, 20d. And paid to the same minstrels on Christmas, 3s 4d. And paid to the same minstrels on the feast of St William the archbishop, 20d. ...

Clothing of the officials and of the others

And paid for the clothing of the city minstrels for the same feast of Pentecost   28s

...

Expenses on the feast of Corpus Christi

And paid on expenses incurred on the feast of Corpus Christi by the mayor, the aldermen, the Twenty-four, and others of the honourable men both on food, bread, and ale consumed by them on this day and on wine red and white, and white apples given and presented to diverse noble and outstanding men then being in the same city with the rent of the Chamber on the same day and the gratuity to the friar preaching on the Friday next following, according to custom

Total 65s 8½d

Necessary expenses, both internal and external

... And paid to the pageant masters of the Coronation of the blessed Virgin Mary of the Ostlers of this city, for support and aid of their costs incurred on this behalf according to custom, 2s. ...

Mercers' Account Rolls MA: D54U

mb 1

...

Forfeits and for the ships

Item, the said master and constables reckon, viz, from the master (of the fraternity) of Corpus Christi, for the occupation of the Great Hall, per annum 6s 8d. ...

York Minster Chamberlains' Rolls YM: E1/43 MP

mb 1
(*as E1/44 above 1472*)

1476
House Books Y: B1

f 19v (*31 May*)
It was agreed and ordered by the common assent and consent of the said council and all the commons there, that from the time of his installation each of the aldermen and of the Twenty-four of

the same city is to have one torch carried by his servant annually
in the procession the Friday, the day after the feast of Corpus
Christi, to the praise of God and the honour of this city. Each of
them (is to do this) under penalty of 40s, to be forfeited and
paid to the use of the Chamber without any pardon or remission
to be had on that account in the future. And that all the other
citizens and inhabitants of this city, both from the guilds and
from the craftsmen, who from devotion or custom are accustomed
to hold and carry their torches, either themselves or through (the
agency of) others, in the said procession annually, or have been
ordered and directed by the said council (so to do), are to
present themselves and go peaceably in their order, manner, and
places, according as he who is common clerk of this city at the
time shall then cause to summon, call, and name, or just as he
shall summon, name, and call each and every one of them to that
effect, under penalty of 40s for each one doing the contrary and
being delinquent to be paid to the said Chamber.

Mercers' Account Rolls   MA: D54V

mb 1

...

From ships
and other
receipts

Item, they reckon from the income received from ships and from
others, viz, from John Waterhouse, pageant master, and his
associates, 2s. And from the master of the Corpus Christi Guild
for the rent of the hall, 6s 8d. ...

Repairs to
the hall

And they paid for the carrying of torches the day after Corpus
Christi   2s
And they paid for the rent of the pageant house to the masters
of Ouse Bridge   12d

...

1477
A/Y Memorandum Book   Y: E20

f 291v

Ordinance for
the pageant of
the Purification
of the blessed
Virgin Mary

In the name of God, amen. In the year of our Lord 1477 and the
seventeenth year of the reign of King Edward the fourth after
the conquest of England, on the advice of John Tonge, then
mayor, and of all the council of the Chamber, (it was ordered)
that the pageant of the Purification of the blessed Virgin Mary

shall play henceforth yearly on the feast of Corpus Christi just as the other pageants (do). And beyond this, it was agreed that those who are the Masons of this city at the time bear the burdens and expenses of the aforesaid pageant and will produce it to be played yearly in a good and fitting manner, in (good) order so that they would be willing to answer before him who is mayor at the time when they were forewarned of it. And that those who are now and shall be at the time the Labourers of this city yearly henceforth, viz, the Faggotbearers, Gardeners, Earthwallers, Pavers, Dikers, and Groundwallers with earth, shall pay and deliver each year from now on on the eve of Corpus Christi in the Council Chamber of this city to those who are the chamberlains of the same at the time, 13s 4d to aid the expenses of that pageant, under penalty of 26s 8d to be equally divided between the Chamber of this city and the repair of the aforesaid pageant, and that, with this done, the aforesaid Labourers be quit of playing any and every pageant within this city from henceforth. And further, that the said Masons will have yearly on the eve of Corpus Christi 13s 4d from those who are the chamberlains of this city at the time, and that the said Masons will produce the said pageant annually and bear henceforth all the expenses and burdens pertaining to the said pageant as though they wish to render yearly to him who is the mayor at the time, and the penalty of forfeiture decreed and provided in the other pageants henceforth. And that the masters of the said Masons' pageant are to go and make the rounds with the aforesaid pageant in the stations according to the ancient custom. And that the said Labourers will choose each year among themselves four men as searchers, and that these will collect from each and every labourer working within this city, its suburbs, and its liberty the aforesaid sum of 13s 4d, and that they will hand over this sum in this Chamber as has been said above under the aforesaid penalty. And that if it happens that any of the aforesaid Labourers at any time should be rebellious and refuse to pay, then the afore-said four men or one of them shall have one sergeant at mace of the Chamber and that sergeant will go with them at all necessary and opportune times by the order of him who is mayor at the time, etc. And that any of the three crafts of the aforesaid Labourers, viz, Earthwallers, Pavers, and Groundwallers are to pay, and any (member) of them is to pay for himself yearly for the said pageant, 4d, and the other Labourers named above, 2d, under pain of 12d, etc, to be paid equally to the Chamber and the said pageant, etc.

Mercers' Account Rolls MA: D54X

mb 1

...

From ships
and others

Item, they received from the master of the Corpus Christi Guild for the hall, 6s 8d. ...

Repairs to the
hall and fees

And they paid for the carrying of the torches on the day after Corpus Christi, 2s.

...

mb 2*

Repairs on the
pageant house

Item, they seek an allocation for repairs made on the pageant house this year, viz, they paid for 7 posts and pans, 5s. And for 24 spars and stanchions, 3s 4d. And for 40 English boards, 5s. And they paid for 1 (piece) of wood to John Skelton, 2s. And for sharplings, 11d. And for 600 double spikings, 2s. And for 150 broad stones, 3d. And they paid for 400 middle spikings, 12d. And for half a hundred weight of iron for crooks and bars, 2s 6d. And for the working of the same iron, 20d. And for cartage of timber, 5d. And they paid for 2 carpenters and 2 assistant tilers at the same place for 13 days, at the price of 20d a day: total, 21s 8d. And for 1 lock with a key, price 4d. And they paid for sawing, 2s.

...

Corpus Christi Account Rolls Y: C99:5

mb 2

...

Allowances

Wherefore the said master seeks to be allowed for various expenses incurred by him in the said year on the general procession, viz, on the day after Corpus Christi. On a payment made to 1 clerk carrying 1 cross, 2d. And for payment made to 4 clerks carrying the baudekin, 8d. And for payment made to 8 men carrying 8 torches, 16d. And for payment made for wax used at the same time on 2 candles, 4d.

Total 2s 6d

...

Corpus Christi Ordinances   Y: G11A*

(*7 June*)

... Item, we establish that the master of the aforesaid fraternity or guild, dressed in a silken cope, shall take his place in the solemn procession of Corpus Christi as the principal presiding officer. And that two of his predecessors, to be elected by him, who earlier had been masters of the same fraternity, shall march with the same (master), one on the right and the other on the left.

Item, we establish and we ordain that in this procession two of the senior wardens of this fraternity, at the determination of the master, bearing white rods in their hands, shall guard carefully the shrine of the body of Christ, and that its remaining four wardens, also bearing white rods in their hands to manage the same procession as participants, shall walk decently and reverently, employ their labours effectively and heed diligently (everything) concerning the same. And we desire that these six wardens wear silken stoles on their necks, designed to distinguish them from their other brothers and for the reverence of the abovesaid body of Christ.

Item, we desire and ordain that every rector and perpetual vicar of the said city of York and any chaplain of the same city (who is a) secular brother of the said fraternity be present in the said procession and march personally in it, dressed in a proper surplice. And that those who know how to sing better stand near those who wear silken copes in the middle of the procession, singing devout praises with them to the most glorious body of Christ, to the best of their ability. And if anyone of these rectors, vicars, or chaplains shall have absented himself from the same procession, unless he can be excused sufficiently at the discretion of the master of the same, he shall thereby incur and pay a penalty of 6d to the use of the said fraternity, to be collected and demanded by the aforesaid master or his immediate successor if they are able to, and if not, by the aforesaid lord, the official of the court of York.

Item, we desire and establish that two chaplains (who are) worthy brothers of the said fraternity be assigned and deputed to singing litanies and other songs suitable for the time in every general procession to be made in the city of York by those who are then the master or wardens of the said fraternity. And that if any chaplain thus assigned shall disdain to obey without a legitimate cause, to be approved or rejected by the master, then as often as he shall have refused thus, he is to incur and pay a penalty of 2d to be applied to the use of the said fraternity and enforced as above. ...

1478
A/Y Memorandum Book Y: E20

f 331v
To all who shall see or hear this writing, (we hope for) eternal deliverance in the lord, from the mayor and commons of the citizens of the city of York. Know that we have conceded and released in return for rent to Henry Watson and Thomas Dicinson, pikemongers, the performance of the play of Corpus Christi yearly in High Ousegate between the buildings now in the tenure of the abovesaid Henry and Thomas, ie, at the east end of Ouse Bridge, the said play to be had and held there from the feast of Corpus Christi AD 1478 for the duration of the next twelve full years following, for a return thence yearly to us, the aforesaid mayor and our successors, viz, into the hands of those who are chamberlains at the time, of 11s of lawful English money for the need of the commons of the aforesaid city, yearly while the aforesaid term lasts, ie, within the next six days after the feast of Corpus Christi, under penalty of loss of the aforesaid play, the present lease not withstanding at all, ie, so that the said play or diversion be not played at all at that site. And we, the foresaid mayor and commons and our successors will warrant and maintain against all persons the said play or diversion for the aforesaid rent of 11s until the end of the aforesaid twelve years as described above. In testimony of which etc.
...

f 332 *(20 September)*
In the name of God, amen. In the 1478th year after the Incarnation of the ever-living God, on the twentieth day of the month of September, the most illustrious, most awesome, as all report, and yet most Christian Edward, by the grace of God, king of England and France and lord of Ireland, with a great throng of dukes, marquesses, earls, barons, and other nobles of the kingdom accompanying him for certain reasons, indeed, with almost all those of greater birth flowing toward him in throngs from all sides, had come from the north towards Pontefract. John Fereby,

at this time the noble mayor of this fair city, together with many of the more noble men of this county had met the aforesaid lord king a little less than two miles beyond Wentbridge and accompanied the said lord king to Pontefract, and there the said mayor and his companions took leave of the said most awesome lord king and the other nobles of the kingdom. The said mayor with his companions and others had come thence to the said city of York and (their) home when one week had scarcely passed.

The same lord king, with very many magnates of the kingdom, came to this city of York and was met by the aforesaid very noble man John Fereby, mayor, the aldermen, and other individual chamberlains who were able to ride, and other quite respectable men of this city, both on horseback and on foot. And gifts had been given to the aforesaid excellent prince and king quite lavishly as is clearly written in the book of this year. And on the twenty-eighth of the same month, by day, he had departed from this fair city to London.

City Chamberlains' Rolls Y : C 3 : 7

mb 1 *(Expenses only)*

...

Rents resolute   And paid to the pageant masters of the Ostlers for a certain annual rent for the support of the pageant of the Coronation of the blessed Virgin Mary in the aforesaid city, as in the previous accounts   2s

...

mb 2

...

And paid to Thomas Gaunt for 1 banner for the Corpus Christi Play at the door of Henry Watson   4d

...

Necessary expenses   And paid to Margaret, seamstress, for the mending of the banners of the Corpus Christi Play   3d

...

mb 1d

...

Gifts and presents for the most illustrious prince, Edward, king of England, and for others, etc	And in money paid by the said accountants for 2 measures of red wine, Gascon wine, pain-demaine, and leavened bread, as well as for 12 cygnets (and) 12 pickerels bought and given to our most illustrious and awesome Edward, by the grace of God, king of England and France; together with (money paid) by order of the whole council of the Chamber from the gratuity (fund) on wine, 'pain demain', (and) pickerel bought and given to the dukes, marquesses, counts, barons, knights, and other servants of the said lord, King Edward, who were with the king himself at his last coming to this city; and on various gratuities in ⟨...⟩ given to various officers of the same king by order of the mayor and the recommendation of the said council in the month of September, as appears under the heading of the same (month) in the paper book of the chamberlains, etc.

£35 5d

...

Clothing of the officials	And paid for 12 yards of russet cloth bought this year for the clothing of 3 minstrels

26s 8d

...

And paid to 6 minstrels of the lord king coming to this city according to custom

20s

Gratuities to minstrels and the servants of lords	And paid to 3 city minstrels as a special gratuity, according to custom, at different times of the year, viz, on Easter, 40d; on Corpus Christi, 20d; on the vigil of St John the Baptist, 20d; on Christmas, 40d; and on (the feast of) St William, 20d; (to the minstrels) attending and being with the mayor for the honour of the city according to custom

11s 8d

And paid to 4 minstrels of the prince of England coming to this city

6s 8d

...

And on expenses incurred this year by the mayor, aldermen, and many others of the council of the Chamber on the feast of Corpus Christi, who were seeing and observing the play in the lodging of Nicholas Bewyk according to custom; together with 40s 4d paid for wine, red and white, given and sent to the knights, ladies, gentry, and nobles then within the city; and also 9s paid for the rent of the Chamber, and 3s 4d paid to a certain person preaching and pronouncing the sermon on the day after the aforesaid feast in the cathedral church of St Peter at York, after the procession had been celebrated according to the custom of the council as it appears item by item in the chamberlain's book, which has been inspected and approved concerning this account ...

Expenses on the feast of Corpus Christi and the vigil of St Blaise, the bishop

£4 18s 6d

Mercers' Account Rolls MA: D 54 Y

mb 1
...

For ships

Item, they reckon for 6s 8d received from the master of the fraternity of Corpus Christi for the rent of the hall

...

And they paid for the carrying of the torches on the day after Corpus Christi in the procession   2s

...

1480
York Minster Chamberlains' Rolls YM: E1/58 MP

mb 1
(as E1/44 above 1472)

1481
Mercers' Account Rolls MA: D 54 Z

mb 1

Necessary expenses

... And they paid for the carrying of the torches on the feast of Corpus Christi 2s. ...

York Minster Chamberlains' Rolls Y M : E 1 / 46 *M P*

mb 2
(as E1/44 above 1472)

1482
House Books Y : B 2-4

f 59v *(31 May)*

...

On this day all those listed agreed that the pact made in the time
of Thomas Wrangwayssh, mayor, about the carrying of torches
on the day after Corpus Christi be observed from this day forward
under the penalty contained therein. And, further, that the
Weavers and the Cordwainers are to go with their torches in the
procession on the day after Corpus Christi in the form given
below. That is to say, one of the Weavers is to begin from the
right and one of the Cordwainers from the left, and then one of
the Cordwainers from the right and one of the Weavers from the
left, and in this way all members of those crafts, etc. And any
craft which shall fail in the foregoing shall forfeit and pay £10 to
the use of the commons or their said bodies for imprisonment
at the mayor's pleasure, etc.

Void because
of the following

...

f 60 *(1 June)*

...

On which day it was ordered by all those above written that all
craftsmen of the city who heretofore out of devotion or habit
used to carry torches in the procession of Corpus Christi on the
day after the same, should go in order, as appears in those
things written below. In the first place, that the Weavers and
Cordwainers are to go in turn, that is, that the Weavers are to
go from the right and the Cordwainers from the left, and that
each craft is to have sixteen torches. And whoever shall default
at any time on the foregoing, let him forfeit £10 to the use of
the commons and their bodies to be imprisoned at the king's
pleasure, etc.

York Minster Chamberlains' Rolls Y M : E 1 / 50 *M P*

mb 2
(as E1/44 above 1472)

1483
York Minster Chamberlains' Rolls YM: E1/53

mb 2

Necessary
expenses

... And for the rent of the chamber above the doors of the (Minster) close where the lords, the dean, and his brothers heard the play of Corpus Christi, 3s 4d, and the play called the Creed Play, 3s 4d: 6s 8d. ...

Richard III Received in the Minster
YM: Vicars Choral Statute Book

p 48*

...

Memorandum that on the twenty-ninth day of the month of August, that is, on the feast of the beheading of St John the Baptist, AD 1483, Richard III, king of England and France, came to the city of York. The queen and the prince accompanied him with many other magnates, both spiritual and temporal: five bishops, of Durham, Worcester, St Asaph, Carlisle, and St David's; the earls of Northumberland, Surrey, and Lincoln; Lords Lovell, Fythew, Stanlay, Strawng', Lylle, Grastoke, and many others. And he was received solemnly by the city with a procession to the chapel of St James-without-the-Walls, and so he entered into the city honourably, (passing) through various spectacles and decorations of the city, as far as the cathedral of St Peter. And there he was honourably received with a procession by the lords, the dean, the canons with all the ministers of the said church in silk copes of a blue colour. Having been sprinkled with holy water and censed at the west door of the church, he said an Our Father (kneeling) upon an ornate stool at the font, and thus a succentor of the vicars began the response 'De Trinitate', that is, 'Honour and Strength', and it was finished by the choir before the steps of the high altar. And then there was a pause for about the space of one 'Our Father' and a 'Hail Mary'; then the dean began the prayers 'And lead us not, etc' for the king. This being done, the dean and canons with the ministers returned to (their) stalls while the 'Amen' was concluded with the organ. And then the psalm 'Te Deum' was begun by the prelate celebrating the office and finished by the choir and organ. And immediately the antiphon 'De Trinitate' was begun by the succentor, that is, 'Thanks be to thee, O God, etc', with the versicle and the prayer 'De Trinitate'. Thus he went into the palace of the lord archbishop.

And on the next feast of the Nativity of blessed Mary following, the king and queen came, crowned, to the procession of the aforesaid church, accompanied by the prince and all the lords, both temporal and spiritual. The bishop of Durham celebrated the office, and the high altar was adorned with twelve silver and golden hangings, along with many other relics of the lord king, which remained there until the sixth hour of the night. And after mass, all returned to the palace, and there the prince was invested (as heir-apparent) by the lord king before lunch in the hall before all. And so they sat at lunch for four hours and there were present the dean, Robert Both, (and) the canons, that is, the treasurer Portyngton, Potman the archdeacon of York, the sub-dean, and four other prebends, ten parsons, twelve vicars, and other ministers of the church.

1484
House Books Y: B 2-4

f 135 *(23 September)*

The lease to Henry Albon and his associates (for) the pageant house

Memorandum that in the same year, the second of the reign of King Richard III, Henry Albon, Henry Wresill, and Richard Shaw, skinners, came before the honourable Thomas Wrangwish, mayor of the city of York, in the Council Chamber, and rented one building in Raton Row, called the pageant house, from the feast of St Martin next after the date of these present (letters) until the end of forty years, in annual rent from it, 12d at the term dates, etc (ie, at Pentecost and Martinmas, see Bridge-masters' Accounts). And the aforesaid Henry, Henry, and Richard, and their assigns will repair, etc, the said building at their own proper expenses and costs. And if it happens that the aforesaid rent of 12d is in arrears, etc ⟨...⟩ for forty days after any term date, etc, then it will be permitted to the said mayor, etc, to repossess, etc, save always that if the aforesaid Henry Albon, etc, shall have made anything anew within that building, or if their assigns shall have (done so), the same Henry, etc, shall repair, etc, all that (is) thus newly made, etc. Nor shall he or they remove any at the end of the term date or at any other time without supervision, licence, etc.

...

York Minster Chamberlains' Rolls   YM: E1/47 PM

mb 2

Necessary
expenses

... And for the rent of the chamber above the doors of the (Minster) close where the lords, the dean, and chapter with the lord archbishop heard the play of Corpus Christi, 5s. ...

YM: E1/52 MP

mb 2
(as E1/44 above 1472)

1485
Mercers' Account Rolls   MA: D54AA

mb 1d

Allowances

... And for the carrying of the torches in the procession of Corpus Christi, 2s. ...

York Minster Chamberlains' Rolls   YM: E1/48 MP

mb 2*
(as E1/44 above 1472)

1486
City Chamberlains' Rolls   Y: C4:1

mb 1

Forfeits with
fines to the
magistrate

And received from ... the craft of Linenweavers, 5s, as forfeiture for not playing the Fergus pageant. ...

mb 2
...

Lease of stations
for the Corpus
Christi Play

And of 10s received from Adam Hudson and his companions for the rent of the first station at Micklegate
And of 12s received from Richard Dicson and from his companions for the rent of the second station
And of 11s 9d received from Adam Barbour and from Richard Miton for the rent of the third station
And of 10s received from Thomas Wells for the rent of the fourth station
And of 11s received from Henry Watson on account of the

indenture for the rent of the fifth station

And of 7s received from Robert King and his companions for the rent of the sixth station

And of 8s received from Roland Robson and his companions for the rent of the seventh station

And of 8s 4d received from William Harpham and his companions for the rent of the eighth station

And of 6s 7d received from Milo Arwom and his companions for the rent of the ninth station

And of 5s received from Lambert Tymanson and his companions for the rent of the tenth station

And of 4s 8d received from Peter Parot and his companions for the rent of the eleventh station

With respect to such cash as was received for the rent of the twelfth station, viz, upon the Pavement, it was not received because it was not let as in the preceding accounts

Total £4 13s 4d

...

mb 3

Rents and repayments

The same accountants reckon that in the cash paid out each year by them to the pageant master of the Coronation of the blessed Virgin Mary to the greater support of the same pageant as in the preceding accounts 2s

...

mb 4

Gratuities to minstrels and (the servants) of lords

...

And on gratuities given to the minstrels of our lord king who were in this city 20s

And on payments given to the city minstrels
annually on Easter, 3s 4d; on Corpus Christi,
20d; on the Nativity of St John the Baptist, 20d; 11s 8d
on Christmas, 3s 4d; and on (the feast of)
St William, 20d, according to custom

...

Expenses
incurred on the
feast of Corpus
Christi

And paid in cash for various victuals and other
expenses incurred this year by the mayor and
aldermen and very many others of the council
of the Chamber on the feast of Corpus Christi,
who were seeing the play in the room of Thomas
Cokke, with 4s for the rent of the same room,   £4 20d
together with divers gifts of wine and other
things given and sent to various ladies, knights,
and other foreigners visiting the city on the same
feast. As it appears item by item in the book of
the said accountants

...

mb 4d

Expenses
incurred
concerning
the visit of
the lord king,
together with
the gift given
to his majesty
in the month
of June

And paid in cash for timber, 60s 15d; for
carpentry, 60s 3d; for mending, 11s 2d; for
cartage of timber, 9s 6d; for various labours by
labourers, 15s 6d; for planks and iron, 11s; for
the loan of 1 pair of organs with their playing,
12d; for keys appropriate for this kind of show,
15s 2d; for the making of two trees and a rosebush, 13s 4d; for silver, gold, green, and similar
paper, 33s 5½d; for crewel thread for the fringes
and the embroidery of the banners, wholesale,
13s 10d; for red buckram, 23s 6d; for 23 ells of
brabant linen cloth, wholesale, 26s 6d; for lawn,
11s; for making robes and hoods, 6s 4d; for
making jackets and a red rose, 5s 4d; for painting
the banners, for painting the shields and other   £35 18s 6d
embroidered cloths, with thread for the same,
43s 9d; for 500 ells of cloth called canvas, at 2½d
an ell, £5 4s 2½d; and for painting the same, £4;
for writing and painting 3 rolls about the visit, 18s;
for thread, wholesale, 3s 2d; for mending 3 scaffolds,
5s; for the payment for the pageant of the Weavers,
4s; for the payment for the singing clerks, 10s; for
various foreign items provided by the clerks, the
managers of the said visit, 8s 5d; for various items
provided by Richard Burgesse, 2s 4d; on the wages
of sir Henry Hudson, the chaplain, 66s 8d; and of
3 other clerks, managing and playing (a play) on the
said visit as appears item by item in the book of the
said accountants, 60s

Gift of the kings

And paid in cash for a gift given to our lord king on his arrival at this city as appears item by item in the book of the said accountants, together with the costs and expenses incurred about that gift as is set out by that book

£30 3s 8d

...

Mercers' Account Rolls MA: D54BB

mb 1
(as D54AA above 1485)

York Minster Chamberlains' Rolls YM: E1/51 MP

mb 2
(as E1/44 above 1472)

1487
Mercers' Account Rolls MA: D54CC

mb 1

Bequests

... And received from the craftsmen of the Bowers for the rent of the pageant house for this year, 2s.

...

Repairs and allowances

Wherefore the same master and constables seek an allocation for expenses incurred this year, viz, they paid for 2 pieces of wood bought for the pageant house, price 6d. And they paid to 2 men for sawing the said wood, 2d. And they paid for 100 double spikings, 4d. And they paid for 2 dozen and for 2 pounds of iron for the bands and hasps and the staples for the abovesaid pageant house, 15d. And they paid to Adam Hudson for making the said bands, hasps, and staples, 8d. And they paid for 2 swales for the said doors, 8d. And they paid for 1 lock and 1 key for the said lock, 4d. And they paid to William Johnson, carpenter, working there for a day and a half, 9d. And they paid to John Gryndon for the cleaning of the said pageant house for a half-day, 2d. And they paid for 36 pounds of wax and rosin for 4 torches of the guild, and for the making of the same, 6s 8d. And they paid to the wardens of Ouse Bridge for the rent of the aforesaid pageant house, 12d. ... And for the carrying of the torches in the Corpus Christi procession according to custom, 2s. ...

1488
Bridgemasters' Account Rolls Y : C85:1

mb 1*

...

Returns and
rents both
within Mickle-
gate and
without Raton
Row and Tofts

And 12d received from the rent of 1 house by the masters of
the pageant of the Skinners of the city of York, paid per annum
at the same times

...

And 12d received for the rent of 1 pageant house of the Mercers
in the same place, paid per annum at the same times
And 12d received for the rent of the pageant house of the Bakers
in the same place, paid per annum at the same times
And 12d received for the rent of the pageant house of the
Tanners in the same place, paid per annum at the same times
And 2s received for the rent of the pageant house of the Carpenters and Cordwainers in the same place, paid at the same
times
And 8d received for the rent of the pageant house of the Goldsmiths in the same place, paid per annum at the same times

...

Mercers' Account Rolls MA: D54DD

Bequests to-
gether with the   mb 1
receipts of   ... And received for the rent of the pageant house 12d.
money for the
pageant house

Repairs includ-   ... And they paid for the carrying of the torches in the Corpus
ing allowances   Christi procession 18d. ...

York Minster Chamberlains' Rolls YM: E1/55 MP

mb 1
(as E1/44 above 1472)

1489
Mercers' Account Rolls MA: D54EE

mb 1
Rent for the
pageant house   ...
together with   And they reckon for the rent of the pageant houses this
bequests   year   nothing

Allowances ... And they paid for carrying torches in front of the procession on the Friday next after the feast of Corpus Christi 18d. ...

1490
House Books Y : B 7

f 5v *(2 July)*
...

On which day, and before those named, there came into the Council Chamber, in full council, Thomas Chapman, John Ellis, William Stubbes and Richard Raby as the manucaptores, and each personally went bail for Richard Rawlyn,. John Pycher, and the other cordwainers who are in the lord king's prison of the city of York, to produce those men, Richard, John, and the other cordwainers, bodily before the mayor within the next seven days following the date of the presents, on pain of forfeiting £20, to be paid to the use of the commons of this city or of a payment of £10 forfeited by those cordwainers for their disobedience in the carrying of torches contrary to the ordinances, etc.

A/Y Memorandum Book Y : E 20

f 296v *(27 November)*
...

This abovewritten ordinance on the Tapiters was cancelled and annulled in the time of John Gylliot, mayor, by his assent and that of the whole council of the Chamber on the twenty-seventh day of November in the sixth year of the reign of King Henry the seventh.

Mercers' Account Rolls MA : D54FF

mb 1
...

Rent for the pageant house And the same accountants reckon for the rent of a pageant house received from the craftsmen of the Bowers and Fletchers this year 12d.

... And (they) paid for carrying the torches in front of the procession on the Friday after the feast of Corpus Christi according to custom 18d. ...

Corpus Christi Account Rolls Y : C99 : 7

mb 3

...

<table>
<tr><td>Allowances</td><td>Wherefore the said master seeks to be allowed for various expenses incurred by him in the said year on the general procession, viz, on the day after Corpus Christi. First, to the clerk carrying the cross before the procession, 2d. Item, paid to 4 clerks carrying the baudekin, 8d. Item, paid to 9 men carrying 9 torches, 18d. Item, paid for the wax to be burned, 6d. And paid to Thomas Bateman and Thomas Hunter, clerks, in the vestry of the Minster, as a gratuity on 2 occasions, 12d. And paid to 2 men carrying the shrine, 4d. And paid for the meal of the master and the 6 wardens around the feast of Corpus Christi and at the end of the reckoning according to custom, 5s.</td></tr>
</table>

...

York Minster Chamberlains' Rolls YM : E1/56 MP

mb 1
(as E1/44 above 1472)

1491
Mercers' Account Rolls MA : D54HH

mb 1

...

<table>
<tr><td>Rent of the pageant (house)</td><td>And they reckon for the rent of a pageant house this year, nothing, because it is the right of the Bowers and Fletchers through the agreement made
 Total: nothing </td></tr>
</table>

<table>
<tr><td>Allowances</td><td>... And they paid for making 3 torches and for the mending of a judas for the feast of Corpus Christi, 10s 4d. And they paid for the carrying of the torches in front of the Corpus Christi procession, 18d. ...</td></tr>
</table>

1492
House Books Y : B7

f 70* *(1 June)*

...

Assembled in the Council Chamber [on the bridge of the Ouse] in the Common Hall. It was agreed that the mayor, each alderman, sheriffs, and each one of the common council will have a torch to carry before the body of our saviour Jesus Christ the day after the day of Corpus Christi, on penalty of a fine for each one aforementioned, 40s, to be paid to the common profit of this city without any pardon. And if the mayor for the time being does not levy all the penalties to have been forfeited, then therefore he will pay the said fines out of his personal goods to use as aforementioned.

Item, the same day it was determined by the said present that each guild, fraternity, trade, and occupation in the same city which long ago has been accustomed to carry torches, will carry the torches of the same guild, fraternity, trade, and occupation according to the ancient custom on the day after Corpus Christi for its honour, properly, etc, and to the honourable custom aforementioned on pain and forfeiture formerly provided for at the first time of the mayoralty ... of Thomas Wranghwys, which pain and forfeiture is 40s from each guild, etc. And moreover, that they will carry their torches in the positions and places to them assigned by the common clerk for the time being.

Cordwainers   Item, the same day it was agreed and determined by all the said present that the Cordwainers in the same city will carry their torches the day after Corpus Christi in the room on the left hand of the Weavers, and the same in any other place on the penalty formerly provided for.

f 85   (21 September)

...

Assembled in the Council Chamber on Ouse Bridge. It was agreed by the said present that the mayor and the chamberlains will cause to be levied all manner of penalties incurred by Roger Appulby and William Barker, merchant, because they failed to carry their torches the day after Corpus Christi just passed according to the ordinance previously made and provided. And also that the said mayor and chamberlains forthwith cause to be levied from the guild of Cordwainers all penalties that they have incurred, because they did not carry their torches the day after the day of Corpus Christi just passed according to the ordinances and against the commandment of the mayor and common council previously made and given. And this to be levied forthwith.

...

Mercers' Account Rolls MA: D54II

mb 1

...

Rent for the pageant house	And furthermore, the abovesaid accountants reckon for the rent of a pageant house 12d

Allowances	... Item, they paid for carrying the torches in front of the procession on the feast of Corpus Christi according to custom, 18d. ...

1493
Mercers' Account Rolls MA: D54KK

mb 1

...

Rent (from) a pageant house	And likewise, the said accountants reckon for the rent of a pageant house this year nothing

Allowances	... Item, they paid for carrying the torches in front of the procession on the feast of Corpus Christi according to custom, 14d. ...

1494
Mercers' Account Rolls MA: D54LL

mb 1

...

And furthermore, the same accountant and the same constables reckon for the rent of a pageant house this year *(blank)*

... Item, they paid for carrying the torches in front of the Corpus Christi procession on the Friday next after the feast of Corpus Christi according to custom, 14d. ...

1496
Mercers' Account Rolls MA: D54NN

mb 1
(as D54LL above 1494, second entry)

Corpus Christi Account Rolls   Y: C99:8

mb 3

...

Allowances Wherefore the said master seeks to be allowed for various expenses incurred by him in the said year on the general procession, viz, on the day after Corpus Christi. First, to 4 clerks carrying the baudekin, 8d. And paid to the clerk carrying the cross before the procession, 2d. And paid to 7 men carrying 7 torches, 14d. And paid for the wax to be burned before the shrine, 4d. And paid to Thomas Bateman and Thomas Hunter, clerks, in the vestry of the Minster as a gratuity, 12d. And paid to 2 men carrying the shrine, 6d. And paid for the meal of the master and the 6 wardens around the feast of Corpus Christi and at the end of the reckoning according to custom, 4s. ...

1497
Mercers' Account Rolls   MA: D5400

mb 1

Allowances ... Item, they paid for carrying the torches before the procession on the Friday next after the feast of Corpus Christi according to custom, 14d. ...

1498
Corpus Christi Account Rolls   Y: C100:1

mb 2

...

Allowances Wherefore the said master seeks to be allowed for various expenses incurred by him in the said year on the general procession, viz, on the day after Corpus Christi. First, to 4 clerks carrying the baudekin, 8d. And paid to the clerk carrying the cross before the procession, 2d. And paid to 7 men carrying 7 torches, 14d. And paid for the wax to be burned before the shrine, 4d. And paid to Thomas Bateman and Thomas Hunter, clerks, in the vestry of the Minster as a gratuity, 12d. And paid to 2 men carrying the shrine, 6d. And paid for the meal of the master and the 6 wardens around the feast of Corpus Christi and at the end of the reckoning according to custom, 5s.

...

And paid for the mending of the 'castles', 2d. ...

1499
House Books Y: B8

f 59 *(12 June)*
...

Item, William Fryston came before the mayor and those present, and he was ordered to appear before them on the following Friday to answer to them for a certain house among the pageant houses which he, together with the searchers of the Weavers, rented from the mayor and the chamberlains at the time of the mayoralty of Thomas Gray for 6s a year. ...

f 64 *(6 September)*
...

On the same day, William Robynson, the alderman of the Weavers, and William Friston (were cited) concerning one building at the pageant houses, the which William Friston afterwards comes and confesses that he had rented the said building. ...

f 64v *(17 September)*
... On the same day, it was ordered to William Friston, alderman of the Weavers, and the other weavers there, that they pay 18s for the rent of one pageant house for the three years that end at the next feast of St Mary [following, and these before the next feast of (St) Mary, and it has been pointed out to them that they should pay the said rent from now on, or that] of which 18s they are to pay 12s at the next feast of (St) Mary and 6s at the feast of St Martin.

City Chamberlains' Rolls Y: C4:4

mb 1

Lease of the stations of the Corpus Christi Play

And concerning the rent of the first station, it is let to William Catterton, etc   4s
And concerning the rent of the second station, it is let to John Nicholson and others, etc   4s
And concerning the rent of the third station, it is let to John Elys, Richard Gibson, and others   6s 5d
And concerning the rent of the fourth station, it is let to Edward de la Kyver and Matthew Cotez and others   5s
And concerning the rent of the fifth station, it is let to Richard Thomson and others, etc   4s

And concerning the rent of the sixth station, it is let to John
Wark and others   3s 11d
And concerning the rent of the seventh station, it is let to Robert
Clyff and others   40d
And concerning the rent of the eighth station, it is let to the
brothers of St Leonard, etc   2s 4d
And concerning the rent of the ninth station, it is let to the wife
of William Sharp and to the wife of *(blank)* Thuayter, etc   40d
And concerning the rent of the tenth station, it is let to Nicholas
Caton and others by indenture, etc   5s
And concerning the rent of the eleventh station, it is let to John
Byrkhed and others   2s 8d
And concerning the rent of the twelfth station, it is let *(blank)*

Total 44s

...

Y : C 4 : 3

mb 1

Rents resolute ... As paid in cash to the pageant masters of the Coronation of
the blessed Virgin Mary for the support of the same pageant as in
the previous accounts   2s
...

mb 1d
...

Gratuities to
minstrels and
to the servants
of lords

And paid in gratuities to the city minstrels according
to custom at various times of the year, viz, (at) Easter,
Corpus Christi, the Nativity of St John the Baptist,   10s
Christmas, and (the feast of) St William for the
honour of the city, aside from the attending masters

And on gratuities given to 6 minstrels of the lord prince in the
month of May this year, etc   10s
...

Clothing of the
officials according And paid to 3 city minstrels for their clothing for Christmas 24s
to custom
...

<table>
<tr><td>Expenses
incurred on
the feast of
Corpus Christi</td><td>And on expenses incurred this year by the mayor, the aldermen, and very many others from the council of the Chamber on the feast of Corpus Christi who were seeing and observing the play in the lodging belonging to the Common Guildhall according to custom, as appears item by item in the paper book of the chamberlain, and also 5s paid for the rent of the Chamber, etc.</td><td>£3 13s 11d</td></tr>
</table>

And paid to a certain doctor of theology preaching a certain sermon on the day after the feast of Corpus Christi as in pre-ceding ⟨years⟩   40d

Total £3 14s 11d

...

Bridgemasters' Account Rolls   Y : C85 :2

mb 1
...

Returns ⟨and⟩ rents both ⟨...⟩

And for the rent of 1 building for the pageant of the Skinners, paid, etc   12d
...

And for the rent of 1 pageant house of the Mercers, paid, ⟨etc⟩   12d
And for the rent of 1 pageant house of the Bakers, paid at the same times   12d
And for the rent of 1 pageant house of the Tanners, paid, etc   ⟨12d⟩
And for the rent of 1 pageant house of the Cordwainers and Carpenters, paid at the same times   2s
And for the rent of 1 pageant house of the Goldsmiths, paid at the same times   8d
...

And for the rent for the pageant house from the Weavers of the city of York in the same place, discharged by them for a period of years, paid, etc   16d
...

Mercers' Account Rolls   MA : D54QQ

mb 1

Allowances

... Item, they paid for carrying the torches on the Friday next after the feast of Corpus Christi 18d. ...

Corpus Christi Account Rolls   Y : 100:2

mb 2

...

Wherefore the said master seeks to be allowed for various expenses incurred by him in the said year, viz, on the general
procession on the day after Corpus Christi. First, paid to the
clerk carrying the cross before the procession, 2d. And paid to
4 clerks carrying the baudekin, 8d. And paid to 7 men carrying
7 torches, 14d. And paid for wax to be burned before the
shrine and on the general commemoration of the dead (in the
chapel of St William) on Ouse Bridge, 6d. And paid to 2 men
carrying the shrine, 6d. And paid to Thomas Bateman and
Thomas Hunter, clerks, in the vestry of the Minster, as a gratuity,
in salary, 12d. And paid for the meal of the master and the 6
wardens around the feast of Corpus Christi and at the end of
this reckoning, 5s. ...

Allowances

1500
Mercers' Account Rolls   MA: D55RR

mb 2d
... Item, paid for the carrying of the torches of the said guild on
the Friday next after the feast of Corpus Christi, 14d. ...

Allowances
according to
custom, includ-
ing the fee of
the beadle and
of the clerk of
the account

1501
City Chamberlains' Rolls   Y : C5:1

mb 2

...

Lease of the
stations of
the Corpus
Christi Play

And concerning the rent of the first station, it is let to William
Catterton and others beyond the station of the common
clerk   3s 11d
And concerning the rent of the second station, it is let to John
Caldbek and others   4s
And concerning the rent of the third station, it is let to Richard
Gibson and others   5s 10d
And concerning the rent of the fourth station, it is let to Thomas
Spicer and others   5s
And concerning the rent of the fifth station, it is let to William

Barker and others   3s 11d

And concerning the rent of the sixth station, it is let to Alan
Staveley and others - cancelled

And concerning the rent of the seventh station, it is let
to Robert Clyff and others. And concerning the rent of   10s
the eighth station, it is let to Alexander Donne and others

And concerning the rent of the ninth holding, it is let to William
Sclater and others   12d

And concerning the rent of the tenth holding, it is let to William
Couke and others   5s 6d

And concerning the rent of the eleventh holding, it is let to
William Catterton and others by indenture   5s

And concerning the rent of the twelfth station, it is let to John
Rothley and others   4s

Total 50s 8d

...

mb 3

Rents resolute   Whence the said accountants seek an allowance
for as much as was paid in cash to the pageant
master of the Coronation of the blessed Virgin   2s
Mary for the support of the same pageant as
in previous accounts

...

mb 3d

...

Gratuities to   Item, paid as a gratuity to the city minstrels
minstrels and   according to custom at various times of the year,
other servants   viz, at Easter, Corpus Christi, the Nativity of St
John the Baptist, (the feast of) St William for   10s
the honour of the city aside from the attending
magistrates

...

Clothing of the   And paid to three city minstrels for their clothing for
officials accord- Christmas
ing to custom   24s

...

Expenses   And on expenses incurred this year by the mayor, the aldermen,
incurred on   and very many others from the council of the Chamber on the
the feast of   feast of Corpus Christi who were seeing and observing the play in
Corpus Christi   the lodging belonging to the Common Guildhall according
to custom, as appears item by item in the paper book of the
chamberlain, and also paid for the rent of the chamber of the

mayor, etc

And paid to a certain doctor of theology preaching a certain sermon on the day after the feast of Corpus Christi as in preceding (years)

Total £4 4s 8d

...

Bridgemasters' Account Rolls Y: C86:1

mb 1

...

Returns and rents both within Micklegate and without Raton Row and the Tofts

And for the rent of 1 building in the same place for the pageant of the Skinners, paid at the same times   12d

...

And for the rent of the pageant house from the Weavers of the city of York in the same place, discharged by them for a period of years   16d

And for the rent of a pageant house of diverse crafts this year, etc   18s

...

And for the rent of the pageant house of the Mercers, 12d. And for the rent of the pageant house of the Bakers, 12d. And for the rent of the pageant house (of the) Tapiters, 12d. And for the rent of the pageant house of the Cordwainers and Carpenters, 2s. And for the rent of the pageant house of the Tanners, paid, etc, 12d. And for the rent of the pageant house of the Goldsmiths, paid, etc, 8d. ...

And for the rent of the pageant house of the Waxchandlers, 8d. And of the pageant of the Coopers, 4d.

...

Mercers' Account Rolls MA: D55SS

Allowances according to custom, including the fee of the beadle and the clerk of the account

mb 3d

... Item, they paid for the carrying of the torches of the said guild of Holy Trinity on the Friday next after the feast of Corpus Christi, 14d. ...

Corpus Christi Account Rolls Y: C100:3

mb 3

...

Allowances

Wherefore the said master seeks to be allowed for various expenses incurred by him in the said year, viz, on the general procession on the Sunday next after the feast of Corpus Christi. First, paid to the clerk carrying the cross before the procession, 2d. And paid to 4 clerks carrying the baudekin, 8d. And paid to 7 men carrying 7 torches, 14d. And paid for wax to be burned before the shrine and on the general commemoration of the dead (in the chapel of St William) on Ouse Bridge, 7d. And paid to 2 men carrying the shrine, 4d. And paid to Thomas Bateman and Thomas Hunter, clerks, in the vestry of the Minster as a gratuity, 12d. And paid for the meal of the master and 6 wardens around the feast of Corpus Christi and at the end of the reckoning according to custom, 5s. ...

And paid to the clerk of Holy Trinity of York, on the Sunday after the feast of Corpus Christi as a gratuity, 2d. ...

Commemorations   And paid for the making of 6 torches this year, 20s 10d.

...

1502
Mercers' Account Rolls MA: D55TT

mb 2d
(*as D54SS above 1501*)

Corpus Christi Account Rolls Y: C100:4

mb 3

Commemorations ... And paid for the making of 6 torches this year, 36s 4d. ...

And the said master seeks to be allowed for various expenses incurred by him in the said year, viz, on the general procession on the day after the feast of Corpus Christi. First, paid to the clerk carrying the cross before the procession, 2d. And paid to 4 clerks carrying the baudekin, 8d. And paid to 7 men carrying

Allowances   7 torches, 14d. And paid for wax to be burned before the shrine and on the general commemoration of the dead (in the chapel of St William) on Ouse Bridge, 2d. And paid to 2 men carrying ⟨the shrine, 4d. And⟩ paid to Thomas Bateman and his companion, clerks, in the vestry of the Minster as a gratuity, 12d. And paid for ⟨...⟩

1503
Bridgemasters' Account Rolls   Y : C86 : 2

mb 1*
...

Returns and rents both within Mickle-gate and without Raton Row and the Tofts

And for the rent of 1 building in the same place for the pageant of the Skinners, paid at the same times   12d
...
And for the rent of the pageant house of the Weavers of the city of York in the same place discharged for a period of years   16d
And for the rent of the pageant house of diverse crafts ⟨...⟩   18s
...

And for the rent of the pageant house of the Mercers, 12d. And for the rent of the pageant house of the Bakers, 12d.
And for the rent of the pageant house of the Tapiters, 12d. And for the rent of the pageant house of the Cordwainers and Carpenters, 2s.
And for the rent of the pageant house of the Tanners, 12d. And for the rent of the pageant house of the Goldsmiths, paid, etc, 8d.
And for the rent of one building in the same place on the land of John Alan   40d
And for the rent of the pageant house (of) the Waxchandlers   8d
And for the rent of the pageant house (of) the Coopers   4d
...

Mercers' Account Rolls   MA : DD55UU

mb 2d
(as D55SS above 1501)

mb 1d

External expenses

... Expenses incurred by Robert Whetley, constable. First, for a half dozen (pieces) of wax, 3s 6d; and for the manufacture of torches, 3s 4d. Expenses by John Albanas, constable. First he paid for 7 dozen (pieces) of rosin for torches, 3s 6d. ...

1504
Mercers' Account Rolls   MA : D55VV

mb 3
(as D55SS above 1501)

And they paid to Henry Marshall for diverse material for painting the pageant 12s 6d. ...

1505
Mercers' Account Rolls MA : D 5 5 WW

mb 4
(as D55SS above 1501)

Corpus Christi Account Rolls Y : C 1 0 0 : 5

mb 3

...

And the said master seeks to be allowed for various expenses incurred by him in the said year, viz, on the general procession on the day after Corpus Christi. First, paid to 4 clerks carrying the baudekin, 8d. Item, to a clerk carrying the cross before the procession, 2d. Item, paid to 2 boys carrying candelabras, 2d. Item, paid to 7 men carrying 7 torches, 14d. Item, paid for wax to be burned before the shrine and on the general commemoration of the dead (in the chapel of St William) on Ouse Bridge, 6d. And paid to 2 men carrying the shrine, 6d. And paid to Thomas Bateman and his companion, clerks of the Minster, as a gratuity, 12d. And paid to the sacristan of Holy Trinity and to the door-keeper of the minster of St Peter of York as a gratuity, 6d. And paid for the meal of the master and the 6 wardens around the feast of Corpus Christi and at the end of the reckoning according to custom, 5s. ...

Allowances for necessary expenses

1506
City Chamberlains' Rolls Y : C 5 : 2

mb 2

...

Lease of the stations of the Corpus Christi Play

And concerning (the rent) of the first station let to Richard Catterton and to others   4s
And concerning the rent of the second station let to John Couper and Caldbeke   6s
And concerning the rent of the third station let *(blank)*   *(blank)*
And concerning the rent of the fourth station let to John Mowbray, William Moresby, Thomas Parker, and others   8d
And concerning the rent of the fifth station let *(blank)*   *(blank)*

And concerning the rent of the sixth station let *(blank)* *(blank)*
And concerning the rent of the seventh station let to the brothers
of St Leonard   12d
And concerning the rent of the eighth holding let *(blank)* *(blank)*
And concerning the rent of the ninth station let *(blank)* *(blank)*
And concerning the rent of the tenth station let to William
Caton, 2s 6d, and to the wife of Wharton, 2s 6d   5s
And concerning the rent of the eleventh station let *(blank)* *(blank)*
And concerning the rent of the twelfth station let *(blank)* *(blank)*
And concerning the rent of the thirteenth station let to Robert
Clyffe   12d

Total 20s

...

mb 3

...

Rents resolute — Item, paid to the support of the pageant of the Coronation of the
blessed Virgin Mary as in preceding (years)   2s

...

mb 4

...

Gratuities to minstrels — And paid to the city minstrels on Easter as in preceding
(years)   40d
And paid to the city minstrels on the feast of Corpus Christi as
in preceding (years)   20d
And paid to the city minstrels on the feast of the Nativity of
St John the Baptist as in preceding (years)   20d
And paid to the minstrels of the lord prince as in preceding
(years)   10s
And paid to the minstrels of the lord king in the month of
August this year as in preceding (years)   20s

...

And paid to the city minstrels on Christmas as in preceding
(years)   40d
And paid to the city minstrels on the feast of St William   20d
And paid to 2 minstrels of Lord de Darcy at the command
of the mayor   20d

...

Clothing of the officials according to custom — And paid to 3 city minstrels for their clothing for Christmas
as in preceding (years)   24s

...

Expenses
incurred on
the feast of
Corpus Christi

And on expenses incurred this year for the mayor,
the aldermen, and very many others of the council
of the Chamber on the feast of Corpus Christi,
who were seeing and observing the play in the
lodging belonging to the Common Guildhall
according to custom, as appears item by item in
the paper book of the chamberlain, and also
paid for the rent of the chamber of the mayor,
etc. And paid to a certain doctor preaching a
certain sermon on the day after Corpus Christi,
and on the expenses of the common clerk

£4 7s 8d

Total £4 7s 8d

Mercers' Account Rolls   M A : D 5 5 X X

mb 2
(as D55SS above 1501)

Corpus Christi Account Rolls   Y : C 1 0 0 : 6

mb 3

...

Payments for the
commemoration
of the dead and
the making of
torches

Allowances and
necessary
expenses

And the said master seeks to be allowed for various necessary
expenses incurred by him this year, viz, on the general procession
on the day after the feast of Corpus Christi. First, paid to a
clerk carrying the cross before the procession, 2d. And paid to
2 boys carrying candelabras, 2d. And paid to 4 clerks carrying
the baudekin, 8d. And paid to 7 men carrying 7 torches, 14d.
And paid for wax to be burned before the shrine and on the
general commemoration of the dead (in the chapel of St William)
on Ouse Bridge, 7d. And paid to 2 men carrying the shrine,
6d. And paid to Thomas Bateman and his companion, clerks of
the Minster, as a gratuity, 12d. And paid to the sacristan of
Holy Trinity, 2d; and to the doorkeeper of the Minster of blessed
Peter of York, 4d, as a gratuity: 6d. And paid for the meal of
the master and the 6 wardens around the feast of Corpus Christi
and at the end of the reckoning according to custom, 5s. ...

And paid for the making of 6 torches, 30s. And paid for the
making of 6 banners for the same torches this year, 5s. ...

York Minster Chamberlains' Rolls   Y M : E 1/60 *M P*

mb 2
(*as E1/44 above 1472*)

1507
Mercers' Account Rolls   M A : D 5 5 Y Y

Allowances
according to
custom including
the fee of the
beadle and the
clerk of the
account

mb 3

... Item, they paid for carrying the torches of the said guild of Holy Trinity on the Friday next after the feast of Corpus Christi 14d. ...

And also they seek to be reimbursed for 40s paid to Thomas Drawswerd, carver, for the pageant of Doomsday
                                        Total 40s

...

1508
City Chamberlains' Rolls   Y : C5 : 3

mb 1

...

Lease of the
stations of
the Corpus
Christi Play

And concerning the rent of the first station let to Richard
Caterton   4s 4d
And concerning the rent of the second station let to John Calbek
and Richard Asheby   6s
And concerning the rent of the third station let to John Elles
and Richard Gibson   5s
And concerning the rent of the fourth station let to John White
and Thomas Parcour   5s
And concerning the rent of the fifth station let to Simon
Vicars   3s 8d
And concerning the rent of the sixth station, it is let to Master
Staveley and others   12d
And concerning the rent of the seventh station let to John Bate-
man and Nicholas Baxster   5s
And concerning the rent of the eighth station let (*blank*) (*blank*)
And concerning the rent of the ninth holding let to William
Cooke   5s
And concerning the rent of the tenth station let to William
Caton   5s

And concerning the rent of the eleventh station let to Doctor
Adrian   3s 4d
And concerning the rent of the twelfth station let to William
Russell and others   3s 4d
And concerning the rent of the thirteenth station *(blank)* nothing

Total 46s 8d

...

mb 3

...

Rents resolute And paid in cash to the support of the pageant of the
Coronation of the blessed Mary as in preceding (years)   2s

...

mb 4
(as C5:2 above 1506)

...

Clothing of
the officials And paid to 3 city minstrels for their clothing for Christmas
according to as in preceding (years)   24s
custom

...

Expenses on And on expenses incurred in this year for the mayor,
the feast of the aldermen, and very many others of the council
Corpus Christi of the Chamber on the feast of Corpus Christi, who
were seeing and observing the play in the lodging
belonging to the Common Guildhall according to
custom, as appears item by item in the paper book of £4 14s 4d
the chamberlain, and also paid for the rent of the
chamber of the mayor, etc. And there was paid to
a certain doctor speaking a certain sermon on the
day after Corpus Christi, and on the expenses of
the common clerk, etc

The total is clear

Mercers' Account Rolls MA: D55ZZ

mb 2
(as D53SS above 1501)

mb 3
... Item, for the manufacture of door bands and crooks for the

Repairs made concerning and upon the above-said buildings

pageant house, 16d. Item, paid to John Whyte for nails for the great hall and the pageant house, 2s. ... Item, for the manufacture of the pageant doors including the labour of the carpenters, 10s. ...

Corpus Christi Account Rolls Y: C101:1

mb 3

...

Allowances for necessary expenses

And the said master seeks to be allowed for various necessary expenses incurred by him this year, viz, on the general procession on the day after the feast of Corpus Christi. First, paid to a clerk carrying the cross before the procession, 2d. And paid to 2 boys carrying candelabras, 2d. And paid to 4 clerks carrying the baudekin, 8d. And paid to 7 men carrying 7 torches, 14d. And paid for wax to be burned before the shrine and on the general commemoration of the dead (in the chapel of St William) on Ouse Bridge, 4d. And paid to 2 men carrying the shrine, 6d. And paid to the clerks of the vestry of the church of St Peter of York as a gratuity, in salary, 12d. And paid for the meal of the master and the 6 wardens around the feast of Corpus Christi and at the end of the reckoning according to custom, 5s. ...

1509
Mercers' Account Rolls MA: D55AAA

Allowances according to custom including the fee of the beadle and of the clerk, accountants

mb 2

... Item for carrying the torches of the said guild on the Friday next after the feast of Corpus Christi, 14d. ...

Repairs made concerning and upon the above-said buildings

... Item, they paid to 1 of the Daubers for a half-day at the pageant garth, 2s. Item, for 1 lock, 1 staple, and 1 pair of door bands for the same house, 7d. ... Item, for 100 fir laths at the pageant house, 5d. ... Item, for 2 wagonloads of earth for the pageant house, 4d. ...

1510
Mercers' Account Rolls MA: D55BBB

mb 2
(as D55AAA above 1509)

York Minster Chamberlains' Rolls Y M : E 1 / 6 1 *MP*

mb 2
*(as E1/44 above 1472 except that the cloth over the head of
St William is specified as a pallium)*

1511
Mercers' Account Rolls M A ; D 5 6 C C C

Allowances
according to
custom, includ-
ing the fee of
the beadle and
of the clerk
of this account

mb 2
... Item, for carrying the torches of the said guild on Friday, the
day after Corpus Christi, 14d. ...

Repairs made
concerning
and upon the
abovesaid
buildings

... Item, they paid to William Vance and his servant, working as
tilers on the Tofts for a day and a half, 15d. ...

Corpus Christi Account Rolls Y : C 1 0 1 : 2

mb 4

...

Allowances
for necessary
expenses

And the said master seeks to be allowed for various necessary
expenses incurred by him this year, viz, on the general procession
on the day after the feast of Corpus Christi. First, paid to a
clerk carrying the cross before the procession, 2d. And paid to
2 boys carrying candelabras, 2d. And paid to 4 clerks carrying
the baudekin, 8d. And paid to 7 men carrying 7 torches, 14d.
And paid for wax to be burned before the shrine and on the
general commemoration of the dead (in the chapel of St William)
on Ouse Bridge, 7d. And paid to 2 men carrying the shrine, 6d.
And paid to the clerks of the vestry of the church of St Peter
of York as a gratuity, 12d. And paid to the sacristan of Holy
Trinity, 2d; and to the doorkeeper of the minster of blessed
Peter of York, 4d: 6d. And paid for the meal of the master and
the 6 wardens around the feast of Corpus Christi and at the end
of this reckoning, according to custom, 5s. ...

York Minster Chamberlains' Rolls Y M : E 1 / 6 1 b *MP*

mb 2*
(as E1/61 above 1510)

1512
Mercers' Account Rolls MA: D56DDD

Allowances according to custom, including the fee of the beadle and of the clerk

mb 2

... And for carrying the torches of the said guild on Friday, the day after Corpus Christi, 14d. ...

Corpus Christi Account Rolls Y: C101:3

mb 4

...

Allowances for necessary expenses

And the said master seeks to be allowed for various necessary expenses incurred by him this year, viz, on the general procession on the day after the feast of Corpus Christi. First, paid to 8 priests carrying the shrine, 8d. And paid to the clerk carrying the cross before the procession, 2d. And paid to 2 boys carrying candelabras, 2d. And paid to 4 clerks carrying the baudekin, 8d. And paid to 7 men carrying 7 torches, 14d. And paid for wax to be burned before the shrine and on the general commemorations of the dead (in the chapel of St William) on Ouse Bridge, 6d. And paid to 2 men carrying the shrine, 6d. And paid to the clerks of the vestry of the church of St Peter of York as a gratuity, 12d. And paid to the sacristans of Holy Trinity, 2d; and to the door-keeper of the minster of blessed Peter of York, 4d: 6d. And paid for the meal of the master and the 6 wardens around the feast of Corpus Christi and at the end of this reckoning, according to custom, 5s. ... And paid for the washing of 8 albs and 8 amices and 8 little cushions belonging to the shrine, 12d. ...

1513
Mercers' Account Rolls MA: D56EEE

mb 2

Allowances according to custom

... And for carrying the torches of the said guild on Friday, the day after Corpus Christi, 14d. ...

1514
Bridgemasters' Account Rolls Y: C86:3

mb 1

...

⟨...⟩

For the rent of 1 building in the same place for the pageant of the Skinners, paid, etc   12d

...

For the rent of 1 pageant (house) of the Weavers in the same
place discharged by them for a period of years, paid, etc   16d
For the rent of a pageant (house) of diverse crafts this year at
the same times   18s

...

For the rent of the pageant house of the Goldsmiths, 8d. Of 1
building in the same place on the land of John Aleyn of the
pageant (house of) the Waxchandlers, 8d. Of the pageant (house
of) the Coopers, 4d. Paid at the same times: 5s
For the rent of the pageant (house) of the Mercers, 12d. Of the
pageant (house) of the Bakers, 12d. Of the pageant (house) of
the Tapiters, 12d. Of the Carpenters, 2s. And the pageant
(house) of the Tanners, 12d.   6s

...

Mercers' Account Rolls   MA: D56FFF

mb 2
(as D56EEE above 1513)

...

Repairs   And for the pageant door, 1 stanchion, and nails 1½d. ...

1515
Mercers' Account Rolls   MA: D56GGG

mb 2
(as D56EEE above 1513)

Corpus Christi Account Rolls   Y: C101:4

mb 2

...

Allowances
for necessary
expenses

And the said master seeks to be allowed for various necessary
expenses incurred by him this year, viz, on the general procession
on the day after the feast of Corpus Christi. First, paid to the
clerk carrying the cross before the procession, 2d. And paid to
2 boys carrying candelabras, 2d. And paid to 4 clerks carrying
the baudekin, 8d. And paid as a gratuity to the chaplains carrying
the shrine, 8d. And paid to 7 men carrying 7 torches, 14d. And
paid for wax to be burned before the shrine on the general

commemoration of the dead (in the chapel of St William) on Ouse Bridge, 18d. And paid to 2 men carrying the shrine, 6d. And paid to the clerks of the vestry church of the minster of blessed Peter as a gratuity, in salary, 12d. And paid to the sacristan of the church of Holy Trinity, 2d. ...

1516
City Chamberlains' Rolls   Y : C6 : 1

mb 1*

...

The lease of the stations of the Corpus Christi Play

And received from the rent of the first station let *(blank) (blank)*
And from the rent of the second station let to Henry Gale, innkeeper ⟨...⟩
And from the rent of the third station let to John Blakey ⟨...⟩
And from the rent of the fourth station let to John White, alderman ⟨...⟩
And from the rent of the fifth station let to John Strins ⟨...⟩
And from the rent of the sixth station let to Alan Staveley, ⟨alderman⟩ ⟨...⟩
And from the rent of the seventh station let *(blank)* *(blank)*
And from the rent of the eighth station ⟨let to⟩ the lord mayor, the aldermen, and others from the council ⟨of the Chamber⟩ ⟨...⟩
And from the rent of the ninth station let ⟨...⟩ ⟨:::⟩
And from the rent of the tenth station let *(blank)* *(blank)*
And from the rent of the eleventh station let *(blank)* *(blank)*
And from the rent of the twelfth station let to Robert G⟨...⟩ ⟨...⟩
And from the masters and brothers of St Leonard's for ⟨...⟩
Hall ⟨...⟩

...

mb 2

...

Rents resolute

And paid in cash to the support of the pageant of the Coronation of the blessed Virgin Mary as in preceding (years) 2s

...

(as C5:2 above 1506 except no prince entry)

Clothing of the officials according to custom

...

And paid to 3 city minstrels for Christmas as in preceding (years) 24s 4d

...

(as C5:3 above 1508; Sum £3 6s 8d)

Mercers' Account Rolls MA: D56HHH

mb 2

... And for carrying the torches of this guild on the day after Corpus Christi, 14d. ...

1517
Mercers' Account Rolls MA: D56III

mb 2
(as D56HHH above 1516)

1518
City Chamberlains' Rolls Y: C6:3

mb 1
(Expenses as C6:1 above 1516. Sum for liveries 27s 4d; sum of expenses Corpus Christi day £4 4s 9½d).

Bridgemasters' Account Rolls Y: C86:4

mb 1

...

⟨...⟩

For the rent of 1 building in the same place for the pageant (house) ⟨of the Skinners, paid, etc   12d⟩

...

For the rent of 1 pageant (house) of the Weavers in the same place ⟨discharged by them for a period of years, paid, etc⟩   12d
For the rent of the pageant house of diverse crafts ⟨this year at the same times⟩   18s

...

For the rent of the pageant house of the Goldsmiths, 8d. Of 1 holding in the same place on the land of John Aleyn of the pageant (house of) the Waxchandlers, 8d. Of the pageant (house of) the Coopers, paid at the same times   5s
For the rent of the pageant (house) of the Mercers, 12d. Of the pageant (house) of the Bakers, 12d. Of the pageant (house) of the Tapiters, 12d. Of the pageant (house) of the Carpenters, 2s. And of the pageant (house) of the Tanners, 12d.   6s

...

Mercers' Account Rolls MA: D56KKK

mb 2
(as D56HHH above 1516)

mb 4

Repairs of lands and buildings

... And for the transport of 4 loads of lime, tiles, and sand to the Tofts, 2d. ... And to the Tofts, 100 thack tiles, 6d. ... And for 2 loads of earth for the building at the Tofts, 6d. ... And paid to Robert Tyler for 100 laths for the pageant green, 5d. ... And paid to John Mason and his assistant working at the pageant garth for three and a half days, 2s 6d. And for the transport of boards to the pageant garth, 1d. ... And for hasps and staples for the pageant garth, 8d. And for 100 laths, 7d. And for the carrying of lime, tiles, and sand, 1d. And for 1 lock for the pageant house, 2d. And for laths, 8d. And for 20 loads of sand, 8d. And paid to John Clynt for the transport of the sand, 4d. And for 2 loads of earth, 6d. And for 100 laths, 7d. And for 4 bushels of plaster, 9d. And paid to William Gllot and to his servant, working five and a half days, 3s 7d. ... And for the cleaning of the pageant house, 2d. ...

1519
Mercers' Account Rolls MA: D56LLL

mb 2
(as D56HHH above 1516, but sum is 12d)

1520
City Chamberlains' Rolls Y: C6:4

mb 1
(as C6:3 above 1518; sum of expenses on Corpus Christi Day £4 11s 4½d)

City Chamberlains' Books Y: CC2

f 21

Lease of the Corpus Christi Play

The first station to the common clerk		*(blank)*
paid	The second station is leased to John Blakey	5s 6d
paid	The third station is leased to Gilbert Walron	4s

paid	The fourth station is leased to Richard Powle	3s 10d
	The fifth station is leased to Miles Robynson, fisherman, paid	2s 8d
paid	The sixth station is leased to the lord mayor and the aldermen, etc, also to Nicholas Baxster	10d
	The seventh station is leased *(blank)*	*(blank)*
	The eighth station is leased *(blank)*	*(blank)*
paid	The ninth station is leased to John Bower	40d
paid	The tenth station is leased to John Lytster	4s 8d
paid	The eleventh station is leased to Alderman Paul Gills - not yet paid	3s
	The twelfth station is leased to Richard Plumpton and John Jameson	2s 8d
	The thirteenth station is leased *(blank)*	*(blank)*

Total 30s 2d examined

f 25

Rents resolute

...

Item, paid to the support of the pageant of the Coronation of the blessed Virgin Mary as in preceding (years) 2s

...

f 28v

Clothing of the officials according to custom

...

Item, paid to the city minstrels at the said (feast) of Christmas 27s 3d

...

Gratuities of minstrels and other servants

First, paid to the city minstrels on Easter as in preceding (years) 40d

Item, paid to the city minstrels on the feast of Corpus Christi as in preceding (years) 20d

Item, paid to the city minstrels on the feast of the Nativity of St John the Baptist, etc 20d

Item, paid to the city minstrels at Christmas as in preceding (years) 40d

Item, paid to the minstrels of the lord king in this year as in preceding (years) 20s

Item, paid to the city minstrels on the feast of St William as in preceding (years)   20d

Total 31s 8d examined

f 29v*

Expenses on the feast of Corpus Christi

First, for ale, 8s 3d. Item, for new ale and for the yeast, 4d. Item, for the yeast for cooking pickerel, 2d. Item, on bread called leavened bread, 3s 6d. Item, on bread for making the trenchers, 8d. Item, on bread called 'Manebrede', 9d. Item, on salt, 1d. Item, on mustard, 4d. Item, on butter, 4d. Item, on mutton, 10d. Item, on 2 sacks of coal called charcoal, 7d. Item, on 7 white cups, 3d. Item, on 3 cheeses called 'Hemingbrough cheese', 13d. Item, on 3 gallons of milk, 3d. Item, on the strawberries, 3d. Item, on 1 white rod, 4d. Item, on 3 pints of honey and ale for the same etc, 10d. Item, on 100 eggs, 9d. Item, on 26 pullets, 2s 2d. Item, on 8 capons, 3s 10½d. Item, on 10 geese, 3s 5d. Item, on 25 pigeons, 12d. Item, on the venison, 8d. Item, on 2 dozen rabbits and 2 shoats, 3s. Item, on beef, 2s 6d. Item, on the quarter of the mutton and on 1 lamb, 21d. Item, on the 3 marrowbones, 6d. Item, on 4 pounds of suet, 4d. Item, on 7 pickerel, 10s 6d. Item, on 200 apples, 3s 10d. Item, on the 4 pecks of flour, 20d. Item, on the hire of the 2 dozen pots, 5d. Item, on wine for the lady mayoress and for her sisters: 1 gallon from the Vintners and 1 gallon from the Bakers according to custom, 2s. Item, on wine for the lord mayor for his companions, the aldermen and the Twenty-four, 7s 8d. Item, on the hire of 6 dozen rough vessels, 18d. Item, on 3 other shoats, 11d. Item, on 1 ounce of saffron, on ¼ (ounce) of pepper, on 6 pounds of sugar, on 1 pound of dates, on 1 pound of prunes, on 1 pound of currants, and on 1 ounce of cloves and of mace, on another 2 ounces of saffron and of ginger, 7s 8d. Item, on bread, on ale, and on wine for the common clerk according to custom, 2s 8d. Item, on the hire of a cook and a provisioner, 2s 4d. Item, on the gratuity for the housekeeper, 8d. Item, on water for the cook, 2d. Item, on the gratuity for the bakers, 4d. Item, on the gratuity for 2 doorkeepers, 8d. Item, on the gratuity for Thomas Sadler for the hanging of the Chamber, 20d. Item, on the nails for the same, 4d. Item, on the gratuity for the daughter of the said Thomas Sadler for her diligent labour, 2d. Item, on 1 key for the door of the buttery, 2d. Item, for the hire of Thomas Flemyng's chamber, 6s 8d.

Sum total of this expense £4 11s 4½d examined

Mercers' Account Rolls MA: D56MMM

mb 3
(as D56HHH above 1516, but sum is 12d)

Corpus Christi Account Rolls Y: C102:1

mb 3-4

...

Allowances for necessary expenses

And the said master seeks to be allowed for various necessary expenses incurred by him this year, viz, on the general procession on the day after the feast of Corpus Christi. First, paid to the clerk carrying the cross before the procession, 2d. And paid to 2 boys carrying candelabras, 2d. And paid to 4 clerks carrying the baudekin, 8d. And paid as a gratuity to 3 cantors, 8d. And paid to 3 sacristans of the minster, 6d. And paid as a gratuity | to the chaplains carrying the shrine, 8d. And as a gratuity to the singing clerks, 12d. And paid to 7 men carrying 7 torches, 14d. And paid to 2 men carrying the shrine, 7d. And paid to the clerks of the church (ie) of the vestry of the church of St Peter as a gratuity, 12d. And paid to the doorkeeper of St Peter's and to the sacristan of Holy Trinity as a gratuity, 8d. ...

1521
City Chamberlains' Rolls Y: CC2

f 58

Lease of the Corpus Christi Play

	The first station to the common clerk	*(blank)*
	The second station is leased to John Myrni and to George Churcheman, skinner	5s
paid	The third station is leased to Gilbert Walron and to William Nauton	4s 4d
	The fourth station is leased to Richard Powle	2s
paid	The fifth station is leased to Miles Robinson and *(blank)*	2s 8d
	The sixth station is leased to the lady mayoress and her sisters	*(blank)*
paid	The seventh station is leased to Mr Alan Stavelay, alderman	12d
paid	The eighth station is leased to John Bateman, notary	40d
	The ninth station is leased to the lord mayor and his brothers, the aldermen	*(blank)*

paid	The tenth station is leased to Richard Styrlay, alderman, bower 40d
paid	The eleventh station is leased to John Lytster 4s 8d
paid	The twelfth station to Paul Gilli and William Cure, aldermen 3s
paid	The thirteenth station is leased to Richard Plumpton, merchant 2s 4d
	The fourteenth station is leased *(blank)*

Total 31s 8d

f 62

Rents resolute

...

Item, paid to the support of the pageant of the Coronation of the blessed Virgin Mary as in preceding (years) 2s

f 65

The clothing of the officials according to custom

...

Item, paid to the city minstrels on Christmas as in preceding (years) 27s

...

Gratuities to the minstrels and the other servants

First, paid to the city minstrels on Easter as in preceding (years) 40d

Item, paid to the minstrels of the lord king this year as in preceding (years) 20s

f 66

Expenses on the feast of Corpus Christi

First, for 3½ dozen pots of ale, 10s 6d. Item, on bread, 5s. Item, on beef, 2s 3d. Item, on wine, 7s. Item, on 10 capons, 4s 4d. Item, on 14 geese called in the vulgar tongue, greengeese, 5d. Item, on 26 pullets, 2s 6d. Item, on butter, 4d. Item, on eggs, 10d. Item, on 3 dozen rabbits, 4s 6d. Item, on 3 shoats, 18d. Item, on 7 pickerel, 10s. Item, on 1 bushel of meal, 2s 8d. Item, on 3 cheeses, 16d. Item, on vinegar and on verjuice, 2d. Item, 2 dozen and 8 pigeons, 14d. Item, on mustard, 4d. Item, on mutton, on suet, on curds, and on milk, 2s 8d. Item, on spices, 5s 6d. Item, on 50 faggots and on the transport of the same, 18d. Item, on 2 sacks of charcoal, 8d. Item, on apples, 15d. Item, on rushes, 4d. Item, on 1 white rod, 4d.

Item, on 2 gallons of wine given by the Bakers and the Vintners according to custom, 16d. Item, on 1 dozen cups, 3d. Item, on the hire of vessels called in the vulgar tongue, 'rough vessels', 4d. Item, on the adjustment of the rents, 2d. Item, on ale, 3d. Item, on wine for the common clerk, 8d. Item, on bread for the same clerk for his dinner, 2d. Item, on ale for the same clerk at the said dinner, 4d. Item, on the hire of a cook and a provisioner, 2s 4d. Item, on the gratuity to the housekeeper, 8d. Item, on water for the said cook, 2d. Item, on a gratuity given to the 2 doorkeepers, 9d. Item, on a gratuity to Thomas Sadler for the hanging of the Chamber for the lord mayor and for his brothers, 20d. Item, on a gratuity to the Bakers according to custom for their labour, 6d. Item, on the nails for the hanging of the said Chamber, 2d. Item, on a gratuity given to the daughter of the said Thomas Sadler, 2d. Item, on the hire of the Chamber for the aforesaid lord mayor and for his brothers, 6s 8d.

Sum total of these expenses £4 9s 3d

Bridgemasters' Account Rolls   Y: C87:1

mb 1

...

Returns and rents both within Micklegate Bar and without and the Tofts

For the rent of 1 building in the same place on the land of the Skinners, paid at the times   12d

...

For the rent of 1 pageant (house) of the Weavers in the same place   16d

For the rent of 1 house of the pageants of diverse crafts lying on pageant green: this year   18s

...

For the rent of the house of the pageants of the Goldsmiths, of 1 building in the same place on the land of John Alen of the pageant (house of) the Waxchandlers, and of the pageant (house of) the Coopers   5s

For the rent of the pageant (house) of the Mercers, 12d. Of the pageant (house) of the Bakers, 12d. Of the pageant (house) of the Tapiters, 12d. Of the pageant (house) of the Carpenters, 2s. And for the pageant (house) of the Tanners, 12d.   6s

...

Mercers' Account Rolls   MA: D56NNN

mb 2*
(as D56HHH above 1516, but sum is 12d)

Repairs of land
and buildings

And for mending the door for the little play, called the pageant door, 2d. And for the mending of 2 organs, called pipes, 2d. ...

1522
City Chamberlains' Books   Y: CC2

f 98
Leasing of the Corpus Christi Play

The first station to the common clerk	*(blank)*
The second station is leased to John Myres and to John Blakey	4s 4d
The third station is leased to John Mason, innholder	*(blank)*
The fourth station is leased to Thomas Warde, barber for 40d received	3s 2d
The fifth station is leased to John Cawdwell, mariner	2s 8d
The sixth station is leased to Dame Agnes Staveley, widow	12d
The seventh station is leased to Reginald Berlay, notary	3s 4d
The eighth station is leased to the lord mayor and his brothers	*(blank)*
The ninth station is leased to *(blank)*	*(blank)*
The tenth station is leased to Richard Stirley, bower	40d
The eleventh station is leased to John Lytster, tailor	4s 8d
The twelfth station is leased to the lady mayoress and her sisters, received	nothing
The thirteenth station is leased to William Galland, girdler	3s paid
The fourteenth station is leased to *(blank)*	*(blank)*

Total 25s 6d

f 104
Rents resolute
...

Item, paid to the support of the pageant of the Coronation of the blessed Virgin Mary   2s
...

f 106v
Clothing of the officials, according to custom

...

Item, paid to the city minstrels for their clothing on the same feast, etc.   27s 4d

...

f 107
Gratuities to the minstrels and the other servants
First, to the city minstrels on Easter as in preceding (years) 3s 4d
Item, paid to the minstrels of the lord king in this year as in preceding (years)   20s
[Item, paid to the city minstrels for their clothing] on Christmas as in preceding (years)   27s 4d
Item, paid to the city minstrels on the feast of Corpus Christi 20d
Item, paid to the city minstrels on the feast of the Nativity of St John the Baptist   20d
Item, paid to the city minstrels on Christmas   3s 4d
Item, paid to the city minstrels on the feast of St William   20d
Total *(blank)*

f 108
Expenses on the feast of Corpus Christi
First, on the bread called in the vulgar tongue leavened bread, on pain-demaine, and on bread called trencher bread, 5s. Item, on 3½ dozen (pots) of ale, 7s. Item, on beef, mutton, and suet, 4s. Item, on 10 capons, 6s 11d. Item, on 12 greengeese, 4s 6d. Item, on 2 dozen and 7 rabbits, 5s 10d. Item, on venison, 2s. Item, on 2 dozen pullets, 20s. Item, on 3 shoats, 17d. Item, on 3 dozen pigeons, 21d. Item, on eggs and butter, 14d. Item, on 1 bushel of wheat, 11d. Item, on 6 pike, 16s. Item, on faggots, 15d. Item, on mustard, on vinegar, and on verjuice, 10½d. Item, on apples, 20d. Item, on red wine, claret, white wine, Rhine (wine), and malmsey, according to the bill on that account, etc, 8s 4d. Item on 1 white rod, 4d. Item, on rushes, 4d. Item, on the hire of vessels, 2s 6d. Item, on milk, curds, and marrow bones, 16d. Item, on ale for the common clerk, 10d. Item, on bread and on wine for the same clerk, 16d. Item, on payment to Thomas Sadler for the hanging of the Chamber of the lord mayor and his brothers, ie, with the nails and benches etc, 2s 2½d. Item, on a gratuity to the cook and to the provisioner of the said mayor, 2s 8d. Item, on a gratuity to 3 porters for

their labour, 14d. Item, on a gratuity for the housekeeper of the said mayor, 8d. Item, on the hire of the Chamber for the said mayor and for his brothers as in preceding (years), 6s 8d. Item, on the cheeses, 3s 6d. Item, on a gratuity given to the baker of the lord mayor for his assiduous labour, 10d.

Sum total of these expenses £4 14s 11d examined

Mercers' Account Rolls MA : D56000

mb 2
(as D56HHH above 1516, but sum is 12d)

1523
City Chamberlains' Books Y : CC2

f 143v

Leasing of the Corpus Christi Play

The first station to the common clerk	*(blank)*
The second station is leased to John Myers, official	3s 4d
The third station is leased to John Ellys, merchant	2s
The fourth station is leased to John Thorneton, merchant	2s
The fifth station is leased to Richard Clyf, bower	2s
The sixth station is leased to no one since it is played before the lord mayor and his brothers	
The seventh station: it is played before the lady mayoress and her sisters	⟨.⟩d
Robert Parkyn, cordwainer	paid 10d
The eighth station is leased to Matthew Tayllour	2s
The ninth station is leased to John Lyster, tailor	3s 8d
The tenth station is leased to Robert Wylde, alderman	12d
The eleventh station is leased to William Galland	2s 8d
The twelfth station is leased *(blank)*	*(blank)*

examined Total 20s 6d

f 147v

Labourers

Alexander Gray, labourer, the pageant master of the Labourers of Bowtham Ward presents Thomas Meryman, labourer, to exercise that office in this year.

John Bramley, labourer, the pageant master of the Labourers in Monk Ward, presents

Thomas Knapton, labourer, to exercise that office in this year.

William Smyth, the pageant master of the Labourers of Micklegate Ward with North Street Postern, presents

Robert Gubbys, labourer, to exercise that office in this year.

f 151

Rents resolute

...

Item, paid to the support of the pageant of the Coronation of the blessed Virgin Mary   2s

...

f 153v

Clothing of the officials according to custom

...

Item, paid to 2 city minstrels for their clothing on Christmas this year [as in preceding (years)]   18s 3d

...

f 154

Gratuities both to the king's minstrels and to those of this city *(as 1452 above, but total is 31s 8d)*

Expenses on the feast of Corpus Christi   *(blank)*

Bridgemasters' Account Rolls   Y : C87:2

mb 1*

...

Returns and rents both within Micklegate Bar and without and the Tofts

For the rent of 1 building in the same place on the land of the Skinners of the said city, paid at the same times   12d

...

For the rent of 1 pageant ⟨...⟩ paid at ⟨the same⟩ times   16d

For the rent of 1 house ⟨of the pageants of diverse⟩ crafts lying on pageant green this year, paid at ⟨the same⟩ times   18s

...

For the rent of the house of the pageants of the Goldsmiths, of 1 building in the same place on the land of John Allen, paid

at the same times, of the pageant (house of) the Waxchandlers
and of the pageant (house of) the Coopers ⟨5s⟩
For the rent of the pageant (house) of the Mercers, 12d. Of the
pageant (house) of the Bakers, 12d. Of the pageant (house) of
the Tapiters, 12d. Of the pageant (house) of the Carpenters, 2s.
⟨And of the pageant (house) of the Tanners,⟩ 12d 6s
...

Mercers' Account Rolls MA: D56PPP

mb 2
(as D56HHH above 1516, but sum is 12d)

1524
City Chamberlains' Books Y: CC2

f 187v
Leasing of the play of Corpus Christi
The first station to the common clerk *(blank)*
The second station is leased to John Blakey for 3s
The third station is leased to John Ellys, merchant, for 2s 4d
The fourth station is leased to James Shipton, merchant,
for 3s 8d
The fifth station is leased to William Nawton, merchant, and to
Cawdewell for 2s
The sixth station is leased to the lord mayor and his
brothers *(blank)*
The seventh station is leased to Ronald Berlay, notary, and Miles
Newton, whereby for the part of the said Ronald, 20d, and for
the part of the said Miles, 8d for the purpose of the
Chamber 2s 3d
x The eighth station is leased to Thomas Flemyng for 2s
x The ninth station is leased to John Clerk, founderer, for 2s
x The tenth station is leased to John Lyster and to Robert Cooke
for 4s
The eleventh station is leased to Robert Wylde, alderman,
for *(blank)*
The twelfth station is leased to *(blank)*, girdler, and *(blank)* 2s
The thirteenth station is leased to no one upon the
Pavement *(blank)*
...

f 194

Rents resolute

...

Item, paid to the support of the pageant of the Coronation of
the blessed Virgin Mary as in preceding (years)   2s

...

f 196v

Clothing according to custom

...

Item, ⟨...⟩ to the city minstrels for their clothing on ⟨...⟩ Christmas
as in preceding (years), etc   27s

...

f 197

Gratuities both of the lord king's minstrels and
of the city minstrels as in preceding (years)

(as 1452 above, but total is 31s 8d)

f 197v

Expenses on the feast of Corpus Christi

First, on bread, 5d. Item, on 10 capons, 6s. Item, on 13 greengeese, 4s. 2½ dozen rabbits, 3s 3d. Item, in payment for
venison, 20d. Item, 2 dozen pullets, 20d. Item, on 3 shoats,
16d. Item, on 3½ dozen pigeons, 5s. Item, on eggs and butter,
14d. Item, on grain, 12d. Item, on spices, on pike, 14s. Item,
on mustard, on vinegar, on verjuice, and on salt, 8d. Item, on
apples, 20d. Item, on cheese, ⟨...⟩ Item, on charcoal, 9d. Item,
on honey, 3d. Item, on faggots, 10d. Item, on 1½ dozen (pots)
of ale, 8s. Item, on beef, mutton, and suet, 4s 6d. Item, on red
wine, claret, white (wine), Rhine (wine), and malmsey, 6s 9d.
Item, on milk, curds, and marrowbones, 16d. Item, on spices,
7s. Item, on hire of vessels, 20d. Item, on wine and bread for
the common clerk, 16d. Item, on a gratuity to the vintners, 8d.
Item, on a gratuity to the bakers, 8d. Item, on a gratuity to the
seneschal of the mayor for his labour and advice, 2s 8d. Item,
on the hire of a cook and a provisioner, 3s. Item, on a gratuity
to Thomas Sadler for the hanging of the Chamber of the aforesaid mayor and his fellow aldermen, etc, 20d. Item, on nails, 3d.
Item, on a gratuity to the housekeeper ⟨...⟩, 8d Item, on a
gratuity to the doorkeepers, 5d. Item, on a white rod, 4d. Item,
on a gratuity ⟨...⟩ of the lord mayor for his labour, 8d.

£4 7s 9d

Mercers' Account Rolls   MA: D56QQQ

mb 2
(as D56HHH above 1516, but sum is 12d)

York Minster Chamberlains' Rolls   YM: E1/62 MP

mb 2
(as E1/61 above 1510)

1525
City Chamberlains' Books   Y: CC2

f 228v

	Leasing of the Corpus Christi Play	
	The first station is leased *(blank)*	*(blank)*
	The second station is leased *(blank)*	2s
	The third station is leased to John Mason, innkeeper, for	4s paid
x	The fourth station is leased to William Nawton	2s
x	The fifth station is leased to Brian Lorde	2s
	The sixth station is leased to Robert Man ⟨...⟩	2s 4d
	The seventh station is leased *(blank)*	*(blank)*
x	The eighth station is leased to Miles Neweton	2s 4d
x	The ninth station is leased to Matthew Hartley, tailor	2s
	The tenth station is leased to John Lyster, tailor	4s 8d
	The eleventh station is leased *(blank)*	*(blank)*

The twelfth station is leased to Robert Hyl, tailor, 12d, and to William Galland, girdler, [12d] in payment for rent but ⟨without setting a precedent⟩   [2s 4d]

The thirteenth station is leased *(blank)*	*(blank)*
The fourteenth station is leased *(blank)*	*(blank)*
The fifteenth station is leased *(blank)*	*(blank)*

f 236
(as f 194 above 1524)

f 239

Clothing

...

Item, paid to the city minstrels for their clothing on Christmas from a new ⟨grant⟩ from the mayor and the council ⟨while his pleasure lasts⟩   40s

Payments both of the minstrels of the lord king
and of the minstrels ⟨of this city⟩
(as 1452 above)

f 240
Expenses on the feast of Corpus Christi
First, on bread, 5d; on pain-demaine with the trencher bread,
9½d; on ale, 10s 3d; on beef, mutton, marrowbones, and suet,
4s 4d; on milk, 4d; on 10 capons, 6s 8d; on ⟨...⟩, 4s 2d; on 2
dozen rabbits, 4s; on pullets, 21d; on 4 shoats, 21d; on 3 dozen
pigeons, 18d; on eggs and butter, 15d; on ⟨...⟩, 15d; on 5 pike,
16s; on mustard, on vinegar, on verjuice, and on salt 6d; on
cheese, 2s; on charcoal, 9d; on faggots, 10d; on claret, on Rhine
(wine), on white (wine), and on malmsey, 6s 2d; on payment for
venison, 3s 4d; on spices, 6s 10½d; on the hire of vessels, 2s 6d;
on spices, 6s 10d; on a gratuity for the vintners, 8d; on a gratuity
to the bakers, 8d; on a gratuity to the seneschal, 2s 8d; on a
gratuity to the cooks, 3s; on a gratuity to the housekeeper ⟨...⟩;
on a gratuity to the bakers, 8d; on rushes and yeast, 6½d; on
wine for the common clerk, 16d; on a gratuity to Thomas Sadler
for the hanging of the Chamber with the nails, 23d; on the
footing of the benches and trestles, 2d; on the hire of cups with
broken 'trusys', 5d; on a gratuity to a certain labourer, 2d; on a
gratuity to the doorkeepers, with a gratuity given to Thomas
Goodbarne, 12d; on the hire of the Chamber, 6s 8d
Total of the aforesaid expenses £5 20½d

Mercers' Account Rolls MA: D57RRR

mb 2
(as D56HHH above 1516, but sum is 12d)

1526
City Chamberlains' Books Y: CC3(1)

p 37
Leasing of the Corpus Christi Play
The first station to the common clerk   *(blank)*
x   The second station is leased thus: to John Blakey, John Cawlebek,
and Richard Esschby   3s 4d
x   The third station is leased thus: to John Wilkynson   4s 6d
x   The fourth station is leased thus: to James Shypton   3s
x   The fifth station is leased thus: to Richard Bayteman   2s 1d

The sixth station is leased thus: to the lord mayor, Brian
Lorde   6d
The seventh station to the duke of Richmond and to his
companions, and from Thomas Wilman for his house, 3d; and
from Archibald Foster, tailor, for his house, 2d; and from Widow
Bekwyth, 4d   9d
x   The eighth station is leased thus: to Matthew Hartley   3s 4d
x   The ninth station is leased thus: to John Lyster   5s
x   The tenth station is leased thus: to Thomas Nycholson   4s
The eleventh station to the lady mayoress   *(blank)*
                    Total 27s 3d

p 61
                    Clothing according to custom

...

Item, paid to the city minstrels for their clothing at Christmas
from a new grant from the mayor and the council while his
pleasure lasts, etc   40s

...

            Payments both of the minstrels of the lord king
            and of the city minstrels as in preceding (years)
(as 1452 above, but total is 31s 8d)

p 63
                Expenses on the feast of Corpus Christi
First, for leavened bread and on pain-demaine, 4s 8d. Item, for
ale, 7s 6d. Item, on beef, 21d. Item, on mutton and marrowbones, 22d. Item, on 11 greengeese, 3s 5d. Item, on capons, 4s.
Item, on pullets, 22d. Item, on shoats, 16d. Item, on pigeons,
12d. Item, on milk and on curds, 2s. Item on *(blank)*
                    Total £3 19s 8½d

Mercers' Account Rolls   MA: D57SSS

mb 2
(as D56HHH above 1516, but sum is 12d)

1527
House Books   Y: B11

f 23*   *(8 October)*

...

note   William Lowrans, tilemaker, by the order of the said mayor was then appointed, and he will be a contributor to the pageant of the Tilers of the said city. And he will only pay with them in everything yearly from henceforth just as they do and not otherwise ...

City Chamberlains' Books   Y : CC 3 (1)

p 133

Leasing of the Corpus Christi Play

	The first station (is) before the common clerk	*(blank)*
	The second station is leased to John Blakey	2s
x	The third station is leased to John Mason and John Wylkynson	4s 6d
x	The fourth station is leased to James Shypton for	3s
	The fifth station is leased to Richard Baytman	22d
	The sixth station is leased before the mayor and his fellows, etc	*(blank)*
x	The seventh station is leased to Reginald Beysley for	3s 4d
x	The eighth station is leased to Thomas Flemyng	2s
x	The ninth station is leased to Matthew Hartley and his companions	3s
	The tenth station is leased to John Lyster, sheriff, and William Mullans, barber	4s 8d
	The eleventh station is leased before the lady mayoress and her sisters, etc	*(blank)*
	The twelfth station is leased to Thomas Nicholson for	4s
	The thirteenth station upon the Pavement is leased to no one	*(blank)*

24s 6d

Total 28s 4d

p 149

...

Labourers

3s 4d to the master, John Blody
⟨...⟩, John Smyth, pageant master   for Gilbert Wylson
of the Labourers of Micklegate

Richard Studley, pageant master
of the Labourers of Walmgate   for Robert Stodderd, recently
Bar   labourer there

(blank) Leday, pageant master of Bootham Bar	for Thomas Halyland, recently master there
John Bell, pageant master of Monk Bar this year	for William Mell, recently master there

p 157

...

Gratuities both for the minstrels of the lord king and of the city minstrels in preceding (years)

First, paid to the city minstrels as a gratuity for the period of Easter as in preceding (years), etc   3s 4d

Item, paid to the minstrels of the lord king on the vigil of St Bartholomew the apostle   20s

23s 4d

Item, paid for the wages of the waits, aside from all things received of this city at that time   17s

To various players at the Common Hall, etc   6s

examined Total 46s 4d

pp 158-9

...

42s 8d
Expenses on the feast of Corpus Christi

First, on the bread called leavened bread, 4s. Item, on the pain-demaine, 12d. Item, on ale, 6s 3d. Item, on beef, 2s. Item, for marrowbones and mutton, 20d. Item, for capons, 4s. Item, for greengeese, 3s 4d. Item, for pullets, 22d. Item, for shoats, 18d. Item, for rabbits, 16d. Item, for butter and milk 6d. Item, for eggs, 10d. Item, for cheese, 16d. Item, for salt and for mustard, 4d. Item, for vinegar and for verjuice, 4d. Item, for honey, 4d. Item, for an ointment box, 4d. Item, for faggots, 2s 8d. Item, for 1 (blank) sacks of charcoal, 4d. Item, for spices, 5s. Item, for pickerel, 13s. Item, for apples, 12d. Item, for the hire of cups, 3d. Item, on the hire of vessels, 2s. Item, for flour from wheat, 14d. Item, for rushes, 6d. Item, for red wine, claret, and white (wine), 6d. Item, to the Bakers of the city for wine according to custom, 8d. Item, for 3 dozen trenchers, 3d. | Item, as a gratuity for 1 'ffowme', 6d. Item, on expenses incurred by Thomas Clerk, deputy of the common clerk for keeping the register over and above bread, ale, and wine, 2s 4d. Item, on a gratuity to the cook, 2s 8d. Item, on a gratuity to the housekeeper, 6d. Item, on a gratuity to the doorkeeper, 3d. Item, on a gratuity to the seneschal, 2s. Item, on a gratuity for the baker, 4d. Item, on a gratuity to the provisioner, 4d. Item, on a gratuity to Thomas Sadler for the hanging of the Chamber, 20d. Item, to John Burton for the white rod, 4d.

£3 16s 9d

       examined Total of the said expenses £3 16s 9d

...

Mercers' Account Rolls MA: D57TTT

mb 2
(as D56HHH above 1516, but sum is 12d)

York Minster Chamberlains' Rolls YM: E1/64 MP

mb 2
(as E1/61 above 1510)

1528
City Chamberlains Rolls Y: C6:6

mb 1*
...

From the rent of the first station, nothing, because the common clerk has it

From the rent of the second station, in the usual place, let thus to James Hopperton   2s 8d

From the rent of the third station, in the usual place, let thus to John Mason   3s 10d

From the rent of the fourth station, in the usual place, let thus to James Shipton, gentleman   2s 8d

Lease of the Corpus Christi Play

From the rent of the fifth station, in the usual place, let thus to Richard Bayteman   2s

From the rent of the sixth station, in the usual place, let thus to Henry Wodde, waxchandler   2s 4d

From the rent of the seventh station, in the usual place, nothing, because the lady mayoress

From the rent of the eighth station, of Archibald Foster for a small part of the rent thence because the lord mayor stood there   8d

From the rent of the ninth station, in the usual place, let thus to Matthew Hartley and to Humphrey Stevynson   3s

From the rent of the tenth station, in the usual place, let thus
to John Lyster   4s 8d
From the rent of the eleventh station, let thus ro Robert Wylde,
alderman   nothing
From the rent of the twelfth station, let thus to Thomas
Nicholson   2s
And from the rent of the thirteenth station on the Pavement
this year   nothing
...

City Chamberlains' Books   Y : CC3(1)

p 232*
Leasing of the Corpus Christi Play
Concerning the first station it is leased etc before the common
clerk   *(blank)*
o   From James Hopperton for the second station   2s 8d
o   From John Mason for the third station   3s 10d
o   From James Shypton for the fourth station   2s 8d
o   From Henry Wode for the sixth station before the aforesaid
Henry   2s 4d
From the seventh station before the lady mayoress   *(blank)*
o   From Richard Bayteman for ⟨...⟩ bunting of the Chamber
⟨...⟩ year   2s
From the sixth station before the lord mayor and his fellows
and from Archibald Foster on the other side of the street   8d
From Matthew Hartley and Humphrey Stevynson, embroiderer,
for rent for the seventh station apportioned to them in
Stonegate   3s
From the eighth station at the gates of the Minster which has
been let thus to John Lyster   4s 8d
From the ninth station at the door of Robert Wyld,
alderman   *(blank)*
From Thomas Nicholson for the tenth station at Goodramgate 2s
Total 23s 10d examined

p 247
...
Labourers

| John Halyfax, pageant master of Walmgate for Richard Studly | Thomas Bemyman, pageant master of Micklegate Ward; for Gilbert Wylson this year |

William Dobson of Jelygate,
pageant master of Bootham Bar

p 254
                Gratuities both for the minstrels of the lord king
                      and of the city minstrels

First, paid to the minstrels of the lord king on the Friday before
the feast of Bartholomew   20s
...

p 255
                  Expenses on the feast of Corpus Christi

First, on bread called leavened bread, 8s. Item, on pain-demaine,
16d. On ale, 18s; on beef, 2s; on mutton, marrowbones, and
suet, 22d; on *(blank)* capons, 5d; on greengeese, 3s 8d; on
pullets, 20s; on shoats, 18d; on *(blank)* rabbits, 2s 4d; on butter
and on milk, 6d; on eggs, 10d; on cheese, 21d; on salt and
mustard, 3d; on vinegar and verjuice, 4d; on honey, 4d; on a kid,
14d; on pike, 16s; on spices, 5d; on pigeons, 8d; on 2 herons,
3d; on a carver, 3d; on apples, 20d; on wine, 7s 9d; on the hire
of cups, 5d; on 2 sacks of charcoal, 6d; on the hire of vessels, 2s;
on faggots, 22d; on a gratuity given to the searchers of the
Bakers, along with the aforesaid pageant masters for a gallon of
wine, 8d; on payment for the said gallon to the searchers of
the Vintners, etc, 8d; on a gratuity to the seneschal, 2s 8d; on
a gratuity to the cook and to the provisioner, 3s; on a gratuity
to the housekeeper, 8d; on a gratuity to the bakers, 4d; on a
gratuity to the doorkeeper along with the hanging of the
Chamber, 12d; on a gratuity to the waits, 16d; to John Burton,
squire of the mayor for the white rod, 4d. On [the feast of]
(blank)
              Total of the aforesaid expenses £4 10s 11d

Bridgemasters' Account Rolls   Y : C87 : 3

mb 1
...

Returns and rents both within Micklegate Bar and without and the Tofts

For the rent of the Skinners of the said city for a building in
the same place, paid at the same times   12d
...
For the rent of 1 pageant house of the Weavers in the same

place, paid ⟨at the same times⟩   16d

...

For the rent of 1 garden recently on the land of John Hall,
alderman, with the pageant (house of) the Chandlers and the
pageant (house of) the Coopers,   5s
For the rent *(blank)* of the Mercers, Bakers, Tapiters, Carpenters,
Tanners, paid at the same times   6s

...

For the rent of 1 house of the pageants of diverse crafts, lying
on pageant green: this year   18s

...

Mercers' Account Rolls   M A : D 5 7 U U U

mb 2
(as D56HHH above 1516, but sum is 12d)

Wax for burning   And for the topping of 6 torches and for 7 dozen (and?) 2
pounds of new stuff and for the manufacture, viz, of the old
stuff, 28s. ...

1529
York Minster Chamberlains' Rolls   Y M : E 1 / 6 6 *M P*

mb 2*
(as E1/61 above 1510)

1533
Corpus Christi Account Rolls   Y : C 1 0 2 : 2

mb 3

...

Necessary   And the said master seeks to be allowed for various necessary
expenses   expenses incurred by him this year, viz, on the general procession
on the day after Corpus Christi. First, paid to clerks carrying
the cross before the procession, 4d. And paid to 2 boys carrying
candelabras, 2d. And paid to 4 clerks carrying the baudekin, 8d.
⟨...⟩ and paid as a gratuity to the cantors, 8d; ⟨...⟩ paid ⟨...⟩ to
the constables of the Hall of the cathedral of St Peter as a gratuity,
12d. And paid to the doorkeeper of St Peter's, 4d. Item, to the
sacristan of Holy Trinity, 4d. And paid to clerks ⟨...⟩, 12d. And
paid to 6 men carrying 6 torches, 12d. And paid to 2 men
carrying the shrine in the chest, 8d. ...

York Minster Chamberlains' Rolls   YM : E1/71a MP

mb 2
(as E1/61 above 1510)

1534
Corpus Christi Account Rolls   Y : C102:3

mb 3

...

Allowances
for necessary
expenses

And the said master seeks to be allowed for various necessary
expenses incurred by him this year, viz, on the general procession
on the day after Corpus Christi. First, paid to the clerk carrying
the cross before the procession, 2d. And paid to 2 boys carrying
candelabras, 2d. And paid to 4 clerks carrying the baudekin, 8d.
And paid to the chaplains carrying the shrine, as a gratuity, 8d.
And paid as a gratuity to the cantors, 8d. And paid to the parish
clerks, singing, 12d. And paid to 6 men carrying 6 torches, 12d.
And paid to 2 men carrying the shrine, 8d. And for expenses
incurred at the same time, 8d. And paid to the clerks of the
vestry of the cathedral church of St Peter as a gratuity, 12d. And
paid to the doorkeeper of St Peter's and to the sacristan of Holy
Trinity as a gratuity, 8d. ...

1535
Corpus Christi Account Rolls   Y : C103:1

mb 3

...

Allowance
for necessary
expenses

And the said master seeks to be allowed for various necessary
expenses incurred by him this year, viz, on the general procession
on the day after Corpus Christi. First, paid to the clerk carrying
the cross before the procession, 2d. And paid to 2 boys carrying
candelabras, 2d. And paid to 4 clerks carrying the baudekin, 8d.
And paid to the chaplains carrying the shrine as a gratuity, 8d.
And paid as a gratuity to the cantors, 8d. And paid to the parish
clerks, singing, 12d. And paid to 6 men carrying 6 torches, 12d.
And paid to 2 men carrying the shrine, 8d. And for expenses
incurred at the same time, 8d. And paid to the clerks of the
vestry of the cathedral church of St Peter as a gratuity, 12d. And
paid to the doorkeeper of St Peter's and to the sacristan of Holy
Trinity as a gratuity, 8d. ...

1536
York Minster Chamberlains' Rolls   Y M : E 1 / 7 0 *MP*

mb 2*
(as E1/61 above 1510)

1538
York Minster Chamberlains' Rolls   Y M : E 1 / 7 3 *PM*

mb 2*
(as E1/61 above 1510)

1541
Corpus Christi Account Rolls   Y : C 1 0 3 : 2

mb 3
...

Allowances for necessary expenses

And the said master seeks to be allowed for various necessary expenses incurred by him this year, viz, on the general procession on the day after Corpus Christi. First, paid to the clerk carrying the cross before the procession, 2d. And paid to 2 boys carrying candelabras, 2d. And paid to 4 clerks carrying the baudekin, 8d. And paid to the chaplains carrying the shrine, 8d. And paid to the parish clerks, singing, 12d. And paid as a gratuity to the cantors, 8d. And paid to 6 men carrying 6 torches, 12d. And paid to 2 men carrying the shrine, 8d. And for expenses (incurred) at the same time, 8d. And paid to the clerks of the vestry of the cathedral church of St Peter as a gratuity, 12d. And paid to the doorkeeper of St Peter's and the parish clerk of the church of Holy Trinity on the High Street, 8d. ... And paid for the meal of the master and the 6 wardens around the feast of Corpus Christi, according to custom, 5s. ...

1546
York Minster Chamberlains' Rolls   Y M : E 1 / 7 4 *MP*

mb 2*
... And paid to John Gachet for his room above the doors of the (Minster) close on Corpus Christi day, 3s 4 ⟨d⟩ ...

1551
A/Y Memorandum Book   Y : E 20

f 292* *(14 August)* *Tapiters*
See the many other ordinances of this craft made on the 14th day of August in the year of our lord the king Edward VI, as they plainly appear in the Book of Thomas Appleyard, then mayor.

First, it was ordered and agreed as much for the common good of all the people of the lord king as for that of the craftsmen of the aforesaid craft, that no craftsman of the abovesaid craft shall work at the same craft, except while the light of day can reasonably suffice him for working with the tool of the said craft called the shuttle, under penalty of 10s to be paid as often as anyone of them has transgressed against the said ordinance, two-thirds to the commons of this city and one-third to the said craft for the upkeep of the pageant and play of Corpus Christi supported by the said craftsmen.

...

f 292v

...

Item, that each master of the abovesaid craft in his own person will go about with the pageant of the said craft on the feast of Corpus Christi, and will work for the control of the same, until the play of the said craft shall have been properly completed in the stations to be assigned and ordered by the city, in accordance with the ordinance of the same city, unless someone of them shall have been hindered by age, weakness, or illness, or by some other lawful and likely cause of release, in which case he will provide and ordain another adequate deputy in his place, and if any of them shall have defaulted in any particular of this ordinance, he is to pay to the commons and to the craft, 12d, to be applied in equal portions, etc.

...

Translations: Appendix 1

f 10v

...

Bakers because
below

[Item, it is ordained and established by common assent of the Bakers of York that no member of their guild shall henceforth sell any small round loaf or round loaf of pain-demaine to any regrater of bread to be placed for sale, on pain of paying half a mark, 40d of it to the Chamber and 40d to the said Bakers' pageant of Corpus Christi.]

...

f 19   *Glovers*

Ordinances of the Glovers

... First, with regard to the first constitution, let it be effected in the following form, that is, that henceforth each member of the said guild who will engage himself as master in their trade will pay on his engagement, 3s 4d to the Chamber of the mayoralty, and to the maintenance of the light of Corpus Christi of the said guild, 5s.

Item, that henceforth no master of the said guild will keep his shop open on Sunday to display or to sell that which pertains to his trade, except on the feast of Pentecost, the common fairs, the feast of St Peter ad Vincula, and the feast of St Michael following thereupon, on pain of 20d to be paid for each forfeiture to the said Chamber of the mayoralty and for the light of Corpus Christi, 20d.

Item that no master of the said guild will engage or assign any apprentice as journeyman during the year following the completion of his term of apprenticeship, until he has worked under hire for one whole year with any master of the said guild and has been found skilful and competent to work in their trade, on pain of 3s 4d to be paid to the Chamber of the mayoralty aforesaid, and to the said light of Corpus Christi, 3s 4d.

f 20v

...

The ordinances of the Chandlers

...

First, that each master who will come to take a place in the said guild, let him be proved competent and knowledgeable to work and take a place in the said guild, and that he will pay upon his entry when he first holds shop and occupies it as master, 6s 8d. That is, one half for the use of the said guild to maintain their said pageant, and the other half to the Council Chamber for the use and profit of the commonalty of the aforementioned city.

...

f 21

Scriveners of Text

...

And that no member of the said guild act contrary to this ordinance in any point aforesaid, he will pay 20s of sterling, that is, 10s to the Council Chamber and 10s to the use of their pageant and the lights of their said guild.

...

f 22

Skinners

...

First, that all the forfeitures which are due in the said guild and are to come, be levied and one half of these paid to the Council Chamber and the other half to the said guild to maintain their pageant and their light.

...

Item, that all upholders people who sell furs within the said city or the suburbs be contributors to pay toward their pageant of Corpus Christi.

Item, if any one of the said guild be rebel or disrupt, speak ill of or disobey the searchers or the pageant masters of the same guild who are at the time duly doing their duty, let him pay 6s 8d, one half to the Chamber and the other half to the said guild, to maintain their pageant and their light. ...

f 22v

Here of the Bowers

...

Item, that if any member of the said guild take an apprentice in the said craft, he will pay on his first entrance to the use of their pageant, 3s 4d.

...

f 26

The ordinances of the Curriers
The same (ordinances are) in the new register

To their honourable lord mayor of the city of York, we entreat you humbly, if it be pleasing to you to consider the poor situation of the said guild of the Curriers of the said city, how they are charged with a pageant of very great costs and too grievous to be borne, for they are people weaker and poorer than they used to be before these times and used to have other support and aid to sustain their said pageant before these times: that is, from each apprentice of the said guild on his first entrance to the said guild, 12d and from each servant who takes pay in the said guild each year, 4d, concerning which they beg, if it be pleasing to you, that henceforth no apprentice be taken in the said guild for a shorter term nor for longer than for six years, and that he will pay on his entrance, in all, 2s. That is, 12d to the use of their said pageant and 12d to the Council Chamber, and each servant per year 4d to the use of their said pageant as it used to be before these times.

  Item, that each master when he is enfranchised and enters the guild for the first time as master, that he will pay to the use of the said pageant, 40d.

...

f 26v*

The ordinances of the Coopers

To their very honourable and very reverent lord mayor of the city of York, your poor concitizens, the Coopers of York, entreat very humbly that as they have a very great charge against their impoverished state to sustain and maintain their pageant and play of this day of Corpus Christi, inasmuch as their guild and they themselves are very poor people, so very distressed as to

possessions, and within a short time their situation has greatly
worsened, and also the Joiners who were with them to maintain
the said pageant have been separated from them, may it please
your very bounteous lordship to make amendment of their said
guild to ordain and allow to be registered before you that whoever henceforth has raised a new shop and first takes an engagement as master in the said city, will pay at his entry 6s 8d, one
half to the Chamber of the mayoralty, the other half to their
searchers of the said guild, to maintain their aforementioned
pageant, and this as an act of charity.

Item, it is ordained by all the craftsmen of Coopercraft aforesaid, that each man of the same guild, and if the said work be
found to be badly done by the searchers of the same guild, that
he will forfeit the pennies as follows: that is, for one bucket not
properly made, 12d, and for each other vessel of the same value,
12d, if it be found faulty in timber or in workmanship. He who
made it or had it made will pay the 12d, one half to the Chamber
of the mayoralty on the Ouse Bridge, and the other half to the
support of their pageant of Corpus Christi.
...

f 29v* *Barbers*

[Item, that those who are aliens or other outsiders (who) practise
medicine or surgery in the city and derive benefit for their
business be contributors to sustain and maintain their said
pageant and their light on pain of 6s 8d, to be paid in the
aforesaid manner.

[Because below   Item, if anyone be rebellious to the said guild concerning
on folio 72]   attendance at their meeting to organize necessary provisions for
their pageant light or other legal ordinance and honest business,
unless he have reasonable excuse, he will pay as appropriate
garnishment one pound of wax for their light.]
...

f 30
            These are the ordinances of the Capmakers of York
...
Item, that anyone in whose possession such manner of false work
be found, each time be fined by 3s, of which 2s will be raised for
the use of the commonalty of the said city, and 12d for the use
of the pageant of the aforementioned Capmakers. ...

f 30v

Cardmakers

To the honourable and wise lords, the mayor and aldermen of
the city of York, let it be shown, if it be pleasing to you, by your
simple neighbours of the commonalty of the aforementioned
city, John Baker, John de Burton, William Orgoner, Thomas
Junour, William de Bredon, Robert de Houeden, Henry del
Chirche, cardmakers, and by the other masters of the guild of
the Cardmakers of the said city, for the common benefit and
in relief and aid of their said guild, which is on the point of
perishing on account of evil people who have fled and taken
themselves out of the said city with goods and chattels of other
loyal people, for whom, by your wise advice and counsel, due
remedy can be made in this way for the future, if it be pleasing
to you: that is, that no such foreigner who has fled or come
from foreign places be put to work in the said guild for more
than two days unless he has sufficient reference for himself by
authentic letters from 'south seal' concerning his life and his
good reputation, or unless he is able to find sufficient pledges
to act as guarantees for him and for his deeds, on pain of 6s 8d,
to be paid to the Chamber and another 6s 8d, to be pageant of
their said guild by him who will be found acting contrary to this
ordinance

...

f 32

[Tanners, Glovers, Parchment workers

...

By which it is ordained that each one of the said craftsmen who
henceforth buy any woolly skins from the said Butchers, except
for those which have their ears, heads, and the wool intact, will
pay for each contravention for which he is found guilty, 3s 4d
to the Chamber of the mayoralty, and another 3s 4d for the
maintenance of the light of Corpus Christi of the guild of the
one in whom the fault is found.]

...

f 33v

Pinmakers' craft First, it is ordained and accepted that no master of the guild of
Pinmakers henceforth take in nor retain any foreigner of the said
guild to work with him, unless he be placed in the said guild to

serve in the manner of apprentice, as is meet by ancient usage and custom and just as is the custom in the city of London for vagrants and vagabonds and in other cities of the realm, on pain of a fine of 40d to the Council Chamber, and 40d to the maintenance of the pageant of the aforementioned guild. ...

f 34

Saddlers

... Firstly, if there should be any debate on a matter concerning their guild by anyone of the abovesaid guild, he who feels himself grieved or abused will reveal his grievance to the masters of the said guild, and they will order redress in due manner according to that which will seem best to them in good faith and reason, and anyone who is found to be rebellious or contrary in this manner will pay to the searchers and governors or the said guild to support the pageant of Corpus Christi, 10s and 5s to the Common Chamber of the mayor and the commonalty of the city of York. ...

ff 45-5v *Dyers*
[Item, that each one who henceforth takes up for the first time the position of master in the said guild, pay from his entry to the pageant masters of the said guild for the use of the pageant and to the Chamber of the mayor of the city, 20s in equal parts. ɪ Item, that each apprentice who will be named and received into the said guild henceforth pay on his entry to the said guild, for the use of the pageant and to the Chamber, 20s.
...
Item, it is accorded and ordained by all the masters aforesaid that he who breaks or contravenes any of these articles named above and for this be convicted by four masters of the said guild will be held to pay forthwith to the said masters of their said pageant for the time being and to the aforementioned Chamber, 20s.]
...

f 51v

Cutlers

... For each time he thus be convicted he will pay 40d, one half to the Council Chamber of the mayoralty, and the other half for the support of their pageant of Corpus Christi. ...

f 58v

Potters

...

Firstly, if any servant of the said guild be found with petty theft to the value of 6d or more, that thereafter no master of the said guild will give him any work to work on, on pain of 20s to be paid to the Chamber of the mayoralty for the use of the commons and for the support of the pageant of Corpus Christi of the said guild in equal portions.

...

f 64

Painters, Stainers, Goldbeaters

...

First, it is ordained and provided that all the masters and crafts-men aforesaid, by their common consent, assemble on the first Sunday after Easter each year to elect their searchers for the coming year, and to make decisions concerning their pageant of Corpus Christi, and to do other things needed for the gover-nance of the said pageant, and that none will absent himself at this time without reasonable cause, on pain of 6s 8d to pay, one half to the Chamber and the other to their guild for the support of their said pageant.

...

Item, if any man of another guild engages in and is accustomed to work in the guilds abovesaid with paintbrush for fulling or any manner of colour, if he be franchised, let him pay to the pageant of the said craftsmen, and if he be not franchised, let him franchise himself and pay to the same pageant on the afore-mentioned penalty each time that he be convicted.

f 76 *Cordwainers*

...

And also since the aforesaid craftsmen bear yearly the heavy expenses and great burdens of their pageant and of the many players in the same and of torches of great beauty in the proces-sion of Corpus Christi Day and in the minster of St Peter at York, and of other expenses more than certain others of the various crafts do, therefore, they seek and humbly request that it might be confirmed and ordered for them for relief of their heavy burdens and expenses, as the Tapiters of this city have by the record and enrolment here in the Chamber, viz, that any Scot or other foreigner who had not been born in the kingdom and land of England coming to this city, and who set up as a master in the aforesaid craft of Cordwainers, that at his first setting up he must pay 40s for the use of the commons of this city, and another 40s to be applied to the aforesaid craft of the Cordwainers.

...

f 77v *Cordwainers*

...

Item, that if anyone of the aforesaid craft has been elected to any office in that craft, whether that of searcher or of master of the guild; or that of any of the four masters holding office for for the pageant and light of Corpus Christi, or for the care of any other materials pertaining by virtue of some office to the good rule and order of the said craft, and if he has refused, objected to, or resisted taking it upon himself and performing it, that then he will lose it and pay 10s sterling under in the aforesaid way.

...

f 90*

Ordinances of the Barbers

First, it was ordered by the unanimous consent and full will of all the masters of the craft of Barbers of this city of York, that none of them would engage in or work at anything or any task pertaining to his craft on any Sunday, except only bleeding men fixed in infirmities and making other cures and remedies for the sick, and if anyone dared to act contrary to this constitution, for each violation he will pay 6s 8d to be applied in equal proportions to the use and profit of the commons and the support of the pageant and burdens of the said craft.

Item, that all foreigners and strangers, whoever they were, practising medicine or the art of surgery within this city who shall receive some payment for their service must contribute yearly to sustain and maintain the aforesaid pageant of the Barbers and their light and the other burdens of the same, under penalty of 6s 8d, to be applied as stated above.

Item, if any one of the aforesaid craft were unco-operative and refused to come to their meetings providing for the necessary order and provision of his pageant and light, or of any other ordinance, when he has been adequately warned by law-abiding and honest men, unless he shall have shown a reasonable excuse, he will lose and pay to the maintenance of the light of the afore-said craft, 3s 4d, as often as he shall have been guilty of this ⟨...⟩, to be paid to the Chamber and the craft.

...

f 90v

...

Item, that the searchers and masters of the pageant of the said craft will be chosen in any year on the next Monday after the Feast of the Nativity of St John the Baptist and on the same Monday, the searchers of the previous year ⟨shall render⟩ their account to the masters of the aforesaid craft then present there, concerning all things occurring in the previous year, under a penalty of 3s 4d as is specified above concerning those who do not come when warned, to be forfeited to the said craft and Chamber.

...

ff 128v-9* *(Marginal note to Fishmongers' ordinance)*
[This penalty of 20s was moderated in the time of William Bowes, mayor, to 6s 8d to the Chamber and 40d to the craft in the power of those who are not tenants of the commons on Foss Bridge, at the will of the mayor, and as to the tenants of the commons ⟨...⟩, for us, let 40d go to the Chamber at the disposition of the mayor and what will content the craft from the 40d.]

f 283
Curriers more after that in the other book on folio 21 with the folio folded over.

® These ordi-
nances are
corrected anew.
Other ordinances
are added to
these new ones
in the time of
mayor Edward
Fawcett

All the masters of the Curriers' craft of this city (beg) their honourable lord, the mayor of this city of York, to consider their poor estate and how yearly they are burdened with a pageant in the Corpus Christi Play and with other burdens all but un-supportable by them, and to graciously grant them that no one of the aforesaid craft may take any apprentice in the said craft for a term less than of six years, under penalty of 6s 8d to be paid in equal portions to the Council Chamber of the city and to the aforesaid craft for the support of their pageant by (any) master who shall have done the contrary, and under the penalty of taking the forfeiture of the apprentice contrary to the term of this ordinance. And that as soon as any master of the aforesaid craft shall have accepted any apprentice, he should pay for him at his first entrance 12d to the aforesaid Chamber and another 12d to the aforesaid craft.

Item, that any assistant who is to be contracted in the aforesaid craft and receiving reward or salary, if he has been an apprentice to that craft in the aforesaid city, shall pay 4d yearly to the masters of the aforesaid pageant, and if he has not been an apprentice, he shall pay 8d yearly to the said pageant.

Item, that any assistant who has well and faithfully served his master in the aforesaid craft for six years or longer according to the term contracted between them shall pay at his first opening of his shop 3s 4d for the support of the aforesaid pageant. And if any foreigner has come to the city to work at the aforesaid craft and was not an apprentice in the aforesaid craft in the aforesaid city, he shall pay 6s 8d to the aforesaid Council Chamber and 6s 8d to the support of their pageant at the first opening of a shop.

...

Translations: Appendix II

Inventories of the Guild of Corpus Christi 1416-1546

1416 Y : C99:1

	mb 1d

Ornaments and tools of the fraternity

Item, the same wardens give an account of the 10 torches belonging to the said fraternity for the veneration of the body of Christ,

Total of torches 10

Standards

And of 6 standards embroidered with chalices to be set about the 6 torches before the dead,

Total of standards 6

'Castles'

And of 10 painted 'castles' with 10 small canvas bags to cover them,

Total of 'castles' 10

Banners

And of 40 embroidered banners, together with 1 canvas bag to put them in, together with papers,

Total of banners 40

(Protective) cloths

And of 10 (protective) cloths of canvas for the carrying of the said 10 torches in the Corpus Christi procession,

Total of cloths 10

Roundelets

And of 3 dozen wooden devices, ie, roundelets, for placing atop the revets,

Total of roundelets 36

Revets

And of 40 revets received from their predecessors,
And of 40 revets bought new.

Cups

And of 48 wooden cups, which are old, worn out, and do not hold liquid,
And of 24 cups bought new,
Total of new cups 24

Napkins

And of 1 linen table napkin, containing 14 ells in length,
And of 2 table napkins, each one containing 13 ells in length,
And of 2 table napkins, each one containing 10 ells in length,
And of 1 table napkin of twill work containing *(blank)* (ells) in length from the gift of sir William de Neuton,

Towel

And of 1 listed towel of twill work containing 14 ells in length from the gift of John Lee and his wife,
Total of napkins 6

Naprons

And of 6 naprons of linen cloth for the chief men,
Total of naprons 6

Cooking pots

And of 1 large cooking pot given by Olive de Cotyngham,
Total of cooking pots 1

Brass pots

And of 1 large brass pot given by Alice de Welton
And of 1 large brass pot given by sir John Crome, lately vicar in the choir of the church of York,
And of 1 large brass pot given by Margaret Sowreby; indeed it is not received as above,
Total of brass pots 3

Tin vessels

And of 6 dozen tin vessels in stock and 1 dish and 2 platters,
And of a half-dozen tin vessels from the bequest of Beatrice Lathom
Total of tin vessels, 6½ dozen in stock,
1 dish and 2 platters

Salt-cellars

And of 18 salt-cellars of pewter,
Total of cellars 18

Cleaning cloths

And of 2 canvas cloths for cleaning the vessels,
Total 2

Chaplets

And of 6 chaplets with 6 other little writings, together with the reasons for the election of the chief men,
Total of chaplets 6

Books of ordinances	And of 2 books, one of the old ordinances and the other of the new, together with the names inscribed, Total of books 2
Letters of indulgences	And of 2 letters of indulgences, 1 from the archbishop of York, and the other from the bishop of Carlisle, Total of letters 2
Boxes	And of 2 boxes and locks for the tools to be kept therein, Total of boxes 2
A piece of silver	And of 1 silver piece from the gift of sir Richard Arowis, former vicar of the church of St Mary-super-Bishophill, Total of pieces 1
Maple cups	And of 1 maple cup decorated with silver from the gift of Agnes Wyman, Total 1
Spoons	And of 2 silver spoons received from sir Thomas Tanfeld, vicar, for his entry, Total of spoons 2

1449-51   Y: C99:3

mb 1

...

Wherefore the said wardens reckon and seek an allowance: and first, for expenses and payments made on the silver shrine with its appurtenances, viz, for 1 jewel, silvered and gilded, called the brooch, set at the top of the bell tower. Item, on roofing and covering of the 4 parts of the same shrine, called izles or roofs, gilded with silver, together with the ornamenting and beautification of the northern side of the same shrine with gold and silver chains and rings. Item, of 1 silver-gilt covering furnished for the large beryl or crystal called the monstrance and wrought by John Stultyng, as they appear together, 4lb 6oz 3½qu in weight of gold and silver for gilding, price 5s the oz, total £13 9s 4½d. And for the improvement of a certain jewel containing the relics of saints, that is, with 1 round foot of silver and gilded, 1½oz in weight, price 7s 6d, with 1 crystalline stone set in the midst of the jewel, price 3s 4d. And of 1 silver-gilt jewel furnished for the beadle in the sign of the fraternity and wrought by the same John Stultyng in the form of 2 angels genuflecting at the tabernacle and supporting the chalice with the Host to the honour of Corpus Christi, as though in the presence of the Father and the Son and the Holy Spirit, as it appears, 8¼oz in weight, price 5s the oz, total 41s 3d. And of 2 larger images, that is to say, of Peter and Paul, gilded with silver with 24 other silvern and enamelled images wrought by George Wylardby, together proportionally, 8oz 3½qu in weight, price 30d the oz, total 22s 2d. Item, paid to the same George for the working of each image, 16d, total 34s 8d. And of 1 golden tabernacle received earlier from stock and here put into the shrine, price 15s. And of 1 golden ring with a sapphire set in it, price 20s. And of another golden ring with a pearl set in it, price 4s. And 1 golden necklace from the gift of the late sir John Castell, price 5s. And of 1 golden necklace from the bequest of Joan Nalton, price 11s 4d. And of 1 silvern necklace set with gilt, price 2s 6d. And of 1 precious stone called adamant set therein, price 10s. And of 1 silvern circlet selected from stock and set on the shrine, price 6s 8d. And of 8 torches made new this year, price 28s 6d. And of 3 lbs of wax in the candles burning around the shrine on the feast of Corpus Christi and now in the chapel of St William, on the general commemorations of the dead during the year, price 2s. And of 1 torch earlier received (and) put in stock, price 3s 4d. And of 5 dozen new cups bought this year, price 3s 4d. And of pewter vessels furnished and renovated this year, viz, 3 dozen platters, 4 dozen dishes, 2 dozen saucers and 20 salt-cellars, price 17s. And of 1 new chest for carrying the shrine separately and keeping it safe, price 7s 2d. And of 1 square device of wayscot furnished for keeping the shrine from the damp and rain, together with 4 poles and other appurtenances, price 5s 8d, together with the battlements upon the bier and 14 other poles for the banners. And for the painting and colouring of the same, 16d. And for 4 valances of blue buckram embroidered with golden chalices and set with golden stars with the fringes of vari-coloured threads, 4s 8d. And of 3 ells of blue buckram for the bordering and binding of 17 large banners, price 18d. And of 1 large square piece of cloth embroidered with the image of the Holy Trinity for protecting the shrine safely, price 3s 4d. And of 6 garlands made this year, price 8d. And of 3 books and other documents furnished for the chaplains singing in the procession, price 12d. And of 2 painted angels holding the aforesaid candles in the chapel of St William, 12d. And of 20d paid to Robert Dewe for the fastening of the aforesaid box and for 4 keys and 4 locks with other necessaries, *(blank)*. And of 15 ells of cloth embroidered with chalices and writings, price 3s 6d. And of 1 other piece of cloth embroidered with the image of St Gregory celebrating the mass before the image of Christ, price 4s 6d. And of 24 revets brought new, price 3s 6d. And of one English book received earlier and now put in store with 17 suitable banners and 8 other accessory banners, and other ornaments furnished in detail for the Creed Play, price £8 2s 10d. And for 2 pieces of matting furnished for covering the benches in the aforesaid hall for the good men sitting there, price 9d. Item, paid to a certain woman for the making of 26 napkins and for the hemming of the aforesaid pieces of cloth, 4d. Item, paid to a certain tailor for the affixing and the bordering of the aforesaid banners, 6d.

Total £35   10s   10½d

1465   BL: Lansdowne MS 403

ff 2-5v

Indeed a statute and provision exists on the wise advice of the brothers of this guild that each person formerly master of the fraternity and its wardens, around the day of their account, shall make available and commit to the care and custody of their succeeding master and wardens the treasure and jewels, with any other goods belonging to the guild which follow in this way. First, on the twenty-second day of the month of October in the year of our Lord 1465, sir William Caber, rector of the church of St Helen, York, formerly master of the said guild, together with those formerly its wardens, have made available to sir Thomas Oureum, rector of the parish church in North Street, York, next the master of the said fraternity, and to its wardens at the time, the jewels written below.

First, the gilded silver shrine, dedicated in honour of the most adored body of Christ, was delivered to the aforesaid sir Thomas Oureum and to the wardens by Lord Thomas Spoford of sacred memory, formerly bishop of Hereford, on the eleventh day of the month of June, viz, on the day of St Barnabas the apostle, in the year of our Lord 1449. Which venerable and pious bishop, indeed, obtained freely and devoutly various jewels and not a few gifts for the decoration of the said holy shrine, as lies exposed plainly in the accounts made afterwards.

The same worthy holy shrine, indeed, is valued at £256.

Item, 1 great and concave crystal called a monstrance, with 2 silver angels, valued at £10 6s 8d

Item, 1 image of the Holy Trinity on the top of the shrine, valued at *(blank)*

Item, 1 tabernacle of gold and pearl, with the image of the blessed Virgin Mary, from the gift of the said Lord Thomas, bishop of Hereford, valued at *(blank)*

Item, 1 great gilded necklace, with stones of blue colour, valued at 5s

Item, another small necklace with 4 leaves around the middle of the shrine 16d

Item, another small necklace with certain writings, valued at 18d

Item, 1 tabernacle of gold and of margarite called pearl, with the image of the blessed Mary Magdalene and with 3 gold rings *(blank)*

Item, 1 ring of beryl valued at *(blank)*

Item, 1 gilded silver lamb of God, with the name of Jesus. Item, a gilded silver image of St Lawrence, with 1 crown circumscribed with margarites 16s 6d

Item, 1 gilded silver shell on the top of the shrine, valued at 3s 6d

Item, another gilded silver shell on the top of the shrine, valued at *(blank)*

Item, 1 belt fixed about at the bottom of the shrine, valued at *(blank)*

Item, 1 gilded silver pyx, arranged for aromatic spices, valued at 26s 8d

Item, 1 ring inscribed with these writings, 'In God is all', valued at 40s

Item, 1 silver belt completely studded, valued at 30s 4d

Item, 1 gold necklace with 1 diamond, valued at 20s

Item, 1 gilded silver tabernacle, with the image of the blessed Virgin Mary enclosed in it, valued at 13s 4d

Item, 1 gold ring, valued at 4s 2d

Item, 1 gilded ring having a precious stone, valued at 3s

Item, 1 gold earring with a gold cross hanging from it, valued at *(blank)*

Item, 1 gilded tabernacle of silver, with an image of the blessed Virgin Mary enclosed in it of gold *(blank)*

Item, 1 stalk of coral from the gift of Robert Wystow *(blank)*

Item, 1 gold ring from the gift of Margaret Balzay *(blank)* |
Item, 3 stalks of coral hanging together on a rope 2s
Item, 2 large gilded silver crucifixes with 2 other smaller gilded crucifixes hanging together on a rope with 2 necklaces of silver with 1 bead of beryl *(blank)*
Item, 1 knob prepared with pearl and with 2 cords, one of which (is) plain, the other enamelled, and with 2 gold rings, one of which is enamelled, and 1 cross of gold with the image of Christ crucified, and together with images of the blessed Virgin Mary, valued at *(blank)*
Item, 1 gilded silver lamb of God, from the gift of Agnes Kylborn 5s
Item, 1 silver crucifix, gilded, valued at 16d
Item, 49 beryls in a certain sack *(blank)*
Item, 1 belt gilded with silver roses, valued at *(blank)*
Item, 1 gold heart with one crown, valued at *(blank)*
Item, 1 stalk of coral gilded at the end, valued at 20d
Item, 1 small silver crucifix, valued at 8d
Item, 1 gold tablet with the image of the Holy Trinity, Christopher, and St Barbara 22s
Item, 1 jewel called mother of pearl, the nativity of our Lord Jesus Christ sculpted in it and placed in a silver gilded setting, valued at 40s
Item, 1 great knob of pearl, priced at 3s 4d
Item, 1 crucifix of silver, with 2 images, valued at 20d
Item, 1 gilded silver shell fixed to the shrine, priced at 4s
Item, 1 tabernacle of gold from the gift of lady Joan Ingylby, priced at 54s 4d
Item, 1 necklace of gold called 'heart of gold' from the gift of Lady Alice Constabyll, his daughter, priced at 20s
Item, 1 black belt from the gift of Lady Margaret Clarevas, priced at 20s
Item, 1 cross of gold with a certain part of the lady's cross enclosed in the same, from the gift of the same Margaret, priced at 30s
Item, 1 gold ring with 1 necklace called 'heart of silver' *(blank)*
Item, 1 necklace called 'heart of gold' from the gift of Katherine Styllynton *(blank)*
Item, 1 gilded necklace of copper from the bequest of John Belamy priced at *(blank)*
Item, 1 gold ring from the bequest of Katherine Burgh, priced at *(blank)*
Item, 1 gilded silver ring from the gift of Elaine Benyng,

priced at   (blank)
Item, 1 gold necklace called 'lamb of God' and 1 gold ring from
the gift of Agnes Shrewodd, priced at   (blank)
Item, 1 silver ring, priced at   (blank)
Item, 1 silver ball called 'musk ball' from the gift of Elaine Gare,
late wife of Thomas Gare, Jr, priced at   50s
Item, 1 gold heart from the gift of Agnes Sherwod, priced at   4s
Item, 1 rosary from the gift of the wife of Thomas Wansforth,
priced at   26s
Item, 1 silver shell, priced at   3s
Item, 1 crucifix from the gift of Agnes Burlay, priced at   5s |
First, 1 gilded rosary of silver containing 75 beads, with 2 great
knobs of pearl, with 1 crucifix, and 2 necklaces with 1 gilded
silver ring, valued at   40s
Item, another large rosary of coral containing the complete
psalter from a lady, with 17 gilded jewels and 1 necklace with
writings of Jesus Christ and with a ring of gold, valued at 48s 10d
Item, another rosary of coral with 14 gilded jewels of silver
containing the complete psalter from a lady, with 1 gilded double
crucifix of silver with 1 knob of pearl, valued at   5s
Item, another rosary of coral with 7 gilded jewels of silver, with
1 stalk of coral, valued at   2s 4d
Item, another rosary of coral with 11 gilded jewels of silver 2s 4d
Item, another rosary with certain beads of silver and certain of
coral, with 2 silver rings and 1 brooch   6s 8d
Item, another rosary with gilded beads of silver, with 1 gilded
double crucifix, valued at   (blank)
Item, 1 small rosary with certain beads of silver and certain
(beads) of coral, with 1 gilded crucifix of silver   4s
Item, 1 rosary of silver from the gift of Margaret Danby, priced
at   6s 8d
Item, 1 gilded shell of silver from the gift of sir Thomas Clyff,
chaplain, priced at   4s 6d
Item, 1 gilded shell of silver, given for the entrance (offering
into the guild) of Agnes Marshall, priced at   4s
Item, 1 rosary of coral with 59 jewels of silver and certain of
them gilded, from the gift of Joan, daughter of Richard Watson,
priced at   10s
Item, 1 gilded shell from the gift of Batilda Wakefelde, priced
at   (blank) |
First, 1 silver goblet, valued at 40s. And 1 silver jewel with a
crystalline stone containing precious relics, viz, part of the

cross of the Lord, part of the vestment of St Thomas, bishop of Canterbury, and part of the habit of St Francis, part (of that) of the glorious duke of Lancaster, and 2 precious stones taken from the little wheel of St Katherine. Sum total of the jewels, 20s. And another jewel of silver gilt in the sign and mark of the guild to be shown publicly to the people on the breast of the beadle, valued at 41s 4d. And common seals of the fraternity, of silver, valued at 12s. And a private seal of silver, valued at 3s 4d. And 1 large goblet of costly stone with a plain gilded silver binding, which goblet of indulgence, indeed, is distinguished with a worthy name, and for this reason, indeed, Lord Richard Scrop, late archbishop of York, of blessed memory, graciously gave forty days of indulgence to penitents and confessed persons who drank soberly with a pure mind, if from this goblet, with moderation and not excessively nor at will. Indeed, the same stone is valued at 40s. Which stone indeed, or goblet, Agnes Wyman, late wife of Henry Wyman, late mayor of the city of York, obtained for the fraternity of Corpus Christi, very devotedly, whose soul rest in perpetual peace, amen. And 1 goblet of precious stone with a gilded binding of silver, valued at 36s 6d. Item, 1 casket, well-bound, under 5 keys, arranged for a store place, and for keeping the documents and the common seal, valued at 26s 8d. |

First, 1 missal received in the time of sir John Fox, master of the guild, 5 marks. Item, 1 vestment of blue cloth and a decorative band of green, powdered with stars of gold, priced at 7s. Item, 1 bag of linen cloth and 1 case of blue cloth, priced at (blank). Item, 1 bag of linen cloth and 1 case of green broad Alexander, priced at (blank). Item, 2 cruets of pewter, valued at 8d, which were all from the gift and bequest of sir John York, Sr, formerly chaplain of the fraternity or guild of Corpus Christi, whose soul please God, amen.

Item, vestments of blue silk called velvet, arranged for the priest, deacon, and subdeacon, with 3 silk copes for their suit, valued at £34. And 1 white vestment of bustian for the priest celebrating mass, valued at 14s. And another vestment of bustian, priced at 6s 8d. And 3 small cloths of the passion of Christ, valued at 16d. And a cloth embroidered with the image of blessed Pope Gregory celebrating mass before the image of the Saviour, valued at 4s 7d. And 7 stoles made anew, arranged for this purpose: that they might be worthy to be worn suitably over the shoulders of the master and of the 6 wardens of the

fraternity in the solemn procession of Corpus Christi, valued at
47s 7d. And 1 vestment of red broad Alexander, valued at 8s.

First, letters patent of the lord king concerning the new
foundation and creation of the fraternity of Corpus Christi,
valued at £10. And other letters of the foundation of the guild,
valued at £6. And 1 gathering of parchment in which are written
copies of the letters patent of the lord king and of the letters of
foundation of the fraternity, valued at 4s. And 1 book containing
old statutes and ordinances, in which book are registered the
names of the brothers and sisters of the guild, valued at 20s. And
1 muniment under the seal of the commons of the city of York,
valued at 6s 8d. And 3 bulls sent from the highest curia, with 2
copies, valued at 20s. And 4 letters of bishops' indulgences,
valued at 10s. And other letters of indulgences which Lord
Thomas Spoforde, formerly bishop of Hereford, conceded to
each priest who said this collect devoutly in the celebration of
masses: 'Omnipotent and eternal God, preservation and life of
the faithful, etc,' with the secret and post-communion, which
collect, secret, and post-communion, indeed, the bishop himself
made and ordained so that he might induce the minds of the
faithful to pray for the brothers and sisters of this guild. And
these letters of indulgence, valued at 10s. And 9 writings of
instruments and documents concerning the mortuary payments
of the priests of the city of York not to be paid, valued at £6.
And if any one has agreed to alienate anything of these indulgences written with good grace and honestly, he should know
that he is ensnared in a sentence of excommunication in the
judgement of God. And 2 writings concerning the rent to be had
for the year in Skeldergate, York, valued at 10s. And 1 breviary
containing 43 gatherings of parchment, valued at 40s. And a
small table for saying graces, valued at 12d. And 22 rolls on
which the accounts of predecessors are inscribed, valued at 22s. |

First, 1 wooden box upon the high altar in the chapel of
St William on Ouse Bridge, valued at £3. And 1 painted gilt
bier for bearing the said shrine in the procession, 6s 8d. And 8
white cushions furnished for the shoulders of those carrying the
shrine, valued at 2s 2d. And 4 images of the evangelists and
16 angels newly painted with shields and rolls, together with 2
copper chalices, gilded, and 2 crystals, for supporting the said
bier and shrine, 38s. And 2 small pieces of buckram cloth
embroidered with gilt chalices for the said bier, and 1 square
wooden canopy and 4 poles, valued at 4s. And a piece of cloth

embroidered with the image of the most high Trinity, valued at 3s. And 4 pieces of blue drapery with chalices and gilt stars, valued at 5s. And 4 linen sacks for keeping 4 hides of the said bier suitably, valued at 6d. And 1 short wooden chest bound with iron for keeping the shrine securely, valued at 8s 8d.

First, the book called original containing the articles of the Catholic faith recently written in the English tongue, valued at £10. And another old book of the same play, 100s. And another book of the same, called in English, the Creed Play, containing 23 quires. And 17 large banners, valued at £4. And 4 smaller banners of red silk, priced at 6s 8d. And 9 other banners called pennons with newly-made shields of the faith and embroidered chalices, valued at 11s 6d. And 24 iron devices called sockets, furnished for the extension of the banners, valued at 4s 6d. And 1 papal mitre, valued at 10d. And 1 royal crown with a sceptre and 1 glove, valued at 6d. And 12 rolls recently written with the articles of the Catholic faith, ı valued at 3s 4d. And 1 small square chest with 1 lock and key for keeping the said banners, valued at 2s. And 2 episcopal mitres, valued at 12d. And 1 key for St Peter and 2 pieces of 1 embroidered tunic, valued at 12d. And 4 other banners called pennons, 3s 4d. And 10 diadems for Christ and the apostles, with 1 mask and 9 other wigs, 6s.

First, 14 torches, valued at *(blank)*. And 3 old judases, valued at 14d. And 12 painted castles and golden chalices and plates of iron belonging to the same castles, valued at 4s. And 34 embroidered banners furnished for the torches, valued at 20s. ı

First, 8 napkins with 2 other second-best napkins, valued at 6s 8d. And 5 other napkins newly made, containing 73 ells, valued at 24s 7d. And 1 towel, valued at 2s. And 2 other smaller towels, valued at 2s 4d. And 24 napkins, valued at 12d. And 6 naprons, valued at 2s. And 9 dozen cups, valued at 5s. And 20 salt-cellars of pewter, valued at 4s. And 60 roundels for the revets, valued at 16d. And 1 small (piece of) linen for the table where the cups are set, valued at 8d. And 64 earthen pots called revets, valued at 9s. And 1 long chest with 3 locks and 3 keys for keeping the said linen cloths, valued at 16s. And another short chest without a covering in the buttery, valued at 12d. And another long chest with 1 key for keeping the said revets, 3s 4d. And another small chest, valued at *(blank)*. And 1 twill napkin containing 8 ells, valued at 6s 8d.

First, 1 large brass pot with 3 long feet, valued at 6s 8d. And another smaller brass pot, valued at 6s 8d. And another brass pot, valued at 3s 8d. And 8 dozen and 10 doublers and 15 dozen dishes, and 2 dishes together with 10 dozen and 1 salt-cellars, valued at £5 13s 4d. And 2 tools called marking irons, valued at 8d. And 1 ladle of brass, priced at 8d. And another ladle, priced at 1d. And 1 fork called a flesh crook, valued at 6d. And a pair of bellows, valued at 3d. And 1 rusty knife of little value, valued at ¼d. And 2 pieces of 1 broken doubler.

Translations: Appendix III

Pater Noster Guild Return, 1388-9

York

Having heard a proclamation made on behalf of the lord king in the city of York, to the effect that our lord the illustrious king and the venerable council are to be informed and notified concerning each and every establishment, foundation, and obligations of fraternities or guilds within the county of York, hence it is that the wardens of the guild of the Lord's prayer, founded in the city of York, notify and certify to the said our lord the king and his excellent council concerning each and every thing that pertains to the foundation and government of the said fraternity in this form: first, as to the cause of the founding of the said fraternity, it should be known that after a certain play on the usefulness of the Lord's prayer was composed, in which play indeed many vices and sins are reproved and virtues commended, and was played in the city of York, it had such and so great an appeal that very many said: Would that this play were established in this city, for the salvation of souls and the solace of the citizens and neighbours. Wherefore, the whole and complete cause of the foundation and association of the brothers of the same fraternity was that that play be managed at future times for the health and reformation of the souls, both of those in charge of that play and of those hearing it. And thus, the principal work of the said fraternity is that the play should be managed to the greater glory of God, the deviser of the said prayer, and for the reproving of sins and vices. And because those continuing in their sins are unfit to call God their father, therefore the said brothers first of all are bound to avoid unworthy associations and occupations, and are to cleave to good and honest occupations. Item, they are bound at their main devotional gatherings to pray especially for the brothers and sisters of the said fraternity, living and dead, praying that the living may be able so to maintain their fraternity that they might deserve to gain the fatherhood of God, and the dead of the brotherhood will be freed all the more quickly from torments by their prayers. Item, they are bound to be present at funerals and burials of deceased brothers and sisters of the said fraternity. And if any brother has nothing of his own for the expenses incurred at the time of his burial, then the rest of his brothers shall cause him to be buried of their own wealth and charity. And if any brother of the said fraternity dies and is buried far from the city, then the rest of his brothers shall cause a memorial mass to be celebrated for him within the city of York. Item, it is forbidden for any brother of the aforesaid fraternity to be so confident of help from the brotherhood that he boldly enters into litigation or fighting, or maintains some unjust cause, under pain of losing all aid and friendship or succour from the aforesaid fraternity. And because all is vain in the congregation of the faithful without some regulated work of charity, therefore the said brothers set out the following clause: that if by chance any one of these brothers be robbed, or their goods or chattels accidentally burned, or they be incarcerated for an unjust reason or brought to the level of poverty by divine visitation, then the rest of his brothers devise charity for him immediately according to his need, as the wardens of the said fraternity think fit, lest by chance he be lost in default of aid. Item, they are bound to hang and maintain in the cathedral church of York one candelabrum with seven lights, which will be lit Sundays and holy days in honour of the seven petitions in the Lord's prayer and to the praise and honour of almighty God, maker of that prayer, and of St Peter, the glorious confessor, and St William, and all the saints. Item, they are bound to look after, and renew whenever necessary, a certain drawing which hangs above a column in the cathedral church aforesaid, next to the above candelabrum and depicts the layout and usefulness of the Lord's prayer. Item, they are bound, whenever the play of the said Lord's prayer is shown in the form of a play in the city of York, to ride with the players of the same through certain principal streets of the city of York and to be dressed in one livery, to give greater ornament to their riding. And some of them are bound to go or ride with those players until the said play be completely

finished, for the peaceful managing of the said play. And once a
year they are to hold a feast together and elect new wardens for
the said fraternity to watch over everything for the new year, and
render to those recently elected wardens a faithful accounting of
all that they have done in the elapsed time towards the work of
the said fraternity. Item, it is ordained that no one is to be
received into the brotherhood of this fraternity until he is
examined by the wardens of the said fraternity, to see whether
he has the will to live honestly and to do for the aforesaid
fraternity and its direction as best he can in agreement with the
said wardens. And because the founders of the said fraternity
knew themselves to be unable to be wise once and for all in the
laying down of regulations, they added at the end of all the said
ordinances the following clause: that whenever and as often as
ever it should by chance happen, that we or our successors,
wardens and brothers of the said fraternity, should become wiser,
none of us or our successors shall be rebellious or resist against
our ordinances or those of our successors, if by chance we or
they should make in the future other new regulations to the
greater glory of God and the succour of the said fraternity. As
a result of this clause, other wardens of the said fraternity added
for the greater glory of God, that a certain chaplain be maintained
and employed to celebrate divine service annually for the said
brothers and sisters of the said fraternity, living and dead, and all
their benefactors. Also the same brothers are wont to gather
together at the end of every six weeks throughout the year to
pray especially for the health of the lord king and the good
governance of the English realm, and for all the brothers and
sisters present and absent, living and dead, and all the benefactors
of the said fraternity or the said brothers. And once a year, they
are wont to have a general mass of the dead for the deceased
brothers and sisters of the said fraternity. Not do any rents of
land, or holdings, or any other chattels, excepting only the
apparatus intended for the use of the said play, belong to the
said fraternity, which apparatus, indeed, cannot in the least
serve any other purpose except only the said play. And there is
one wooden chest belonging to the said fraternity to hold the
said apparatus. Because the seals of the wardens of the said
fraternity are unknown to many, we the said wardens have
procured the seal of the vicar general of the spiritualities of the
venerable father in God, the Lord Thomas, archbishop of York,
primate of England and legate of the apostolic see, which we

wardens have affixed to these letters. And we Richard of Thoren, resident canon of the church of York and vicar general of the spiritualities of the aforesaid venerable father, at the behest of the said fraternity and in witness of all the foregoing, have affixed to the present letter the seal which we use in our office as vicar general.

Given at York, 21 January, 1388.

End-notes

1 Reg. 10 f 264
We have provided what we consider the essential parts of the constitution to put the prohibition in context.

2 M2/6/c f 29
These accounts run from 29 September to 29 September. The feast of St Leonard is 6 November.

2 E/1/1 *MP* mb 2
The chamberlains' accounts were made up twice a year at Pentecost and Martinmas. The double entries such as this one are for the feast of the translation of St William on the Sunday after Epiphany (6 January) and Pentecost. The single entries are for the feast of St William on 8 June.

3 M2/6/c f 44v
The upper left-hand corner of the folio has crumbled away and been repaired.

3 E20 f 3
Many ordinances in this MS are undated. They are gathered together in Appendix I in the order in which they occur in the MS.

6 E1/9 *MP* mb 4
There is damage to the MS along the right edge of this membrane.

6 C47/46/454
See Appendix III for the complete document.

7 E1/14 *PM* mb 2
The interlineation 'Translac*ion*is' is in error. The intended feast is 8 June.

7 E20 f 46
'in nouo registro' refers to the later part of E20, see p xx.

8 E1/17 *MP* mb 2
Damp stains have obliterated part of the writing on this roll.

8 E20 f 17v
The cross reference here is to the ordinance for the play on f 19v (p 10). This reference and the
series of references to other ordinances concerning the play found at the beginning of the entry on
f 19v are not accurate according to the modern foliation of E20. They are, however, generally
accurate in the medieval foliation, made before many leaves were inserted into the codex. The
first gathering consists of twelve leaves but the modern numbering begins on the old fly-leaf, so
that modern foliation numbers the first gathering 2-13 rather than the original 1-12. At the end of
the first gathering, an additional leaf has been inserted. This has been numbered in the modern
hand f 14. The second gathering, then, originally began with f 13, but begins with f 15 in modern
foliation. The original second gathering was again one of twelve leaves. Nothing has been added in
the first half of the gathering so that the reference on modern f 17v (medieval f 15v) 'plus in
se*cun*di folio seq*uenti*' is a reference to modern f 19v (medieval f 17v) and the first reference on
modern f 19v 'plus de eode*m* in se*cun*do folio pre*ce*de*nti*' is merely a cross reference. The second
reference to the torches 'in iiij. fol*io* pre*ce*de*nti*' takes the reader back to modern f 15 (medieval
f 13). This reference is, however, mistaken since the reference is on modern f 16v (medieval
f 14v), p 12. The scribe seems to have made the common error of writing iiij for iij. If all the
insertions into the book are taken into account, 'in cxij*m*o fol*io* seque*nti*', the third reference on
f 19v, leads accurately to modern f 148v (medieval f 129), p 13. This is confirmed by the reference
on that folio back to xvij, ie, modern f 19v. The final reference to the ordo paginarum 'in fine
hui*us* libri' was originally accurate, since that gathering appeared near the end of the *maior registrum*.

10 E1/27 *MP* mb 2
E1/26 is a copy of this roll.

12 *York Plays*, xxix
A second reading of this roll is given by Angelo Raine: 'My father used to have in his possession
the only existing account roll of this guild, for the year 1399, and from this roll I made extracts ...
The only reference to a play in the account roll is the "ludus doctorum".' (Angelo Raine, *Medieval
York* [London, 1955], 91-2).

13 E20 f 42
The first ordinance of the Spurriers and Lorimers concerning the pageant is cancelled. Further
down the folio and written over the earlier ordinances in a later hand is a note concerning the
involvement of the Hatmakers in the pageant of Christ and the Doctors. The note is dated by the
mayoral year of Richard York, 1468 or 1481. Cross references appear under the later dates.

14 E1/37 *MP* mb 2
E1/35 is a copy of this roll.

15 Lansdowne MS 403 f 17v
Red faces have been drawn in the bowls of the o's in 'Co*n*stitu*tio*' (l 17).

16 E20 ff 65v, 68
The vertical line (l 17) marks the last words on f 65v; the continuation of the entry is on the
bottom of f 68 under French ordinances in another hand. Two other folios have been interleaved here.

16 E20 ff 252v-5
This 'ordo gathering' has been published in part by Drake in *Eboracum*, Smith in *York Plays* and Davies in *Extracts*. More recently, Martin Stevens and Margaret Dorrell Rogerson published the entire gathering in *Modern Philology*, fully annotated with a translation. Rather than repeat that edition, we have chosen here to represent the MS more properly in its present state of preservation. Besides the flood damage, ff 253-4 have split (or been deliberately slashed) from the bottom half way up the folios. The breaks have been patched with paper, now discolouring and obliterating the writing underneath. Other holes in the parchment are similarly patched. We have printed what is now visible and given the readings of earlier editors in footnotes. Unless otherwise indicated, the readings in the first list are from Smith, in the second from Davies. We have not attempted to reproduce the complex variety of braces and lines connecting craft names and pageant descriptions. Although the second list (which is undated) has traditionally been assumed to be later than the first, we have preserved the gathering intact. The hands are similar, though not identical. The second list (on f 255) is in two columns.

27 C99:1 mb 1-1d
We have chosen the form 'torch*ea*' rather than 'torch*ia*' or 'torch' for our expansions because, although the three forms all appear in these accounts, elsewhere in this collection the 'ea' form is more common.
     C99:2, a copy of C99:1, for the entry on l 17, p 27 reads: 'Et in factura & *pro* lichino eo*run*dem ij s.'

28 E20 ff 187v-8
The first words in every line of f 187v have been washed way. Words have been supplied from Sellers, *York Memorandum Book* II, 63-4. The long list of names of citizens attending the meeting (included in this document as in later House Book entries) has not been reproduced.

30 E20 ff 75v, 78
These ordinances of the Cordwainers are dated only by the mayoral year of William Bowes. Bowes was mayor also in 1427-8 and 1442-3. Cross references appear under those dates.

32 E20 f 43v
This folio has been repaired. The entry is under preservative. 'in viij^{mo} fol*io* *pre*cedent*i*' refers to ordinances of the Tapiters on f 33 not included in this selection.

33 E20 ff 57v, 64v
These ordinances of the Plasterers and also those of the Fishers and Mariners are dated only by the mayoral year of Thomas Gare. Gare was mayor also in 1433-4. A cross reference appears under that date.

36 VC Box XII
The dating of this document is approximate. Dated by Albert Chambers, 'The vicars choral.'

37 Vq 1x
The dating is approximate. Dated by Albert Chambers. For Robert Scrueton, see p 44.

40 E20 f 283
A marginal note in a late sixteenth-century hand indicates that these ordinances were redrawn during the mayoralty of Edward Fawcett (1598).

40 C82:2 mb 1
The Bridgemasters' Accounts were made up annually, but payment was expected on two days, Pentecost and Martinmas. The terms referred to, therefore, in these rolls are the times of the year when the rent was paid. The rentals in this first roll, except for the entry concerning the Skinners and Dyers, do not specify that these are pageant house rents. However, the entries are enough like those from 1428, where pageant houses are specified, to warrant the assumption that they do concern pageant houses.

41 E20 f 279
The reference forward is to the Walkers' Guild on modern f 300, not reproduced in this selection.

42 E20 ff 278-8v
The grammar of the marginal heading on f 278v is internally contradictory. The general sense of the heading, although apparently written in the same hand as the major entry, is not consistent with the sense of the entry.

45 E20 f 287v
Most final 'r's' end with a flourish. Some 'y's' are dotted.

47 E20 f 21v
The parchment is now so washed away that the writing is indecipherable.

48 E20 f 283v
Tape over the centre heading covers the ends of many words. 'suspendebat & crepuit medius' (l 31), cf Acts 1:18.

50 A15
A15, the actual sealed document concerning the agreement, has been chosen as the base text rather than the version copied into E20A.

53 E20A f 119v
Upper and lower case 'w's' are hard to distinguish in this hand. Most final 'r's' have flourishes added.

55 D63
The endorsement on this document is in a different but contemporary hand.

58 D53A mb 6
A paper account survives for this year in D63. There is no significant difference except for 'dwrres' (l 4): the paper account has 'durres'. Sellers, in *York Mercers*, 49, misreads 'awrres' for 'dwrres'.

61   C82:11 mb 1
This is all that remains from the entry. The roll is badly torn as well as faded.

61   D19 f 9
Dr Sellers (*York Mercers*, 82) implies that this document is dated 1488. But she makes no clear distinction between this entry on f 9 of the Chartulary and the note of the election of John Shawe as master in 1488 on f 9v, which is in a different and later hand. The will of one of the constables named, William Bluefront, was probated 26 June 1447. (Collins, *Index of the Wills in the York Registry 1389-1514*, Yorkshire Archaeological and Topographical Association, Record Series VI (1888), 19). Thomas Scauceby, who is named master of the company in the document, held that office only once before 1447, in 1443. This document must therefore be dated 1443.

Transcription of the 1443 ordinance in the Chartulary and Minute Book is complicated by the fact that it has been overwritten in a late nineteenth-century hand. The first published version of this entry was by Rev C. Kerry, 'Discovery of the Register and Chartulary of the Mercers' Company, York,' *The Antiquary*, 269, and wrongly indicates that the pageant masters of the Mercers were in charge of the Pater Noster Play. Dr Sellers did not have the MS in her possession when she prepared her edition of the Mercers' documents and at first relied on a transcription provided by Sir Henry Bemrose of Derby. The MS was recovered shortly before publication and Dr Sellers corrected the earlier work; she, too, transcribed 'paternoster play', (Sellers, *York Mercers*, 82). But consideration of the MS under ultra-violet light has shown that the original entry (ll 29-30) was not 'þe paternoster play' but 'þair play'.

The overwriter does not appear to have been familiar with fifteenth-century script and made several errors when retracing the words of the entry. He used punctuation not in use in 1443: hyphens in 'pater noster-play' (ll 29-30) and 'be-langes' (ll 30-1), and a colon after 'þto' (l 31). He also dotted the letter 'i' and was apparently unable to distinguish between the letters 'i' and 'r' in some cases as 'r' is dotted in 'Bluefront,' (l 25), 'forth' (l 29), 'receyue' (l 30) and 'Cristi' (l 38). In line 22 he wrote 'who' for what must have been originally 'whol', in line 25 'Gaing' for original 'Gaunt' (William Gaunt is named as a constable in the 1443 Compotus Roll, Box D53), and 'þ'to' for original 'þto' in line 31. Under ultra-violet light what appears to be 'þe þat' noster-play' in the overwritten version can be seen to have been originally 'þair play'. The overwriter traced 'þe' over the 'þa' of 'þair' and 'þat' noster-' over the 'ir' (the 'r' in 'þair' is a long 'r'). The words 'þat' noster-' extend into the right-hand margin and the line is half an inch longer than any other in the entry.

62   E20A ff 121-1v
Otiose flourishes on 'm' and 'n' have been ignored.

65   CC1 p 26
The only meaning given for 'waferer' in the *OED* is 'a maker or seller of wafers or thin cakes'. The constant appearance of these men in these lists suggests, perhaps, that the word may also have the force of 'wayfarer' or 'vagabond'.

73   MS Bodley 857 f 1v
This poem on the fly-leaf of Bodley 857 is the only example in this collection of Latin verse recording a ceremonial visit. The superlineations have been retained because the metre would be destroyed if those between lines 37 and 39 were lowered to the line. The interlineation between

lines 39 and 40 is in the nature of a gloss. These are in a different hand from the poem itself. The couplets are linked although they do not rhyme.

80 C99:3 mb 2d
The entry is badly faded.

84 C83:4 mb 1
The declension of the Latin form of 'mercer' varies between second, where the genitive plural is 'mercer*orum*', and third, where the genitive plural is 'mercer*um*'. Where the intended declension is unclear, we have expanded according to the practice of the formula.

91 D63
The financial crisis recorded in this document allows us to date it 1461. In that year (see above), there is an entry in the compotus roll of the company making up the exact sum needed by the pageant masters in excess of the pageant money collected (30s 4½d). The only problem here is that the roll speaks of 'Thome Nandyke et socijs suis Magistris Pagine'. Thomas Nandyke is not one of the names that appear on this document as pageant master. Three of the four named pageant masters were Henry Williamson, John Bosswell and Thomas Skotton. Nandyke was made free in the same year as Williamson (34 Henry VI, 1455-6), one year before Bosswell and two before Skotton (Collins, *Freemen*, 175-6, 178). They were all young men in 1461 and possibly the pageant masters, finding themselves in financial difficulties, prevailed upon their friend Thomas Nandyke to present their case to the company. Corroborative evidence that this document belongs to 1461 is found in the appearance of the name of John Gudale in the list of names and amounts on the front of the document. It was the custom for such a list to be written before the collection was made and the amounts entered as they were received. No amount appears against Gudale's name. His will was probated 21 April 1461 (Collins, *Wills*, 71). He apparently died between the time the list of members was drawn up and the pageant money collected.

92 E20 f 293v
Otiose marks above nasals are omitted here. Upper and lower case 'w' are hard to distinguish in this hand.

93 C3:3 mb 1
The fourth station is identified in this account as being opposite the church of St John the Baptist. This is the church of St John Ouse Bridge and is identified by Drake as St John the Evangelist (*Eboracum*, 235).

95 D63
This document and the next must be considered together. They share the same pageant masters John Leghtlop, William Thelle, and Richard Sawer. Leghtlop became a member of the Mercers' Guild in 1459 and Sawer in 1462. (Sellers, *York Mercers*, 70). Richard Sawer was a clerk and would have been admitted to the guild as a special member. His admission in 1462 gives us the earliest possible date for these documents. They clearly refer to two different years, and, since they name the same men as masters, it is likely that they refer to two consecutive years. One of these documents refers to the making of the second pageant. The account dated 1461 (see p 91), makes no mention of it; but the account dated 1464 (see p 97), speaks of 'nayls to both pagyants'.

These documents must come after 1461 and before 1464. Since one mentions the second pageant and the other does not, this account must belong to 1462 and the next to 1463.

97   Sellers, *York Mercers*, p 72
Dr Sellers mistakenly dates this 1472 (*York Mercers*, 71). She prints together with this document, the list of pageant silver collected from the same document headed 'this is the rakynyng of our pageant silver reseyved be the handes of Thomas Wrangwyshe, Thomas Maryott and John Lokwod in the yere Thomas Neylson beyng mayor'. She assumes that the three men named in the heading were the master and constables of the company. Wrangwyshe was master of the company in 1472, but neither Maryott nor Lokwod were constables. On all other accounts the men named are the pageant masters. Thomas Neylson was twice mayor but his years of office were 32 Henry VI (1453) and 4 Edward IV (1464). The final evidence refuting the date of 1472 is found in the pageant silver list. Thomas Scauceby, the first member of the company listed, died in 1471 (Collins, *Wills*, 146). He appears in the list as having contributed 6d to the expense of the pageant. Once the date 1472 is discarded, we are left with 1453 and 1464. Richard Sawer, clerk, who joined the company in 1462 (see above note to p 95), appears in the list. This document must be dated 1464.

99   D63
The list on the inner leaves of this document is dated 1467.

107   E20 ff 295v-6
Dots on the line are scattered throughout the text.

108   E20A f 147v
This ordinance dates from either 1475-6 or 1483-4, the two mayoral terms of Thomas Wrangwish. A cross reference appears under the later date.

114   E20A f 195A
Collated with B1 f 68. E20A has been chosen as the base text because it is the registered copy.

115   D54X mb 2
The scribe wrote 'at p' for 'at price', possibly on the analogy of 'appre*ciatur*'.

116   G11A
G11A has been chosen as the base text because, although both G11 and G11A seem to be copies of a third original, G11A is the formal, sealed document.

118   E20 ff 304v, 296v
Upper and lower case 'a' are hard to distinguish in this hand.

127   E20 ff 367v-8
Collated with the copy of the Carpenters' ordinances from E55A f 4. The E20 version is chosen as the base text because it is probably the earlier text and the one officially entered in the civic book.

128 E20 f 379
The actual foliation is 380a in present position. The MS was misbound after pencilled foliation designated this folio 379. Upper and lower case 'a' are hard to distinguish in this hand.

131 E20 f 52v
This document has been interleaved in the MS.

132 Vicars Choral Statute Book p 48
The Vicars Choral Statute Book was chosen as the base text for the collation since it was begun in 1421. M2/2/c is a collection of material written down in the sixteenth century.

136 E20 f 74v
The entry is upside down at the foot of the folio and cancelled in brown ink.

137 E1/48 MP mb 2
The membrane is damaged along the right edge of this account.

137 B6 f 12v
The two marginal headings are in the same hand. The English heading is in the far left margin; the French between the list of those present at the meeting and the text of the entry.

138 B6 ff 15v-18
Some 'ion' words end with a flourish, some do not. As there is no apparent logic to their occurrence, all flourishes have been treated as otiose. Although Drake suggests that the mythical founder of York should be called 'Ebrank' (*Eboracum*, 489), the weight of the evidence seems to be on the side of 'Ebrauk' even when (as in p 140, l 5) there are four minims producing the spelling 'Ebrauuk'.

143 B6 f 18
In the MS roughly drawn braces link lines ending 'gudely'/'victoriously', 'benyngne'/'condigne'; 'pleasing'/'reynyng'. 'I pray in this space' (l 10) is set off to the right opposite the first four lines of the passage and has been inserted in its proper context. 'I shall sew to my sone to send you his grace' (l 14) appears on the right as well, opposite the last three lines and has been dealt with in the same way.

146 Cotton Julius B XII ff 10-13v
The scribe of this manuscript ended many words with a final flourish. Such flourishes have been deemed otiose. The speech of Our Lady (p 149) is written as the House Book version.

152 E20A f 162
This last ordinance was agreed to in 1487-8 and enrolled in 1491-2.

152 B6 f 92
Here, as frequently in the English text, the collective term is abbreviated as 'Coialtie' (p 153, l 6), probably on the analogy of 'Coitis' in Latin. Although it is possible that the scribes intended 'Comminaltie', when the word 'common' is written out, it is spelled as it is in modern usage. We

have, therefore, expanded the form as 'Commonialtie'.

154   B6 ff104v-5
Most of the House Book entries concerning the visit of Henry VII in 1487 are not minutes, but discursive accounts, apparently written after the fact, of the events surrounding the Simnell rebellion. In March this year the city council heard of the coming rebellion and asked the king for money and men to defend the walls. Lambert Simnell was refused entry and the attack of Lord Scrope of Bolton on 11 June was turned back. The Corpus Christi Play was postponed because of the rebellion and performed on 5 August when the king came to the city.

157   C85:1 mb 1
The change in the formula in the Skinners' entry reflects the arrangement made by Henry Albon, Henry Wresill and Richard Shaw by the mayor and council on 23 September 1484 (see p 134).

160   E20 f 302
Between f 301 and f 303 is part of a paper page numbered f 302 and containing what appears to be a copy of a House Book entry concerning the Tapiters. The page is cut before the completion of the formula at the end of the entry represented in the transcription by '...' (l 39). The second entry (beginning Item) is on a full page of E20 also numbered f 302 and is under the inserted fragment. Both versions are similar to a version in B7 f 17.

164   B7 f 70
The word 'dee' (ll 30, 32, 34, 35; see also p 166, l 38) has been left unexpanded in the text because we are unsure of the form intended. Kelham, in A Dictionary of the Norman or Old French Language (London, 1779), lists 'dee' as a verbal adjective meaning 'to have been', but none of the more recent dictionaries consulted includes such a form. Other possibilities have been suggested: the expansion 'dees' might be related to AN 'dels', a contraction of 'de les', used absolutely; or, the adverb 'deuement', a fourteenth-fifteenth century form of 'dûment' ('duly: in due time, properly'), fits the sense of the passage, although it would be an unusual expansion of the MS 'deꝺ'.

174   B7 f 100v
The MS is badly faded. B7 has been chosen as the base text because it is earlier than E22.

176   B7 f 109v
Upper and lower case 'a' are difficult to distinguish in this hand.

177   B7 f 135
The MS is badly faded.

178   B7 f 136v
Both 'þ' and 'y' are in use for the sound 'th' during this section of the MS. The scribe of f 135 uses 'y'; the scribe of f 136v uses 'þ'.

182   B8 f 101-1v
At the top of f 101v is the following running head: 'xvᵒ die Decembre anno Henrici vij'.

185 E20A f 201v
Collated with B8 f 80v. The registered copy is taken as the base text.

190 B9 f 3
The address and signature are written beside one another in the MS and separated from the main body of the text.

193 B9 ff 4v, 5-7v, 8
Upper and lower case 'a' are difficult to distinguish in this hand. On f 6v, a 'C' appears midway between the two lines of the MS at the beginning of the recorder's speech. See also Bodleian MS Gough Yorkshire 2 for a short version of this visit.

199 C86:2 mb 1
This is the first appearance (ll 29-30) of John Alan, who has a special relationship with the Goldsmiths, Coopers and Waxchandlers in subsequent entries.

204 B9 f 37
This entry appears on the same folio with the minutes of the meeting of 16 August 1507, written in a very different hand.

209 E1/61b MP mb 2
There is no heading for this entry on the roll.

213 C6:1 mb 1-2
The roll is badly water damaged and cannot be read, even under ultra-violet light.

221 CC2 f 29v
The punctus after each sum in this list has the force of a comma.

223 B10 f 18v
William Darson (l 35) is written in a different ink and hand, and is apparently a real signature.

226 D56NNN mb 2
'organum' (l 40) is listed as a second declension noun in R.E. Latham, *Revised Medieval Latin Word-List* (London, 1965), 325.

227 B10 f 43
The MS from 'coien Counsaill' (l 25) for common council is without a brevigraph and may be connected by analogy to 'coialtie'. This scribe frequently writes 'coien' for common, sometimes without the brevigraph, sometimes with the terminal 'n' abbreviated (see B10 f 116v, l 16, p 239).

230 MS Add 220/2 f 27
This entry and those for 1525 (f 44v) and 1528 (f 74) are from Elizabeth Brunskill's transcription of the lost original (see Introduction, p xxxviii). It refers, perhaps, to a song or act performed by the underclerk (see 1538-9, PR Y/MS 3 f 35).

233   C87:2   mb 1
The second entry is probably that for the Weavers (see above C87:1, 1521).

239   B10   f 116A
Folio 116A is a separate piece of paper pasted on the bottom of f 116v with the words 'Extractus Robertus payerson se' written on the left-hand edge in an earlier hand, at right angles to the text. It has been damaged and repaired.

242   B11   f 23
This entry ends, 'Nec cum alia arte istius Ciuitatis pro diuersis consideracionibus dictum maiorem movent &c. & precipue pro certa Tegula per ipsum vsque reparacione communis Crane & aliarum terrarum predicte Ciuitatis &c.' A formula is being cited here. Since we do not have the formula, neither the Latin sentence nor an attempted English translation will make sense.

246   C6:6   mb 1
The right-hand edge where the 'summa' should be is irregularly damaged by a rodent.

247   CC3(1)   p 232
The circles in the left margin are probably indications of payments.

248   CC3(1)   p 254
On p 254 of CC3 the scribe has written both the normal heading for minstrels (here reproduced) and half-way down the page the normal heading for the payment to other civic officials. Only the single item concerning the king's minstrels was entered.

250   B11   ff 67-7v
Upper and lower case 'a' are difficult to distinguish in this hand. '... & on the markett day / Provyded ...' (ll 37-8): the virgule could be mistaken for a kind of semi-colon but it is probable that the scribe's pen slipped in making the stroke. The virgule is his usual means of punctuation.

251   E1/66 MP   mb 2
The roll is fragmentary at the right edge.

252   B11   f 97v
The signature 'Thomas wyllyson' (p 253, l 4) is preceded by two marks.

254   C87:4   mb 1
The scribe appears to have mistaken the word 'pistoribus' (bakers) and 'piscatoribus' (fishermen). The 'ffishers' appear here (l 9) for the first time and subsequently for five rolls covering ten years. Their place is then retaken by the Bakers. We know from their accounts that the Bakers regularly paid the shilling rent until after 1642. The fishermen appear nowhere else in these rolls. A mistranslation is the probable explanation.

254   D57XXX   mb 2
This roll and the four subsequent ones have what is apparently a meaningless 'SS' added to the marginal heading.

256   B13   ff 24-4v
At the bottom of f 24 is written 'plus in dorso'.

262   E1/70 *MP*   mb 2
The roll is fragmentary at the right edge.

266   E1/73 *PM*   mb 2
The roll is fragmentary at the right edge.

268   PR Y/MS 3   f 41v
This entry is on a piece of paper stitched to the bottom of the folio.

272   B15   ff 36-6v
This entry is followed by further injunctions to the city officials to oversee the work.

273   B15   ff 57-8v
'Inven*ci*on of the holy Crosse' (p 274, l 12) is apparently an error for the Exaltation of the Holy
Cross. The first letter of 'poore' (p 274, l 30) corresponds to the 'p' of 'pleasor' (p 274, l 38),
although an 's' would suit the context better.

275   B15   ff 56-6v
At the bottom of f 56 is written 'plus in dors'.

278   PR Y/MS 3   f 54
This entry is on a small piece of paper stitched to the bottom of the folio.

289   E1/74 *MP*   mb 2
Repair of the roll covers the 'd' on line 5.

290   D58M(a)   mb 1-2
All subsequent headings indicate revenue from properties listed by a street name (here Felter
Lane). Later rents from Peterlane Little and Toft Green are among receipts of the company.

296   B20   Endpapers
The letter is bound into the endpapers of B20. The endorsement 'Vynteners An order taken
12th March 1551' is written in a different hand from the letter.

300   B20   f 67
The original sentence read, '... that they shold haue rydden apon myddsom*er* even wit*h* their
officers and a nombre and at other tymes ...' The original scribe then decided to specify the other
times and inserted '⸜' in the text and '⸜ Corpus *christ*i day' in the left margin; '⸜.' in the text and
'⸜. and saynt petre even' in the left margin and then cancelled 'and at other tymes'.

300   E20   f 292
In the top left-hand corner: '⟨...⟩ ordinaciones reformant ⟨...⟩ Chris*to*fero Harbert ⟨...⟩'.

302   Add MS 33852 f 12

The heading of the entry beginning f 12 contains a blank where the regnal year should be. The
next entry, containing the long pageant house and pageant repair list, is dated 19 December,
1 Mary. It must, therefore, refer to the Corpus Christi Day, 1553. Following it is an entry beginning on f 14 (the badly stained folio) dated 6 Edward VI or 1552. No specific mention of the
playing of the pageant occurs in this account. This is consonant with the cancellation of the play
that year by the council because of the plague. The accounts for 1553 and 1552 seem, then, to
be reversed, with the 1553 accounts inserted on a blank leaf and a half. The accounts beginning
on f 12, then, must be for 1551, a year when the play was played and the only year not specifically
dated in this sequence.

303   B20 f 100

The heading for the entry at the bottom left-hand corner of f 100 has a hand drawn to point to
this entry.

303   B20 f 100v

'Alsoo' is written in the top right-hand corner of B100v. It is not a catch-word and seems to have
no relation to the text.

306   Add MS 33852 f 15

The final items on f 15 are written under the 'summa' in a different hand, possibly that of the
auditor.

307   B21 f F

The first gathering of B21 is badly water damaged.

308   B21 f 16

Although E22 is a registered copy, this text is the earlier version of the ordinance. An even later
revision of the Blacksmiths' ordinances dated 1 June 1674 (E22 f 330v) continues to refer to
money collected for the support of the activities of the craft as Pageant Silver.

310   B21 f 43

The cancellation (ll 29-30) is made by underlining with dots rather than striking through.

312   B21 f 52v

Following the entry there are two pages left blank for ordinances not made up.

312   B21 f 57

The scribe has emended his text. He seems to have first written 'apon / reasonable consideracion
and / good aduyse it was agreed ...' He then cancelled 'apon', inserted 'by' and indicated the
reversal of 'good aduyse' and 'reasonable consideracion' by the use of superscript '.a.' and '.b.'
The new phrasing is 'by / good aduyse (and) reasonable consideracion it was agreed ...'

320   Add MS 33852 ff 17v, 19v

The accounting system for the expenses in 1554 is unique in this MS. The expenses are placed
under months beginning with January. The payment to the players is recorded under January

and the payment for their dinner under December. Both expenses were incurred 24 May.

321   D59T(a) mb 1-2
Box D82 contains two paper drafts of the torch-bearing entry and for the same entry in 1556.
Box D73 contains paper drafts of the Butchers and Bowers payments for 1555-7, 1559, 1561,
1563, 1564-9, 1571, 1574-83 and 1586.

322   Add MS 33852 f 20v
The final item on f 20v is written under the 'summa'.

324   B22 f 67v
The MS is badly faded at the margin.

334   E20A f 221v
The registered copy is taken as the base text.

344   C91:2 mb 1
A paper draft exists of this entry.

346   Add MS 33852 f 24
The final items on f 24 are in different ink, apparently in the hand of the auditor who also altered
the 'summa'.

347   Add MS 33852 f 24v-5v
A second hand apparently added the pageant master entry at the end of Expenses rather than
Receipts, realized his mistake and cancelled it, placing the entry at the end of the Receipts. The
name of Lancelot Coupland appears written in full in both entries, spelled 'laneslate'. The scribe
of the main entry has a brevigraph over 'lans', but as further appearances of the man's name in
adjacent folios are variously spelled, no expansion has been attempted.

348   B24 f 57
This paragraph and the next one were copied into the book on f 57v and then cancelled, suggesting
that the clerk kept a rough copy of the minutes and copied them later into the book.

353   B24 f 106a
This is the original letter written by Hutton's scribe in a rather Italianate hand, signed by Hutton
himself in a darker ink. The letter is badly damaged on the edges but has been repaired. The copy
of the endorsement written at the foot of f 106a is in the hand of the scribe who wrote the f 106v
entry. The hand is difficult and his strange Arabic '4' has lead earlier editors (including ourselves)
to misread '40' for 'to' (l 30) and '24' for '27' (l 36). The reading of '40' and '24' is correct and
solves the problem of possible misdating since 24 March would be 1567 for the scribe, but 27
March would be 1568.

357   Add MS 33852 ff 33v-4
A draft of this account appears at the end of the MS, ff 65-6

368 B25 ff 27-7v
This text is chosen as the base text rather than the copy in the Ecclesiastical Commission Minutes (BI: HC A.B.7 ff 41-1v) because of the context recording the action of the council. The scribe wrote the name Eymis (p 369, l 31) clearly. The original signature preserved in HC A.B.7 may be Kymis. Neither of these two names appears in the Freemen's lists.

370 E20A ff 230-1
B/Y, the earlier registered version, is taken as the base text.

372 C93:1 mb 2
This year the Foss Bridge Accounts were amalgamated with the Ouse Bridge Accounts. The pageant house entries from this roll on are in the fourth entry in each roll.

375 D60M(b) mb 2d
There is a note of Jackson's default in D62.

380 D60N(b) mb 2d
There is a note in D62 of Peter Hall's release and defaults in pageant money by Richard Hewton and Alan Herbert.

381 C7:2 mb 4
Moore and Balderston (two of the waits named in l 21) had been fined in Quarter Sessions in 1571 (Y: F3 f 23). Clerke (a third wait, l 22) stood surety for an offender 26 June 1593 (Y: F6 f 122v).

385 E22 ff 142v-3v
Robert Hewit, here named as master of minstrels (l 19), appears frequently in subsequent records and three times in the Quarter Sessions Books: 14 March 1571 (Y: F3 f 16), 23 January 1573 (Y: F3 f 72) and again 11 February 1583 (Y: F3 f 719).

390 D60Q(b) mb 2
There is a note in D77 indicating a payment of 6d to the Bridgemasters for the half of the rest due at Pentecost.

395 Add MS 33852 f 61
The auditors' report after the accounts for this year contains what seem to be the marks of four of the men named as auditors and the signatures of Langton and Hudson. This is the last regular entry in the MS. The last seven folios contain various decisions of the company dated variously and not in sequence from 1570-94. The draft of the 1569 account appears on ff 65-6. The only other references to pageant and minstrel activity appear on f 67. The entry is undated and incomplete, and written in a hand unlike any other in the MS. The entries are as follows:

...

Item Lad doune to mynstrels at tomas slaters   viij d

...

Item for nales & nalyng of *our* pagyn huse dore   iij d

...
Item farme of *our* paggyne huse   xij d
...
It*em* gyve to mynstryls of Trenite sunday   ⟨...⟩

They may refer to some year between 1580 and 1585 when BL Add MS 34604 begins.

395   QQ80/4/1 f 1v
QQ80/4/1 and QQ80/4/2 are close copies of each other with little to distinguish between them.
QQ80/4/1 has been chosen as the base text because it has a slightly fuller text.

398   D60T(b) mb 1
In a paper account for that year in box D62 is a note of a continuing 10s default by Richard
Hutton.

399   B28 f 40v
The marginal heading here, although apparently written in the same hand as the entry, does not
accurately reflect the content of the entry. The heading and others in this section are in slightly
darker ink, suggesting that the scribe wrote the headings later for easy reference.

400   B28 ff 70-1v
An antiquarian copy of these ordinances appears in Bodl. Rawlinson 450 f 388v.

401   B28 f 78v
Robert Collier was indicted, along with several others, for drinking in an unlicensed house, 26 July
1583 (Y; F4 f 3). A bond of £10 was set for him 1 February 1584 (Y: F4 ff 2-2v). On 23 July
1585 he was arraigned for an unspecified offence and bound over until the next session (Y: F4
f 113v).

408   B28 f 157
Tenniswodd appears twice in the Sessions Books for 1583 (Y: F4 ff 24v, 26v).

412   C94:3 mb 2
C94:4 is a paper draft of this roll.

413   D61W(b) mb 2d
Three years of defaults for the Butchers and Bowers are noted in the paper account for this year
in D62.

416   CC6(1) f 1v
This is the city's copy of the agreement bound into the endpapers of CC6. The mark between
'Robt' and 'hewit' at the end of the entry seems to represent his mark.

421   CC6(1) f 90
This is the last folio of CC6(1); a new type of paper is used.

424   Add MS 34604 f 4
The accounts in this book were made up either on 1 August or on 25 July. We have arbitrarily chosen the second of the two years for the dating.

426   E56 p 4
This entry is the first of many with some names changing yearly until 1644. Until 1595 the formula remains as printed here. From 1596 'pageant money' of journeymen is referred to as 'custom money'. From 1608 'pageant money' of the Ainsty (a suburb of York) is referred to as 'Ainsty money'.

427   PR Y/MG 19 p 60
Some words in this book are glossed in a modern hand.

431   D61Z(b) mb 2d
Six years back rent from the Butchers and Bowers is noted under a heading of 'Defaults' in paper account in D62, along with an arrear of 2s 2d noted against Richard Herbert for his pageant money and 10s against William Hancok for his.

432   PR Y/MCS 17 ff 9v-10
Some words in this book are glossed in a modern hand. The original scribe sometimes writes both a majuscule 'F' and a miniscule 'f' where 'ff' would be expected.

435   CC6(3) f 55v
Thomas Graves, wait, had appeared before the court of Quarter Sessions on 11 February 1583 as Thomas Grave, musician. He was bound over for an unspecified offence.

435   CC6(3) f 74
'William halley ... Maiour' (p 436, ll 5-10) is written on a note pasted to the bottom of the page.

438   QQ80/2/1 f 2
The Bricklayers regularly paid for minstrels at celebrations held on St James' Day (25 July); St Luke's Day (18 October); and Plough Day (the Monday after Epiphany – 6 January). The accounts seem to run normally from St James to St James and so span the year under which they appear in the text and the next one. The entry for 1589 is thus for 1589-90. Many early accounts are cancelled.

441   E22 f 109
The registered copy is taken as the base text.

441   CC7(1) f 57
This folio is fragmented at the edges.

442   D61C(c) mb 1
After this roll, all references to pageants and pageant houses disappear from the Mercers' records. The ceremonial Venison Feast continues and is arranged by the 'pageant masters' for many years, but the use of the title has ceased to have any playmaking significance.

446   QQ80/2/1 f 7
These entries are expenses although they appear under a 'receipts' heading.

461   QQ80/2/1 f 20
A draft of this account appears on f 15v.

465   Add MS 34604 ff 31-3v
The MS entry is misdated 1593-4.

471   Add MS 34604 f 36v
The amount received from the pageant masters for Maundy Bread was originally written for both masters. John Milner apparently defaulted. The sum was then altered as follows: 'vj s' cancelled; 'viij d' altered to 'iij s iiij d', thus dividing the total in half.

475   C9:1 mb 4d
MS very faded. Only this entry is legible.

482   CC9(2) p 108
The superlineation (l 17) is hard to decipher. It seems to mean 'delivered to in person'.

483   C95:5 mb 2
This is a paper draft.

489   Add MS 34604 f 45
The illegible letters on this page have been obliterated by ink showing through from the verso side.

503   PR Y/HTG p 158
This entry is puzzling since James I did not pass through York until 16 April 1603 and Holy Trinity Goodramgate records three ringings for the king in 1603 (see p 513).

506   B32 f 250
Following this excerpt are one hundred and fifty names of citizens divided by parish.

512   E40 f 118
Collated with QQ80/4/1 f 9v and QQ80/4/2 f 9. E40 has been chosen as the base text because of the context provided for the ordinances.

518   QQ80/2/1 f 48v
Dated by mayoral year. Several experimental hands appear on these folios.

522   QQ80/2/1 f 53
From ff 50v-96v many dots, having no apparent function, appear between words.

526   E22 ff 136-6v
The headings are in a column ruled off from the text. The entries appear to be numbered in the

margin between text and column. The number 6 appears opposite the first entry and 7 opposite the entry below, headed 'Electinge of pageante masters'.

528 CC13(2) f 44v
'for' is written after the cancellation and above 'To'.

532 QQ80/2/1 f 63
A draft of this account appears on f 57.

540 QQ80/2/1 f 70
The names of the three pageant masters are in the heading for the year. See also 1613 (f 74).

541 Add MS 34604 ff 84-5v
The action taken by the auditors from their note on f 84 indicates that the company must have agreed to disallow the use of its funds for minstrels and wine. Pageant dinners had been discontinued in 1608. The Bakers continued to receive rent from William Wright until 1644 (f 139) and pay some form of pageant house rent until 1651 (f 164). Officers of the company called pageant masters continued to be elected until at least 1761 when BL Add MS 34604 ends.

549 B34 ff 118-20v
(p 552, l 25) 'O nimium fortunati ...': cf Vergil, *Georgicon II*, 458, where the complete text is as follows:

'O fortunatos nimium, si sua bona norint, / agricolas, quibus ipsa procul discordibus armis / fundit humo facilem victum tellus!'

(Oh most fortunate, if they only knew their blessings, are the countrymen for whom, far from clashing arms, the most righteous earth pours forth those things, easy sustenance from the soil.)

559 PR Y/MS 2 f 92
This entry actually appears under the accounts for 1616, although the king's visit was April 1617.

565 CC17(2) f 69-70
This single folio is numbered '69-70' in MS.

572 QQ80/2/1 f 94v
This is apparently a draft of the account appearing on ff 102-2v. See below.

572 QQ80/2/1 f 102v
On f 103v there is a cancelled draft for 1630.

575 QQ80/2/1 f 108
ff 108v-122v are taken up with miscellaneous fines, agreements, apprenticeships, etc of the company for various years. Dinners are mentioned, but no minstrels.

579 CC20(2) ff 17, 18
In these books, initials appear beside various entries. These may be the initials of the individual scribes.

581 CC20(4) f 31
The folio is torn (or burned?) away at the right-hand margin.

583 B35 ff 208-11
The catchword 'highnesse' (p 584, l 42) is omitted from the text. The catchword 'And' (p 590, l 22) is omitted from the text.

595 B35 f 284v
The beginning of the entry is dated 30 June 1635. The note at the bottom of the page and the next entry are dated 7 August.

596 C19:1 mb 3
In this entry and in C19:2 and C19:3, the sums have been copied in Arabic form in later hands.

597 CC22(1) ff 18-31
This book has been badly flood damaged.

600 B36 ff 28-31
The catchword 'in' (p 601, l 17) and the catchwords ('the', 'occasions', M*aiestes*') for ff 29v-30v have been omitted from the text.

607 CC22(3) ff 23, 25, 41-1v
There are holes in the middle of these entries.

End-notes Appendix I

620 E20 f 26v
Otiose flourishes occur regularly over 'n' in this hand.

620 E20 f 29v
The reference is to ordinances on ff 90-90v. See p 625.

621 E20 f 31
This was once a separate ordinance now inserted into the book. Stitch marks are visible on the left-hand side. In this script, otiose flourishes appear on final 'r's'.

625 E20 f 90
There is a long English side note here dated 1592, indicating that new ordinances had been written into 'le black pap*er* booke'.

626 E20 ff 128v-9
In this hand 'y' and 'þ' are the same letter form, except that 'y's' are dotted.

End-notes Appendix II

640   Lansdowne MS 403 ff 7-8v
Frequent dots that have no apparent function occur throughout this passage.

End-notes Appendix V

651   D19 f 11v
D19, the Chartulary of the Mercers, is foliated in both a renaissance and modern hand. The folios containing the names of the pageant masters for 1488-90 are foliated in a modern hand. The old foliation begins again in 1492. Dates given are editorial.

Abbreviations

abl	ablative	M L	medieval Latin
acc	accusative	n	noun
act	active	nom	nominative
adj	adjective	nt	neuter
adv	adverb	part	participle
C L	classical Latin	pass	passive
conj	conjunction	perf	perfect
dat	dative	phr	phrase
eccl	ecclesiastical	pl	plural
E G	English Glossary	pp	past participle
f	feminine	pr	present
fut	future	prep	preposition
gen	genitive	pron	pronoun
imper	imperative	prp	present participle
impers	impersonal	rel	relative
ind	indicative	sg	single
indecl	indeclinable	subj	subjunctive
inf	infinitive	tr	transitive
intr	intransitive	v	verb
m	masculine	vb	verbal

Glossaries

The glossaries are intended to make the documents as accessible as possible to the reader. English words (especially craft names) which occur in Latin or Anglo-Norman passages are found in the English glossary, although words not easily recognized as English have been listed alphabetically in the appropriate glossary with a cross reference to the English (EG).

Words are included in the Latin glossary if they are not to be found in Lewis and Short, *A Latin Dictionary* (Oxford, 1897), the standard reference work for classical Latin. Words listed in Lewis and Short which have had a change or restriction of meaning in medieval Latin are also cited. Homonyms from Lewis and Short are included to avoid confusion with medieval Latin words. Many words in these documents are common classical Latin words using medieval spellings. Such variations have not been considered significant, ie, as producing new words. They are:

> ML *c* for CL *t* before *i*
> ML *cc* for CL *ct* before *i*
> ML *d* for CL *t* in a final position
> ML *e* for CL *ae* or *oe*
> ML *ff* for CL *f*, especially in an initial position
> ML addition of *h*
> ML omission of CL *h*
> ML *n* for CL *m* before *m* or *n*
> intrusion of ML *p* in the CL consonant cluster *mn* or *ms*
> ML doubling of CL single consonants and singling of CL double consonants

In addition, medieval Latin words can vary in spelling by alternation between *i* and *e* before another vowel. Scribal practice has been followed in such cases, as well as with *i/j* and *u/v* variants.

Words or phrases which may be unfamiliar to a reader of modern French are included in the Anglo-Norman glossary. Some Anglo-Norman words beginning with *d'* or *l'* in the text do so as a result of elision of a preceding *de* or *le, la* with the initial vowel. Such words are glossed under their initial vowel. Where the gender of a noun has been impossible to determine, the uncertainty is indicated by a question mark (?). Headwords have been chosen according to frequency of usage. All variant spellings are listed.

Forms of English words interesting from a purely phonological or morphological point of view have generally not been included in the English glossary. It is assumed that the reader is familiar with common spelling alternations (eg, medial and final *d/th*, initial *en/in*) in otherwise easily understood words. Where variant spellings of the same form occur, the first spelling in alphabetical order has normally been chosen as headword. However, where this would result in an odd or rare spelling becoming a headword, a more common spelling has been given precedence. Spellings separated from their main entries by more than two intervening ones have been cross referenced.

In the Latin glossary, headwords are given in the standard form: ie, nouns are listed by nominative, genitive, and gender; adjectives by the terminations in the nominative singular; verbs by their principal parts. Where the same word occurs in spellings which differ according to the list above, the most common spelling is designated as standard and used for the headword. Some scribal errors in spelling are footnoted in the text; others are to be found listed separately in the glossary. Anomalous inflectional forms are dealt with in one of two ways: they are listed separately and cross referenced to the main entry or, if they follow the headword alphabetically, they are listed under that headword and set apart by bold-face type.

Manuscript capitalization has been ignored. Only the first three occurrences of each word are given with page and line number separated by an oblique stroke. If the word occurs in marginalia, this is indicated by a lower-case *m* following the page and line reference.

Works consulted:

Craigie, Sir William A. et al. *A Dictionary of the Older Scottish Tongue from the twelfth century to the end of the seventeenth.* Parts I-XXIX. Chicago, 1931-77.

Du Cange, Charles du Fresne. *Glossarium mediae et infimae latinitatis.* 6 vols. Paris, 1733.

Godefroy, Frédéric. *Dictionnaire de l'ancienne langue française et de tous ses dialectes du ixe au xve siècle.* 10 vols. Paris, 1880-1902.

Greimas, A.J. *Dictionnaire de l'ancien français jusqu'au milieu du xive siècle.* 2nd ed. Paris, 1968.

Kelham, Robert. *A Dictionary of the Norman or Old French Language.* London, 1779.

Kurath, Hans and Sherman M. Kuhn. *Middle English Dictionary.* Fascicules A.1-M.4. Ann Arbor, 1952-77 (The files in Ann Arbor have been consulted for later letters as well).

Latham, R.E. *Dictionary of Medieval Latin from British Sources.* Fascicule 1, A-B. London, 1975.

— *Revised Medieval Latin Word-list from British and Irish Sources.* London, 1965.

Lewis, Charlton T. and Charles Short. *A Latin Dictionary.* Oxford, 1879.

The Compact Edition of the Oxford English Dictionary. 2 vols. New York, 1971.

Latin Glossary

abusus, -us *n m* abuse, misuse 16/17

accidia, -e *n f* sloth (vice) 12/39

acer, acris, acre *adj* See **vinum**

adamond EG

adhero, -ere, -si, -sum *v tr* adhere to, engage in 645/29

adtunc *adv* then 106/22, 122/19

agnus, -i *n m* lamb 20/25, 20/27, 222/7; — **dei** *n phr* literally, lamb of God; a piece of flatwork jewellery in the shape of a lamb, symbolically an icon of Christ 634/17, 635/9, 636/1, etc; EG, **agnus**

affecto, -are, -avi *v intr* be affected, moved (by feelings, emotions, etc) 48/5

agrus, -a, -um *adj* from **acer, acris, acre** See **vinum**

aieris, -is *nf* weather 51/10

aisiamentum, -i *n nt* easement, accommodation 79/37, 90/17, 90/30, etc

aldermannus, -i *n m* alderman 12/16, 37/30, 38/1, etc

aliqualiter *adv* in some way, in any way 646/13

alliceo, -ere, -ui, -citum *v tr* induce 638/28

allocacio, -onis *n f* allocation, allotment, allowance 115/42, 116/18m, 137/13m, etc

allocacionies *n f nom pl* for **allocaciones** 238/32m, 241/27m, 244/37m, etc See **allocacio**

alloco, -are, -avi, -atum *v tr* allocate (funds) 12/40, 39/23, 116/18 etc

allutarius, -i *n m* cordwainer 30/10, 32/37, 40/31, etc

almarialum, -i *n nt* 3/32 See **armarialum**

altare, -aris *n nt* altar 18/9, 133/12 summum

— *n phr* high altar 97/40, 638/40

altra *adj f sg* syncopated form of **altera** the other (of two) 247/15

amyttus, -i, *n m* amice, square of white linen on shoulders of celebrant priest 211/6

anglicanus, -a, -um *adj* English 78/16, 78/29, 80/8, etc

anglice *adv* in the English language 35/4, 98/19

anglicus, -a, -um *adj* English 32/17

annuatim *adv* yearly 12/3, 17/7, 29/16, etc; **annuiatim** 52/34

antiphona, -e *n f* antiphon 133/5

apostolicus, -a, -um *adj* apostolic; **apostolica sedes** *n phr* apostolic see, the holy see, ie, Rome 647/36

apparator, -oris *n m* overseer, manager 79/30

apparelum, -i *n nt* fittings, gear 133/12

apparicio, -onis *n f* apparition, appearance 26/17, 26/18, 26/19, etc

appendo, -ere, -endi, -ensum *v tr* affix (a seal) 36/32, 52/22

applico, -are, -avi, -atum *v tr* pay (a sum of money) to 16/23, 29/8, 29/22, etc

apprecio, -are, -avi, -atum *v tr* value, appraise 98/1, 98/4, 98/10, etc

apprenticiatus, -us *n m* apprenticeship 31/34, 32/2

apprenticius, -i *n m* apprentice 31/33, 32/17, 35/18, etc

arcuarius, -i *n m* bower 164/14

aretro *adv* in arrears 36/12

armarialum, -i *n nt* cupboard 3/33

armigerus, -i *n m* squire 69/26, 71/39, 71/40, etc

ars, artis *n f* craft, guild 31/34, 32/16, 34/40, etc

artefex, -icis *n m* 156/15, 161/16 See artifex

articulus, -i *n m* article of faith 98/16, 98/27, 639/16, etc

artifex, -icis *n m* craftsman 28/28, 31/4, 31/13, etc

artificialis, -e *adj* made with skill or craft; pertaining to a craft guild 2/6

artificium, -i *n nt* craft guild 5/13, 8/23, 16/22, etc

artificum, -i *n nt* 31/38, 37/28 See artificium

ascensio, -onis *n f* ascension 26/20

asculto, -are, -avi, -atum *v tr* listen 117/5

assensio, -onis *n f* 66/40 See ascensio

assertus, -a, -um *adj* the aforesaid 120/21

assignatus, -i *n m* an assignee 134/28, 134/34

associacio, -onis *n f* association 6/40

assumpcio, -onis *n f* assumption (of the Virgin Mary) 26/24

ataris *n nt gen sg* for altaris 132/29 See altare

attempto, -are, -avi, -atum *v tr* attempt, attack 16/25

attendo, -ere, -i, -ensum *v tr* attend, accompany 116/38, 122/5, 132/15, etc

attornum, -i *n nt* attorney, proxy 87/15

aucus, -i *n m* goose 222/4, 225/24; — viridis *n phr* green (or young) goose 229/30, 235/9, 241/17-18, etc

augustinius, -a, -um *adj* Augustinian See frater

auricalcus, -a, -um *adj* brazen 640/19

auricallcatus, -a, -um *adj* brazen 68/30

aurifaber, -bri *n m* goldsmith 35/34, 35/39, 40/35, etc

avantagium, -i *n nt* gain, profit 34/9

ave *n indecl* the prayer Ave Maria 132/30

avisamentum, -i *n nt* advice, consideration 34/3, 34/27, 39/31, etc

azinus, -i *n m* ass, donkey 18/28

baiualatorium, -i *n nt* bier 98/2, 98/7, 98/9, etc

ballivus, -i *n m* a bailiff 8/22

barbitonsus, -i *n m* barber 625/11, 625/14, 625/26

baro, -onis *n m* baron 60/27, 65/7, 66/14, etc

barra, -e *n f* bar 9/15, 9/23, 9/26, etc

batellus, -i *n m* boat 33/40

baudekyn, bawdewkyn EG

beatus, -a, -um *adj* blessed; *with a proper noun,* Saint 3/33, 11/37, 26/22, etc

beda, -e *n f* bead 635/4, 636/29, 636/31, etc

bedellus, -i *n m* beadle 185/28, 188/33, 189/38, etc

beldellus, -i *n m* 210/23 See bedellus

benedictus *n indecl* the versicle benedictus qui venit from the canon of the mass 20/15

benedictus, -a, um *adj* having been blessed 483/16; aqua benedicta *n phr* holy water 132/26

benivole *adv* kindly, benevolently 48/13

berillum, -i *n nt* beryl, or a similar precious stone; a high quality glass or crystal, used to glaze windows and monstrances 51/15, 631/27, 634/16, etc

billa, -e *n f* billet 9/37, 229/37

blandrellum, -i *n nt* white apple 106/21

blodius, -a, -um *adj* blue 74/21, 82/10, 83/8, etc

boitria, -e *n f* buttery 79/37

boldius, -a, -um *adj* 98/11, 639/12 See blodius

boscus, -i *n m* firewood 18/9

boses EG

bovinus, -a, -um *adj* bovine See carnis

bowere EG

brabannia, -e *n f* brabant 145/24

broggator, -ris *n m* broker 46/9, 46/10, 46/15 See also EG broggours

brotherinus, -i *n m* embroidery 145/22

bukysyn EG

bulla, -e *n f* a (papal) bull 638/19

burdalexander, burdealexander EG

bustiane, -anis *n nt* bustian, coarse cloth 638/1

calix, calicis *n f* chalice 27/32, 98/6, 98/8, etc

camera, -e *n f* room, chamber 102/9, 106/23, 122/20, etc; — consilij *n phr, or simply* camera the council chamber of the city council 8/24, 12/4, 29/18, etc

camerarius, -i *n m* chamberlain, a member of the council chamber 12/5, 29/7, 29/20, etc

campanile, -is *n nt* little bell 631/22

cancello, -are, -avi, -atum *v tr* cancel (a document, an agreement) 7/35m, 161/6

canonicus, -i *n m* canon (ie, of a cathedral) 132/24, 133/2, 133/17, etc

canonicus, -a, -um *adj* canonical 73/36

capa, -e *n f* cape, cope (eccl vestment) 116/32, 117/13

capella, -e *n f* chapel 51/25, 51/34, 52/2, etc

capellanus, -i *n m* chaplain 15/18, 51/30, 52/21, etc

capillum, -i *n nt* chapel 102/8

capitalis, -e *adj* chief 41/31

capitulum, -i *n nt* (cathedral) chapter 10/32, 12/32, 103/29, etc

capucium, -i *n nt* hood, cowl 145/25

cariagia, -e *n f* cartage 116/7, 145/15

caritative *adv* charitably 646/7, 646/21

caritativus, -a, -um *adj* charitable 646/15

carnifex, -icis *n m* butcher 31/14, 31/15, 31/24, etc

carniprivium, -i *n nt* Lent 69/9

carnis, -is *n f* flesh, meat 9/19, 47/11; — **bouina** *n phr* beef 222/6, 225/23, 229/29, etc; — **bouium** beef 79/4; — **bouum** beef 235/16-117; — **ouium** lamb 79/4; — **mutulium** mutton 221/37, 225/30-1, 229/29, etc; — **vitulorum** veal 79/4

carpentaria, -e *n f* carpentry 145/14

carpentarinus, -a, -um *adj* pertaining to carpentry or carpenters 9/25

carpentarius, -i *n m* carpenter 32/37, 33/3, 41/35, etc; **carpenterius** 9/27

castellum, -i *n nt* castle, part of a torch 27/36, 98/35, 179/25, etc

catallum, -i *n nt* chattel 7/9, 646/18, 647/28

cathedralis, -is *n m* cathedral 102/8, 122/22, 254/31, etc

catholicus, -a, -um *adj* Catholic 50/22, 98/17, 98/27, etc

causo, -are, -avi, -atum *v tr* cause 47/36, 48/2

cautelose *adv* carefully 80/2

cedula, -e *n f* document, schedule 632/35

celatura, -e *n f* canopy 98/9, 639/9

celebracio, -onis *n f* celebration (of a mass or a holy day) 638/24

celebro, -are, -avi, -atum *v tr* celebrate (a mass or holy day) 1/18, 2/14, 122/23, etc

cementarius, -i *n m* mason 33/20, 33/21m, 33/29, etc

cenapium, -i *n nt* mustard 221/36, 225/30, 229/36, etc

ceptrum, -i *n nt* sceptre 98/25, 639/26

cera, -e *n f* wax (used in torches) 27/16, 91/11, 104/2, etc

cera *n f* 465/42 See **sera**

cericum, -i *n nt* silk 78/20

cericus, -a, -um *adj* silken 80/4

cernicum, -i *n nt* silk 132/25

cerotecarius, -i *n m* glover 617/14

certifico, -are, avi, -atum *v tr* make certain, certify 645/6, 645/13

cervicallum, -i *n nt* little pillow, little cushion 211/7

chaloners EG

chaplettes EG

chariours EG

cheuerons EG

chivalerus, -i *n m* knight 66/27, 67/8, 67/24, etc

chorum, -i *n nt* choir 1/18, 73/37, 132/29, etc

cimiterium, -i *n nt* churchyard, cemetary 85/6

ciphus, -i *n m* cup 79/20, 629/18, 629/20, etc

circumauratus, -a, -um *adj* gilt all around 635/21

circumceptus, -a, -um *adj* encircled 634/19

circumforincius, -i *n m* bordering 632/31

circuo, -ere, -i *v intr* go around 49/23, 50/14, 79/24, etc

cirotheca, -e *n f* glove 98/26

cirpus, -i *n m* rushes (sometimes used as lights; sometimes strewn on the floor as a covering) 1/7, 225/34, 229/39, etc

claretus, -a, -um *adj* See **vinum**

clausura, -e *n f* the closing, clasp, catch (of a box) 52/5

clava, -e *n f* key 116/10

clava, -e *n f* mace 17/6, 113/28 See also **serviens**

clavacio, -onis *n f* nailing (specifically the nailing

of Christ to the cross) 26/12, 37/21

clavecorda, -e *n f* clavichord 89/31

clavis, -is *n f* key 9/22, 52/5, 52/6, etc

clavus, -i *n m* key 156/27

clericus, -i *n m* ecclesiastical clerk 79/29, 116/20, 116/21, etc; — **communis** *n phr* common or town clerk 17/2, 109/40, 187/6, etc

coartifex, -icis *n m* fellow-craftsman 37/25

cocliar, -aris *n nt* spoon 634/20, 634/22, 635/24, etc

cocus, -i *n m* cook 42/15, 79/16; — **communis** *n phr* town cook 42/17

collecta, -e *n f* collect 638/24, 638/26

coloracio, -onis *n f* colouring 632/27

comerarios *n m acc pl* for **camerarios** 33/26 See **camerarius**

comes, -itis *n m* earl 66/9, 67/8, 67/18, etc **cometibus** *dat pl* 132/18

comitatus, -us *n m* county 87/11, 645/9

comitissa, -e *n f* countess 94/35

commestio, -onis *n f* meal, feast 646/38

communio, -onis *n f* communion, ie, reception of the sacrament 20/30

communis, -e *adj* common, pertaining to the community 11/36, 17/2, 28/18, etc

communitas, -tatis *n f* the commons, the community 8/24, 12/7, 12/17, etc

compilatus, -a, -um *adj* compiled 17/2, 68/28, 88/4, etc

compoto, -are, -avi, -atum *v tr* 161/15, 176/5, 631/19, etc See **computo**

compotum, -i *n nt* account 38/35, 40/12, 121/8, etc

computo, -are, -avi, -atum *v tr* reckon, make or give an accounting 9/14, 27/15, 103/42, etc

concavatus, -a, -um *adj* concave 634/2

concensu *n m abl sg* for **consensu** consent 109/26

concepcio, -onis *n f* conception (ie, of a child) 76/36

concino, -ere, -ui *v tr* sing together 117/24

conclavo, -are, -avi, -atum *v tr* nail one thing to another 22/5

conductio, -ionis *n f* production (of a play) 101/26; hire 91/8

confluo, -ere, -i, -itum *v tr* flow together (of a

large group of people) 120/19

confrater, -tris *n m* fellow member (male) of a religious confraternity 6/40, 15/34, 51/5, etc

confraternitas, -tatis *n f* confraternity 645/31

congregacio, -onis *n f* congregation, general meeting 90/18, 91/1, 625/29, etc

conpacio, -onis *n f* agreement, contract 79/3

conquestum, -i *n nt* conquest 6/3, 12/14, 17/1, etc

consoror, -oris *n f* fellow member (female) of a religious confraternity 645/30, 646/4, 647/17, etc

constabularius,-i *n m* constable 106/36, 156/18, 177/23, etc

constitucio, -onis *n f* decree or constitution of any body, whether a guild or the city council 15/17, 28/22, 30/36, etc

contradiccio, -onis *n f* contradiction, gainsaying 41/40

contribuo, -ere, -i, -tum *v tr* contribute 35/14

contributarius, -i *n m* contributor 31/7, 31/9, 64/30, etc

contributorius, -a, -um *adj* contributory 31/17, 33/30, 34/2, etc

convive *n declension and gender unknown* feast 25/36

coocum, -i *n nt* (?) coconut 79/11

cooperacio, -onis *n f* covering 631/23

coopertolium, -i *n nt* cover, lid 640/10

cooperturium, -i *n nt* cover 631/26

cooportura, -e *n f* cover 52/6

copia, -e *n f* copy 88/3, 638/14

cor, cordis *n nt* (?) heart-shaped ornament of precious metal 635/5, 635/14, 636/6, etc

coronacio, -onis *n f* coronation 26/9, 26/25, 54/33, etc

corporax, -acis *n gender unknown* (?) corporal 637/33, 637/34

corureours, couureours E G

creacio, -onis *n f* creation 25/9

creo, -are, -avi, -atum *v tr* create (someone) in an office or dignity 133/15

crod E G

crokes, crukes E G

croude, crowde E G

crucifixum, -i *n nt* crucifix 635/2, 635/7, 635/11, etc

cruettes EG

crulez EG

curdes EG

curia, -e *n f* court, whether of justice or of courtiers 117/21

curialitas, -tatis *n f* gratuity 2/20m, 3/40m, 10/32, etc curialetate *abl sg* 12/32

currallo *n nt abl sg* for corrallo 634/41; *of* corrallum coral

curriculum, -i *n nt* course 120/28

curyour, cuuryours EG

custagium, -i *n nt* costs 146/4

custodia, -e *n f* custody 40/14, 633/20; — pagine *n phr* office of pageant master 243/13, 243/16, 243/20, etc

custos, -odis *n m* warden 3/17, 4/1, 4/16, etc; — pagine *n phr* pageant master 247/32, 247/33, 247/36-7, etc

data, -e *n f* date 86/15, 134/26, 159/25, etc

dealbatus, -a, -um *adj* white 15/25

deauratio, -onis *n f* gilding 631/29

debilis, -e *adj* weak, worn-out, faint (of writing) 88/4, 629/18

debity *adj gen sg* for debiti; *of* debitus, -a, -um owing, owed 631/29

decanus, -i *n m* dean (of a cathedral chapter) 132/3, 132/24, 132/30, etc

decetero *adv* henceforth 1/18, 2/2, 34/31, etc

delibero, -are, -avi, -atum *v tr* deliver something to someone 5/39; *in pass* pay back (a sum) 42/6; delivero 17/5

demanda, -e *n f* demand, claim 36/18

denarius, -i *n m* penny, pence 15/35, 29/7, 29/9, etc

dentriculus, -i *n m* pickerel 221/33, 222/9, 225/27, etc

dentrix, -icis *n m* pike 229/35, 235/13, 237/37

deporto, -are, -avi, -atum *v tr* wear 117/13, 638/9

deposicio, -onis *n f* deposition (of the body or relics of a saint) 103/31, 103/34, 107/6, etc

depredo, -are, -avi, -atum *v tr* rob someone of something *(with double acc)* 646/17

deputatus, -a, -um *adj & perf part pass* deputized, having been sent in the place of another 244/21, 301/24

desposicio, -onis *n f* 208/37, 208/41 See deposicio

di. *abbreviation of* dimidium a half 30/16, 79/3, 83/36, etc

diademz EG

dies, diei *n f* day; one of the days of the week 1/27, 2/1, 2/29, etc; — dominica *n phr* Sunday 34/34; in dies daily 48/4; — lune Monday 69/9, 75/29; — marcis (*or* martis) Tuesday 69/13, 71/11, 71/12; — veneris Friday 1/27

dimissio, -onis *n f* lease, the act of leasing 36/17, 120/2, 134/21m, etc

dimitto, -ere, dimisi, dimissum *v tr* send away 21/18, 25/22; *often in phr* dimittere ad firmam lease out, rent out 35/33, 35/34m, 36/23, etc

disposicio, -onis *n f* disposition, decision 29/11, 30/3, 209/39, etc

districtio, -onis *n f* distraint 38/20, 42/4

distringo, -ere, -i, -inctum *v tr* distrain 38/14, 38/15

doctor, -oris *n m* learned man, especially one learned in theology or law 18/14, 19/19, 25/31, etc

domina, -e *n f* lady (title) 52/11, 68/3, 75/19, etc

dominicus, -a, -um *adj* pertaining to the Lord, See dies 34/34 and oracio 6/32, 7/2; pertaining to a lord, See panis 60/31, 65/11, 74/30, etc

dominus, -i *n m* lord (title), (applied not only to peers and bishops, but to Benedictine monks, members of a cathedral chapter, and priests) 3/31, 9/17m, 9/31, etc

dompni *n m gen sg, probably from* dominus, -i lord 632/8

domus, -us *or* -ui *n f* house, home 5/18, 5/25, 5/26, etc; *also in phr* — pagine *or* paginarum pageant house, or house of the pageants 42/10, 46/22, 46/25, etc

donatum, -i *n nt* gift 66/3

doubeler E G

draghtlouers E G

ductura, -e *n f* transporting, moving 218/31, 218/36, 219/5, etc

ducus, -us *n m* duke 637/10

duodenum, -i *n nt* dozen 28/5, 91/11, 91/12, etc

dux, ducis *n m* duke 60/26, 65/6, 66/13, etc

dyademaunt E G

dyademz E G

educcio, -onis *n f* production (of a play or pageant) 87/28

effectualiter *adv* effectually 117/4

electio, -onis *n f* choice 34/4; election 5/20, 630/27

eligo, -ere, elegi, electum *v tr* choose (by election), elect 34/12, 39/15, 40/9, etc

emendacio, -onis *n f* mending, repair 6/38, 9/22, 54/35, etc

eneus, -a, -um *adj* made of brass 640/15, 640/16

ereus, -a, -um *adj* made of copper 630/1m, 630/1, 630/2, etc

erigo, -ere, erexi, erectum *v tr* raise, erect, put up (a shop, etc) 35/16, 35/21

evidencia, -e *n f* evidence, proof 637/28, 638/30

ex nunc *adv* henceforth 32/21

exannuo, -ere, -i, -atum *v tr* approve 122/26

excecutore *n m abl sg* 133/4, 133/11 See executor

excessiuus, -a, -um *adj* excessive 47/30

executor, -oris *n m* executor (of a will) 5/24, 87/19, 88/7, etc

exemium, -i *n nt* gift 120/33, 145/6, 145/15m, etc

exemius, -a, -um *adj* excellent 120/34

exemua *n nt nom pl* for exemia 121/26m See exemium

eximinum *n nt nom pl* for exemium 146/4 See exemium

exopposito *adv* on the opposite side 93/21, 93/27, 101/8, etc

expansio, -onis *n f* stretching out (specifically of Christ on the cross) 26/12, 37/21

expenca, -e *n f* for expensa expenses 203/17, 203/19m, 207/1m, etc

exspensa, -e *n f* for expensa expenses 124/41m, 237/21

extraho, -ere, -axi, -actum *v tr* draw out (a sword from its sheath) 64/27

extunc *adv* thenceforth 33/30, 36/6, 87/30, etc

fabrica, -e *n f* fabric (of a church, etc) 88/18

fasticulum, -i *n nt* faggot 225/32, 244/13, 248/20, etc

feodum, -i *n nt* fee 115/38m, 185/28, 188/33, etc

feretrum, -i *n nt* bier 23/24; reliquary or shrine in which the sacrament was carried in Corpus Christi procession 51/32, 73/39, 79/34, etc; feratrum, -i 210/34, 210/38, 213/2, etc

feria, -e *n f* weekday 14/9

festivus, -a, -um *adj* festal, festive, pertaining to a feast day 2/2, 50/24, 51/11, etc

ffeuers E G

ffounders, ffoundours E G

ffuystours E G

fincio, -onis *n f* affixing, sewing on 78/32

finis, -is *n m* end, finish 11/1, 11/33, 11/34, etc; point (of a dagger) 64/28

finis, -is *n gender unknown* fine, assessment 143/34m

firma, -e *n f* lease, rent 3/17, 35/33, 36/28, etc See dimitto See also E G farme

flammeolum, -i *n nt* woman's veil, specifically Veronica's veil 21/32

fleubotamo, -are, -avi, -atum *v tr* let blood 625/17

focalium, -i *n nt* fuel 9/19

folium, -i *n nt* page, folio 8/24m, 10/39, 10/40, etc

fons, fontis *n m* fountain, spring 85/4; baptismal font 132/27

forinsicus, -a, -um *adj* foreign, strange, external 41/7, 47/11; forincecus, -a, -um 200/2m, 200/15m; forincicus, -a, -um 90/17m,

90/29m, 90/33m, etc

forisfacio, -ere, -feci, -fectum *v tr* forfeit 109/
32, 126/21, 159/27, etc

forisfactura, -e *n f* forfeit, forfeiture 106/36m,
113/17, 143/34m, etc

forisfacturum, -i *n nt* forfeit, forfeiture 143/34

formula, -e *n f* bench 79/21 See also EG formes

foundours EG

fourbours EG

fourmez EG

frater, -ris *n m* member of a fraternity 50/33,
87/39; member of a religious order 4/16;
fratres augustini *n phr* Augustinian friars
85/20, 102/7; fratres predicantes (*or*
predicati) Friars Preacher (Dominicans)
35/37, 106/23; fratres sancti leonardi
brothers of St Leonard's Hospital, Augustinian monks 180/25

fraternitas, -tatis *n f* fraternity, confraternity
6/31, 6/41, 7/8, etc

frengium, -i *n nt* fringe 145/21

fullitura, -e *n f* fulling (of cloth) 41/13

fullitus, -a, -um *adj* fulled (cloth) 41/6, 41/10

fundacio, -onis *n f* foundation (of an organization), founding 6/31, 61/40, 638/11

fundator, -oris *n m* founder 647/4

fursperres EG

fustinula, -e *n f* 'fleshcrook', a sort of fork or
hook for removing meat from a pot 640/20

garcio, -onis *n m* boy, servant 18/9, 76/2

gardianum, -i *n nt* garden 85/4, 85/8

garlandum, -i *n nt* garland 632/34

garnest EG

garniamentum, -i *n nt* garment, livery 12/18

garsio, -onis *n m* 75/26 See garcio

gaudium, -i *n nt* joy 18/34, 51/20

gaudium, -i *n nt* gaud (an ornament) 636/16,
636/19, 636/23, etc

geistour EG

generosus, -i *n m* person of good birth, member
of the gentry 74/32, 83/25

genuflecto, -are, -avi, -aturum *v intr* genuflect
631/36

gestrum, -i *n nt* dagger 64/20, 64/25, 64/28

gilda, -e *n f* craft guild 12/15; religious guild
68/27, 115/34, 116/31, etc

giro, -are, -avi, atum *v tr* turn 79/19

gracia, -e *n f* thanks 50/24; grace 33/6, 52/14;
gracias tibi deus *n phr* antiphon beginning
'Thanks to thee, O God' 133/6

grenegeys EG

grossum, -i *n nt only in idiom* in grosso wholesale 64/21, 91/15, 145/22, etc

gubernaturum, -i *n nt* governing, organizing,
directing 6/39, 6/42, 645/24, etc

guihald, guyhald EG

hangyng EG

haraldus, -i *n m* herald 55/1m, 55/1, 65/38, etc

hausorium, -i *n nt* ladle 640/19

hespum, -i *n nt* hasp (of a door) 219/1 See
also EG hespis

hibitu *n f abl sg* for habitu monastic habit
637/9

honor virtus *n phr* beginning of a liturgical
hymn used as a title, the *responsorium* for
Trinity 132/28-9

hospicale *n nt acc sg* for hospitale 92/33 See
hospitale

hospicium, -i *n nt* lodging 122/16; — communis
aule (or Guildhall) *n phr* specifically rooms
above the arch of the Guildhall let at Corpus
Christi to the dignitaries of the city 181/21,
188/2, 203/20, etc

hospitalarium, -i *n nt* hospital 85/20

hospitale, -is *n nt* hospital 12/22, 27/21

hospito, -are, -avi, -atum *v tr* house, store 5/15,
5/18, 9/21, etc

hostia, -e *n f* consecrated Host 631/37

huiusmodi *indecl adj* of this kind, such 15/25,
29/9, 29/12, etc

iacio, -ere, ieci *v intr* lie 18/27, 35/36, 226/21,
etc; *used transitively in* cause to lie, lay out
64/26

iakettes EG

immediate *adv* immediately 133/5

immediatus, -a, -um *adj* immediate 117/20

imperpetuum *adv* perpetually, always 49/12, 50/7, 113/3, etc

imposterum *adv* henceforward 38/36, 51/8

imprisonamentum, -i *n nt* imprisonment 42/7

imprisono, -are, avi, -atum *v tr* imprison, jail 33/2

inantea *adv* henceforward 38/4

incarnatio, -onis *n f* incarnation 120/12

incontrarium *adv* to the contrary, otherwise 8/23

incurro, -ere, -i, incursum *v tr* incur (a penalty) 39/24, 117/18, 117/30, etc

indentura, -e *n f* indenture 35/32, 36/32, 52/22, etc

indifferens, -entis *adj* disinterested 49/5

indulgencia, -e *n f* indulgence (ecclesiastical) 630/36, 630/37m, 637/22, etc

indulgencialis, -e *adj* pertaining to indulgence 637/17

infuturum *adv* in the future, henceforward 34/39, 109/34

inhabilis, -e *adj* disqualified 645/26

insolidum *adv* collectively 87/20

instancia, -e *n f* instance, insistence 48/9, 88/6

institutio, -onis *n f* institution, act of instituting 20/27, 37/13

intendo, -ere, -i, -um *v tr* hear 122/15, 181/21, 188/2, etc

interludium, -i *n nt* interlude (dramatic) 2/21, 44/38, 44/40

intimans, -antis *adj* beloved 21/28

introitus, -us *n m* entrance, especially of a member into a guild or of a cleric into his church 36/1, 36/26, 627/11, etc

intromitto, -ere, intromisi, intromissum *v tr* enter, join (ie, a shop or business) 35/16, 35/22; se — in *v phr* meddle in 38/36

inveteratis, -e *adj* old, worn out 88/3, 629/18

iocale, -is *n nt* jewel, precious object 631/21, 631/31, 631/33, etc

irrotulamentum, -i *n nt* enrolment 624/29

iudassez EG

iugulator, -oris *n m* juggler 71/17

kambesmyth EG

kidberers EG

knoppum, -i *n nt* knob, boss 635/22

kyde EG

laborator, -oris *n m* labourer, workman 112/40, 113/9, 113/20, etc

lagena, -e *n f* gallon 83/36, 221/40, 222/12, etc

laminum, -i *n nt* plates of metal or strips of leather 98/36, 639/36

lanceolum, -i *n nt* small lance, small shaft (ie, for banners) 98/10, 639/10; lanciolis 632/25, 632/26

latoners EG

laudum, -i *n nt* praise 50/24, 60/33, 65/13, etc

lawne EG

legacio, -onis *n f* legacy 632/9

letania, -e *n f* litany 117/24

lettera, -e *n f* 630/36, 638/11 See littera

levacio, -onis *n f* raising up, elevating; — christi (or crucifixi) *n phr* erecting of the cross on Golgotha 26/13, 37/22; — shoppe raising, erecting of a shop or business 31/36, 627/20, 627/25

levo, -are, -avi, -atum *v tr* raise, levy (money, etc) 3/17, 72/29m; — shoppam *v phr* raise or erect a shop 31/35

liberacio, -onis *n f* livery 12/15m, 12/19

liberata, -e *n f* livery 54/38m, 54/39, 64/41m, etc

liberatura, -e *n f* livery 86/5

libero, -are, -avi, -atum *v tr* deliver, hand over, leave (in a will) 12/2, 12/8, 29/16, etc

libertas, -atis *n f* franchise or liberty of a town, privileged area 32/22, 35/17, 46/13, etc

libitum, -i *n nt, in phr* ad libitum at (one's) pleasure, at will 42/19, 52/1

licencia, -e *n f* permission, licence, sanction 84/35, 85/5m, 93/20, etc

lictus, -i *n m* honest man 625/31

ligamen, -minis *n nt* rope, tie 635/1, 635/3

limitacio, -onis *n f* command, direction 116/37

limito, are, -avi, -atum *v tr* assign, appoint, assess 30/23, 30/24 littera, -e *n f* letter 638/13, 638/14, 638/15, etc

lixa, -e *n m* provisioner 222/20, 225/41, 244/26

lodium, -i *n nt* louver (architectural term) 41/26, 41/31, 41/38, etc

louers E G

ludiculum, -i *n nt* 'pageant', literally, little play 226/39

luditor, -oris *n m* player, performer 243/36

ludo, -ere, -i, -sum *v tr* play or perform a play 8/21, 9/18, 18/29, etc

ludus, -i *n m* play, especially the full cycle of pageants making up the Corpus Christi Play 2/5, 3/31, 6/32, etc

lumen, -inis *n nt* light carried in the Corpus Christi procession, processional torch or candle 6/4, 51/17, 64/13, etc

luminarium, -i *n nt* light carried in the Corpus Christi procession, processional torch or candle 15/33, 15/37, 646/23, etc

lumners E G

lusio, -onis *n f* playing or performing of a play 85/7m, 85/10, 86/18, etc

lusor, -oris *n m* player, performer 7/3, 7/7, 65/40, etc

lusus, -i *n m* play, especially the full cycle of pageants making up the Corpus Christi Play 6/34, 11/30, 84/36, etc

luter E G

lyma, -e *n f* (*alternate form of* lymus) lime 218/31, 219/2

magister, -tri *n m* title of address for gentleman or university graduate, Mr 5/39m, 5/40, 44/38, etc; master craftsman in a craft guild 30/12, 30/15, 30/23, etc; — pagine *n phr* pageant master, one of the men chosen yearly to oversee the planning and production of a guild's pageant 38/11, 40/10, 47/12, etc

magnas, -atis *n m* magnate, great man 120/29, 132/16

maior, -oris *n m* mayor (of the city) 5/20, 6/42, 8/22, etc

maior, maius *adj* greater, larger, older (of persons) 6/42, 41/12, 54/2, etc; major (of expenses) 27/15m

maioratissa, -e *n f* mayor's wife, mayoress 243/2

maioratus, -us *n m* mayoralty 36/30, 179/36

maiorissa, -e *n f* mayor's wife, mayoress 106/2

malvess', malvesset' *adj of indeterminate ending* See vinum

mansus, -i *n m* house 73/41

manucaptor, -oris *n m* one who acts as bail or security, mainpernor 5/23, 159/20

manucipio, -ere, -cepi, -ceptum *v tr* go bail, be a mainpernor 159/21

manuteneo, -ere, -ui, -tum *v tr* support, maintain 625/25, 646/13

manutergium, -i *n nt* towel 640/2

mappa, -e *n f* napkin 629/24, 629/25, 629/27, etc

marchio, -onis *n m* marquess 120/16

marcius, -i *n m* March 71/11

marcus, -i *n m* mark (monetary term) 30/16, 637/31

marinarius, -i *n m* sailor 33/40, 34/3m, 34/4, etc

marybonum, -i *n nt* marrow bone 248/12 See also E G marybones

mearemium, -i *n nt* 145/13 See meremium

medio, -are, -avi, -aturum *v intr* intervene, mediate 49/1, 52/14

meldetum, -i *n nt* motley cloth 82/10 See also E G meld

mercer, -is *n m* mercer, shopkeeper, seller of small wares 84/15, 86/30, 88/30, etc See also E G marcer

mercerius, -i *n m* mercer, shopkeeper, seller of small wares 181/39

mercerus, -i *n m* mercer, shopkeeper, seller of small wares 40/27, 46/29, 57/24, etc See also E G marcer

mercerye E G

mercimonium, -i *n nt* trade, goods 2/5, 64/34

meremium, -i *n nt* timber 9/15, 145/15

miles, militis *n m* soldier 19/16, 20/21, 20/32, etc; knight 60/27, 65/7, 66/10, etc

miliare, -aris *n nt* milestone, (by extension) mile 120/22

ministrallus, -i *n m* minstrel 2/20, 2/28, 2/34,
  etc
minutus, -a, -um *adj* minor 2/34m, 3/26m,
  4/8m, etc
missa, -e *n f* mass (eccl) 133/14, 633/1, 638/2,
  etc
missale, -is *n nt* missal 637/30
mitra, -e *n f* mitre (eccl) 74/4, 98/24, 98/29,
  etc
moderamen, -inis *n nt* moderation, measure
  637/20
modium, -i *n m* dry measure, bushel 229/34
modum, -i *n nt* way, means 12/8, 15/18,
  633/22, etc
modum, -i *n nt* dry measure, bushel 225/28
monasterium, -i *n nt* monastery 27/21; — s.
  petri *n phr* (or unmodified) the Minster,
  York Minster 11/37, 28/39, 79/35, etc;
  monesterium, -i 189/26, 190/13, 202/4,
  etc
monimentum, -i *n nt* muniment 638/18
monisterium, -i *n nt* 202/5 See monasterium
monstrum, -i *n nt* showing forth, show 145/19
mortuarium, -i *n nt* mortuary payment 638/30
muirrum, -i *n nt* 637/16 See murra
murenula, -e *n f* earring 634/37
murra, -e *n f* maple 631/6, 637/22, 637/23,
  etc; murrum, -i *n nt* 637/26
murray E G
musterdevelers E G
mustrance, mustraunce E G
mutulis, -is *n m* See carnis

nacio, -onis *n f* nation 32/21
napeones E G
nobilis, -is *n m* nobleman, one of noble rank
  106/22, 122/19
nona, -e *n f* noon, nones (eccl) 30/13
notarius, -i *n m* notary 234/1
noticia, -e *n f* designation, distinguishing mark
  637/12
notificio, -ere, -feci, -fectum *v tr* notify 645/6,
  645/12
novus, -a, -um *adj* new 7/35m, 9/'7, 41/26, etc;

de — *prep phr* anew 98/22, 104/2, 134/35, etc

ob. *abbreviation of* obolus, -i *n m* half-penny
  104/3, 106/25, 145/21, etc
obitus, -us *n m* service of commemoration of
  the dead 182/28, 189/24, 190/10, etc
occupacio, -onis *n f* occupation (of a place of
  business, of a shop) 31/36, 32/25, 40/12, etc
occupo, -are, -avi, -atum *v tr* occupy or set up
  (a shop), work (at a trade), hold an office
  31/35, 32/3, 32/21, etc
officia, -e *n f* office (eccl), mass 133/4
officialis, -is *n m* official, especially of an
  ecclesiastical court 117/21
officiarius, -i *n m* officer 106/16m, 121/33,
  181/16m, etc
officium, -i *n nt* office (eccl), mass 133/11;
  office, duty 625/1, 647/40
operacio, -onis *n f* working (of metal, etc)
  116/7, 632/3
oracio, -onis *n f* prayer 7/1, 133/6, 645/15,
  etc; — dominica *n phr* the Lord's prayer
  6/32, 7/2
oraculum, -i *n nt* holy or sacred utterance 37/24
ordinacio, -onis *n f* ordinance (of any body)
  10/38, 12/13m, 16/24, etc
ordino, -are, -avi, -atum *v tr* order, decree 2/1,
  12/1, 12/15, etc
ordium, -i *n nt* (variant spelling of hordeum)
  barley 79/22
oreginalis, -e *adj* original, authentic 88/19
orforay E G
ornatura, -e *n f* ornamenting 631/24
ostensio, -onis *n f* manifestation; — Veronice
  n phr appearance of the image of Christ on
  Veronica's veil 26/10
ostillarius, -i *n m* ostler 101/25, 121/5
ovis, -is *n m* 79/4 See carnis

pagina, -e *n f* page (possibly) 68/28; pageant,
  one of the individual episodes constituting
  the Corpus Christi Play 8/20, 16/38, 37/20,

etc; pageant, one of the pageant wagons upon which the plays were performed 3/20, 5/15, 35/12, etc (frequently ambiguous) See also Bridgemasters' Accounts.

paginus, -i *n m* pageant 226/24, 233/11, 243/17, etc See also pagina

pallium, -i *n nt* pall (eccl vesture) 208/39, 210/2, 236/3, etc

palpo, -are, -avi, -atum *v tr* touch 23/7

panis, -is *n m* bread 9/18; — dominicus *n phr* pain-demaine, finest quality white wheat bread 60/31, 65/11, 74/30, etc; — levand' leavened bread 78/37, 221/34, 244/5, etc; — subtilis light bread 78/38

papa, -e *n m* pope, the bishop of Rome 638/5

papalis, -e *adj* papal 98/25, 639/25

papirus, -a, -um *adj* 121/36 See paupirius

parasceve *n indecl* Good Friday 1/28

parcella, -e *n f* portion, item, detail 246/29

parcellatim *adv* item by item 122/24, 145/40, 146/3, etc

parcellum, -i *n nt* portion, item, detail 78/31, 145/37, 633/5, etc

pardonacio, -onis *n f* pardon 109/33

parisiensis, -e *adj* Parisian, relating to Paris; — candela *n phr* Paris candle 31/1, 31/6, 31/15, etc

parochialis, -e *adj* parish, parochial 255/42, 261/30, 277/40, etc

pars, partis *n f* part, party (legal) 5/11, 5/13, 12/25, etc

parsona, -e *n m* parson, priest 133/19

passio, -onis *n f* passion, especially the passion of Christ 638/4

pastura, -e *n f* feeding, pasturage (of domestic animals) 79/22

pater noster *n phr* the prayer 'Our Father' 99/5-6, 132/27, 132/30, etc

paupirius, -a, -um *adj* paper, made of paper 181/23, 188/3, 203/22, etc

paupirus, -i *n m* paper 145/20, 218/2, 220/13, etc

pavimentum, -i *n nt* the Pavement (see frontispiece) 29/1, 85/28, 106/2, etc
paviamentum, -i *n nt* 11/39

pecia, -e *n f* piece 98/11, 98/30, 631/1, etc

pedester, -tris *n m* footman 94/16

pellipariarum *n m gen pl* for pelllipariorum 211/21 See pelliparius

pelliparius, -i *n m* skinner 31/4, 40/22, 46/22, etc

pellis, -is *n m* hide, sheet (of parchment) 9/37, 98/13, 639/13, etc

pelter EG

peltrum, -i *n nt* pewter 640/5

pendicio, -onis *n f* hanging, decorating with hangings 244/27, 248/25

pennons, pennonz EG

peregrinus, -i *n m* traveller, pilgrim 23/3, 26/18, 73/34

pergamenum, -i *n nt* parchment 9/37, 80/7, 638/14, etc

perimpleo, -ere, -evi, -etum *v tr* fulfill completely 5/22, 38/30, 48/8, etc

pessoners EG

petecularius, -i *n m* fletcher 164/14

peticio, -onis *n f* petition 646/23

peto, -ere, peti, petitum *v tr* seek 12/40, 78/36, 79/27, etc

petra, -e *n f* stone (as a measure of weight) 103/18

pincerna, -e *n f* housekeeper 222/20, 226/1, 230/5, etc

pinctura, -e *n f* painting 145/27

piscenarius, -i *n m* fishmonger 33/40, 34/3m, 34/5, etc

pistior, -oris *n m* baker 182/1

pisto, -are, -avi, -atum *v tr* bake 42/22

pistor, -oris *n m* baker 5/12, 16/18, 16/22, etc

pixis, -is *n m* pyx 634/26

plasterarius, -i *n m* plasterer 33/21, 33/27, 33/32, etc

plasteratura, -e *n f* plastering 39/8, 39/10, 39/20

plaustratum, -i *n nt* wagon-load 208/18

plegius, -i *n m* pledge, bond, one who acts as a surety 5/23, 6/5

plenarie *adv* fully 31/33, 36/7, 38/23, etc

plenarius, -a, -um *adj* complete, plenary 119/36

plenus, -a, -um *adj* full 6/40, 29/25, 645/22; *in idiom* in pleno consilij in full council 159/19

poketta, -e *n f* bag, pouch 27/36, 638/26 See also EG **poket**

pontificalis, -e *adj* pontifical, pertaining to a bishop or especially to the pope 1/31

pontificatus, -us *n m* pontificate, the state of being a bishop or especially a pope 74/4

portator, -oris *n m, form of* **portitor** bearer, carrier 230/4

portiforium, -i *n nt* portable breviary 58/19; **portiferum, -i** *n nt* 638/36

postcommunis, -is *n m* postcommunion verse sung in the mass 638/26, 638/27

potacio, -onis *n f* drinking 27/23

potellus, -i *n m* pottle, a liquid measure 79/12

prebendarius, -i *n m* prebend (eccl) 133/19

precessionans, -antis *prp* going in advance, going before 117/3

precio, -are, -avi, -atum *v tr* price (goods) 98/21, 635/22, 635/24, etc

preculare, -is *n m* bead; **par precularum** *n phr* rosary 636/7, 636/11, 637/1, etc

prelatus, -i *n m* prelate (eccl) 74/4, 94/33, 133/4

premunio, -ire, -ivi, -itum *v tr* forewarn, cite (legal) 8/22, 18/1, 49/9, etc

presbeteris *n m abl pl* for **presbiteris**, of **presbiter** priest 210/33

presens *adj* present, actual 32/39, 41/30, 117/10, etc

presentacio, -onis *n f* presentation 1/9, 25/24, 25/28, etc

presentatibus *adj f abl pl* for **presentibus** 86/16 See **presens**

presento, -are, -avi, -atum *v tr* present, give 64/36, 94/32

presur EG

primas, -atis *n m* primate (eccl) 647/36

princepe *n m abl sg* for **principe** 132/15, 133/9 See **princeps**

princeps, -cipis *n m* prince 74/9, 121/27m, 133/15, etc

prioratus, -us *n m* priory 28/31

prisona, -e *n f* prison 126/8, 159/22

procescio, -onis *n f, form of* **processio** procession 15/18, 109/39, 132/24, etc

processionaliter *adv* processionally, in a pro-

cession 15/19, 15/34

proclamacio, -onis *n f* proclamation 24/20, 46/10, 645/5

procuro, -are, -avi, -atum *v tr* procure 30/11

produco, -ere, -i, -ctum *v tr* put on, produce (a play) 28/28, 34/6, 34/9, etc

productio, -onis *n f* production (of a play) 31/23, 47/13

proporcionaliter *adv* proportionally 54/1

propricietur *v pres subj pass 3 sg* for **propicietur** of **propicio** be favourable or merciful to (with dat) 80/10

psalterium, -i *n nt* psalter 636/16, 636/20

pultrum, -i *n nt* pewter 630/18, 632/19

punctum, -i *n nt* point, particular 49/35

purgacio, -onis *n f* cleaning 156/29

quarta, -e *n f* farthing 104/3, 640/23

quarterium, -i *n nt* quarter 15/36, 35/38

quaternus, -i *n m* quire (of pages) 98/19, 638/13, 639/19

quietus, -um *adj* quit (of some obligation) 33/35, 42/24, 48/17, etc

quilibet, quelibet, quodlibet *indefinite pron* any one, each one 15/35, 31/21, 32/2, etc

quiscumque, quidcumque *indefinite rel* whoever, whatever 52/8

rasemus, -i *n m* raisin 79/11

ray, rayes, rays EG

receiptis *perf part f abl pl* for **receptis** of **recipio, -ere, -i, -ceptum** receive 111/23

recepcio, -onis *n f* receipts (accounting) 73/18m, 90/16m, 90/29m, etc

recescebant *v imperfect ind act 3 pl* for **recessebant** of **recesso, -ere, -i, -cessum** go back, return 133/2

recognosco, -ere, -novi, -nitum *v tr* recall, recognize, hence acknowledge 33/5

recordum, -i *n nt* record, report 49/38

recreamen, -minis *n nt* refreshment, restoration 74/9

rector, -is *n m* rector (eccl) 117/8, 117/15, 633/27, etc

redditus, -us *n m* rent, revenue 7/8, 36/11, 144/25m, etc; — resolutus *n phr* 180/39-40m, 187/25-6m, 202/34-5m, etc; *or* resolucio — rent resolute (paid out by landlord) 94/3-4m, 101/25-6m, 121/5m, etc

reddo, -ere, -idi, -itum *v tr* return, pay 36/7, 119/36, 134/27, etc; — compotum *v phr* render an account 40/12

refectio, -onis *n f* refection, dining 161/35, 178/38, 179/22, etc

reformacio, -onis *n f* restoration, reformation 33/24, 37/15

regalea, -eum *n nt pl* things or actions belonging to a king 74/1

regardum, -i *n nt* customary payment, gratuity 103/29, 106/23, 107/4, etc; regardium, -i *n nt* 255/40, 261/28

registro, -are, -avi, -atum *v tr* enter in the record, register 17/3, 26/27, 46/16, etc

registrum, -i *n nt* register, record 7/37m, 29/2; the MS of the Corpus Christi Play 244/22

regratarius, -i *n m* regrater, one who buys up goods, especially victuals, for resale at an inflated price 16/20

rehabeo, -ere, -ui, -itum *v tr* regain or recover 36/16

reintro, -are, -avi, -atum *v tr* re-enter 134/33

relicta, -e *n f* relict, widow 100/41

reliquia, -e *n f* relic (of a saint, etc) 631/31, 637/7

renay' *adj of indeterminate ending* See vinum

reparacio, -onis *n f* repair 5/14, 5/26, 35/13, etc

reportacio, -onis *n f* recarrying, carrying back 9/15

residenciarius, -i *n m* residentiary; canonicus — residentiary canon 647/38

resolucio, -onis *n f* payment 144/26m See also redditus

resolvo, -ere, -i, -solutum *v tr* pay 144/25, 180/40m, 187/26m, etc

responsorium, -i *n nt* response (liturgical) 132/28

retallia, -e *n f in phr* per retalliam retail (opposed to in grosso wholesale 64/29) 31/16, 42/19,

53/38, etc

retroactus, -a, -um *adj* past 633/37

reuettes, reuetts EG

rewardum, -i *n nt* 161/34, 178/37, 179/21, etc See regardum

rosum, -i *n nt* rosebush 145/19, 635/13

rotulum, -i *n nt* roll 78/27, 98/5, 98/26, etc

roundeletes, roundelettes EG

rub rosar EG

rubius, -a, -um *adj* for rubeus, -a, -um See vinum

rubrus, -a, -um *adj* red See vinum

rumpuat' *adj of indeterminate ending* 229/37 See vinum

russetum, -i *n nt* russet 121/38

sacramentum, -i *n nt* sacrament, especially the eucharist 15/33, 20/29, 51/14, etc

sacrista, -e *n m* sacristan 202/4, 204/9, 209/27, etc

salsamentum, -i *n nt* sauce, savoury, condiment 31/26

salsarius, -i *n m* saucemaker 30/36, 30/39, 31/5, etc

sannapa, -e *n f* protective cloth 28/1m, 28/1, 28/3, etc

saphirum, -i *n nt* sapphire 632/6

sarracio, -onis *n f* sawing 116/11, 145/14

saunders EG

saveron EG

scabellum, -i *n nt* stool, bench 132/26

scannum, -i *n nt* bench 79/23

scissor, -oris *n m* (?) carver of meat 248/18

scotus, -i *n m* Scot 624/30

scrutator, -oris *n m* searcher, inspection officer of a craft guild 36/3, 36/18, 36/20, etc

scrutium, -i *n nt* inspection 41/6

secreta, -e *n f* the Secret, one of the prayers of mass 638/26

secta, -e *n f* suit of clothes, also a livery 7/5, 12/19

secta, -e *n f* suit (legal), petition 47/33

secularis, -e *adj* secular, lay 117/10

secus, -a, -um *adj* for cecus, -a, -um blind 70/27, 70/31

sedis, -is *n f* see of a bishop; — **apostolica** *n phr* the holy see 647/36

sedula, -e *n f* schedule 17/5

sellarius, -i *n m* saddler 622/32 See also E G sellers

senescallus, -i *n m* seneschal 235/22, 238/2, 244/25, etc

senistra, -e *n f form of* **sinistra, -e** left side, left hand 116/36, 126/4, 126/5, etc

sentencia, -e *n f* sentence, phrase 80/4; sentence (legal) 638/34

septima, -e *n f* (?) week 120/27

sera, -e *n f* lock 98/28, 639/28

serkelett E G

sermo, -onis *n m* sermon 122/21, 181/27, 188/6, etc

sertus, -a, -um *adj for* **certus, -a, -um** fixed, determined, sure 29/34

serveourz E G

serviens, -ntis *n m* servant 30/11, 30/14, 39/19, etc; — **ad clavam** *n phr* sergeant at mace (a municipal officer) 17/6, 113/28

servisia, -e *n f* ale, beer 106/20

shoppa, -e *n f* shop, place of business 31/34, 34/32, 35/15, etc

shotill E G

sicamorus, -i *n m* sycamore 20/17

sigilleus, -i *n m* seal 637/14

sigillum, -i *n nt* seal 36/30, 36/31, 52/17, etc; — **privatum** *n phr* privy seal 637/15

sigmentus, -i *n m* cygnet 121/24

sinapium, -i *n nt* mustard 31/26

sinautem *conj* but if, if however 51/11

singularis, -e *adj* individual, singular, matchless, remarkable 29/35, 29/40, 50/29, etc

sirurgia, -e *n f* surgery 625/23

sissor, -is *n m* tailor 78/32, 633/10

situo, -are, -avi, -atum *v tr* place, set, situate 37/31, 640/7

skafalda, -e *n f* scaffold, scaffolding 29/5, 29/13

societas, -tatis *n f* association, companionship, acquaintance 645/28

solacium, -i *n nt* refreshment 49/18, 49/24, 50/15

solidus, -i *n m* shilling 2/14, 32/27, 38/10, etc

solidus, -a, -um *adj* firm 15/26

solomodo *adv* only, alone 52/8

soror, -is *n f* sister, especially a female fellow-member of a religious guild 15/35, 50/33, 87/39, etc

species, -erum *n f pl* spices 225/31, 235/13, 235/19, etc

specifico, -are, -avi, -atum *v tr* specify, set out specifically 626/5

spicebus *n f abl pl for* **speciebus** 79/9 See species

spiritualia, -ium *n nt pl* spiritualities (eccl) 132/16, 133/10, 647/34, etc

spoliacio, -onis *n f* despoiling, especially the harrowing of hell 26/15

stalla, -e *n f* stall 133/2

stallagium, -i *n nt* site of a market stall 120/3

stancheon E G

stannum, -i *n nt* bench 633/7

staunchons E G

staurum, -i *n nt* store, stock 78/29, 632/5, 632/12, etc

stene E G

stenours, steynours E G

sterlingus, -i *n m* sterling, silver money 32/28, 33/12, 36/9, etc

stipatus, -a, -um *adj* studded 634/30

stipendium, -i *n nt* wages 222/20, 225/41, 235/23, etc

stola, -e *n f* vestment, stole 117/6, 638/6

stultus, -i *n m* fool (ie, jester) 66/36, 67/19

subdecanus, -i *n m* subdean (of a cathedral chapter) 133/19

submitto, -ere, -isi, -issum *v tr* submit; **se submittere** (with dat) *v phr* submit oneself to 30/2, 41/25

succentor, -oris *n m* succentor 132/27, 133/5

superfilatus, -a, -um *adj* folded over 626/37

superpelicius, -i *n m* surplice 15/18, 117/12

superveniens, -entis *adj* visiting, incoming 9/32, 145/9

supervideo, -ere, -i, -visum *v tr* supervise 49/29, 50/13

supervisus, -us *n m* supervision 134/37, 134/38

supportacio, -onis *n f* upkeep, maintenance 30/16, 32/26, 35/20, etc

suspensio, -onis *n f* hanging 26/7

swallis E G

tabernaculum, -i *n nt* tabernacle, shrine,
  receptacle for the Host 631/36, 632/4,
  634/5, etc

tabula, -e *n f* table 79/14; plank 79/21,
  145/16

taliqui, -que, -quod *rel adj* such 144/18

talliaunders E G

tannator, -oris *n m* tanner 40/25, 46/25, 57/28,
  etc; tannarum *gen pl* for tannatorum 249/4

tapitarius, -i *n m* tapiter 32/12m, 32/13,
  32/22, etc; tapitarium *gen pl* 218/20

tapiterus, -i *n m* tapiter 81/23, 84/21 See also
  E G tapiter

tapitor, -oris *n m* tapiter 226/29, 233/15,
  249/3 See also E G tapiter

te deum *n phr* the hymn Te Deum 133/3-4

tectura, -e *n f* covering, roofing 631/22

tegularius, -i *n m* tiler 33/21, 33/22m, 33/32,
  etc

tegulator, -oris *n m* tiler 41/37

tegulatura, -e *n f* tiling 39/8, 39/13, 39/20, etc

tegulo, -are, -avi, -atum *v tr* tile 116/9;
  teguliantibus *prp m pl abl* for tegulantibus
  209/11

tempus, -oris *n nt* time *in phr* pro tempore
  existens 35/26, 38/23-4, 42/8, etc; pro
  tempore esse 29/11, 35/25, 38/26-7, etc
  for the time being

tenementum, -i *n nt* building 3/20, 7/9, 29/37,
  etc

tenura, -e *n f* holding 84/37, 93/22, 119/32

terminus, -i *n m* term (period of time) 31/30,
  31/33; term of an agreement 40/23, 40/25,
  40/27, etc; term of service 32/2

thesauraria, -e *n f* treasurer 73/41

thesaurarius, -i *n m* treasurer 133/18

thurifico, -are, -avi, -atum *v tr* cense 132/26

tibuvnell, tibuvner E G

toga, -e *n f* cassock, gown 89/30, 145/25

tondeo, -ere, totondi, tonsum *v tr* shear (cloth)
  41/9, 41/10, 41/12

tonsor, -oris *n m* shearer 41/6m, 41/11,
  41/14

tonsura, -e *n f* shearing (of cloth) 86/8

torchea, -e *n f* torch 6/1, 10/40, 12/23, etc;
  torcha, -e 89/4, 156/33, 157/26, etc;
  torta, -e 52/32, 109/29, 126/20, etc

transitus, -us *n m* passage, journey, (as a euphe-
  mism) death 21/29, 26/22

transsumptum, -i *n nt* copy 638/20

tregitour E G

trenchours E G

trestez E G

turnours E G

turnulus, -i *n m* wheel 637/11

unacum *prep* together with 65/14, 94/31,
  121/26, etc

uncia, -e *n f* ounce 222/16, 222/17, 222/18

unguella, -e *n f* perfume or ointment box
  244/13

vadium, -i *n nt* wages, pay 145/38; vadis *n nt
  abl pl* for vadiis 243/34

valauncez, valencez E G

vellowett E G

venustacio, -onis *n f* beautifying 631/24

veredis, -e *adj* 248/13, 637/32 See viridis

verrours E G

versiculum, -i *n nt* versicle (eccl) 133/6

verum *n nt acc sg* for verutum spit for roasting
  79/19

vestabuli *n nt gen sg form of* vestibuli 207/40
  See vestibulum

vestiarium, -i *n nt* vestry 161/33, 178/36,
  179/20, etc

vestibulum, -i *n nt* vestry 209/26, 211/1,
  213/2, etc

vestura, -e *n f* clothing 60/22m, 74/21m,
  82/2m, etc

veytagium, -i *n nt* 248/15 See virgetum

vicarius, -i *n m* vicar 117/8, 117/15, 132/28,
  etc

vicecomes, -itis *n m* sheriff 12/16

vigilans, -antis *prp act* keeping vigil; **vigilante matheo** *abl absolute* poetic locution for, on the eve of the feast of St Matthew 73/34

vigilia, -e *n f* vigil, eve (eccl) 12/2, 24/20, 29/16, etc

viginis *n f abl pl* for **vaganis** of **vagina, -e** sheath, scabbard 64/26

vinum, -i *n nt* wine 9/19; — **acre** *n phr* vinegar 79/12; — **agrum** vinegar 225/29, 229/36, 235/14, etc; — **album** white wine 83/36; — **claretum** claret 237/39; — **dulce** sweet wine 53/39, 54/3; — **malvess'** malmsey 229/37, 235/18, 237/39; — **rubrum** red wine 106/21, 244/18; — **rubium** red wine 121/23; — **renay'** Rhenish wine 237/39; — **rumpuat'** Rhine wine 229/37

virga, -e *n f* yard (unit of measure) 121/38; rod, staff 117/2

virgetum, -i *n nt* verjuice 225/29, 229/36, 235/14, etc

viridis, -e *adj* green See **aucus**

vitulus, -i *n m* See **carnis**

vyntarius, -i *n m* vintner 53/40, 54/1

wanyons EG

warantizo, -are, -avi, -atum *v tr* warrant 36/29, 120/7

wattes. waytes EG

xlma, -e *abbreviation for* **quadragesima, -e** *n f* Lent (literally, forty) 66/17, 75/29

yemalis, -e *adj* pertaining to winter, winter 54/38m, 54/39, 60/23m, etc

yems, yemis *n m* winter 36/5, 36/10

zinzeber, zinzebris *n m* ginger 79/8

zonarius, -i *n m* girdler 68/29

Anglo-Norman Glossary

adonques *conj* thereafter 164/34, 623/32;
 adonsque 301/1
afferant *n m* share, proportion, what belongs
 to one 4/24; **afferauntz** *pl* 622/14
affiert *v impers* it belongs, it is meet 13/7,
 13/8, 622/25
annexis *pp pl* attached, joined, annexed 11/16
appartenance *n f* mechanical accessories 618/23
appartenant *pr p* pertaining to, belonging to
 6/12
arraie *n f* gear, furnishing, equipment 15/3
assauoir *v inf & prep* for **à savoir** *only in phr*
 cest assauoir that is to say 8/41, 618/21,
 620/23; **cestassauoir** 13/10, 618/12, 619/
 31, etc
atchate *v pr 3 sg* buys 622/13
attentz *pp* convicted, adjudged, found guilty
 622/15; **atteynt** 623/15; **atteynte** 624/18;
 atteyntez 6/17
auoir *n m* wealth, riches, possessions 619/30
auxi *conj* also 14/33, 14/37; **auxint** 166/32,
 620/10

bille *n f* billet 11/16, 14/37 See also E G
boltis E G
bowers E G
busoignable *adj* necessary, convenient 624/8

card(e)makers E G

cardemakercrafte E G
cedulle *n f* schedule 11/16
cestassauoir See **assauoir**
chaunces *n f pl* breeches, hose 13/40
chaundelers E G
cheiez *pp* fallen 14/21
cire *n f* wax 620/40
coilleront *v fut 3 pl* will collect 4/23
coillet *n f* collection, levy, impost 4/38
conciteinz *n m pl* fellow-citizens 620/5
costages *n m pl* costs 4/26, 11/4, 619/28 See
 also E G
coupercraft E G
coupers E G
couuereours E G
curyour E G

darrein passe *adj phr* in temporal expressions,
 it indicates a day or feast recently past;
 iour de corpus christi darrein passe the day
 of Corpus Christi just past 166/36
darres *n m pl* arrows 6/13
dasore *adv* See **desore**
dee' 164/30, 164/34, 164/35, etc See p 875
 end-note to B7 f 70
deinez *prep* within, inside (of space or time)
 618/34; **deinz** 164/27, 166/27, 620/33, etc;
 dedeinz 620/9
demaigne *n f* Sunday 624/5
demesme *prep & adj* for **de mesme** of the same
 11/3, 11/11

demesne *adj* one's own, personal, that which belongs to one 164/35

deperir *v inf & prep* for **de perir** *in phr* **en poynt deperir** on the point of dying 621/21

desicome *conj* inasmuch as 620/8

desore *adv, form of* **desor** from now on 623/6; *in phr* **desore en auaunt** 14/23, 623/10; **dasore enauaunt** 13/42

desormes *adv* henceforth 6/11, 10/21, 620/14, etc

despensur *n m* expenditure, disbursement 4/26

disease *n f* trouble, inconvenience, distress 11/8

distourbe *v pr 3 sg* disturb 618/37

dorra *v fut 3 sg* shall give or dispose 623/33

dubbers E G

duement *adv* duly, properly 14/21, 618/39, 620/24; **dument** 622/37

eide *n m* aid, help 619/30, 621/21

eint *adv* before, previously 166/32, 166/38

elieux *adj pl* chosen 14/26

encontinent *adv* forthwith 166/33

encourge *v pres subj 3 sg* encourage 11/19; **encourgent** 11/20; **encourgentz** 11/23

endomage *pp* damaged 47/19

enpaire *prep phr* **en peior** to the worse, *in phr* **est moult enpaire** is much worsened 620/10

ensy *adv* 623/24 See **issint**

entour *prep* around, about 11/4

entz *adv, in phr* **ascun entz** any of them 6/16

escu *n m* type of round roll or loaf of bread 617/7

eslier *v inf* choose 624/6

esperoner *n m* spurrier, maker of spurs 13/5; **esporoner** 13/7

estate *n f* state, condition 619/26

estes *n m pl* shafts (of arrows) 6/18

eteant *prp* being 164/33, 165/4

eut *demonstrative pron gen pl* of these 617/8

eut *v perf 3 sg* has been (auxiliary v) 164/39

eyns *n pl* eyes 622/14

ferra *v fut 3 sg* shall do, make 11/19, 47/18

ferront *v fut 3 pl* shall do, make 166/29, 166/33; (occasionally in a more Latin sense) shall bear, as in **ferront toutes les costages** shall bear all the costs 4/25; **ferrount** 8/40, 11/19

ffleccher, ffletchers E G

fist *v perf 3 sg* did made 620/26

fisyk *n f* medicine, physic 620/32

foith *n m & f* time, occasion 6/16, 624/18; **foithe** 621/8; **foitz** 8/40, 623/24

foreins *adj pl* foreign, strange 621/27

forspris *conj* except 617/22

freynt *v pres subj 3 sg* break 623/14

gaunters E G

goldbetours E G

greuee *pp* hurt, grieved 622/35

hauntera *v fut 3 sg* shall enter 619/40

hors de *prep phr* outside of 621/22

horspris *prep* except 14/2

hosyers E G

houres *n f pl* hour, time 11/15; **hures** 619/30, 619/31, 619/39

ia dez *adv phr* once 166/31-2

illeoques *adv* there 15/1

importables *adj pl* insupportable, greater than can be borne 619/28

issint *adv* in such a manner, thus 164/34

iue *n m* play 11/25, 14/1, 620/7

iuer *n m* play 11/4

iuers *n m pl* players 11/22

iuez *pp* presented a play 11/5; **iueez** 11/14, 11/25

iunours E G

larcyn *n m* theft, stolen goods 623/31

laynuz *adj pl* woolly, wool-covered 622/13

leyne *n f* wool 13/42

leyns *n pl* See **eyns**

lisible *adj* lawful, permissible 620/39

lorymer EG

lower *n (?)* fee 619/33

lumer *n m* light, illumination, usually one of the torches called 'lights' of the Corpus Christi procession 5/3, 618/32, 618/41, etc

mateigner *v inf* maintain 620/7

mayneprener *v inf* receive a guarantee 621/30

maynes *n f pl* hands; **es queux maynes** *phr* in whose hands, in whose possession 621/7

medie *v pr 3 sg* disobeys, gainsays 618/37

merisme *n m* timber 620/25

mieult *adv* best 622/37; **mieltz** 10/25

mistre *n m* craft, occupation 617/17, 617/21, 617/3 See also EG **mystery**

moneie *n f* current coin 4/38, 4/40

monstrer *v inf* show, reveal 6/14, 617/21; **monstrent** *pr 3 pl* 621/16; **monstera** *fut 3 sg* 622/36

moult *adv* much 620/10

my *n f, used with* **ne** *as an emphatic negative* **ne ... my** 11/25, 14/21, 14/35

nuresaunce *n f* nourishment 11/28

occupier *v inf* take a place in 618/8, 618/10; **occupiera** *fut 3 sg* 617/17, 618/11

oeps *n m* use, profit 7/36, 8/42, 16/31, etc; **oops** 14/34

orailles *n f pl* ears 622/14

ordeignaunce *n f* order, ordinance 10/22, 620/39, 621/33, etc; **ordeignance** 13/9; **ordeignances** *pl* 11/18

ordeigner *v inf* order, prepare, ordain 11/13, 620/13, 620/38, etc

oue *prep* with 14/27, 623/31, 624/15, etc;

ouesqez 619/28, 620/11, 621/23, etc; **ouesque** 13/41

oueraigne *n f* work 6/12, 620/21, 620/25, etc

ouere *n f* work 11/26

ouerer *v inf* work 13/6, 618/9, 621/27; **ouer** *perf 3 sg* 13/6; **ouerera** *fut 3 sg* 6/11; **ouerez** *perf 2 pl* 14/22

ouesque, ouesqez See **oue**

oultre *adv, in phr* **la valu de vj d ou oultre** the value of 6d or more 623/32

oustez *pp* having passed by, passed out (of something), having finished or terminated (a connection) 620/11

owels *adj pl* equal 5/3, 623/9, 623/36

pagyne *n m* pageant, one of the components of the play cycle of Corpus Christi 7/36, 8/43, 10/24, etc; **pagyn** 4/25, 4/26; **pagine** 620/38; **pagant** 4/39; **pagaunt** 624/16, 624/18; **pagent** 624/7, 624/9, 624/12, etc; **pagentz** 11/4, 11/7, 11/10, etc See also EG **padgeant**

parchemyners EG

payn demayn *n m phr* pain-demaine, finest wheat bread 617/7

pensel *n m(?)* paintbrush 624/15

pestours *n m pl* bakers 617/5, 617/9

peyne *n f* penalty, pain 6/14, 7/35, 13/8, etc; **payn** 164/31, 165/2, 617/7, etc; **payne** 11/20, 11/23, 164/43; **paynez** 164/34; **peyn** 617/24, 624/10, 624/18

pleignet *v pres subj 3 pl* complain 14/30

pleiser *v inf* please, be pleasing (to) 619/34, 621/16, 621/25; **pleser** 619/26; **please** 620/12, **pleise** *pr 3 sg* 11/10

poet *v pr 3 sg* can 621/24

pousez *adj pl* weak 619/29

poynt *n m* point 621/21; **poyint** 618/21; **poyntes** 15/2

prist *v perf 3 sg* took 619/33

purra *v fut 3 sg* will be able 621/30; **purrount** *fut 3 pl* will be able 11/5

purueu *pp* provided 624/4

qestoient *phr* qi estoient who were 620/10

queux *rel pron* whose, the which, which 8/39, 11/5, 621/7; **quex** 166/34

regratir *n m* regrater, one who buys out the available supply of a commodity for resale at a profit 617/7

repairauncez *prp* returning, repairing to 11/9, 11/27

resceu *pp* received 623/10

resceyuera *v fut 3 sg* will receive 617/27

roundel *n m* round cake 617/7

sagement *adv* wisely 164/42

sercheours, serchour, serchours E G

setes *n f pl* arrows, shafts 6/13

si bien *adv phr, in idiom* si bien de ... come de as much according to ... as according to 620/9

sicome *conj* as, just as 14/38, 622/26

sinon q' *conj* except that, unless 620/40; **sinoun q'** 622/13, 622/24

soleit *v impers 3 sg* is accustomed (to) 619/39; **soleient** *3 pl* 619/29

stanours E G

suppliount *v pr 3 pl* request, beg 11/3, 11/24, 619/25; **suppliont** 619/34, 620/5

suppoiale *n f(?)* support 619/30

supportteller *v inf* support 623/2

suppoweler *v inf* support, sustain 10/24

tapiters, tapitours E G

task *n m* prescribing, assignment, task 617/28

teigne *v pr subj 3 sg* hold, retain 622/23

tiel *adj* such, of such a kind 621/26; **tiele** 621/7

tochaunt *prp* touching, pertaining to 622/34

tondours, toundours E G

tresbountinouse *adj sg* very generous 620/12

tutdys *adj* at all times, every day 14/20

vacabundes *n m pl* vagabonds 622/27

veisynes *n m pl* neighbours 621/16

vphalderes E G

English Glossary

abatyd *pp* reduced 326/19

able *v inf* prepare, make ready 109/15

abling dynner *n phr* dinner given when a new member of a guild is legally empowered to practise a craft 522/17; **ablyng dynnir** 372/7; **habling dinner** 439/12, 439/18; **hablinge dynner** 457/3-4

accept *pp* approved, received as offered 137/38

accustumes *n pl* toll charges 108/3

adamond *n* adamant (either diamond or load-stone) 632/11

afallen *v inf* occur 183/8

afferant *n* share, proportion 53/18

affiance *n* faith 142/9, 150/2

agaynesay *v inf* speak against 53/32

agnus *n* figure of a lamb bearing a cross or flag 640/32, 641/14

alemon reuett *n phr* almain-rivet, a kind of light armour, partly made of overlapping plates sliding on rivets 473/40; **allmayn revett** 365/43-366/1; **alman revet** 468/13; **almane reveit** 439/27; **almanravet** 434/30, 462/42; **aulmanrevet** 468/20

alleanly *adv* 'alonely', exclusively 626/16

allegeance *n* allegation 45/31

allmayn revett, alman revet, almane reveit, almanravet See **alemon reuett**

almoner *n* official distributor of alms 606/27, 607/10

amercyed *pp* fined 190/27

ammove *v inf* remove from a position 109/17

amynd *imper v phr* have mind, think 268/24, 270/13, 278/14, etc; **a mynd** 266/41

anameld *pp* enamelled 635/6; **anamelde** 635/7

ancyant *n* ensign, flag 411/33, 411/34, 411/39; **auncient** 464/17, 469/19, 480/32; **auncyent** 419/23

angel noblez *n phr pl* gold coins of a new issue of the noble, worth a varying amount, having as their device the archangel Michael 193/29

angells *n pl* angel nobles 508/12, 508/14, 508/15; **angels** 194/11 See **angel noblez**

apploied *pp* applied (or employed?) 173/24

archetricline *n* president or 'ruler' of a feast 351/31

armynge *prp* forming part of one's arms 433/5

arrered *pp* put up, erected 110/33

assenced *v perf 3 sg* censed (offered incense to) 196/8

assocyate *v inf* act as assistant to 366/39

assufferayn *n* sovereign 149/4

astylwod *n* astel, wood in slips 79/15

aubes *n pl* albs (white vestments reaching to the feet) 55/25

aulmanrevet See **alemon reuett**

auncient, auncyent See **ancyant**

awe *v pr 3 pl* ought to 24/27, 53/10

back gownes *n phr pl* gowns covering only the back 585/21; **backgownes** 601/27

balettboke *n* ballad book 89/31

band *n* hinge 288/28, 377/15; **bandes** *pl* 103/19, 156/23, 156/25, etc barker *n* tanner 5/23, 111/14; barkers *pl* 25/9

barward *n* bear-keeper who leads the animal about for public exhibition 330/16, 409/34, 521/5; barwood 378/22, 378/26; bearward 539/25; barwardes *pl* 270/39, 271/5, 383/23m, etc; bearewardes 501/18, 517/33, 521/3, etc; bearwardes 509/15, 523/20m, 528/6m, etc; berewardes 488/18, 536/39

baslards *n pl* of a species of hanger or dagger, usually worn at the girdle 124/11

bather *adj gen pl* both 45/40, 45/41; bother 173/19

bawdkyn *n* canopy made of cloth of gold and silk 116/22, 161/31, 182/26, etc; baudekyn 79/28; bawdewykyn 178/32, 179/16

baxsters *n pl* bakers (male or female) 192/19, 192/24, 192/30, etc

bayn *n* one who makes a proclamation 327/24

bearward, bearewardes, bearwardes See barward

behof *n* benefit 335/36; behoof 386/10

berall *n* beryl, a transparent precious stone 643/21, 643/22, 643/25, etc; birall 641/5, 641/16, 642/10; byrall 640/32

bere *n* bier 632/26

berewardes See barward

besene *adj* arrayed 146/29, 146/31

besuch *v pr 1 sg* beseech 140/19; besuching *prp* 154/36, 155/22

bett *pp* embossed 56/6

beylles *n pl* cross-bars 309/21

billettes *n pl* notices 287/26, 297/13, 303/11, etc; billetes 307/14; billyttes 293/21; byllettes 295/9

billman *n* soldier or watchman armed with a bill or halberd 432/36

birall See berall

black bill *n phr* type of halberd 434/17, 519/8; blacke bill 433/21, 474/5; blacke byll 445/8; blake bille 474/28

blak gard *n* body of the lowest menials in the royal household 276/23

boge *n* budge, a kind of fur consisting of lamb's skin with the wool dressed outwards 185/5

bolbakers See bowlbakers

bollers *n pl* makers of bowls 26/9, 48/33; bullars 300/5, 304/13

boltis *n pl* short arrows 6/13

bolyon *n* ornamental fringe 195/20, 195/24

bone *n* bane, proclamation of a play (sg of banns) 177/36

borde *n* table for meals 151/11

boses *n pl* rounded ornaments 68/31; bosses 334/12

botellers *n pl* makers of leather and metal vessels for liquids 20/8; bottellers 356/12(2)

botelles *n pl* bundles (of hay) 114/29(2), 344/5(2), etc; bottelles 144/13(2)

bother See bather

botherenes dyner See brotherin dinner

bower *n* maker of bows 228/26, 324/24; bowyer 224/33, 319/41; boweres *pl* 156/15, 161/16; bowers 21/2, 26/3, 291/11, etc; bowyers 322/36

bowlbakers *n pl* those who make bowls 309/9, 321/38, 323/10, etc; bolbakers 295/27; bowlbaikers 320/14; bowllbakers 293/39

bowrne ledders, bowrnledders, bowrnleders See burnleder

brages *n pl* large nails 377/3

brandreth *n* swing 55/34

breke *n* brick 376/39

breviat *n* short account 552/21

breweer wyn *n phr* wine made by brewers (?) 410/40

broderer *n* embroiderer 247/19

broggours *n pl* brokers, purveyors (of wool) 23/1

brotherin dinner *n phr* dinner given for members of a guild 494/26; botherenes dyner 518/17; brotheringe dynner 529/40-1; brothern dynner 548/41; brothernge dynner 576/4

bucasyn *n* bocasin, a kind of fine buckram 632/27; bukasyn 632/30; bukysyn 98/8, 639/8

buklermakers *n pl* makers of bucklers (small shields carried at the back) 10/41, 20/23

bullars See bollers

bultyd loof *n phr* loaf of bread made of sifted flour 377/29

bulyons *n pl* convex ornaments on girdles, books or harnesses 137/3

burdalexander *n* a kind of costly silk cloth from

the Near East 638/10; **burdealexander** 637/34

burdes *n pl* boards 97/18, 99/38, 99/42, etc

burne *n* water from a stream or well 317/10

burnleder *n* drawer of water from streams or wells 364/26; **bowrne ledders** *pl* 288/22; **bowrnledders** 309/7; **bowrnleders** 321/37; **burneleders** 425/16; **burnleders** 292/31, 323/12; **burnlede(.)s** 291/13

bustiane *n* cotton fabric of foreign origin 638/3

butt *n* cask for ale or wine 582/41m, 582/42, 589/36; **buttes** *pl* 599/11

byllettes See **billettes**

byrall See **berall**

byrkes *n pl* birches 410/34, 425/31

callever *n* caliver, a kind of light musket 432/32, 433/24, 447/32, etc; **calever** 434/23; **kalevver** 439/31; **callevers** *pl* 432/38, 434/28, 448/11, etc; **caleeuers** 499/10; **caleuers** 474/1; **caleveres** 445/5; **calevers** 365/33, 468/10; **caliuers** 520/3; **calivers** 485/28, 491/3; **callivers** 492/8; **callyvers** 414/29, 481/14, 519/6; **calyuers** 457/41m

cappers *n pl* makers of caps 258/23, 260/26, 307/33, etc

cardemakercrafte *n* guild of cardmakers 621/40 See also **cordmaker**

cardemakers, cardmakers See **cordmaker**

carlelaxaes *n pl* Carlisle axes, a kind of battle-axe 32/40; **carlill axes** 24/24

carolus *n* a gold piece struck in the reign of Charles I 582/22, 587/30, 603/38; **carelous** 599/7

castes *n pl* units of quantities of bread made at one time 137/40

castyls *n pl* upper rims of torches, shaped like castle turrets 58/7, 58/9

catche *n* strongly built, two-masted vessel 415/25, 415/28; **katche** 415/31; **katches** *pl* 415/33

ceeled *pp* wainscoted 328/15

chaffer *n* trade 62/28

chalenged *v perf 3 pl* demanded 45/10

chaloners *n pl* makers of blankets and bed-spreads 24/7, 24/17

chamlet *n* costly eastern fabric or imitation of it 130/40

chandelars *n pl* makers and sellers of candles 304/32, 342/9, 356/2; **chaundelers** 25/24, 618/6; **chaundellers** 18/33; **chaundlers** 249/2

chanoignes *n pl* canons 146/42

chapes *n pl* the metal plates or mountings of scabbards or sheaths 136/29, 137/3; **cheapes** 448/12

chaplettes *n pl* wreaths for the head 96/16, 630/26, 630/26m, etc

chapman *n* merchant or dealer 64/11, 131/35, 131/36; **chapmen** *pl* 131/38, 251/5

chariours *n pl* chargers, platters 630/10, 630/16

chartt *n* small cart 241/40, 242/8

chauelers *n pl* wigs 55/22; **cheualers** 80/6; **cheualerz** 78/23; **cheuelers** 55/24, 55/27

cheapes See **chapes**

cheuerons *n pl* wigs 98/33, 639/33

chyffes *n pl* tops, ie, wigs 242/12

chyne *n* chain 642/21; **chynes** *pl* 413/36

clarr *n* claret 54/10

clene lentyn *n phr* Lent 118/31

clute *n* flat-headed nail used to fasten the 'wain-clout' or iron covering of the axle-tree of a wagon 309/38; **clottes** *pl* 309/18; **clowtes** 421/20

cociticinz *n pl* fellow citizens 170/24, 170/26 See also **concitesyns**

cognisans *n* coat of arms, badge 349/8; **coninzant** 580/20; **conisent** 453/20; **connysans** 460/14; **conysent** 453/19, 499/25; **cognizances** *pl* 582/31, 599/27; **cognysances** 368/18; **conisantes** 453/30, 453/31m, 453/32; **connysantes** 416/34; **connysayntes** 416/30; **conysentes** 453/24

colour of title *n phr prima facie* right 355/29

comfettes *n pl* sweetmeats made of some fruit, root, etc and preserved with sugar 149/36; **cumfettes** 141/40

comitt *v inf* consign to prison 560/9; **comitt** *pp* 560/7, 560/15; **committ** 159/33

commonialtie *n* commons 112/16, 119/15, 119/22, etc; **commolitie** 349/32; **commonaltie** 611/36; **commonaltye** 551/9; **commonialte** 62/41; **commonialtye** 153/24; **communalte** 130/23; **communaltie** 138/1; **communaltye** 154/39

comoned *pp* communicated 193/6, 201/15; **commoned** 197/20; **commonyng** *vb n* 193/10

compers *n pl* fellow members 172/30, 173/6

comprimyt *v perf 3 pl* compromitted, bound (legal) 183/14

conceyttes *n pl* fancy devices 273/10

concitesyns *n pl* fellow citizens 172/18; **concitezeyns** 53/6 See also **cociticinz**

condigne *adj* worthy 141/16, 143/9, 149/26; **conding** 148/21

condiscended *pp* agreed 326/12

conducte *pp* directed 109/19

confect *pp* made up by a combination of ingredients, especially spices 125/24; **confectes** 54/9, 54/17

coninzant, conisent, conisantes, connysans, connysantes, connysayntes See **cognisans**

connye See **cony**

contennce *n pl* contents 172/2

contentacion *n* satisfying 158/31

conueance *n* conveyance, management 138/23

convoce *v inf* make of one voice 143/9; **convok** 149/26

cony *n* rabbit fur 250/23(2), 250/32, etc; **connye** 505/12; **conys** *pl* 250/32, 250/35(2), etc

conysent, conysentes See **cognisans**

corceleit See **corslet**

cordewanere *n* shoemaker 33/3; **cordwaner** 105/31; **cordyner** 231/30, 264/35; **cordeners** *pl* 162/26; **cordewenerez** 159/32; **cordeweners** 126/3, 126/4(2), etc; **cordewers** 126/1; **cordineres** 483/11; **cordiners** 509/40, 516/30, 544/32, etc; **cordwaners** 20/33, 24/9, 24/16, etc; **cordwayners** 173/3, 173/27, 173/31, etc; **cordweners** 163/8, 163/15, 163/34, etc; **cordwerners** 167/34; **cordyners** 227/9, 258/22, 260/24, etc

cordmaker *n* maker of cards for combing wool

136/25; **cardemakers** *pl* 17/20, 25/11, 136/23, etc; **cardmakers** 621/19, 621/20 See also **cardemakercrafte**

corse *n* ribbon or band of silk (or other material) serving as ground for ornamentation and used as a girdle 641/20, 641/26, 641/28, etc

corslet *n* piece of defensive body armour 434/5, 463/8, 519/39, etc; **corceleit** 439/27; **corselett** 365/43; **corsletett** 473/39; **corslett** 445/2; **corslytt** 519/12; **corselettes** *pl* 406/6, 406/12; **corseletes** 432/26, 432/30, 433/30, etc; **corslets** 468/8; **corslettes** 445/1, 448/13, 473/38, etc; **corslytes** 519/5

corureours See **curyour**

costages *n pl* expenses 45/41 See also Anglo-Norman Glossary

coster *n* hanging, curtain 55/29, 55/32; **costers** *pl* 55/31(2)

coterelles *n pl* bolts used for fastening 55/34

coupercraft *n* guild of cowpers 620/19 See also **cowpers**

couureours See **curyour**

cowper *n* maker and repairer of casks, tubs, buckets, etc 357/8; **coupers** *pl* 17/27, 25/13, 102/38, etc; **cowpars** 450/8; **cowpers** 218/18, 258/7, 260/11, etc

crayer *n* small trading vessel 415/25, 415/28, 415/31; **crayers** *pl* 415/32

crod *n* curd 241/20; **croude** 229/40; **crowde** 235/18; **curdes** *pl* 255/31

crouke *n* hook from which a door is hung 346/2; **crokes** *pl* 103/19, 103/20, 207/23; **croukes** 377/15; **crukes** 116/6, 309/31, 309/34

croyser *n* cross-bearer 152/4

cruche *n* staff 196/16(2)

cruettes *n pl* cruets, small vials or bottles for liquids 637/35

crukes See **crouke**

crulez *n* crewel (a thin worsted yarn) 145/21

cumfettes See **comfettes**

curate *n* cuirass, piece of armour for the body 474/23; **curatt** 445/4; **curatte** 445/1, 519/6; **curett** 473/41

curdes See **crod**

curtall See **doble curtall**

curyour *n* one who colours and dresses tanned leather 627/1; **corureours** *pl* 25/35; **couuereours** 619/23, 619/27; **couureours** 19/32; **curryers** 260/28; **curyers** 258/25, 417/36, 422/21; **cuuryours** 626/36

cutchions See **scutchin**

dawkes *n pl* dalks, pins, brooches, buckles 137/4

dellwys *n gen* devil's 96/19

demened *pp* governed, directed 53/30

devince *v inf* conquer 150/6; **devincede** *pp* 150/14

diademe *n* crown 55/29; **diademes** *pl* 55/26, 55/27; **diademz** 80/6; **dyadems** 309/22, 325/10; **dyademz** 78/22; **dyodemes** 358/15; **dyodyms** 285/5

dilate *v inf* relate, describe 551/42

dissavaunce *n* retreat, retrogression 142/27; **dissaveaunce** 150/20

distresse *n in phr* **tuke distresse** distrained, caused legal seizure of chattels 45/15; **distresses** *pl* 416/13; **distressez** 167/15

distreyt *n* distraint, legal seizure of goods 276/5

disworship *n* dishonour 62/29

dobers *n pl* renovaters of old cloth or clothing 208/15; **dubbers** 14/2, 23/9

dobill ... spykyngs, doble spykynges See **dubyll spykyng**

doble curtall *n phr* obsolete musical instrument, a kind of bassoon 499/30-1

dore bandes *n phr pl* hinges 208/17; **dorebandes** 207/23

dorray *adj* bright yellow 160/35; **dorrey** 160/40

doubeler *n* large plate or dish 640/23; **doblers** *pl* 640/16; **dublers** 129/11, 342/28, 632/20

dowlyng *vb n* dowelling, fastening with a headless pin, peg or bolt of wood, metal or other material 322/2

draffe *n* dregs 361/37, 361/39

draghtlouers *n pl* arrangements of overlapping

boards or glass slips for the purpose of ventilation 41/27, 41/32

dubbers See **dobers**

dubble *v inf* repeat 360/12

dublers See **doubeler**

dubyll spykyng *n phr* spike-nail of double size 99/42; **dobill' ... spykyngs** *pl* 103/21; **doble spykynges** 376/30; **dubbyll spikynges** 156/22; **duble spykyngs** 116/4 See also **midill spykyngs, syngill spykyngs**

dyademaunt *n* crown 635/14

dyadems, dyademz See **diademe**

dykers *n pl* those who make and repair ditches 113/1, 115/17

dyodemes, dyodyms See **diademe**

easbourd *n* Baltic timber 376/28; **esbordes** *pl* 309/26

easement *n* food and lodging 409/15m; **easment** 315/26; **eisement** 82/21; **eysment** 97/32

egelome *n* edge-loom, any tool with a sharp edge 175/32

egetoile *n* edge-tool, any tool with a sharp edge 175/34; **egetole** 174/27, 174/29; **egetolez** *pl* 174/25

eisement See **easement**

empied *pp* 'impaid', paid fully 240/7

enconuenientes *n pl* disagreements 183/7; **inconuenientes** 183/19

engrosse *v pr 3 sg* concentrate in one's own possession 342/16

enhablinge *vb n* giving of legal authority or power 387/41m; **enhablyng** 337/27m

enioyeth *v pr 3 sg* makes glad 148/6

enlawed *v perf 3 pl* brought within the authority of the law 159/33; **enlawed** *pp* 159/4

ensence *v inf* instruct 148/25; **insence** 141/21

entermellyng *vb n* concern, business 250/19

entiled *pp* entered (?) 178/14

erthe wallers *n phr pl* builders of walls and foundations from soil 113/1; **erthwallers** 113/31, 115/16

esbordes See **easbourd**

estreated *pp* exacted 400/29

exilite *n* poorness, poverty 173/28

extemyng *prp* estimating the value of, esteeming 643/13; **exteamyd** *pp* 642/36

eysment See easement

faced *pp* trimmed 505/12

faines *n pl* fines 173/1

fane *n* flag, banner 55/41, 196/34; **faynes** *pl* 273/8

farme *n* fixed payment 96/17, 254/5, 254/7, etc; **ferme** 192/6, 320/3, 321/23, etc; **ffarme** 266/5, 282/19, 282/21, etc; **fferm** 294/16, 295/33, 321/43, etc; **fferme** 267/40, 267/42, 345/1, etc; **ffirme** 373/4; **firme** 382/3, 382/4, 390/3, etc; **fyrme** 413/9, 442/21; *in phr* farm(.)old quantity of land held as a farm 245/38; **firme hold** 343/27; **farmes** *pl in phr* rentes and farmes (ie, rents) 284/11m; **fermes** 379/17m, 477/2m, 483/6m, etc; **ffarmes** 255/14m, 266/6m, 282/19, etc; **ffermes** 267/40m, 305/36m, 329/2m, etc; **ffirmes** 450/2m, 533/37m; **firmes** 394/13m, 398/12m, 402/21m, etc; **firms** 446/2m; **fyrmes** 471/22m

ffeuers *n pl* smiths 19/29

ffewler *n* supplier of fuel 251/15

fflagons *n pl* large vessels for drink at table 590/31

ffleccher *n* maker and seller of arrows 6/11; **fflecheres** *pl* 161/16; **ffletcheres** 561/29; **ffletchers** 6/9, 260/38; **flecchers** 21/3; **fletchers** 258/32, 422/27, 422/34

fflorisshers *n pl* decorators and illuminators of books 152/13

fforerydinge *prp* riding ahead 411/21

fforeyner *n* one not of the town 335/13; **foreyner** 375/7; **forreynar** 370/28; **forreyner** 385/29; **fforanders** *pl* 302/7; **fforenars** 335/12m; **fforeyners** 385/28m; **fforrandars** 286/27; **fforranders** 288/22; **fforreners** 291/13, 292/31; **fforreynors** 129/15m; **fforreynours** 129/14; **foreynars** 342/31

ffounders *n pl* casters of metal 18/20;

ffoundours 18/23; **ffownderers** 258/27; **foinderers** 417/22; **founderers** 260/30, 422/12; **foundours** 25/22

ffowme *n* error for 'founce' (?) (base for a dish) 244/20

ffullars *n pl* those who beat cloth (to clean or thicken it) 330/11; **ffullers** 17/23, 24/8, 24/17; **ffullourz** 186/29

ffurnytour See furniture

ffuystours *n pl* makers of saddle-trees 22/21

flax *n* flask for gun-powder 462/41, 468/14, 475/19, etc; **flask** 485/31; **flaske** 434/14, 479/27; **fluxe** 448/36; **flaskes** *pl* 479/26; **flaxes** 445/5, 474/24

fleschcroke *n* hook for removing meat from a pot 640/21

foot cloth *n phr* a large, richly ornamental cloth laid over the back of a horse and hanging down to the ground on both sides 588/9; **footcloth** 604/11, 604/13; **foote-cloath** 612/8; **footecloth** 588/6; **foot clothes** *pl* 583/28; **footclothes** 608/41

forant *adj & n* of another town 118/20, 123/10, 128/12, etc; **fforeyne** 342/32m; **foraigne** 385/35; **forayne** 335/19; **forein** 176/23; **foreine** 111/14; **foren** 131/35; **forent** 112/4, 153/9; **foreyn** 170/33, 216/25, 300/7, etc; **foreyne** 367/35; **forren** 294/38; **fforren** of another guild 330/7, 424/17; **fforrand** 97/31m; **forand** 97/34m

forefrontes *n pl* principal faces or foremost parts of buildings 283/16

forfacte *v inf* forfeit, have to pay 414/7, 416/3, 435/12, etc; **forefacte** 427/27; **forfact** 400/5, 401/13, 407/3; **forfacted** *pp* 527/7

formelle *v inf* bespeak, mention beforehand 250/42

formes *n pl* benches 318/9; **fourmes** 230/2; **fourmez** 238/6

fotiue *adj* cherishing, warming; by extension, friendly (or votive, devout (?)) 552/18

fourbours *n pl* furbishers (those who remove rust and polish) 25/14

fourmes, fourmez See formes

furniture *n* armour and weapons of war 400/4,

400/23, 414/6, etc; **furnetor** 445/10;
ffurnytour decorating 327/33; **furnetoure**
accessories 474/25; **furnetur** 473/42,
474/1; **furneture** 439/28, 439/31; **furniter**
519/13; **furnitoure** 427/26; **furnytoure**
518/38; **furnyture** equipping 332/15
furr deales *n phr pl* slices sawn from log of fir
606/23
fursperres *n pl* fir spars 9/23
fylour *n* fulling (?) 624/15

garn *n* yarn or worsted 119/12; **garnez** *pl*
119/7
garnest *pp* stocked, provided 630/9, 630/15
garth *n* small enclosed area 218/35, 219/1(2),
etc; **garthe** 208/16
gaudes *n pl* larger and more ornamental beads
placed between the decades of aves in a
rosary 641/4, 642/3, 642/16, etc; **gaudesse**
640/40, 642/5; **gaudez** 640/36, 641/2,
641/33, etc; **gaudies** 643/43, 644/19,
644/25, etc; **gaudz** 642/9, 642/19; **gawdes**
640/38
gaunters *n pl* glovers or glove makers 17/35,
622/10
geistour *n* gester, reciter of *gestes* 75/26, 77/12
gemmoy *n* gemel, double ring 641/14;
gemmows *pl* 641/2
gerre *v inf* cause to 56/2
gestes *n pl* various stages of a journey, usually
applied to royal progresses 193/37
girdler *n* belt maker or maker of small metal
items appended to belts 136/30; **gyrdler**
227/7; **gerdlers** *pl* 136/40; **girdellers** 19/16,
24/9, 24/17; **girdlars** 312/8, 312/13, 355/
28; **girdlers** 136/32, 137/6, 258/38; **gyrdelers**
25/30; **gyrdellers** 107/21; **gyrdlers** 217/8,
261/1, 292/12
glasier *n* glazier or burnisher of leather 133/31,
263/35; **glasiars** *pl* 297/42, 298/2, 298/3;
glasiers 22/19, 297/40; **glasyars** 297/41;
glasyers 258/16, 260/21
goldbeters *n pl* makers of gold leaf 19/4;
goldbetours 624/2

grenegeys *n pl* green geese (young geese) 225/25
grevys *n pl* grievances 252/29
grewand *prp* made from fruit (applied to wine)
54/9; **grewyng** 53/34, 54/16; **growing**
125/23
grootes *n pl* English coins originally worth
four pence 643/19
grose ware *n phr* simple knives (?) 124/11
ground wallers *n phr pl* builders of wall foundations 113/1; **groundwallers** 113/32,
115/17
growing See **grewand**
guihald *n* guildhall 181/22, 203/21, 207/4;
guyhald 188/2
gyrdler, gyrdelers, gyrdellers, gyrdlers See
girdler
gyrsys *v pr 3 sg* saddles 134/10

habling, hablinge See **abling**
haisters See **haster**
halbarde *n* halberd, military weapon consisting
of a sharp-edged blade ending in a point,
and a spearhead mounted on a handle 474/
23; **halbartt** 445/3; **halbert** 407/20;
halbertes *pl* 492/8, 614/17; **holbertes**
481/14
hamydown *n* a kind of purse 107/19
hangyng *vb n* decoration with hanging or
tapestries 230/1, 235/24, 238/5; **hingyng**
222/23; **hyngyng** 226/6
harden *n* coarse fabric made from hards (coarser
parts of flax or hemp separated in hackling)
216/11
harnes *n* defensive or body armour 285/39,
285/42, 300/23, etc; **harnesse** 302/39,
355/38m, 478/27, etc; **harnis** 452/10;
harnys 413/26; **hernas** 24/26; **hernesse**
263/11; **hernis** 427/15
harnessed *pp* armoured 323/40, 332/40,
355/40, etc; **harnesed** 341/4, 341/11m;
harnest mounted 641/24, 641/28, 641/29,
etc
hartshorners *n pl* horners (q v) 25/38
haster *n* manufacturer of hair cloth or horsehair

ropes 153/1; **haisters** *pl* 153/8, 153/11; **hasters** 153/1; **hayrestars** 300/4, 304/12; **hayresters** 48/33, 49/19, 49/26, etc; **haysters** 153/4; **heirsters** 186/25

hauour *n* haviour, substance, wealth 200/27

hayng *vb n* having (or hieing (?)) 96/7

hayrestars, hayresters, haysters See **haster**

hearse *n* ordinarily a structure for carrying clothes and candles over a coffin 423/6

hegh *adj in phr* in hegh and in lawe in high and low, in all points 45/21-2

heirsters See **haster**

hekilles *n pl* instruments for combing or scutching flax or hemp 128/14

hernas, hernesse, hernis See **harnes**

hespis *n pl* hasps, devices for fastening doors 219/1; **hespssees** 156/23; **hespsses** 156/25

heuedes *n pl* flat ends of barrels 53/27

hewke *n* hook 479/26

hingyng See **hangyng**

holbertes See **halberde**

holfe *n* half 612/40

holling pipes *n phr pl* hollow pipes, (or perhaps bagpipes) 470/16

horners *n pl* manufacturers of small items from horns 20/24, 185/21, 185/21m

horslodes *n pl* horseloads (?) 250/22

hosier *n* maker of hose or underclothing 201/7; **hosiers** *pl* 297/22; **hosyers** 13/36m, 13/40, 18/11, etc; **hoysyers** 422/9

hostelars *n pl* innkeepers 114/25, 344/1; **hostilers** 23/31, 106/28; **hostlers** 26/25m, 26/26m; **hostylars** 344/10; **ostelars** 114/33; **ostelers** 114/4, 114/17

hosyercraft *n* craft of hosiers 13/40 See also **hosier**

hunts vps *n phr pl* early morning songs, originally used to awaken huntsmen 388/31; **huntsvps** 388/32; **hunt ys up** 470/8; **hunt ys vp** 470/12

hupes *n pl* circular bands used for wheels 421/18; **huppes** 325/13

hyngyng See **hangyng**

iacke *n* sleeveless tunic, usually made of quilted leather, used for body armour 468/19, 474/7

iaggyd *adj* cut into jags for ornament 267/32

iakettes *n pl* jackets of some kind 145/26

ilez *n pl* roofing of some kind 631/23

ilkon *pron* each one 25/6, 186/39

incontinent *adv* immediately 167/17

inconuenientes See **enconuenientes**

insence See **ensence**

instant *adj* next following 452/30, 463/31; **instante** 435/4, 458/30; **instant** present 327/13

intermyt *v inf* concern 174/26

ioyned brede *n phr* bread joined into a number of shapes, or 'enjoined' bread, ie, made according to order or assize (?) 78/38-9

iudas *n* Paschal candlestick 164/18; **iudassez** *pl* 98/35, 639/35

iuelles *n pl* ornaments (not jewels) 642/35, 644/36, 644/37, etc; **iowelles** 640/28

iunours *n pl* joiners 620/10

kalevver See **callever**

kambesmyth *n* comb maker 49/4

katche, katches See **catche**

keile *n* flat-bottomed vessel 415/25, 415/28, 415/31; **keiles** *pl* 415/33

kersey *n* kind of coarse, narrow cloth, woven from long wool, usually ribbed 460/13

keybandes *n pl* cases used for keys, key-rings 105/8

kidberer *n* carrier of faggots or sticks of wood for fuel 108/33; **kidberers** *pl* 113/1, 115/16

kilne hares *n phr pl* kiln cloths (on which grain was laid for drying) 153/3, 153/9-10; **kilne heris** 153/14

kinges evill *n phr* scrofula 556/30, 607/6

kittyng *vb n* cutting 230/34

knight marshall *n phr* officer of the royal household, who had judicial cognizance within it 155/38; **knyght marshall** 151/35

knop *n* ornamental protuberance 640/39; **knopp** 635/22, 636/22; **knoppes** *pl* 137/3, 644/25; **knoppis** 636/13

kunne *v inf* know 353/6

kyde *n* faggot, wood-stick 248/16; **kyddes** *pl*
  376/35

laith *n* barn (?) 284/20

lambefell *n* lamb's skin 185/4, 185/5

lambefurres *n pl* wool 185/6

larged *pp in phr* in larged freed 159/4

laton *n* latten, a mixed metal of yellow colour,
  either identical with, or closely resembling
  brass 55/41, 137/5

latoners *n pl* makers of and workers in latten
  22/3, 26/13, 37/19, etc

latt *n* thin, narrow strip of wood used to form a
  groundwork upon which to fasten the slates
  or tiles of a roof or the plaster of a wall or
  ceiling, and in the construction of lattice or
  trellis work 288/30; **lattes** *pl* 96/2, 129/15,
  208/17, etc

latt nales *n phr pl* nails used for fastening laths
  376/31, 376/41 See also **latt**

lawde *n* praise 275/23

lawe *adj in phr* in hegh and in lawe See **hegh**

lawne *n* fine linen, resembling cambric 145/24

leades *n pl* lead roofs 408/10, 408/11

leghys *n pl* ledges, transverse bars of wood fixed
  on a door 309/30

lett *n* hindrance 240/3

lettyng *vb n* hindering 119/7, 192/18

leydes *n pl* fields or lands 272/22

listed *pp* bordered, edged 629/31

litt *v inf* colour, dye 119/7; **lit** *pr sub 3 sg*
  119/11

littester *n* dyer 5/13; **lytster** 100/13; **litsters** *pl*
  108/18; **lysters** 210/15; **lytsters** 108/19,
  210/11, 422/29; **lyttesters** 26/5

lommers *n pl* illuminators 152/12; **lumners**
  23/6

lone *n* loin 316/31; **lune** 317/3

lorymer *n* manufacturer of bits and metal
  mountings for horses' bridles 13/5, 13/8;
  lorymars *pl* 311/26; **lorymers** 19/20,
  176/17m

louers *n pl* draught louvers 41/18 See also
  draghtlouers

lowse *pp* loosened 449/29

lowte *v inf* bow 139/32

lumners See **lommers**

lune See **lone**

luter *n* lute player 70/29, 71/34, 76/21

lybartes *n pl* lions 416/31, 416/33(2); **lybertes**
  416/32

lymeburnar *n* maker of lime by burning lime-
  stone 370/28

lymeted *pp* specified 168/33; **lymited** 386/3;
  lymyted 335/29

lyn loyme *n phr* linen loom 268/42

lysters, lytster, lytsters, lyttesters See **littester**

maine bread See **maynebrede**

maini *adj in phr* in maini into many parts (or
  'in money'(?)) 412/11m

mande bred *n phr* bread distributed at a maundy
  (ceremony of washing the feet of the poor)
  293/2; **mandy bred** 294/26, 325/32-3;
  manndye breade 425/38-9; **maundye bread**
  472/1; **maundye breade** 465/32; **mawndye
  bread** 477/22, 477/26-7, 483/27-8;
  mawndye breade 460/36, 489/7

manebrede See **maynebrede**

marcer *n* shopkeeper, seller of small wares
  375/18; **marcers** *pl* 255/18; **merceres** 95/4;
  mercers 24/3, 26/26, 186/38, etc; **mercres**
  61/28; **mersers** 55/9

markin iron *n phr* branding iron (?) 468/16-17;
  markyngirens *pl* 640/19

marmusett *n* monkey 94/19

marshalles *n pl* horse-tenders, farmers 59/30;
  marshalls 124/1, 124/4; **marsshalles** 59/34;
  marsshals 16/5, 19/13, 25/29, etc

marybones *n pl* marrow bones 222/8, 229/40,
  235/19, etc; **marybonis** 248/12; **mary-
  boones** 244/7

maundith *n* maundy, church ceremony celebrating the king's age by washing the feet
  of the poor 606/20

maundye bread, maundye breade, mawndye
  bread, mawndye breade See **mande bred**

maundye dynner *n phr* dinner given at a maundy 425/7-8 See also **mande bred**

maynebrede *n* bread of the finest quality, pain-demaine 137/39, 280/42, 317/17; **maine bread** 556/17, 557/4; **manebrede** 221/35; **maynbread** 326/33, 372/13, 411/4, etc; **maynbred** 420/28; **mayne bred** 288/35; **skallop of maynebrede** *n phr* bread made in the shape of a cockleshell 280/37

meld *n* motley cloth 89/30

melde *n* motley, mixed-coloured cloth 65/2, 101/39

mell *v pr 1 pl in phr* **mell wyth** deal with 53/12

merceres, mercers, mercres See **marcer**

mercerye *n* area where small wares are sold, market 85/26, 93/37

mere mocionz *n phr pl* of their own accords, without the help of anyone else 192/9

mersers See **marcer**

midill spykyngs *n pl* spike-nails of medium size 116/5-6 See also **dubyll spykyng, syngill spykyngs**

milners *n pl* millers 21/18, 26/11, 212/15, etc; **myliners** 422/31; **mylners** 212/13m, 217/11, 217/12, etc

misteres, misteries See **mystery**

monemakers *n pl* minters 19/5

moninge *vb n* monishing, warning 385/35

morryon *n* kind of helmet for soldiers, without beaver or visor 445/11; **moryones** *pl* 445/6

motions *n pl* puppet shows 592/41

mowledes *n pl* shoes for armour (?) 474/25 See also **mowles**

mowles *n pl* shoes for armour (?) 519/10

moyte *n* half 251/13, 251/14, 257/24, etc

murray *n* murrey (purple-red or blood-red) 86/2, 139/18; **murrey** 138/1

musce ball *n phr* ball receptacle for musk 636/4; **muste ball** 642/29

musterdevelers *n pl* articles made of a kind of grey woollen cloth 94/26; **musterdivyles** 130/25

mustrance *n* monstrance 631/27; **mustraunce** 634/2

myliners, mylners See **milners**

mysehauyd *v perf 3 pl* misbehaved (reflexive)

159/9

myssay *v pr subj 3 sg* speak evil against 185/15

mystery *n* trade guild 338/1; **mysterye** 296/29; **misteres** *pl* 212/15; **misteries** 268/36; **mysteriez** 174/15; **mysteryes** 215/42, 216/5; **mystyrs** 127/16

naffe *n* wagon roof (?)(ordinarily, the hub of a wheel) 55/36

naprons *n pl* aprons 629/36, 629/36m, 629/38; **napeones** 640/4

nares *n pl* error for snares (?) 410/6

nattez *n pl* matting 633/6

naylers *n pl* makers of nails 19/17

ne before *adv phr* nigh before 140/41, 141/39

noiues *n pl* knives 124/10

notors *n pl* writers of musical scores 152/12

nowch See **owche**

nowteshote, nowtshott See **outeshote**

noyse *n* set of horns 349/25, 349/31

obles *n pl* obleys, thin cakes of pastry, wafers 149/35

oeps *n* use, benefit, profit 46/4

offerantes *n pl* oblations, offerings 169/9

ordinary *n* book of guild ordinances 591/29, 591/31; **ordynarie** 512/31; **ordynary** 512/25; **ordinaries** *pl* 508/31

orfeuers *n pl* goldsmiths 19/3

orforay *n* orphrey, ornamental band 637/32

ostelars, ostelers See **hostelars**

oþering *n* contraction of 'other' and 'thing' 110/18; **oþeringes** *pl* 110/16

outeshote *n* building extension 394/19, 402/28, 404/24, etc; **nowteshote** 288/5, 292/16; **nowtshott** 306/6; **outeshott** 450/8, 524/31; **outshot** 493/16; **outshote** 428/2; **outshott** 564/16; **owteshot** 329/8; **owteshote** 284/19, 286/11, 290/36, etc; **owteshott** 319/34, 345/8, 350/8; **owtshote** 339/32; **owtshott** 546/12, 558/34, 565/29, etc; **owttshott** 372/32; 〈...〉**shote** 566/22

owche *n* gold setting for a stone (or a clasp (?))
642/15; nowch 635/5; owchesse *pl* 641/10

padgeant *n* one of the individual episodes constituting the Corpus Christi play; one of the
pageant wagons upon which plays were
performed (frequently ambiguous); pachent
16/7m; padgaunt 290/42; padgeant 136/18,
136/26, 136/32, etc; padgeaunt 152/19,
292/22; padgeaunte 293/30; padgen 320/
14; padgian 347/29; padgiane 350/42;
padgiant 152/35, 153/22, 459/26, etc;
padgiante 547/12; padgient 459/24, 564/
11, 564/12, etc; padging 364/18; padgion
395/14, 395/20, 395/34, etc; padgon 424/
31; padgone 384/30; padgyan 347/36, 347/
38; padgyant 379/39, 379/40; padgyon
395/30; padg⟨.⟩ent 564/9; padione 384/32,
384/33, 390/20, etc; padȝhand 16/7;
pagand 45/13, 95/36, 96/17, etc; pagant
61/35, 91/20, 91/36, etc; pagantt 91/34;
pagaunt 250/30, 250/31m, 252/40, etc;
pageand 45/11, 68/16, 73/23, etc; pageant
45/37, 45/40, 54/15, etc; pageante 82/38,
388/41m, 526/26m, etc; pagean⟨.⟩ 60/8;
pageaunt 108/19, 108/21, 108/23, etc;
pageaunte 411/21, 411/30, 412/3; pagen
285/3; pagend 104/14, 104/31, 106/27, etc;
pagende 102/43, 104/27, 104/36, etc; pagent
53/11, 55/12, 55/14, etc; paggan 345/33,
345/40; paggand 292/30; paggayn 345/35;
paggeant 364/37; paggeaunt 364/27;
paggen 295/17; paghant 134/6; pagiant
114/17, 115/8, 131/35, etc; pagiante 82/27,
299/13, 299/33, etc; pagiaunt 25/4, 107/21,
107/25, etc; pagiaunte 260/16, 306/16;
pagient 82/31, 133/28, 267/42, etc; pagion
456/2, 456/14, 456/25, etc; pagione 496/
41; pagyand .207/23, 207/25, 290/35, etc;
pagyant 62/6, 97/12, 97/24, etc; pagyante
380/2; pagyaunt 208/18, 208/19, 290/29,
etc; pagyent 267/40, 268/5, 350/37; pagyn
347/23; pagyne 347/41; pagynt 374/3;
pagyon 296/24, 380/17, 380/19, etc; paiant

149/11, 175/36, 227/35; paiaunt 127/35,
147/6, 148/11, etc; paiaunte 260/15;
paidgion 425/37, 428/36; paieant 268/40,
281/21, 281/25; paieaunt 272/24, 272/30;
paigeant 304/31, 304/36, 305/15; paigiaunt
175/2; paigon 380/15; paigyant 371/10,
371/11; pajand 100/6, 100/15, 100/16;
paujand 99/33, 99/40; pawgand 421/18,
421/28; payant 175/31; paygeant 239/38;
paygent 266/5, 266/7, 266/12, etc; paygon
331/11; paygyant 343/3, 382/16; pacentes
pl 24/29; padgeantes 136/25; padgons
446/35; paganddes 96/7; pagantes 421/3;
pagants 61/36; pageantes 25/6, 60/7,
115/9, etc; pageantez 24/37; pageants
124/21; pageantz 124/6, 297/25, 297/38,
etc; pagentes 109/12, 254/11, 255/21, etc;
pagentz 24/35; pagiantes 263/36, 298/24,
299/3, etc; pagyantes 97/21, 97/24, 282/
26; pagyants 97/18; pagyauntes 291/40;
paiauntes 250/1, 252/15; pawgands 421/
21; paygentes 266/12; padgions *gen* 395/15
pakthrede *n* stout thread or twine 96/5
pans *n pl in phr* postes & pans beams which
rest on the posts of a house and support
the rafters 116/2
parcell gylte *adj phr* partly gilded 644/20,
644/38
parchemeners *n pl* parchmenters, makers or
sellers of parchment 25/19, 39/32, 39/33m;
parchemyners 18/8, 622/10
pariching *n* parish 138/32
party geld *n phr* gold leaf 91/32
pastill *n* little pie or pasty (?) 78/38
patenmakers *n pl* makers of pattens (overshoes
or sandals worn to raise shoes out of mud
or water) 20/5
paujand, pawgand, pawgands, payant, paygant,
paygeant, paygent, paygentes, paygon,
paygyant See padgeant
pavessez *n pl* shields 145/27
payned *pp* fined 251/9
pees *n pl* coats of coarse cloth worn by men
554/20, 582/29, 588/7, etc
pellour *n* fur 185/6, 185/7; pellur 185/8
pelter *n* skinner 5/12

pennaunt *n* pendant 641/20, 641/22, 641/24, etc; **pennaunte** 641/26

pennons *n pl* triangular flags 98/21, 98/31, 639/22, etc; **penonz** 80/5

pension *n* payment for services 82/21

perceyue *v inf* obtain, receive 108/18, 192/20; **perceyve** 135/5; **percieue** 108/22; **perseve** 128/12; **perceyued** *pp* 173/23

perfornesyng *vb n* perfurnishing, trimming 185/8

perryng *vb n* appearing (erroneous gloss) 26/3

perseve See **perceyue**

personelles *n pl* parcels, ie, individual pieces 640/28

pessoners *n pl* fishmongers 18/5

peyre *v pr 1 sg* appear 140/4

pikemongers *n pl* dealers in pike and other fresh-water fish 119/30

plat *n* plan, plot 276/39

plummers *n pl* makers of leaden articles and sellers of lead 20/4, 25/37

poke *n* peck 114/28, 114/29

poket *n* sack or bag 27/40, 628/31; **pokettis** *pl* 27/36, 628/26

polle *n in phr* **by polle** according to number of persons 298/3

pomaunder *n* case for pomander perfume (mixture of aromatic substances, usually made into a ball) 644/11, 644/27

pontificalibus *n pl* bishop's robes, pontificals 152/5

potell *n* half-gallon 420/34; **pottell** 317/3, 317/19; **pottle** 532/25, 532/33

potters *n pl* makers and sellers of earthenware 23/16, 26/21, 26/29, etc

pottyng stang *n phr* pole used for putting the wagon 96/6

preceptes *n pl* written orders, warrants 400/6, 414/8, 445/18, etc

precessed *v perf 3 pl* went before 54/24

precessions See **pressession**

prehemenences *n pl* distinguishing privileges 552/39; **preheminences** 553/16

premisses *n pl* things aforementioned 114/31, 124/17, 173/26, etc; **premissez** 112/14, 114/15, 123/18, etc; **premysez** 171/6, 183/15

preordiniance *n* previously established order 142/12; **preordynance** 150/5

preparate *pp* prepared 141/14, 148/19

pressession *n* possible error for procession 126/34; **precessions** *pl* 146/40

presur *n* cupboard, clothes press 636/35

procintes *n pl* precincts, area nearby 114/11, 344/3; **procynctes** 114/27

promytted *v perf 3 pl* promised 216/1

prose *n in phr* **in prose** in rhymed as opposed to quantitative verse (?) 139/37, 141/7

provision *n* foresight 148/17

pryknote *n* musical notation 58/18

purede *pp* refined 149/6

pursevantes *n pl* attendants 578/40m, 580/9m, 581/13m, etc; **purseuants** 580/35; **purseyvantes** 577/24; **pursivantes** 597/7; **pursuivantes** 578/8

purvie *v inf* provide 131/10

puters *n pl* those who 'put' or propel a wagon 91/40; **putters** 372/11

pynnar *n* manufacturer of pins and other small wire articles 332/9; **pynner** 340/39, 340/40m; **pynnars** *pl* 332/10, 332/11, 332/13, etc; **pynners** 22/2, 37/19, 38/5, etc

pynnercrafte *n* guild of pinners 37/38, 38/26, 38/35, etc See also **pynnar**

quartrons *n pl* quarters (of a pound) 411/3

quere *n* choir 150/27, 150/28, 150/31, etc; **queare** 432/19; **quiere** 538/9; **quire** 568/33, 571/7, 606/31; **quyer** 588/17

queristers *n pl* choristers 423/17

questours *n pl* pardoners 23/8

quiere, quire, quyer See **quere**

qwre *n* wire 294/17

ratable *adj* calculated according to a scale 583/10

ratablie *adv* proportionately 415/40; **ratebly** 328/31

ray *n* kind of striped cloth 86/2, 86/7; **rayes** *pl*

83/6, 86/8; **rays** 60/22, 64/43

rebell *adj* disobedient to authority 107/30, 118/25, 123/17, etc

recoursede *v perf 1 sg* came 147/17; **recoursid** 140/7

reees *n pl* reeds or rews (burrs for rivets) (?) 92/4

regalitie *n* royal jurisdiction 147/13; **rigalitie** 140/3

regesly *adv* 'rageously', in a furious or angry manner 148/30; **regosly** 141/26

regynall *n* contraction of 'original' 330/10, 331/1

reherced *pp* mentioned 164/1, 201/14; **rehersed** 78/1, 118/26, 183/41, etc

remised *pp* remitted (money) 108/8

reparell *v inf* repair 134/6; **reparellyng** *vb n* 304/8

reseant *adj* resident 162/26

resolute *adj* paid 331/19m, 331/32m, 340/11m, etc; **resolut** 442/21m

reuett, reveit, revet, revett See **alemon reuett**

reuettes *n pl* earthenware receptacles for wax 28/6, 28/9, 28/9m, etc; **reuetts** 79/20

revestre *n* vestry 468/19

revet *n* almain-rivet 451/43 See also **alemon reuett**

rigalitie See **regalitie**

ripeley *adv* with mature consideration 171/25

rough vessell *n phr pl* crudely finished vessels 225/37; **rugh vessells** 222/15

roundeletes *n pl* ornamental circles 28/5; **roundelettes** 28/5m, 28/7; **roundels** 640/5

routh *n* ox hide 111/15

roves *n pl* roofs 631/24

royd lyeht *n phr* light dedicated to the Cross 219/20

rub rosar *n phr* red rose 145/26

rugh vessells See **rough vessell**

ryall *n* gold coin worth ten shillings originally 643/18

ryge tyle *n phr* tile used for roofing the ridge of a building 377/7

rype *adj* considered 192/16; **ryppe** 183/17

ryshebearinges *n pl* ceremonies of carrying rushes and garlands to the church and

strewing the floor or decorating the walls with them 358/30

sackbutt *n* instrument consisting of a brass trumpet with a trombone slide 567/26; **sagbutt** 506/39; **sagbuttes** *pl* 443/13, 447/22

sadde *adj* dark, deep 274/7

safferon *n* orange-red product used for colouring and flavouring 316/34; **saveron** 222/16, 222/18

safure *n* sapphire 643/6

sagbutt, sagbuttes See **sackbutt**

salars *n pl* cellars 630/20; **salers** 79/14, 630/ 18m, 630/18; **salerz** 632/21

sallett oyll *n phr* oil used in preparing sallets (helmets) 440/5; **sellit oyle** 467/41

salsemakercrafte *n* guild of saucemakers 30/41 See also **salsemakers**

salsemakers *n pl* saucemakers 30/39, 48/30, 49/7, etc

samell *n* samite or sendal (?), rich silk cloth 596/8

sandeleders *n pl* transporters of sand used for building 192/5, 192/27, 291/13; **sand leders** 292/31; **sandleders** 192/21, 286/27, 288/22; **ssandledders** 302/8; **ssandleders** 293/40

sandeledinge *vb n* transportation of sand for building 428/38

sappe lattes *n phr pl* fir laths 208/17 See also **latt**

sarke *n* garment worn next to the skin, shirt 95/6; **sirke** 55/29; **sarkkes** 96/14; **serkes** 92/6, 97/15, 97/20; **sirkes** 55/22, 55/23

saunders *n pl* horse-parsley ('Alexanders') 79/11

saveron See **safferon**

sawers *n pl* sawyers, sawers of timber 22/27, 127/14, 127/26, etc; **sawiers** 19/17

scalers *n pl* makers of scales 20/22

scearchers, scerchers See **searcher**

scherlynges *n pl* shearlings, fleeces of sheep that have been once shorn 185/5

schocheons See **scutchin**

schorers *n pl* props, supports 468/11

schotes *n pl* levies of some kind 293/11

sciens *n* craft 334/8, 385/20, 385/27, etc;
scyens 268/41, 337/21

scoringesticke *n* scourer (ramrod fitted with a
wad for cleaning out the bore of a gun)
458/8

scutchin *n* escutcheon, shield on which a coat
of arms is depicted 449/15; skutcheon
324/6; skutchion 416/32, 416/33, 416/34;
skutcion 416/31; cutchions *pl* 416/23;
schocheons 608/11; scutchons 290/11,
318/20, 413/36; scutchoons 338/39;
scutcyons 284/2; skotchons 318/28;
skottchons 318/18; skutchions 416/29,
416/35; skutchons 318/23

scyens See sciens

seachers See searcher

search, searche See serch

searched See serche

searcher *n* official appointed by a guild to
enforce its regulations 386/7, 386/8, 391/
14, etc; serchar 335/33, 335/34, 337/37;
sersour 152/25, 252/33, 252/34, etc;
scearchers *pl* 384/25; scerchers 306/34;
seachers 390/29; searchares 447/6;
searchars 461/34; searcherees 494/19;
searcheres 461/27, 497/31, 503/8, etc;
searchers 299/34, 378/36, 380/39, etc;
searches 391/5; searchres 404/6; searshers
298/41; seircheors 159/2; seircheour 159/
12; seircheours 118/30, 118/34, 118/35,
etc; seirchers 158/31; seirchours 123/27;
serchars 114/25, 304/40, 308/13, etc;
sercheours 16/9, 104/27, 104/30, etc;
serchers 239/42, 240/7, 296/21, etc;
serchiours 102/42, 103/2; serchours 45/36,
53/21, 62/35, etc; serchourz 127/35, 175/
33; sersors 167/9; sersours 108/15, 111/5,
111/13, etc; sersourz 204/37, 216/10;
serssours 163/15, 163/34, 168/1, etc;
serssourz 163/27; sersurs 185/15; sessors
463/21; sessours 163/40; sherchers 296/19,
374/25; sherchours 53/25; searchares *gen*
447/6; searchars 461/34; searcheres 450/
42, 451/2, 461/42, etc; searcherees 494/19;
searcheres 494/16; searchers 473/11,

494/8, 497/38; serchers 374/31; surrsers
97/2

sellerage *n* provision of cellars 599/29

sellers *n pl* saddlers 22/18

sellit oyle See sallett oyll

sennett *n* sennight, period of seven days 246/10

serch *n* examination for the purpose of en-
forcing guild regulations 54/21, 114/10,
175/33, etc; search 129/14m; searche
342/31m; serce 227/11; serche 45/37,
114/26, 124/10, etc; serse 108/10; sherch
54/9, 54/12

serchar, serchars, sercheours, serchers,
serchiours, serchours, serchourz See searcher

serche *v inf* examine in accordance with guild
regulations 62/36, 109/11, 124/12, etc;
searche 441/22; serched *perf 3 pl* 53/23;
searched *pp* 129/15; serched 342/32;
serchyd 251/21; sersed 108/15; serchyng
vb n 53/20

serkelett *n* ornamental headband 632/12

serkes See sarke

serse See serch

sersed See serche

sersors, sersour, sersours, sersourz, serssours,
serssourz, sersurs See searcher

serveourz *n pl* servers, assistants 21/20

sessors, sessours See searcher

s[h]ewed *v perf 3 sg* served 151/4

seynt Iames shelles *n phr pl* cockleshells from
shrine of St James Major of Compostella
644/28-9

shalme *n* musical instrument of the oboe class
333/13, 333/15m, 348/40, etc; shawme
347/14; shalmes *pl* 349/25, 361/13

shamylles *n pl* shambles, market (for fish)
294/40

sharplyngs *n pl* kind of nail 116/4

shawme See shalme

sherch See serch

sherchers, sherchours See searcher

sheremen *n pl* shearers of woollen cloth to remove
nap 214/35m; shermen 26/10, 214/36

shethers *n pl* makers of sheaths 10/41, 20/21,
64/22

shobokilles *n pl* shoe buckles 128/26

shoghyrs *n pl* soldiers (?) 131/16

shotill *n* weaving shuttle 301/7

sircote *n* surcoat (outer garment of rich material worn by people of rank) 150/38

sirke, sirkes See sarke

sivin *prp* following (?) 466/42m

skalep *n* vessel resembling a cockle-shell, used in baptism 641/17, 642/20

skallop See maynebrede

skeppez *n pl* skeps, units of dry measure 79/14

skotchons, skottchons See scutchin

skourer *n* wad or sponge for cleaning the bore of a gun 448/37

skule *n* head-piece 439/29; skulles *pl* 474/27, 519/8

skutcheon, skutchion, skutchions, skutchons, skutcion See scutchin

sledmen *n pl* transporters of goods by land (distinct from porters) 258/41, 261/7, 307/25, etc; sledmens *gen pl* 307/30

slyke *adj* such 622/6

solynges *n pl* sills, horizontal beams (?) 103/17

sotheron clothe *n phr* cloth from the south (?) 227/22; sudderon clothe 205/29; sutheron clothe 249/30, 249/36; suttherin clothe 230/35

sowyng *vb n* sawing 91/22

spannall *n* spinal, a textile fabric 97/20; spenall 91/30

spicers *n pl* apothecaries 18/15, 25/21, 54/8, etc; spiceres 54/6

spikynges, spykyng, spykynges, spykyngs See dubyll spykyng, midill spykyngs, syngill spykyngs

sporiers *n pl* makers of spurs 19/20; sporryours 356/12m, 356/12; sporyers 25/31, 258/17, 260/23; sporyourz 176/16m; spurriours 311/26; spurriourz 311/25m; spuryers 417/9, 422/18

ssandledders, ssandleders See sandeleders

staith *n* wharf 313/38, 415/26, 415/39; stahe 118/18

stalled *pp* installed 197/21

stallegyd *pp* made to pay a toll for the privilege of erecting a stall 251/3

stamett *n* some woollen fabric 520/42, 523/41,

528/28; stanit 536/33

stancheon *n* upright bar or support 212/6; stanschns *pl* 91/21; staunchons 116/2

stang See pottyng stang

stanit See stamett

stanours See steynours

stapyll *n* bent rod used for holding the hasp or hook for securing a door 208/16; stapilles *pl* 156/25; staples 219/1; stapylles 156/23

stayes *n pl* props, supports 91/24

stene *n* stone 116/5

stenours See steynours

stenyng *vb n* painting coloured designs on cloth 78/8; steynyng 9/14

sternes *n pl* stars 55/37, 55/39; sternez 641/25

steynourcrafte *n* craft of stainers 37/41 See also steynours

steynours *n pl* painters of coloured designs on cloth 37/19, 38/4, 38/8, etc; stanours 624/2; stenours 37/11

stocke *n* sum of money set aside to provide for certain expenses 526/13; stockes *pl* 541/8, 547/33

stockmony *n* sum of money set aside to provide for certain expenses 511/15

stoopes *n pl* stoops, pillars 609/5, 609/9; stoupes 583/18; stulpes 611/13, 614/4

stothez *n pl* knobs, studs 641/32; stuthes 641/23

stowres *n pl* stowers, stakes, posts 99/41

strake *n* section of the iron rim of a cart-wheel 288/28, 309/19; stroke 425/10; strokes *pl* 421/25

streyne *v inf* distrain, legally force to make satisfaction 93/9

stubules *n pl* staples or stubs (thick nails) (or 'stopels', steps (?)) 421/21

stulpes See stoopes

stuthes See stothez

sty *v inf* ascend 55/35

suckett *n* fruit preserved in sugar 411/2

sudderon clothe See sotheron clothe

surceasse *v inf* desist 297/4

surdaunt *prp* arising 170/26, 170/36

surnap *n* towel for washing hands 151/36

surrsers See searcher

sutheron clothe, suttherin clothe See sotheron
clothe

swallis *n pl* laths, planks 156/25

swilk *adj* such 54/12; swylk 54/21

sye *n* tow or oakum used for caulking 153/10

syght *n* show, spectacle 130/32

symnell *n* bread made of fine flour, prepared by
boiling, sometimes with subsequent baking
78/38

syngill spykyngs *n pl* spike-nail of 'single' size
103/21 See also dubyll spykyng, midill
spykyngs

syviars *n pl* sieve makers 300/5, 304/13

tache *n* clasp or hook 643/36

tale *n in phr* by weight & tale by weight and
count 324/7

talliaunders *n pl* either tailors or edge-tool
makers 23/12

tapiter *n* weaver of tapestry 87/11, 136/25;
tapitour 160/38, 161/2; tapiteres *pl* 107/
39, 108/12; tapiters 26/4, 107/35, 108/2,
etc; tapitors 282/23, 290/32; tapitours
119/5, 119/11m, 160/34, etc; tappiters
546/7, 558/29, 564/11, etc; tapytours
258/35, 284/15, 286/13, etc

tarrecte *v int* contraction of 'to aret' (to
impute) 162/39

tawny *n* cloth of brown colour with predomi-
nance of yellow or orange 274/7, 582/20

teildes *n pl* tents, pavilions 153/3, 153/10

temer *n* timber 294/8

tenour *n* wording 153/1, 163/9, 171/37, etc;
tenor 491/28

text wryghters, textwriters, textwryters See
tixtwriter

thak teell *n phr* roofing tile 218/32; thake
theyll 309/25

thekyng *vb n* thacking, covering with tiles
377/8

theyll See thak teell

throwe *v inf* shape on a potter's lathe 129/11;
throwinge *pp* 129/6

tibuvnell *n* taborner, drummer (?) 72/26;

tibuvner 72/27

tielhouses *n pl* 'tile housers' (?), those who
cover houses with tiles 217/12; tielhousez
212/13

tincler *n* mender of pots and pans, tinker 128/
14; tynclars *pl* 344/24; tynklers 223/34

tipstaves *n pl* staff with a metal tip carried as a
badge by certain officials 464/6; an official
bearing a tipped staff 599/41; tipstaffes
543/11; tipstaues 614/29

tixtwriter *n* professional writer of text-hand
105/29; text wryghters *pl* 312/7; textwriters
314/36

tolle dysshes *n phr pl* dishes or bowls used for
measuring the toll of grain at a mill 305/9

tondours *n pl* shearers 14/16m

tope *n* head, those in leading position 212/20

touch box *n* box for 'touch-powder' or priming
powder 499/2; tuchebox 432/33, 447/33,
462/41; touch boxes *pl* 499/10-11; tuch
boxes 445/5, 468/10, 474/24; tutch boxes
519/7

tournours See turnars

trappour *n* covering for a horse, made of metal
or leather and used for defence 195/20;
trappours *pl* 195/24

trauers *n* dispute 170/14, 215/40; travers 170/
16, 252/24; traves 254/19

trauesse *n* traverse, compartment 197/17

travaux *n pl* (?) *in phr* hangyng in travaux
remaining in dispute 136/17

traves See trauers

treangle *n* ornament or piece of jewellery in a
triangular form 643/36

tregitour *n* juggler 70/7

trencherd brede *n phr* bread made of unsifted
flour, used as a plate or platter 78/39;
trenchirbrede 229/28; trenchourbrede
237/31

trenchours *n pl* pieces of bread used as platters
221/35

trestez *n pl* trestles, benches 79/21

trestyls *n pl* benches 238/6

treuelies *n pl* trevallies, signals made by drum-
beats 513/34

tromppez *n pl* trumpets 95/14; trompys 242/

3; trumpes 55/25

trusys *n pl* handles or decorations (?) 238/7

tuch boxes, tuchebox, tutch boxes See touch box

turnars *n pl* those who fashion wood, metal, bone, etc on a lathe 129/8, 129/13, 300/4, etc; tournours 26/9, 152/12; turnares 129/12; turners 129/5m, 129/10

tynclars, tynklers See tincler

uerynnes *n* weariness 605/26

vpsett *n* setting up of business 110/29, 227/9; vpsettes *pl* 110/29

vyal *n* viol (musical instrument having five to seven strings, played with a bow) 571/6; vyall 571/5

vyntener *n* taverner 296/18; vynter 184/22; vinteners *pl* 248/23; vinters 130/1; vintyners 235/21, 238/1; vyntenars 311/40, 311/42m; vynteners 239/39, 239/42, 296/12, etc; vyntenors 351/31; vynterners 316/40; vynters 19/25, 53/6, 53/21; vyntyners 222/12, 225/35, 280/36

vytell *n* food, victuals 251/17; vitaylles *pl* 326/1

valauncez *n pl* piece of drapery attached lengthwise to a canopy or altar-cloth so as to hang vertically 98/11, 639/11; valencez 632/27

vambraces *n pl* defensive armour for the forearm 432/27, 468/8

varmelon *n* vermilion used as a pigment 318/18

vavasour *n* feudal tenant below a baron 146/36

vellowett *n* velvet 637/39

vergyos *n* verjuice (acid of sour fruit) 317/11

verrours *n pl* glaziers 22/20

veserne *n* vizor mask 55/29; wesseren 241/39; vesenes *pl* 55/22; vesernes 55/21, 55/24, 55/26; wesserons 242/9

viace *n* vice, mechanical device 139/30, 141/38

vinteners, vinters, vintyners See vyntener

visards *n pl* masks 423/12

vitaylles See vytell

vitellers *n pl* suppliers of victuals and provisions 251/16

vncouenable *adj* inappropriate 622/5

voide *n* emptying of chamber 151/36

vpayn *contraction of* upon pain 60/10; vppayn 63/7; vppon 269/13

vphaldster *n* dealer in small wares or second-hand articles 619/17 See also vpholder

vpholder *n* dealer in small wares or second-hand articles 108/23; vphalderes *pl* 13/41; vphalders 185/11, 618/34 See also vphaldster

vppayn, vppon See vpayn

wadmen *n pl* packers of wadding (or woodmen (?)) 23/2

waferer *n* waferer, itinerant seller of wafers 66/3, 66/4, 66/18, etc; waferrer 92/32; wafferer 66/20, 66/35, 67/19, etc; waffereres *pl* 75/29

waffrons *n pl* wafers 142/35

waite *n* musician 143/20, 143/24, 408/20m, etc; wait 346/26; wate 405/17m, 405/17, 418/30, etc; wayte 333/19, 349/7, 349/12, etc; waitees *pl* 611/10; waites 143/18, 280/10, 280/11, etc; waittes 267/22; wates 239/6, 239/10, 239/28, etc; wattes 239/24, 243/34, 295/31, etc; waytes 54/39m, 60/24, 72/30, etc; waytez 60/22; wayttes 135/21, 253/8, 267/18, etc; waites *gen pl* 453/30m, 454/10, 459/34, etc; wates 454/10m, 463/16, 479/41m, etc; waytes 575/16, 580/3, 593/16

walkers *n pl* fullers 25/12, 249/41, 258/5, etc

waltir leadirs See waterleders

wanyons *n pl* wagon-loads (?) 79/22

wapentack *n* subdivision of certain English shires, corresponding to the hundred of other counties 600/35; wapentyk 274/10, 274/16

washardscarlet *n* scarlet 'washer' cloth 612/31

wate, wates, wattes See waite

waterleders *n pl* carters of water 20/27, 21/13, 26/1, etc; waltir leadirs 320/15; watter ledders 302/8; watterledders 293/39; watterleders 192/5, 192/26

wax chandelars *n phr pl* makers and sellers of wax candles 356/2; waxchandelars 356/2m, 356/6; waxchaundelers 188/26; wexchaundlers 218/17

wayte, waytes, waytez, wayttes See waite

websterseruauntz *n pl* servants of weavers 24/16

weders *n pl* male sheep 137/41

weffers *n pl* weavers 210/16

wendes *n pl* apparatus for winding, windlasses 242/9

wesseren, wesserons See veserne

wexchaundlers See wax chandelars

whitchaundlers *n pl* makers of white candles 217/9

wiflers *n pl* persons used to hold back the spectators 464/7, 469/15, 481/27

wiredrawers *n pl* makers of pins and other wire articles 128/31; wyerdrawers 128/6, 128/39; wyredrawers 128/24

wirship *n* honour 24/27

wo *adj* grieved 275/4

wolpakkers *n pl* packers of wool for transportation or sale 23/2, 26/18

wyerdrawers, wyredrawers See wiredrawers

wyndrawers *n pl* transporters of wine 22/32; wynedrawers 26/17

ypocras *n* cordial drink made of wine flavoured with spices 54/10

Indexes

The Subject Index is designed to be used with the Introduction. When a subject occurs regularly in a set of documents, a general reference is given rather than many page numbers. To find the specific references, consult the lists of documents in the Introduction. For example, page numbers are given for all references to the Corpus Christi Guild that occur in documents other than the Corpus Christi account rolls, followed by a general reference. The accounts are listed and dated on pp xxxiii-xxxiv.

In the Place & Name Index, places are listed before names (eg, Leicester, city of, is cited before Leicester, Duke of). Place names and titles in such formulaic constructions as the title of the sovereign are not indexed. Other place names and titles appear in both indexes in their modern form where this is ascertainable, followed by a selection of variant spellings. Surnames are cited in the most common or simplest form and are followed by a list of all the variant spellings that occur in the text. Trade names appearing as surnames are so treated. No indication is given of the frequency with which a name appears on a given page. Names whose first element is 'Saint' have been indexed under 'S'. The u/v orthographic distinction has been retained and all residual genitive inflectional endings are included as variant spellings. However, all proper names have been capitalized and 'ff' has been rendered 'F' when it appears in a headword. The pattern followed for ordering page references is as follows: name with no modifier, royalty, peerage in descending order, ecclesiastical authorities, civic officials, personal designation of status (eg, widow or master), modernized Christian names in alphabetical order.

Subject Index

A/Y Memorandum Book, discussion of xvii,
   xix-xx, xxvi, xliii
Actors See Players
Admiral's Men See Lord Admiral, men of
Albany, Lord, players of 533, 536
Aldermen See York, City Council of
Allerton, minstrel from 67
Ancient See York, ancient of
Angels 17-19, 23-4, 55, 78, 92, 95-7, 242
Animals, strange: baboon 524; cow 524;
   marmoset 94
Armour, dressing of 374, 434, 437, 439-40,
   440, 447-9, 451-2, 458, 462, 467-8, 474-5,
   478-9, 485, 490, 495, 498-9, 504, 513-14,
   516, 519-20
Armourers See Craft Guilds
Assise, players at 482
Auditors, for Corpus Christi Play 109
Awdelay, Lord, minstrels of 330
Axletree 97, 99

B/Y Memorandum Book, discussion of xvii,
   xix-xx, xliii
Baboons 524
Bakers See Craft Guilds
Banners and pennants 56, 58, 78, 91, 145, 155,
   196, 273, 632, 637, 639 See also Corpus
   Christi Guild, banners of; Corpus Christi
   Play, banners of; Creed Play, banners of
Banquets, civic 78-9, 325-6, 406, 589-90, 606
   See also Chamberlains' Account Books
   from 1520

Barbers See Craft Guilds
Barkers See Craft Guilds, Tanners
Bartley, Lord, players of 517
Baxsters See Craft Guilds, Bakers
Bearwards 270, 330, 378, 409, 521, 539
Beauchamp, Lord, players of 441
Beaumond, Lord, minstrels of 71, 72, 76
Beef Breakfasts 492-3
Bell-ringers 503, 513-14, 594, 610, 612
Bethom, Edward de, minstrels of 76
Beverley, minstrels from 69, 71, 76
Billets See Corpus Christi Play, billets of
Blacksmiths See Craft Guilds, Smiths
Bladesmiths See Craft Guilds
Blessed Virgin Mary, feast of 180; guild of 216;
   images of 634; light of 219
Bodleian Library xl, xlii
Bollers See Craft Guilds
Bolton, Lord of, minstrels of 71
Book-binders See Craft Guilds, Parchment-
   makers
Books See Plays and play books; Song books
Borthwick Institute of Historical Research
   xxxviii-xxxix
Bosworth Field, battle of x
Bottlers See Craft Guilds
Bowers and Fletchers See Craft Guilds
Bowes, William, minstrel of 67
Bowlmakers See Craft Guilds, Bollers
Boy Bishop 1
Bricklayers See Craft Guilds
Bridgemasters' Accounts, discussion of xxii,
   xxiv-xxv

British Library xxix-xxx, xxxii-xxxiii, xli, xlii
Brounflete, Henry, minstrel of 69, 71
Buckingham, Duke of, minstrels of 67, 70
Bull Ring 406
Burrow, Lord, players of 460
Butchers See Craft Guilds
Butler, John, minstrel of 75

Cambridge, Lord of, minstrels of 66
Candlemas (2 February) 40, 399
Capmakers See Craft Guilds, Hatmakers
Cardmakers See Craft Guilds
Carols 266 See also Singers and singing
Carpenters See Craft Guilds
Carters See Craft Guilds
Cartwrights See Craft Guilds
Carvers See Craft Guilds
Chaloners See Craft Guilds
Chamberlains' Account Books, discussion of
    xx-xxii, xxiv; reference to 188, 203, 207,
    214, 218, 339, 381, 383, 389, 394, 398, 402
Chamberlains' Account Rolls, discussion of
    xx-xxiii
Champions 411
Chandlers See Craft Guilds
Chandos, Lord, players of 430, 496
Cheworth, Thomas, minstrels of 69, 75
Chronicler, royal 594, 595
Churchwardens' Accounts, discussion of xv,
    xxxvii-xxxix
Churchyards, prohibition against playing in
    358
Civil War ix
Clavichord 89
Clerks, as players or directors 92, 99-100
Clifford, Lord, minstrels of 66, 67, 69, 71, 75
Coblers See Craft Guilds
Commissioners, of Henry VIII 642
Common Clerk See York, Common Clerk of
Conyers, Christopher, minstrel of 71
Cooks See Craft Guilds
Coopers See Craft Guilds
Cordwainers See Craft Guilds
Corn merchants See Craft Guilds

Cornets 443, 447, 578, 583, 585, 601
Corpus Christi, day of (Thursday after Trinity)
    xii, xxi, 4, 11, 37, 59-60, 61, 95, 97, 100,
    104, 110, 158, 201, 249, 252, 253, 259,
    263, 265, 280, 282, 285, 286, 289, 291,
    292, 294, 297, 300, 302, 307, 310, 312,
    313, 315, 320, 322-3, 325, 326, 327, 332,
    333, 338, 341, 343, 378, 389, 620
Corpus Christi, day of, Sheriffs riding on xii,
    262, 285, 302-3, 307, 323, 332-3, 341, 356,
    365 See also York, Sheriffs of
Corpus Christi, day after 12, 29, 32, 127, 158,
    159, 161, 163, 164, 165, 166, 167, 168,
    188, 203, 207, 259, 265, 292 See also
    Mercers' Accounts after 1476; Corpus
    Christi Accounts after 1476
Corpus Christi, feast of xv, xix, xxi, xxxv,
    xxxix, xliii, 1-2, 4, 15, 28-30, 32-3, 41, 51,
    55, 64, 68, 108, 115, 126, 128, 152, 183,
    299, 333 See also City Chamberlains'
    Accounts 1396-1569
Corpus Christi, guild of xvi, xxvi, xxxii-xxxiv,
    xliii, 15, 50-2, 68, 73, 77, 82, 87-8, 90-1, 97,
    103, 106, 111, 115, 122, 177, 186, 200,
    283, 285, 317, 628-44 See also Corpus
    Christi Accounts
Corpus Christi, guild of, banners of 27, 204,
    628, 632
Corpus Christi, guild of, master of 106, 111,
    115, 122, 177, 178, 200, 238, 283, 285 See
    also Corpus Christi Accounts
Corpus Christi, Host carried in procession of
    6, 164
Corpus Christi, pageants used in other plays
    or shows 145, 272, 353, 366, 411, 419, 421
Corpus Christi, shrine of xix, xxxii, 51, 79, 98,
    116-17, 118, 631-2, 635, 638-40, 642-4
    See also Corpus Christi Accounts
Corpus Christi, Sunday after 40, 189
Corpus Christi, torches of xxvi, 5-6, 12, 15, 24,
    26, 27, 46, 50-2, 59, 64, 89, 96, 98, 108,
    109, 118, 124, 125-7, 159-60, 163, 173,
    183, 210, 245, 250, 252, 262, 268, 270,
    289, 298, 310-11, 313, 320, 324, 617-18,
    620-1, 622, 624-5, 628, 632, 660, 670, 679
    See also Mercers', Bakers' and Corpus Christi

Guild Accounts

Corpus Christi, vigil of 12, 24, 29, 38, 49, 113, 115

Corpus Christi Play ix, xiv, xv, xvi-xvii, xviii, xix, xxi-xxii, xxvi, 8, 10-11, 13-14, 16-26, 28-32, 34-5, 42-4, 46, 47, 50, 53, 60, 62, 64, 87, 109, 119-20, 121, 127, 132, 135, 153, 154, 176, 212, 256-8, 259, 262, 279, 287, 293, 295, 297-8, 303, 307, 310, 314, 320, 323, 327, 328, 331-2, 338, 339, 340, 341, 351, 352, 355, 356, 390, 392-3, 619 See also station lists in Chamberlains' Accounts See also individual pageants

Corpus Christi Play, banners of 9, 12, 29, 121

Corpus Christi Play, billets of 9, 14, 17, 287, 293, 295, 297, 303, 310, 320, 322, 323, 340, 341, 351, 355

Corpus Christi Play, pageants of
— Abraham and Isaac (Parchmentmakers) 18, 25, 39, 622, 661
— Agony and Betrayal (Cordwainers) 20, 26, 30, 227, 395-6, 672
— Annunciation to Mary (Spicers) 18, 25, 54, 662
— Annunciation to the Shepherds See Offering of the Shepherds
— Appearance of Christ to Mary Magdalene (Winedrawers) 22, 26, 679
— Appearance of Christ to the Pilgrims See Travellers to Emmaus
— Ascension (Tailors) 4, 23, 26, 166, 201, 249, 298-9, 313, 680
— Assigning of work to Adam See Expulsion from the Garden
— Assumption of the Virgin (Weavers) 23, 26, 245, 268-9, 291-2, 293, 297, 307, 331-2, 683-4; used for royal entry, 1486 142, 145, 149
— Baptism of Christ (Barbers) 19, 25, 620-1, 666
— Birth of Christ See Nativity
— Building of Noah's Ark (Shipwrights) 18, 25, 660
— Cain killing Abel (Glovers) 17, 25, 105, 660
— Christ and the Doctors (Spurriers and Lorimers) 13, 19, 25, 176, 264, 311, 356, 665-6

Corpus Christi Play, pageants of
— Condemnation of Christ by Pilate (Tilemakers) xxxv, 21, 26, 36, 37, 44, 48-50, 675
— Conspiracy (Cutlers) 20, 25, 64, 123-4, 131, 169, 185, 623, 670-1, 682
— Coronation of the Virgin (Mayor, etc; Innholders) xxi, 23, 26, 101, 106, 114, 121, 133-4, 144, 180, 187, 202, 206, 213, 219, 221, 225, 228, 232, 234, 236-7, 265, 267, 279, 291-2, 293, 297, 315, 331-2, 343-4, 419, 684-5; used for Midsummer Show, 1585 419
— Creation sequence See Creation of Adam and Eve, Creation of Heaven and Earth, Expulsion from the Garden, Fall of Man, Prohibition of Tree of Knowledge, Work of Five Days
— Creation of Adam and Eve (Cardmakers) 17, 25, 136, 249-50, 621-2, 658-9
— Creation of Heaven and Earth (Barkers) 17, 25, 110-11, 657
— Crucifixion (Pinners, Painters, Latteners) 22, 26, 37-8, 128, 223, 332, 340, 344, 622, 624, 676, 677
— Death of Christ See Mortificacio
— Death of Mary (Drapers) 23, 26, 166, 201, 205, 227, 230, 249, 291-2, 293, 297, 313, 331-2, 681-2
— Deceit of the Devil in the form of a serpent See Fall of Man
— Descent of the Holy Spirit See Pentecost
— Doomsday (Mercers) xxvi, xxvii, 24, 26, 685; used in royal entry, 1541 272 See also Mercers' documents
— Doubting Thomas (Scriveners) 23, 26, 152, 312, 314, 618, 679-80
— Entry into Jerusalem (Skinners) 20, 25, 184-5, 214, 215, 304, 400-1, 618, 670
— Exodus See Pharaoh with Moses
— Expulsion from the Garden (Armourers) 17, 25, 62-3, 104-5, 378-9, 659-60
— Fall of Man (Coopers) 17, 25, 102-3, 620, 659
— Fergus (Masons, Linenweavers) 23, 26, 47-8, 110, 136, 143, 215-7, 663, 678, 682-3

Corpus Christi Play, pageants of
— First Trial before Pilate (Tapiters) 21, 26, 32-3, 107-8, 110, 118-19, 136, 160-1, 300-1, 672-3
— Flight into Egypt (Marshals) 16, 19, 25, 45-6, 59-60, 123-4, 664-5
— Gethsemane See Agony and Betrayal
— Joseph's Troubles about Mary (Founderers) 18, 25, 662
— Hanging of Judas (Saucemakers) 21, 26, 30-2, 48-50, 212, 217, 674
— Harrowing of Hell (Saddlers) 10, 22, 26, 297-8, 622-3, 677-8
— Herod questioning the Three Kings (Goldsmiths -— 1431-2; Masons 1431-2 - 1561(?); Minstrels after 1561) 19, 25, 47-8, 334, 337-8, 388-9, 663
— Jew blaspheming hearse of Virgin See Fergus
— Last Supper (Bakers) xxix, 16, 20, 25, 191-3, 315, 617, 671; used in Pater Noster Play, 1572 372; used in Midsummer Interlude, 1585 420, 425 See also Bakers' Accounts 1544-1609
— Marriage in Cana (Vintners) 19, 25, 53-4, 125, 129-30, 239-40, 296-7, 311-12, 351, 666-7
— Mortificacio (Butchers) 22, 26, 47, 227, 250, 294-5, 677
— Nativity (Tile-thatchers) 18, 25, 33, 39, 41-2, 242, 662
— Noah's Ark during the Flood (Fishers and Mariners) 18, 25, 33-4, 118, 333-4, 415-16, 626, 660-l See also Building Noah's Ark
— Offering of the Shepherds (Chandlers) 18, 25, 304, 342, 356, 618, 663
— Offering of the Three Kings See Herod questioning the Three Kings
— Parting the Garments of Christ (Millers) 21, 26, 212, 674 See also Crucifixion
— Pentecost (Potters) 23, 26, 623, 681
— Pharaoh with Moses (Hosiers) 10, 13-14, 18, 25, 661
— Presentation of Christ in the Temple See Purification of the Virgin
— Prohibition of the Tree of Knowledge

Corpus Christi Play, pageants of
(Fullers) 17, 25, 249-50, 330, 659
— Purification of the Virgin (Hospital of St Leonard, Masons, Hatmakers, Labourers) xxii, 19, 25, 112-13, 351, 664
— Raising of Christ on the Mountain See Crucifixion
— Raising of Lazarus (Hatmakers) 20, 25, 176, 307, 351, 621, 669
— Remorse of Judas (Cooks) 21, 26, 191-3, 250-1, 674 See also Hanging of Judas
— Resurrection (Carpenters) 22, 26, 41-2, 92-3, 126-7, 136, 182-4, 204-5, 252-3, 342, 380-1, 678
— Road to Calvary (Shearers) 14, 21, 26, 41, 214, 675
— Sacrifice of Isaac See Abraham and Isaac
— Scourging and crowning with Thorns (Turners and Bowlmakers) 21, 26, 129, 152, 311, 675
— Second Trial before Pilate See Condemnation of Christ by Pilate
— Simon the Leper (Ironmongers) 20, 25, 34-5, 153, 351, 357, 668-9
— Slaughter of the Innocents (Girdlers) 19, 25, 68, 107, 136-7, 217, 312, 314, 355, 665
— Stretching out and nailing of Christ See Crucifixion
— Temptation in the Wilderness (Smiths) 19, 25, 45-6, 59-60, 123-4, 174-5, 252-3, 667-8
— Thomas the Apostle See Doubting Thomas
— Transfiguration (Curriers) 19, 25, 40, 619, 668
— Travellers to Emmaus (Wool-packers; Sledmen) 23, 26, 307, 321, 679
— Trial before Caiaphas (Bowers and Fletchers) 6, 8-9, 21, 26, 619, 672
— Trial before Herod (Dyers) 21, 26, 111-12, 623, 673
— Washing of Apostles' Feet See Last Supper
— Woman taken in Adultery (Plumbers; Capmakers) 20, 25, 669
— Work of Five Days (Plasterers and Bricklayers) 7, 16, 17, 25, 33, 39, 104, 658
Corpus Christi Play, register of 244, 263, 278, 280, 313, 317, 324, 330-1, 351, 390

Corpus Christi Play, room for Mayor and council See Rooms, for viewing plays

Corpus Christi Play, stations of See Stations, for playing

Corpus Christi Procession xvi, 5-6, 15, 24, 32-3, 46, 59-60, 82, 96, 108, 116-17, 125-6, 158-9, 162, 167-8, 169-74, 186, 210, 252-3, 262, 269, 270, 283, 289, 298, 310-11, 320, 324, 625 See also Mercers' Accounts, Corpus Christi Accounts

Corpus Christi Procession, singers in 223, 254, 255, 261, 277

Costumes See Gloves, as articles of costuming; Mercers' Pageant Accounts; Corpus Christi inventories (Appendix II)

Council of the North ix, x, xl, xli, 191, 322, 367, 550, 553

Couchers See Craft Guilds

Craft Guilds, general xiii-xiv, xviii, 8, 10-11, 17, 24, 28-9, 109, 125-6, 164-5, 186, 190, 193-7, 256-61, 272, 344, 353

Craft Guilds, searchers of xiii-xiv See also individual craft guilds

Craft Guilds
— Armourers (Expulsion from Garden) 17, 25, 62-3, 104-5, 258, 260, 378-9, 417, 422, 659-60
— Bakers (Last Supper) xiv, xvi, xxix-xxx, xliii, 16, 20, 25, 186, 191-3, 222, 225, 235, 238, 244, 248, 258, 280, 315, 316, 417, 420, 422, 617, 671 See also Bridge-masters' Accounts, Bakers' Accounts
— Barbers (Baptism) 19, 25, 258, 260, 417, 422, 620-1, 666
— Barkers See Tanners
— Baxsters See Bakers
— Blacksmiths See Smiths
— Bladesmiths 20, 64, 123-4, 174-5, 185, 260, 308, 417, 422
— Bollers (Scourging and crowning with Thorns) 26, 300, 304, 675
— Book-binders See Parchmentmakers
— Bottlers 20, 356, 666
— Bowers and Fletchers (Trial before Caiaphas) xxvi, 6, 8-9, 21, 26, 250, 260, 291, 417, 422, 619, 672 See also Mercers' Accounts

Craft Guilds
  from 1554
— Bowlbakers 293, 295, 309, 320, 321, 323, 324
— Bricklayers (The Work of Five Days) xvi, xxxi, xliii, 7, 17, 25, 33, 39, 104, 370, 417, 421, 658 See also Bricklayers' Accounts 1589-1629
— Brokers of Wool 23, 46
— Bucklermakers 20 See also Bladesmiths
— Burnleders 288, 291, 292, 309, 321, 323, 425
— Butchers (Mortificacio) xxvi, 22, 26, 31, 47, 186, 227, 250, 295, 417, 422, 466, 622, 674, 677 See also Mercers' Accounts after 1547
— Capmakers See Hatmakers
— Cardmakers (Creation of Adam and Eve) 17, 25, 136, 249-50, 621-2, 626, 659
— Carpenters (Resurrection) xxxi-xxxii, 22, 24, 26, 32, 41-2, 92-3, 126-7, 136, 182-4, 186, 190, 204-5, 227, 252-3, 258, 261, 272-3, 311, 312-13, 342, 380-1, 417, 421, 662, 678-9, 682 See also Bridgemasters' Accounts
— Carters 214, 675
— Cartwrights 127, 182-4, 204-5, 678
— Carvers 127, 252-3, 275-6, 279, 312, 678
— Chaloners 24
— Chandlers (Offering of the Shepherds) 18, 25, 30-2, 217, 304, 342, 356, 618, 663, 665, 674, 684 See also Bridgemasters' Accounts 1501-28
— Coblers 24, 96-7, 160, 186, 298
— Common Carriers See Carters
— Cooks (Remorse of Judas) 21, 26, 191-3, 250-1, 660-1, 671, 674
— Coopers (Fall of Man) 17, 25, 102-3, 258, 260, 417, 422, 620, 659 See also Bridge-masters' Accounts from 1544
— Cordwainers (Agony and Betrayal) xxx-xxxi, 20, 24, 26, 30, 125-6, 158-9, 162-4, 165, 166-8, 169-74, 186, 227, 258, 260, 395-6, 417, 422, 512-13, 544-5, 624-5, 672 See also Bridgemasters' Accounts
— Corn Merchants 312, 680
— Couchers See Tapiters

Craft Guilds

— Curriers (Transfiguration) 19, 25, 40, 258, 260, 417, 422, 619, 668
— Cutlers (Conspiracy) 20, 24, 25, 64, 123-4, 131, 169, 185, 216, 258, 260, 417, 422, 623, 670-1, 682
— Dikers 113, 115
— Drapers (Death of Mary) 13, 23, 26, 166, 201, 205, 227, 230, 249, 258, 260, 291-2, 293, 297, 313, 331-2, 417, 422, 680, 681-2
— Dubbers 14, 208
— Dyers or Litsters (Trial before Herod) 21, 26, 108, 111-12, 210, 258, 260, 623, 673
— Earthwallers 113, 115
— Fletchers See Bowers and Fletchers
— Flourishers 152
— Fishers and Mariners (Noah's Ark during the Flood) 18, 25, 33-4, 118, 186, 333, 415-16, 417, 422, 626, 660-1
— Founderers (Joseph's Troubles about Mary) 18, 25, 258, 422, 662
— Fullers or Walkers (Prohibition of Tree of Knowledge) 17, 24, 41, 186, 249-50, 258, 260, 330, 417, 422, 659
— Furbishers See Armourers
— Gardeners 113, 115
— Girdlers (Slaughter of the Innocents) 19, 25, 68, 107, 136-7, 217, 258, 261, 312, 314, 355, 417, 422, 665, 668, 672, 674
— Glaziers (Harrowing of Hell) 22, 258, 260, 297, 678
— Glovers (Cain and Abel) 17, 25, 26, 105, 186, 258, 260, 417, 422, 617-18, 622, 660
— Goldbeaters See Goldsmiths
— Goldsmiths (Herod questioning the Three Kings until 1431-2; Presentation of Magi) 19, 25, 35-6, 47-8, 258, 261, 334, 417, 422, 624, 663, 664, 676, 677 See Bridgemasters' Accounts until 1524
— Ground wallers 113, 115
— Haberdashers See Hatmakers
— Hartshorners 25
— Hatmakers (Purification of the Virgin; Raising of Lazarus; Woman taken in Adultery) 20, 176-7, 258, 260, 307, 351, 356, 422, 621, 669, 677, 679

Craft Guilds

— Hayresters 48-50, 152-3, 186, 300, 304, 674, 675
— Horners 20, 185, 671
— Hosiers (Pharaoh) 13-14, 18, 25, 258, 260, 297, 422, 661, 680, 681
— Hostilers See Innkeepers
— Innkeepers (Coronation of the Virgin) xxi, 23, 26, 114, 121, 133-4, 246, 265, 267, 279, 297, 315, 330-1, 342, 343, 356, 417, 419, 422, 663, 684-5
— Ironmongers (Simon the Leper) 20, 25, 34-5, 153, 340, 351, 355, 357, 665, 668-9
— Joiners 22, 127, 252-3, 271, 311, 312, 380-1, 417, 421, 678
— Kidberers 108, 113, 115
— Labourers (Purification of the Virgin) xxii, 113, 115, 263, 273, 294, 419, 452, 664 For pageant masters see Chamberlains' Account Books 1523, 1525, 1527, 1528, 1538, 1542, 1554, 1559
— Latteners (Crucifixion) 22, 26, 37-8, 676, 677
— Linenweavers (Fergus) 23, 108, 110, 123, 136, 143, 169, 215-17, 245, 268-9, 658, 671, 673, 682-3 See also Weavers
— Litsters See Dyers
— Locksmiths See Smiths
— Lorimers 13 See also Spurriers
— Luminers See Scriveners
— Lymeburners See Plasterers
— Mariners See Fishers and Mariners
— Marshals (Flight into Egypt) 16, 19, 25, 45-6, 59-60, 123-4, 422, 664-5
— Masons (Fergus, Herod questioning the Three Kings, Purification) xxii, 19, 25, 47-8, 112-13, 115, 263, 334, 338, 389, 658, 663, 664, 682
— Mercers and Merchants (Doomsday) xiii-xiv, xxvi-xxix, xxxii, 24, 26, 53, 64, 105, 107, 258, 260-1, 272, 401, 417, 422, 665, 685 See also **Mercers' Hall; Pageant House**, Mercers'; Bridgemasters' Accounts, Mercers' Accounts
— Millers (Parting of Christ's Garments) 21, 26, 212, 217, 258, 260, 325, 417, 422, 663

Craft Guilds

665, 674, 676

— Minstrels and Musicians (Herod and the Three Kings after 1561) 312, 334-8, 385-9, 391, 508, 591-2, 663 See also **Minstrels; Musicians**

— Nailers 19, 665

— Ostlers See Innkeepers

— Painters (Crucifixion) 22, 26, 37-8, 223, 258, 272, 332, 340, 404, 417, 422, 624, 676 See also Pinners

— Parchmentmakers (Abraham and Isaac) 18, 25, 39, 258, 260, 325, 417, 422, 622, 661

— Pattenmakers 20

— Pavers 113, 115

— Pelterers See Skinners

— Pewterers 18, 258, 260, 662

— Pinners (Crucifixion) xxix, 37-8, 128, 223, 332, 340, 344, 622, 676 See also Painters

— Plasterers, Tilers and Bricklayers See Bricklayers

— Plumbers (Woman taken in Adultery) 20, 25

— Potters (Pentecost) 23, 26, 417, 422, 623, 680, 681

— Pouchmakers 20

— Poultry sellers 250-1, 674, 677

— Roofers See Tile-thatchers

— Ropers 21, 129, 152-3, 186, 304, 311, 342, 675

— Saddlers (Harrowing of Hell) 10, 22, 26, 258, 260, 297-8, 417, 622, 666, 677-8

— Sandcarters See Sandleaders

— Sandleaders 192, 286, 288, 291, 293, 302, 671

— Saucemakers (Hanging of Judas) 26, 30-2, 48-50, 212, 217, 663, 665, 674

— Sawyers 19, 22, 127, 136, 678, 682

— Scalers 20

— Scriveners (Doubting Thomas) 23, 26, 152, 312, 314, 618, 679-80

— Sellers 22 See also Saddlers

— Servers 21

— Shearmen (Road to Calvary) 14, 26, 41, 214, 675-6

— Sheathers 10, 20, 64, 670

Craft Guilds

— Shipwrights (Building of the Ark) 18, 25, 422, 660

— Skinners (Entry into Jerusalem) 20, 25, 32-3, 184-5, 214-5, 304, 400-1, 419, 618, 670 See also Bridgemasters' Accounts

— Sledmen (Travellers to Emmaus) 258, 261, 307, 321, 664, 669, 679

— Smiths (Temptation in the Wilderness) 19, 25, 45-6, 59-60, 123-4, 174-5, 186, 252, 258, 263, 308, 417, 422, 664, 667-8, 670 See also Bladesmiths

— Spicers (Annunciation to Mary) 18, 25, 54, 662

— Spurriers and Lorimers (Christ and the Doctors) 13, 19, 25, 176, 258, 260, 264, 311, 356, 417, 422, 665-6

— Stainers See Painters

— Tailors (Ascension) xxvii, 4, 23, 26, 166, 186, 201, 205, 249, 260, 289, 297, 299, 313, 417, 419, 422, 680

— Tanners (Creation of Heaven and Earth) 17, 25, 110-11, 374-5, 417, 421, 622, 657 See also Bridgemasters' Accounts

— Tapiters (First Trial before Pilate) 21, 26, 32, 107-8, 110, 118-19, 136, 160-1, 300-1, 417, 422, 576, 624, 658, 672-3, 682 See also Bridgemasters' Accounts

— Taverners 25 See also Vintners

— Textwriters, Luminers, Turners and Flourishers See Scriveners

— Tile-thatchers (Nativity) 18, 25, 33, 39, 41-2, 104, 242, 309, 370, 377, 417, 422, 662

— Tilemakers (Condemnation of Christ by Pilate) xxxv, xxxvii, 21, 26, 36, 37, 44, 48-50, 212, 217, 258, 260, 351, 674, 675

— Tinklers 223, 344, 676

— Turners (Scourging and crowning with Thorns) 26, 129, 152, 300, 304, 311, 342, 674, 675

— Upholders 13, 618

— Vestmentmakers (Entry into Jerusalem) 20, 214, 215, 670

— Vintners (Marriage Feast at Cana) 19, 53-4, 125, 129-30, 222, 225, 235, 238, 239-40,

Craft Guilds
248, 280, 296-7, 311-12, 316, 351, 417,
422, 666-7, 685 See also **Taverners**
— Wadmen 23
— Walkers See **Fullers**
— Watercarters See **Waterleaders**
— Waterleaders 21, 26, 192, 293, 302, 671,
674
— Weavers (Assumption of the Virgin) xxxii,
23, 26, 123, 125-6, 158-9, 163, 164-5, 168-
74, 179, 186, 210, 215-17, 245, 260, 268-9,
291-2, 297, 307, 671, 683; rental of pageant
for royal entry, 1486 141-2, 145, 149 See
also **Linenweavers**
— Whitchandlers See **Chandlers**
— Winedrawers (Appearance of Christ to Mary
Magdalene) 22, 26, 679
— Wiredrawers See **Pinners**
— Wool-packers See **Sledmen**
— Woollen Weavers See **Weavers**
— Wrights See **Carpenters**
Creed Play ix, xv-xvi, xxxii-xxxiii, 68, 78, 87-8,
98, 130-1, 132, 177, 200, 236, 238, 257,
285, 340, 348, 352-3, 633, 639
Creed Play, banners of 78, 98, 633, 639
Curriers See **Craft Guilds**
Curtall, double (form of bassoon) 499
Cutlers See **Craft Guilds**

Dacre, Lord, minstrels of 68, 72
Dancing 358, 592
Darby, Lord, players of 471
Darcy, Lord, minstrels of 75, 203; players
of 455, 471
Devils 55, 96, 241
Deynshire, Earl of, minstrels of 76
Diadems 55, 285, 309, 358
Dissolution of religious houses and guilds x,
xiv, xv, xvi, xxxii
Dorchester, Marquis of, minstrels of 67
Dragon (in ridings) 319
Drapers See **Craft Guilds**
Drums and Drummers 410-11, 419, 427, 444,
452, 462, 464, 469, 474, 481, 491-2, 495,

498, 509, 520, 592, 608
Dudley, Lord, players of 517, 524; trumpeters
of 507, 509
Durham, Bishop of, minstrels of 66, 75
Durham, minstrels from 66, 75
Dyers See **Craft Guilds**

E Memorandum Book, discussion of xix-xx
Earl Marshall of England 604
Easter, day after 624
Ebrauk, mythical founder of York 73, 139-40,
142, 147-8, 552, 583
Ecclesiastical Commission xl-xli, 368-9
Egremont, Lord of, minstrels of 77
Epiphany, feast of 1, 72
Erandale, Earl of, minstrels of 69
Essex, Lord, musicians of 471; players of 382,
409, 430, 435
Eueres, William, minstrels of 71
Evers, Lord, players of 509, 528
Exeter, Duke of, minstrels of 66, 69, 71

Fifes 481, 492
Fishers and Mariners See **Craft Guilds**
Fitz Hugh, Lord, minstrels of 69, 71, 73, 75
Fitz William, William, minstrels of 66
Fletchers See **Craft Guilds**, Bowers and
Fletchers
Flourishers See **Craft Guilds**, Scriveners
Founderers See **Craft Guilds**
France, minstrels from 66
Franchise or liberties of City 53, 110, 138,
170, 171, 335, 385
Friaries, Augustinian 169; Preaching 35
Friars 146; Augustinian 85, 102; Preaching
106; White 259
Fullers See **Craft Guilds**
Furbishers See **Craft Guilds**, Armourers

Garter, order of 151-2

Gascoigne, William, minstrel of 77
Girdlers See Craft Guilds
Glaziers See Craft Guilds
Gloucester, Duke of, minstrels of 67
Glovers See Craft Guilds
Gloves, as articles of costuming 97, 100, 230, 238, 249, 266, 268, 270, 278, 281, 282, 287
Goldbeaters See Craft Guilds, Goldsmiths
Goldsmiths See Craft Guilds
Good Friday 1
Grafton's Interlude 405-8, 414-15, 417-23
Gray, Lord, minstrels of 69
Graystock, Lord, minstrels of 66, 69, 71
Guild Hall See York, Common Hall

Haberdashers See Craft Guilds, Hatmakers
Harness, riding in 285, 297, 300, 302, 307, 323, 332, 341, 356, 365, 374, 413, 427, 452, 478
Haryngton, Lord, minstrels of 70, 71, 76; John, minstrels of 69, 71, 73; Thomas, minstrels of 72
Hasters See Craft Guilds, Hayresters
Hatmakers See Craft Guilds
Hell-mouth, part of Doomsday pageant 55, 242
Holy Trinity, Guild of xiv, 107 See also Craft Guilds, Mercers
Holy Trinity Hall See Mercers' Hall
Honourable Men 9, 12, 29, 38, 54, 60, 65 See also York, City Council of
Horners See Craft Guilds
Horsefair, scholars of, players 382
Hosiers See Craft Guilds
Hostelers See Craft Guilds, Innkeepers
Houghton, Baronet, bearward of 539
House Books, discussion of xvii-xix
Hungarians 443
Hunsdon, Lord, players of 397
'Hunt is up' 388, 470

Innkeepers See Craft Guilds

Instruments, musical xvi, 333, 335, 347, 361, 363, 385, 409, 432, 470, 480 See also Cornets; Organs; Reeds; Sackbuts; Shalms; Trumpets and Trumpeters; Viols
Interlude xvi, xxx, xxxiv, 2, 44, 384-5, 397, 399, 414
Ironmongers See Craft Guilds

Jesters 75, 77
Joiners See Craft Guilds
Joly Wat and Malkyn 70, 72
Journeymen 123, 183
Jugglers 71, 76, 592

Keys, of the city 140, 514, 551, 582, 586, 599, 601, 609
King, minstrels of xvi, 9, 60, 67, 70, 72, 74, 76, 80, 81, 84, 94, 101, 144, 203, 206, 214, 217, 220, 221, 225, 229, 232, 234, 237, 241, 243, 248, 259, 271; players of 581, 593 See also Revels, His Majesty's; trumpeters of 276, 507, 608, 615; tumbler of 581
King of Scotland, musicians of the 486
King's evil 556, 607
Knaresborough, minstrel from 67

Labourers See Craft Guilds
Lady Elizabeth, players of 538
Lancashire men, players 382
Latteners See Craft Guilds
Leicester, Lord, players of 436
Leicester, minstrels from 69
Lennox, Lord, trumpeters of 521, 524
Lent 69, 109, 118, 190, 326, 351, 373, 553
Lescrope, Lord, minstrels of See Scrope
Licensing, of minstrels 508, 592; of players 384-5, 405, 522, 538, 576, 592-3; for showing baboons 524
Lincoln, Lord, players of 488, 501

Lincoln, minstrels from 66

Linenweavers See **Craft Guilds**

Litsters See **Craft Guilds**, Dyers

Liturgical drama, York Minster 1

Livery, of waits xiii, xvi, xviii, xxi See also City Chamberlains' Accounts

Locksmiths See **Craft Guilds**, Smiths

London, minstrels from 69, 75

Lord Admiral, men of 430, 455, 509

Lord Chamberlain of England 550, 554, 588; trumpeters of 539

Lord Chancellor of England 151; players of 528

Lord Lieutenant of England 486

Lord President of the North xv, 322, 367, 486, 514, 550, 578, 587, 596; musicians of 399; trumpeter of 400

Lord Privy Seal, players of 269

Lords of Misrule, prohibition of 358

Ludi See **Plays**

Lumer See **Corpus Christi**, torches of

Luminers See **Craft Guilds**, Scriveners

Lumley, Thomas, minstrel of 66; William, minstrel of 66

Lute players 70, 75

Lymeburners See **Craft Guilds**, Plasterers

Mace, ceremonial xi, 155, 184, 194, 196, 197, 198, 514, 554, 583, 586, 588-9, 599, 601-2, 604, 605, 607, 609

Main bread, shield of 137, 280, 284, 286, 288, 291, 292, 294, 302, 307, 310, 317, 322, 323, 326, 358, 372, 411, 420, 556-7

Market 85, 93, 101, 111-12, 166, 344

Marmoset (monkey), belonging to Henry VI 94

Marshals See **Craft Guilds**

Masks 55, 98, 241, 423

Masons See **Craft Guilds**

Maulyuerer, William, minstrels of 70, 71, 75

Maundy bread 293, 294, 325, 425, 460, 465, 472, 477, 483, 489

Maundy Thursday, ceremony 606

May Day 393

May games, prohibition of 358

Mercers See **Craft Guilds**

Mercers' Hall xxvi, xxxii, 61, 90, 91, 103-4, 106, 111, 115, 122, 207

Merchant Adventurers, Worshipful Company of vii, xxvi-xxvii, xlii See also **Craft Guilds**, Mercers

Merchant Taylors See **Craft Guilds**, Tailors

Metham, Thomas, minstrel of 66

Middilton, Richard, minstrels of 71; Thomas de, minstrels of 76

Midsummer, sheriffs riding at 297, 302-3, 307, 323, 332, 333, 341, 333, 341, 393, 396, 399-400, 403, 405-6, 409, 427, 429, 435, 440, 441, 445, 449, 452-3, 458-9, 463-4, 468-9, 480-1, 491-2

Midsummer Show xv-xvi, xxii, xxxviii, 326, 396, 399-400, 405-12, 414-25, 427, 429, 435, 439, 440-1, 445, 449, 451, 452-3, 458-9, 463-4, 468-9, 478, 479, 480-1, 485, 490, 491-2, 495

Millers See **Craft Guilds**

Minstrels xvi, xxi-xxv, xxvi-xxx, xxxiv, 3, 9, 65-77, 80-1, 83, 92, 94, 101, 121-2, 134-5, 144, 181, 202-3, 206, 213-14, 217, 219-20, 225, 229, 232, 234-5, 237, 240-1, 243, 259, 270-1, 293, 294, 302, 306, 312, 322, 330, 334-8, 358, 385-9, 391, 451, 535, 541, 663; of the queen 271; of the king xvi, 9, 60, 67, 70, 72, 74, 76, 80, 81, 94, 101, 144, 203, 206, 214, 217, 220, 221, 225, 229, 232, 234, 237, 241, 243, 248, 259, 271; of the prince 122, 181, 203, 206; of the Duke of Buckingham 67, 70; of the Duke of Exeter 66, 69, 71; of the Duke of Gloucester 67; of the Duke of Norfolk 66, 71, 75; of the Duke of York 66, 70, 72-3, 85; of the Marquis of Dorchester 67; of the Earl of Erandale 69; of the Earl of Deynshire 76; of the Earl of Northumberland 67, 69, 70, 72, 76; of the Earl of Salisbury 66, 69, 70, 71, 72, 75, 77; of the Earl of Westmorland 66, 72, 76; of Lord Awdelay 330; of Lord Beaumond 71, 72, 76; of the Lord of Bolton 71; of Lord Clifford 66, 67, 69, 71, 75; of lord Dacre 68, 72; of Lord Darcy 75, 203; of the Lord of Egremont 77; of

Minstrels

Lord Fitz Hugh 69, 71, 73, 75; of Lord Gray 69; of Lord Graystock 66, 69, 71; of Lord Haryngton 70, 71, 76 See also Thomas Harrington or John Heryngton; of Henry Percy, Lord of Poynings 70, 76; of the Lord of Say 72; of Lord Scrope of Bolton 67, 70, 75; of the Lord of Suffolk 70, 72, 76; of the Lord of Wells 66; of Lord Willoughby 66, 70, 72; of the Bishop of Durham 66, 75; of the Lord of Cambridge 66; of Edward de Bethom 76; of William Bowes 67; of Henry Brounflete 69, 71; of John Butler 75; of Thomas Cheworth 69, 75; of Christopher Conyers 71; of William Eueres 71; of William Fitz William 66; of William Gascoigne 77; of Thomas Harrington 72; of John Heryngton 69, 71, 73; of Thomas Lumley 66; of William Lumley 66; of William Maulyuerer 70, 71, 75; of Thomas Metham 66; of Thomas de Middilton 76; of Richard Middilton 71; of Richard Musgrefe 67; of Alexander Neuyll 75; of Thomas Neuyll 69, 75; of Robert Oghtred 66; of Robert Ogle 68, 71; of John Penyngton 67; of John Percy of Cleveland 72; of Thomas Percy 72; of William Plompton 68, 72, 75; of Thomas Pudsay 70; of Ralph Puddeszay 65-6, 70-1; of William Puddesay 75; of Nicholas Radclyff 73; of Thomas Rampston 76; of Robert Roos 66; of William Rowes 76; of John Savage 66, 72, 75; of John Saynell 77; of Walter Tailboys 69, 75-6; of John Talbot 76; from Allerton 67; from Beverley 69, 71, 76; from Durham 66, 75; from France 66; from Knaresborough 67; from Leicester 69; from Lincoln 66; from London 69, 75; from Newcastle-upon-Tyne 66, 69; from the North 72; from Nottingham 237; from Pocklington 69; blind 66, 70, 76; story teller 76 See also **York**, waits of; **Musicians**; **Craft Guilds**, Minstrels; York Minster Chamberlains' Accounts, St Leonard's Hospital Accounts, Bakers' Account Books, Bricklayers' Account Book

Minstrelsy 147, 334-8, 385-9

Monsters See **Animals**, strange

Monteagles, Lord, players of 488

Moot halls, as playing places 538

Morden, Lord, players of 455

Morris dancing, prohibition of 358

Musgrefe, Richard, minstrel of 67

Musical instruments See **Instruments**, musical

Musicians xvi, 334-8, 385-9, 391, 399, 423, 469-70, 507, 535-6, 591-2; of the King of Scotland 486; of James I 509; of the Lord President 399; of Lord Essex 471 See also **Minstrels**

Nailers See **Craft Guilds**

Nativity play, liturgical 1

Neuyll, Alexander, minstrels of 75; Thomas, minstrels of 69, 75

Newcastle, minstrels from 66, 69

Norfolk, Duke of, minstrels of 66, 71, 75

North Yorkshire County Library See **York**, City Archives

Northumberland, Earl of, minstrels of 67, 69, 70, 72, 76

Nottingham, minstrels from 237

Oghtred, Robert, minstrels of 66

Ogle, Robert, minstrels of 68, 71; Lord, players of 455

Ordo paginarum 11, 16-26

Organs, playing 133, 145, 150, 226, 571

Ouse River, flood of, 1898 xvii, xx; personification of 549, 554-5, 558; water of 79, 171

Oxford, Lord, players of 419; trumpeters of 539

Pageant xix, xxii, 139, 147, 149, 178, 192, 272, 304, 318, 405, 411-12, 423 See also **Corpus Christi Play**; Appendix VI

Pageant house xix, xxii, xxvi, xxix, 3, 5,

35-6, 39, 179, 191-2 See also Bridgemasters' Accounts, Mercers' Accounts, Bakers' Accounts

Pageant house, Mercers' 376

Pageant masters xiv, xxvi, xxix, 16, 38, 40, 45, 47, 49, 53, 55, 60, 61, 104, 111, 118, 124, 127, 128, 152, 153, 157, 166, 177, 180, 183, 227, 230, 258, 294, 299, 304, 327-8, 340, 343, 374, 375, 376, 377, 510, 526-7, 545

Pageant money xiv, 128, 129, 185, 190-1, 205, 216, 227, 230-1, 239-40, 249, 250, 257-61, 264, 295, 297, 299, 300, 303, 304, 305, 313, 327, 328, 340, 344, 353, 355, 368, 370, 380, 395-6, 426

Pageant silver See Pageant money

Pageants, order of See Ordo paginarum

Painters See Craft Guilds

Parchmentmakers See Craft Guilds

Pardoners 23

Paris candles 30-2, 663

Parish documents, discussion of xxxvii-xxxix

Paschal lamb, Bakers' pageant of the Last Supper 309, 325

Passion of Christ, symbols of 55

Pater Noster Guild xiv, xvi, xxxiv, 6-7, 12, 645-8 See also St Anthony, Guild of

Pater Noster Play xvi, xxvi, xxxiv, 6-7, 12, 99, 178, 262, 327-8, 365, 366-7, 368, 377-8, 645-8; banners of 328

Patrons See Travelling players; Minstrels and individual names

Pembroke, Lord, players of 455, 491

Penyngton, John, minstrels of 67

Percy, Henry, Lord of Poynings, minstrels of 70, 76; knight, minstrels of 70; John, minstrels of 72; Thomas, minstrel of 72

Pilgrimage of Grace x

Pinners and Painters See Craft Guilds

Pipes 226

Plague 295, 327, 479

Plasterers See Craft Guilds, Bricklayers

Play See Corpus Christi; Creed; Pater Noster; St Denys; St George; St James; Vineyard; Grafton's Interlude

Player, king and queen 318

Players xxi, xxxiv, 7, 9, 25, 54, 66, 67, 69-70, 72, 76, 77, 91, 95, 96, 97, 99, 109, 243, 287, 288, 292, 294, 302, 310, 314, 320, 322, 323, 325, 326, 331, 353, 358, 392, 399, 411, 415, 419, 423, 432, 449, 479, 482, 507, 530-1, 554-5, 558, 563, 573, 576, 593, 597, 624; of York 65, 476, 530-1, 549 See also Queen's players; Travelling players; York Minster Chamberlains' Accounts 1472-1538

Players, not to play 464, 479, 481, 482, 486, 501, 528

Playhouse 530-1

Playing gear 334, 353 See also Creed Play; Grafton's Interlude; Mercers' Accounts, Bakers' Accounts

Playing places 449, 464-5, 530-1, 538 See also York, Common Hall; Stations, for playing

Plays and play-books 1, 3, 378, 384-5, 449

Plompton, William, minstrels of 68, 72, 75

Plumbers See Craft Guilds

Pocklington, minstrels from 69

Potters See Craft Guilds

Poulterers See Craft Guilds, Poultry sellers

Poultry sellers See Craft Guilds

Poynings, Lord of, minstrels of 76

Prince, minstrels of 122, 181, 203, 206; players of 568; trumpeters of 608, 615

Processions 146, 150, 168, 196, 310-11, 320-1, 326-7 See also Corpus Christi Procession

Public Record Office, documents in xxxii-xxxiv, xlii

Pudsay, Ralph, minstrel of 65, 66, 70-1; Thomas, minstrels of 70; William, minstrel of 75

Pullen, John scholars of (players) 418

Purification of Virgin, feast of See Candlemas

Quarter Session, Court of xxv-xxvi

Queen's bears 378

Queen's players 409, 413, 430, 449, 451, 455, 462, 464, 471, 473, 481, 482, 487, 488, 501, 521, 522, 564

Questours 23

Radclyff, Nicholas, minstrel of 73
Rampston, Thomas, minstrel of 76
Recorder of York See York, Recorder of
Reeds (pipes) 55
Rehearsing players 95, 99
Religious Guilds xiv, xxxiv See also Corpus
    Christi, guild of; Holy Trinity, guild of;
    Pater Noster Guild; St Christopher, guild of
Revels, His Majesty's 580, 593
Ridings See Sheriffs' Ridings; Yule, riding of
Rods, ceremonial 195, 197-8, 259, 280, 317,
    492, 514, 549, 584, 600-1
Rooms, for viewing play; Mayor and Council:
    Corpus Christi Play 102, 106, 122, 145,
    181, 188, 203, 207, 214, 217-18, 220, 222,
    226, 230, 238, 259, 265, 267, 279, 315,
    339; —: Pater Noster Play 328; —: Mid-
    summer Interlude 406, 415; Dean and
    Chapter 132, 135, 289
Roos, Robert, minstrel of 66
Ropers See Craft Guilds
Rowes, William, minstrel of 76
Royal visits xiii, xvii, xxi, 9 (Richard II), 73
    -4 (Henry VI), 121 (Edward IV), 130,
    132-3 (Richard III), 137-43, 145-52 (Henry
    VII), 193-8 (Princess Margaret), 271-6
    (Henry VIII), 504-8, 514-15, 549-57 (James
    I), 581-93, 599-607 (Charles I)
Rushbearing, prohibition of 358
Rutland, Earl of, trumpeter of 539

Sackbuts 443, 447, 506, 567
Saddlers See Craft Guilds
St Anthony, guild of xiv, xvi, 178, 327, 365,
    377, 535 See also Pater Noster Guild;
    hall of xxix, 335, 386, 535; — as playing
    place 449 See also Bakers' Accounts for
    1585; hospital of xxxiv
St Barnabas, feast of (11 June) 36
St Bartholomew, feast of (24 August) 248

St Blaise, feast of (3 February) x, xii, xxi
St Christopher, guild of xvi, 68, 101
St Denys, play of xvi, 88; players of the parish
    of xvi, 77
St Edward, translation of (13 October) 74
St George, guild of See St Christopher, guild
    of; riding of xvi, 289, 310, 311, 318, 320,
    326-7
St James, play of xvi, 68
St John the Baptist, feast of (24 June) 67, 70
    See also Chamberlains' Accounts
St Katherine, image of 644
St Leonard, canons of 146-7; feast of (6 Nov-
    ember) 2, 3-4, 92; hospital of xvi, xxxiv-
    xxxv, xxxix, 2, 3-4, 12, 19, 25, 85, 92, 101,
    180, 213, 664 See also Corpus Christi Play,
    Purification of the Virgin
St Martin, feast of (11 November) 180
St Mary See Blessed Virgin Mary
St Peter, keys for 98
St Peter's Part xxxv See also York Minster,
    Dean and Chapter
St Stephen, feast of (26 December) 30
St Thomas, hospital of xxxii, xxxiii See also
    Corpus Christi, guild of; play of 649-50
    See also Corpus Christi Play
St Valentine, feast of (14 February) 69
St William, feasts of (8 June and Sunday
    after Epiphany) xiii, xxxv, xliii See also
    York Minster Chamberlains' Rolls; shrine
    of 150, 196
Salisbury, Earl of, minstrels of 66, 69, 70, 71,
    72, 75, 77
Sandcarters See Craft Guilds, Sandleaders
Saucemakers See Craft Guilds
Savage, John, minstrels of 66, 72, 75
Sawyers See Craft Guilds
Say, Lord of, minstrel of 72
Saynell, John, minstrels of 77
Scaffolds 29, 145, 271, 507, 606
Scholars of Horsefair, players 382
Scholars of John Pullen, players 418
Schoolhouses, as playing places 538
Schoolmaster See Grafton's Interlude
Scriveners See Craft Guilds
Scrope, Lord of Bolton, minstrel of 67, 70, 75

Scutcheons 284, 290, 318, 324, 338, 413, 416, 449, 608

Searchers See **Craft Guilds**, searchers of

Sermon, preached day after Corpus Christi 188, 203, 207, 259, 265, 279

Servers See **Craft Guilds**, Turners

Shalms 333, 347, 348, 349, 361

Shearer See **Craft Guilds**, Shearmen

Shearmen See **Craft Guilds**

Sheathers See **Craft Guilds**

Sheriffs 193, 549 See also **York**, Sheriffs of

Sheriffs' riding xii, xvi-xvii, 215, 223-4, 228, 365, 393 See also **Corpus Christi**, day of, Sheriffs riding on; **Midsummer**, Sheriffs riding at

Shield See **Main bread**

Shipwrights See **Craft Guilds**

Show of armour, on St Peter's Eve (28 June) 448, 458, 462, 467-9, 479, 480-1, 485; Friday before St Peter's Eve 463; Wednesday after St Peter 491 See also **Midsummer Show**

Singers and singing 196, 266, 268, 272, 278, 282-3, 287, 385, 422-3, 535, 588, 606

Skinners See **Craft Guilds**

Sledmen See **Craft Guilds**

Smiths See **Craft Guilds**

Song-books 58, 89

Songs 333, 365, 399, 423, 432, 535 See also **Singers and singing**

Sonnets 535

Spicers See **Craft Guilds**

Spurriers and Lorimers See **Craft Guilds**

Stafford, Lord, players of 382, 403, 430, 509; trumpeters of 517

Stations, for playing xxi, xxii, 8, 10-12, 119-20, 298, 311, 356, 366, 406 See also **Chamberlains' Accounts**

Sudder, Lord, players of 494

Suffolk, Lord, minstrels of 70, 72, 76; players of 269, 436

Summer lords and ladies, prohibition of 358

Summergame light 219

Sussex, Lord, players of 273, 396, 430, 435, 455

Sword, civic and ceremonial xlii, 514-15, 550, 551, 554, 555, 556, 583, 585-6, 588, 589, 590-1, 601-2, 604-5, 606, 609

Taborer 94

Tailboys, Walter, minstrels of 69, 75, 76

Tailors See **Craft Guilds**

Talbot, John, minstrel of 76

Tanners See **Craft Guilds**

Tapiters See **Craft Guilds**

Taverners See **Craft Guilds**, Vintners

Textwriters See **Craft Guilds**, Scriveners

Theatre See **Playhouse**

Tile-thatchers See **Craft Guilds**

Tilemakers See **Craft Guilds**

Tilers See **Craft Guilds**, Bricklayers

Tinklers See **Craft Guilds**

Torches, ceremonial See **Corpus Christi**, torches of

Town Halls, as playing places 538

Travelling players xvi, xviii, 419, 449, 573, 576; of the Queen 409, 413, 430, 449, 451, 455, 462, 464, 471, 473, 481, 482, 487, 488, 501, 521, 522, 564; of the King 581, 593 See also **Revels**, His Majesty's; of Lady Elizabeth 538; of the Prince 271, 568; of the Lord Admiral 430, 455, 509; of the Lord Chancellor 528; of the Lord Privy Seal 269; of Lord Albany 533, 536; of Lord Bartley 517; of Lord Beauchamp 441; of Lord Burrow 460; of Lord Chandos 430, 496; of Lord Darby 471; of Lord Darcy 455, 471; of Lord Essex 382, 409, 430, 435; of Lord Evers 509, 528; of Lord Hunsdon 397, of Lord Leicester 436; of Lord Lincoln 488, 501; of Lord Monteagles 488; of Lord Morden 455; of Lord Ogle 455; of Lord Oxford 419; of Lord Pembroke 455, 491; of Lord Stafford 382, 403, 430, 509; of Lord Sudder 494; of Lord Suffolk 269, 436; of Lord Sussex 273, 396, 430, 435, 455; of Lord Willoughby 464; of Lord Worcester 418, 442, 455, 464, 486, 488; scholars of Horsefair 382; scholars of John Pullen 418; in assize week 482

Treasurer of England 194
Trumpets and Trumpeters 24, 67, 70, 242, 411, 514, 545, 550, 563, 568, 580, 583, 592; of the king 276, 507, 608, 615; of the prince 608, 615; of the Lord Chamberlain 539; of Lord Dudley 507, 509; of Lord Lennox 521, 524; of Lord Oxford 539; of Lord Rutland 539; of Lord Stafford 517
Tumblers 581, 592
Turks 563
Turners See Craft Guilds

Upholders See Craft Guilds

Vestmentmakers See Craft Guilds
Vineyard, play of xvi, 60
Vintners See Craft Guilds
Viols 571

Wafferers 66-8, 69-73, 92
Waits See York, Waits of
Walkers See Craft Guilds, Fullers
War of the Roses x
Watercarters See Craft Guilds, Waterleaders
Waterleaders See Craft Guilds
Weavers See Craft Guilds
Wells, Lord of, minstrel of 66
Westmorland, Earl of, minstrels of 66, 71, 76
Whitchandlers See Craft Guilds, Chandlers
Wiflers 464, 469, 481, 492
Wigs 55, 98, 639
Willoughby, Lord, minstrels of 70, 72; players of 464; Hugh, minstrels of 66
Wills, discussion of xxxix-xl
Winedrawers See Craft Guilds
Wings, of angels 55, 95, 96, 242
Wiredrawers See Craft Guilds, Pinners
Wool-packers See Craft Guilds, Sledmen
Wool-sellers See Craft Guilds, Brokers of Wool
Woollen Weavers See Craft Guilds, Weavers

Worcester, Lord, players of 418, 442, 455, 464, 486, 488
Wrights See Craft Guilds, Carpenters

York, Aldermen of See York, City Council of
York, ancient of 411, 464, 469, 480
York, arms of 12, 29, 506, 549, 554, 580, 582, 587, 600, 603, 604, 609
York, Bailiffs of xi, 8
York, Bridgemasters of xii, xix, xx, xxi, xxii, xxiv-xxv, xxvi, xliii, 3, 35-6, 130, 135, 310, See also Bridgemasters' Accounts, Mercers' Accounts, Bakers' Accounts
York, Chamberlains of xii, xvi, xxi-xxiv, xliii, 12, 13, 29, 38, 113, 115, 119, 122, 130, 135, 139, 153, 158, 163, 167, 169, 173, 179, 184, 223, 253, 256, 271, 272, 273, 276, 282, 290, 294, 303, 317, 328, 348, 352-3, 357, 368, 399, 400, 401, 403, 406, 414, 424, 453, 464, 482, 506, 508, 584, 585, 589, 590, 596, 598, 600, 605, 606, 607, 608, 670, 684 See also Chamberlains' Accounts
York, City Archives xvii-xxvi, xlii
York, City Council of x-xiv, xvi, 4, 8, 11, 12, 13, 29, 32, 33, 34, 37, 41, 47, 48, 54, 59, 65, 74, 80, 83, 86, 93, 94, 102, 106, 109, 112-13, 119, 120, 122, 123, 126-7, 130, 131, 135, 136, 138-9, 145, 153, 154, 159, 164, 165, 167, 169, 170-1, 181, 186, 187, 193, 198, 201, 203, 204, 207, 213, 215, 216, 217, 220, 222, 224, 227, 236, 239, 251, 253, 257, 264, 270, 274, 275, 278, 279, 282, 291, 296-7, 314, 315, 324, 325-6, 327, 328, 333, 335, 339, 342, 344, 349, 351, 353, 355, 365, 366-8, 378, 385, 393, 396, 399, 400, 405, 406, 409, 410, 411, 421, 445, 463, 480, 481, 485, 486, 491, 492, 505-6, 507, 508, 512-13, 514-15, 550-1, 554, 556, 567, 579, 581-5, 587-91, 596, 601, 605-7, 608-9, 611-12, 613-14, 618, 619, 621
York, Common Clerk of xiii, 17, 165, 184, 187, 207, 220, 222, 224, 225, 228, 229,

231, 233, 235, 238, 240, 242, 246, 247, 262, 263, 278, 280, 282, 290, 313, 317, 330, 351, 508, 513

York, Common Hall xi, 155, 164, 169, 181, 198, 200, 204, 259, 276, 311, 312, 408, 452, 505, 508; as outside playing place 11, 28, 141, 236, 264, 272, 278, 298, 314, 315, 414; as inside playing place xvi, 243, 384-5, 397, 399, 409, 419, 430, 435-6, 441-2, 449, 465, 471, 476, 487, 488, 491, 501, 521

York, Community of (Commonalty or the Commons) xii-xiii, 5, 8, 11-12, 16, 28, 30, 31-2, 34, 35, 38, 42, 51, 62-3, 72, 109, 112, 119, 130, 138, 143, 153, 154, 158, 178, 183, 195, 197, 215, 223, 256, 271, 274, 296, 301, 354, 392-3, 399, 505, 514, 551, 586, 617, 621, 623, 626

York, Corporation of 530, 551, 554, 567, 586, 590, 600

York, Court of Quarter Session xxv-xxvi

York, Deputy Common Clerk of xiii, 68, 244

York, Duke of, minstrels of 66, 70, 72, 73, 85

York, Lady Mayoress of 106, 222, 224, 228, 231, 240, 243, 246, 247, 264, 279, 310, 321, 326, 406, 414, 420

York, Magistrates of xxv, 469, 560

York, Mayor of x-xiv, xxi, 5, 8, 9, 11, 12, 13, 14, 17, 24, 26, 28-9, 31, 33, 34, 35-6, 37-8, 39, 41-2, 43-4, 45, 47, 51-2, 53, 54, 59, 62, 64, 65, 74, 80, 82, 86, 93, 94, 96, 102, 106, 107-8, 109, 110, 111, 112-13, 115, 118-20, 123, 125-6, 128, 129, 130, 134, 137-9, 145, 153-6, 158-61, 162, 163-7, 168-74, 175, 176, 177, 179, 182-4, 189, 191, 192-8, 200-1, 204, 214-15, 223, 226, 230, 236, 237, 238, 239, 240, 242, 246, 247-8, 250, 252, 253, 259, 267, 284, 285, 289-90, 291, 297-8, 300, 310, 321, 322, 325, 326, 328, 330, 333-4, 335, 338, 342, 346-7, 349, 351, 353-4, 356, 363, 365-70, 372, 378, 381, 385, 389, 391, 393, 397, 399-400, 401, 405,

409, 410-11, 413, 416, 420-1, 436, 441, 449, 463, 470, 475, 480, 482, 486, 491, 499, 501, 505-6, 508, 511, 512, 520, 550-2, 554-7, 559-60, 567, 575, 582-93, 596, 599, 601, 608-9, 611-12, 613-14, 626, 666, 681, 684

York, players of 65, 476, 549

York, province of x, xv, 358, 369

York, Receivers' Rolls xxii

York, Recorder of xiii, 118, 146, 154, 193-8, 274-5, 486, 505, 508, 550-4, 556, 582, 583, 585-90, 599, 601-7, 609, 611

York, Sergeants of xiii, 95, 118, 135, 154, 167, 169, 184, 195, 514, 551, 588, 604

York, Sheriffs of xi-xii, 24, 138, 146, 154, 170, 172, 184, 193, 195-8, 215, 236, 239, 263, 270, 276, 285, 290, 300, 302, 400, 410, 441, 463, 469, 480-1, 486, 491, 507, 549-51, 556, 579, 583-5, 589-91, 596, 600-1, 604-7, 612, 626 See also **Sheriffs' riding**

York, Waits of xiii, xvi, xxi, xxii, 134-5, 143, 200, 239, 318, 324, 333, 347, 348-9, 362, 363, 368, 387, 391, 397, 399, 405, 408, 413, 449, 453-4, 459, 469-70, 475, 479-80, 485-6, 492-3, 495, 496, 499-500, 507-8, 535, 541, 550, 567-9, 579, 585, 591-2, 596, 601, 609, 614 See also **Chamberlains' Accounts;** book of 134-5, 453, 463, 479-80, 485-6

York Cycle See **Corpus Christi Play**

York Minster, Chamberlains of xxxv-xxxvi, xliii

York Minster, Choristers and Choir 150-1, 399, 423, 432, 538, 568, 571, 606

York Minster, Dean and Chapter xv, xxxv-xxxvi, 132, 135, 150-1

York Minster, Dean of 132, 135, 150-1, 353-4, 390

York Minster, Library xxx-xxxi, xxxv-xxxvi, xxxix, xlii

York Minster, Vicars Choral xv, xxxv, xxxvii, 36-7, 44, 675

Yule, riding of xvi, xl-xli, 359-62, 368-9

Place and Name Index

Acomb Moor (Acome Moore) 590

Acredd (Acrides), Robert 537, 540, 559

Addeson (Addison, Addyson) 413, 427; John 433, 437; Thomas 434

Adenett, William 279

Adriano, Doctor 206

Ainsty (Aynesty, Aynsty) 193, 274, 600, 604

Albarras, John 200

Albone (Albon), Henry 134

Aldercorn, John 652

Aldestanemore (Aldestanemor), John 34, 45

Alexander, Sir Walter 589

Allan (Alan, Alen, Aleyni, Allen, Allyn), Mr 356, 378; Hugh 654; John 199, 211, 218, 226, 233; Robert 654; William 654

Allanson, William 585

Allenbye (Allandbye), James 428, 431, 437, 438, 442, 488, 493

Allerton 67

Allerton, Robert 45

Alne, William 16

Ambler, Christopher 433, 434

Ametson 328

Amplefrith, Simon 654

Amyas, Mr 131

Anderson, Thomas 111-12

Androe 271

Androwe, Thomas 433

Anne, Queen 132, 133; of Denmark 507, 508, 514

Applebye (Appilby, Applebyes, Appulby, Apulby), Bartholomew 422, 507; Robert 46; Roger 165, 166

Appleyard (Apleyard, Apleyerd, Appleyardes, Appleyerd, Appleyerdes), Alderman 314, 414, 418; Mr 356; Thomas 305, 339, 652

Archer 444, 474

Ardington, Nicholas 654

Ardyen, Mr 276

Arkindale (Arkedell, Arkendaile, Arkindaile, Arkindall, Arkindelle), Mr 443; John 395, 461, 511; Martin 439, 467, 493, 494; Robert 483, 502

Arowis, Richard 631

Arundell and Surrey, Thomas Earl of 604

Arwom, Miles 144

Ase, John 41

Ashburn, Christopher 369

Asheby (Esschby), Richard 205, 240

Aske, John 391, 655

Askwith (Askwithe, Asquith, Asquyth), Sir Robert 560; Lord Mayor, Robert 551; Alderman 406, 506, 528, 533, 536, 539, 541, 543, 545; Robert 470, 480

Aslaby, George 366, 372, 655

Asper, John 53

Assaphensis See St Asaph

Atherton, Mr 409

Atkinson (Atkynson, Atkynsone), Adam 277; James 653; John 338; Thomas 653

Atkirk (Atkirke), Anthony 652; George 652

Avyson, Nicholas 330

Awdelay, Lord 330

Awkland, Richard 325

Aylde, Thomas 101

Aynley (Aynlay), Richard 296, 297, 315

Babthorp, Rado 85

Bachelar (Bacheler, Bachilor), Henry 111; John 653

Baggergate (Baggeryete) 67

Bailley, Thomas 228

Baills 265

Baker, John 621; Ralph 653

Balderston (Balderstome, Baltherston, Bawderston, Bawderstone), John 381, 383, 389, 393, 397, 402, 408, 409, 410, 419, 430; Peter 532, 542, 543, 559

Ball, William 99

Balland, William 231

Balzay, Margaret 634

Banester (Bannester, Banyster), Henry 394, 473, 655

Bankhouse (Bankhows), Thomas 184, 201, 653

Barbour, Adam 144; John 105; Thomas 93, 101

Barker, Thomas 424, 656; William 165, 166, 187, 652

Barston, John 410

Barton, John 559-60; William 45

Barwick, Robert 611

Bateman (Bayteman, Baytman), John 206, 224; Richard 240, 242, 246, 247; Thomas 161, 178, 179, 182, 189, 190, 202, 204

Bawde, John 105

Bawderstone See Balderston

Baxster, Nicholas 206, 220

Bayne, Francis 654, 655

Beachame, Lord 441

Beale, Mr 611

Bean, Mr 272

Beaumont (Beamond, Beaumond), Viscount 72, 75; Lord 71, 76

Beckwith (Beckith, Beckwithe, Beckwyth, Bekwith, Bekwyth), Alderman 406, 414, 480; Alderman William 366-7; Mr 314; Widow 240; Christopher 418, 463, 655; James 372, 655; Leonard 375, 655; William 652

Bedale, Alan de 35-6; William 55

Bedford, Robert 34

Beese, John 93

Beke, Thomas 426

Bekynghm, Robert 652

Belamy, John 635

Bell, John '243; Miles 652

Bellesthorpp, John 273

Belt, Sir William 590; William 585

Bemyman, Thomas 247

Bennittes, Doctor 484

Benson, John 651

Benyng, Elaine 635

Berlay, Reginald 228; Ronald 234

Bernyngham, John 52

Best, James 324, 325

Bethom, Sir Edward de 76

Beuerlay, Thomas 91, 92

Beverley (Beueraci, Beuerl', Beuerley, Beuerlaci, Beuerlaco) 69, 71, 73, 76, 613

Bewyk (Bewik), Nicholas 105, 122; William 170

Beysley, Reginald 242

Bilbowe (Bylbowes), John 463; Robert 314

Bilbrough Cross (Bilburgh Crose, Bilburghcrosse) 138, 139

Bille, Nicholas 105

Birkby (Birkbie, Byrkby), Mayor 436; Alderman 414, 418, 463, 480; Peter 343

Birnand, Mr 356, 366

Bishopfield (Bysshopfeyld) 256

Bishophill (Bischophill, Byshope Hill, Bushophill) 519; parish of 445; church of St Mary on 631

Bishopthorpe xv, 556, 590

Blades, James 230

Blakburn, Nicholas 84

Blakey, John 213, 220, 228, 233, 240, 242, 278

Blanchyrd, Thomas 654

Bland, James 398, 655

Blayds, Christopher 395

Blenkarne, Mr 508; Thomas 463

Blody, John 243

Bluefront, William 61

Bluther, Henry 184

Blyth (Blythe), Andrew 133, 134; Richard 654

Blythman, Ninian 305

Bogg, John 265

Bolron, John 33, 41

Bolton, John 51; Robert 49, 50; Thomas 27
See also **Scrope**

Bondhill Row (Bondall Rawe) 550

Bonsfeilde (Bonsfeld), Mr 482; John 480

Bootham Bar (Boothombar, Bowdome Barr,
Bowtham Barre, Bowthome Barr, Bowthum-
barre) 197, 198, 243, 247, 273, 505, 507,
582, 599, 611

Bootham Ward (Boothomeward, Bothomeward,
Bowthome Ward) 319, 330, 407, 408, 599,
607, 611

Boroughbridge (Burghbrigge, Burghbrygge)
190, 191

Bossall, Richard 652

Bosswell, John 92

Both, Dean Robert 133

Bouland, William 84

Bower, John 220

Bowes, Sir William 67; Mayor William 31, 45,
59, 626

Bowlmer (Bowemer), Thomas 434, 465, 466

Bracebrig, Mayor Thomas 49

Bradley, Richard 469, 470, 476, 482, 488,
496, 500, 501, 509, 517, 520, 523, 527,
528, 535, 536, 538, 541; Thomas 501, 509

Brady, John 426

Bramley, John 232

Brand, Wilfred 404, 655

Branthwate (Brathwaite, Braythwhaite),
Edward 444; John 327; Thomas 542

Braye, Richard 461

Brearey (Breray), Councillor 613; Sheriff
Christopher 600; Richard 264; William 507

Bredon, William de 621

Brekles Mylnys 130

Bridlington 73

Brigg (Brigge, Bryg), Adam del 11, 28; John
37; William 27

Brignall, Thomas 85

Broddes, Thomas 313

Brooke (Broke, Brook), Alderman 432, 485;
Sheriff 410; Percival 480, 485, 507, 655;
Robert 366, 378, 654

Brougham Castle, Westmorland 556

Brounflete, Henry 69, 71; John 34

Brown (Browne), Anthony 151; William 111

Brownlesse (Brownles), John 460, 461; William
521

Bryg See **Brigg**

Bubwyth, Sir Roger 52

Bucke, Mr 514

Buckingham (Bukyngham, Bukynham), Duke
of 67, 70

Bukton, Thomas de 5, 24, 26

Bull 72; John 66

Bullocke, William 345

Burdon, Robert 27; Simon 419

Burgesse (Burges), Richard 130, 145

Burgh (Burghe), Sir Thomas 151; Ambrose
385; Katherine 635

Burghbrigge, Burbrygge See **Boroughbridge**

Burkes, William 434

Burleigh (Burlay), Lord 514, 515; Agnes 636

Burnes, Robert 442

Burnett (Burnet, Burnytt) 167; Robert 463,
656

Burrowe, Lord 460

Burton (de Burton) 26, 38, 42, 46, 50, 52; Mr
259; John 244, 248, 621; Robert 576;
Roger 17; Thomas 529, 540, 543, 652;
William 347, 389, 428, 439, 447, 472, 655

Busfeld, John 418

Butler (Butteller), Sir John 75; Robert 93,
105

Buttercram, John 34

Buttirwyk, Walter 27

Buxnell, Thomas 72, 73

Bylbowes See **Bilbowe**

Bynglay, Thomas 85

Bynkes, Adam 653

Byrkby See **Birkby**

Byrkhead (Byrkhed), Brian 394, 410, 655;
John 180

Caber, William 633

Calbek (Caldbeke) 202; John 187, 205

Calome, Mr 333

Calton, Anthony 398, 655; Simon 33

Cambridge (Cantabrig'), Lord 66

Candell, John 89
Cankerd, William 274
Carl, Thomas 325
Carlisle (Carlile) 605
Carlisle (Carliolensis, Karliel), Earl of 591;
    Lord 590; Bishop of 132, 630
Caruour, Phillip 85
Castlegate (Castelgate) 11, 28, 313
Catlynson, Thomas 651
Caton, Nicholas 180; William 202, 206
Catryk (Catrik), John 73, 82, 85
Catterton (Caterton), Richard 202, 205;
    William 180, 187
Catton, John de 5
Caue, John 37
Caward (Cawarbe, Cawood), James 488, 489,
    502
Cawdewell (Cawdwell) 233; John 228
Cawlebek, John 240
Cay See Key
Chaloner, Thomas 167, 173, 174
Chambers (Chambre), John 357, 497, 654;
    Oswald 653
Chandos (Shandes. Shandoze), Lord 430, 496
Chapman, Richard 374; Thomas 159
Charles I ix, xvii, 581-91, 599-614
Chater, Mr 595; George 596
Chaundeler, Margaret 58
Chaw See Shaw
Chawmer, John 451
Cheworth, Thomas 69, 75
Cheyne, Sir John 151
Chirche, Henry del 621
Chomley (Chamley, Cholmelay, Cholmlay)
    Richard 169-73
Christ Church (Kryskyrk) 130
Churcheman, George 224
Chymnay (Chymney), Alderman William 198;
    William 94
Clark See Clerk
Clarvas (Clarevas, Clarvax), Giles 651, 652;
    Margaret 635
Clayton, Mr 281; Henry 87; Ralph 272, 279
Clerk (Clark, Clarke, Clarkes, Clerck, Clerke,
    Clerkees, Clerkes) 426; Christopher 277;
    John 167, 234, 317, 330, 351, 374, 381,
383, 389, 393, 397, 402, 408-9, 430, 435,
    454, 460, 469-70, 525; Nicholas 72, 351,
    363, 376; Richard 376, 377, 483; Robert
    75, 654; Thomas 244, 426; William 99, 100
Cleueland' See Percy
Clifford (Cliffordes, de Clyfford, Clyfforde),
    Lord 66, 69, 71, 75, 76, 153, 553, 588-91,
    604-5; Richard 170, 172-3
Clifton (Cliffton) 197, 507
Clifton Ingges 556
Clifton (Clyffton, Clyfton), wife 291;
    William 37, 38
Clorus, Emperor Constantine 602
Clydero, Richard 273
Clyff (Clyf, Clyffe), Richard 231; Robert 180,
    187, 202; Thomas 636
Clyfton See Clifton
Clynt, John 219
Coattes, Thomas 653
Cocke See Cook
Coiltman (Coltman), Thomas 433, 437
Coke, Cokke See Cook
Coldwell, Gilbert 436, 656
Coliar (Colyer), Christopher 273; Robert 401
Colliergate (Cellyergate, Coliargate, Colyergate)
    279, 314, 357
Collinson, John 654
Collyweston (Colyweston) 193
Colthirst (Colthirste), Mr 408, 409, 415, 420;
    Thomas 411
Comgilton, Robert 143
Commendell, Robert 498
Common Hall Gates 272, 298, 328, 339, 356,
    366, 406, 583
Coney Street (Conestreet, Connyngstreyt,
    Conyenx Strete, Conyngstrete, Quonyenx
    Strete) 11, 28, 93, 101, 141, 149, 155, 272,
    298, 305, 313, 314, 357, 406
Consett (Concett, Consytt), Christopher 375,
    512-13, 655
Constabyll, Alice 635
Constantine See Clorus
Conyers, Christopher 71; William 198
Cook (Cocke, Coke, Cokke, Cook, Cooke,
    Couke, Cowke, Cuke), Mr 279; Miles 277,
    652; Peter 117-18, 172; Robert 234, 651;

Roland 316; Thomas 37, 145; William 187, 206, 502 See also **Cowkes**
Copley, Thomas 398, 655
Cotez, Matthew 180
Cotyngham, Olive de 629
Coulton, Mr 611
Couper See **Cowper**
Couret, Mr 481, 482
Cowke See **Cook**
Cowkes (Cokx), Steven (?) 293
Cowper (Couper), Alderman 581, 582, 609; George 405, 408; Henry 450; John 202, 481; Walter 265; William 37, 653
Cowpland (Coupeland, Coupland), George 654; Lancelot 347; William 41
Crake (Crak) 167, 168, 173-4
Crathorn, Mayor Thomas 64
Crauen (de Crauen), John 9, 52
Crawforth (Craforth, Croforth), Mr 340; Percival 300, 303, 335
Creswick (Cresswicke, Creswicke, Criswicke) 495, 498, 504; John 485; Oswald 514, 519
Criplinge, John 395
Cristallson, James 473
Croft (Crofte), Marmaduke 600; William 37
Croklyn, Richard 101
Crome, John 630
Crosbie, Edward 490; James 410
Crosse, James 383, 655
Cuilsby, Richard 651
Cuke See **Cook**
Cumberland (Comberland), Earl of 515, 550, 553-4, 556-7, 605; Francis, Earl of 550
Cunnysburgh, Thomas 33
Cunsby, William 33
Cunyng, Henry 130
Cure, Nicholas 241; William 224
Curtays (Curteys), Thomas 55, 85
Custanee, Thomas 238
Cuthberte (Cutberd) 411, 423
Cymney See **Chymnay**

Dacre' (Dacr'), Lord 68, 72
Dam, Thomas 53

Damfort, Mr 514
Danby, Margaret 636
Darcy (Darcies, Darsie), Lord 75, 203, 455, 471
Darling, John 653
Darson, William 223
Darte, Lawrence 436
Dauidensis See **St David's**
Davyll, George 654
Dawson (Dauson), Mr 609; Bartholomew 652; George 652; John 434; Margaret 231; Robert 404, 655; Thomas 613; William 418
Dayson, Mr 257
Daystern, John 79
del Style See **Style**
Dent, Christopher 430, 435, 449; Robert 462; Thomas 496, 497
Derby (Darbie, Darby), Earl of 330; Lord 471
Dernwater, William 86
Dewe, Robert 632
Deynshire, Earl of 76
Dickinson (Dicinson, Diconson, Dycconson, Dyckonson), Anthony 314; George 313; Henry 652; Thomas 119, 614
Dishley, Mr 593
Dixon (Dickson, Dicson, Dixson, Dycsson, Dykson) 317; James 433; John 295, 472; Nicholas 264, 542; Richard 143, 450; William 540, 546
Doblay, Christopher 87
Dobson, Mr 289; Henry 654; William 247
Dodsworth (Dodisworthes, Dodsworthes), Anthony 537, 544; Giles 563, 572
Dogeson (Dogeshon, Dogeso), Mr 270, 289; John 216; William 268
Doncaster 600
Donne, Alexander 187
Donnynge, George 424
Donyngton 67
Dorchester (Dorcetr'), Marquis of 67
Dove (Doves), Mrs 576; Thomas 519
Drawswerd, Thomas 188, 205
Drax, William 37
Drewrie, Roger 273
Dringhouses (Dringhowsis) 139
Dromer, Arthur 410, 419

Dudley (Dudleys), Lord 507, 509, 517, 524
Duffeld, John de 5
Dunwell, Robert 204
Dunyng, George 656
Dunyngton, Thomas 654
Durem, Thomas 33
Durham (Dunelm', Dunelmie) 66, 73, 75, 156, 364
Durham (Dorham, Dunellmensis, Dunelm', Dunelmensis), Lord 75; Bishop of 66, 69, 74, 76, 132-3, 196
Dyckonson See Dickinson
Dycsson, Dykson See Dixon
Dyneley, Mr 349
Dynns 572
Dyonist 572

Easton, Edward 569
Ebor', Edward (Archbishop of York) 369
Eden, Anthony 273, 653
Edinburgh (Edenbrough, Edenburgh) 549, 584
Edmund (Edmond) 263; Archbishop of York 369
Edward II xlii
Edward III xlii
Edward IV ix, x, xi, xvii, 118, 120, 121
Edward VI (Prynce Edward) 275
Edward (Edwardes), Lawrence 428, 656
Edwyn, Oswyn 653
Egremont, Baron 77
Elden, Robert 277; William 653
Elizabeth I 504
Ellerd, Thomas 654
Ellis (Elles, Ellys, Elys), John 159, 180, 199, 205, 231, 233, 278, 318; Robert 573
Ellwycke, James 654
Elton, William 593
Elwald (Elwolde), John 189; Robert 652
Emmyngburgh See Hemingbrough
Emondson (Eminsonnes), Martin 461, 466; William 271
Emson, Roger 160
Erandale, Earl of 69
Eshe (Esshe) 217; John 654

Eshwray, John 167
Esschby See Asheby
Essex (Essikes, Essix), Earl of 382, 409, 430, 435, 471; George 184; Richard 239
Esyngwald, Mayor Thomas 39
Etton, William 537, 540
Eueres, Sir William 71
Evenwod, John 87
Exeter (Dexistr', Excester, Excextr', Exestr'), Duke of 69, 70, 71; Lord 66
Exilbe, Edward 655
Eymis, Thomas 369
Eyre, John 654

Fairewether (ffairwether, ffareweddrs) 313; Mr 609, 611, 613
Fale, Thomas 347
Farlay, Fabian 654; William 654
Farmery See Fermery
Fawcett (ffawcet, Fawsett), Edward 418, 463, 627; Roland 480
Fawkes, Mr 357
Felter Lane (ffalter Layne, ffelterlayn, ffelter-layne) 290, 292, 293, 295, 321, 322, 324, 331, 340, 341, 343
Fereby (fferiby), John 118, 120; Robert 34
Fermery (Farmery), John 428, 656
Ferrour, Richard 33
Fish Shambles (ffyshe shamylles) 294
Fisher (ffissher, ffysher), John 389, 419, 655; Thomas 651
Fishergate Mill (ffyschergayte Mylne) 277
Fitt, Thomas 87
Fitz Hugh (ffitzhugh, Fythew), Lord 69, 71, 73, 75, 132
Fitz William, William 66, 75
Flambaute, Christopher 547
Flanders 53
Flemyng, John 275-6, 277; Thomas 222, 234, 242, 259, 265, 267, 271, 279, 281
Flesh Shambles (fflesshamels) 30
Flesshner, Thomas 87
Fletcheres, Tristram 561
Folneby, Thomas 189

Fons, Robert 224
Fordayne, Christopher 433
Forester (Forster), Edward 172; Henry 35-6
Foss Bridge xii, xxii, 49, 294, 626
Fossgate xxvi
Foster, Archibald 240, 246, 247
Fouldes, John 76
Foulford, John 93
Fountains, Abbot of 85, 151
Fox (Foxe), John 87-8, 637; Thomas 265
Foxgill, William 463
France 66, 448
Frankland, William 421
Freesleye, William 416
Fresby (ffrysbe), William 383, 418, 655
Friston (ffryston), William 179, 180
Fulford (ffulfoord) 274
Fuster, William 654
Fynch, Thomas 189
Fysher See Fisher
Fythew See Fitz Hugh

Gachet, John 289
Gaing, William 61
Gaittes See Gayte
Gale (Gayle, Gaylls), Mr 257, 279, 298, 314;
    Henry 213
Galland, William 228, 236
Gannton, John 79
Gardiner, Hugo 34
Gare, Elaine 636; Thomas 33, 34; Thomas
    Jr 636
Garland, John 481
Garth, James 652; John 424, 425
Gascoigne, William 77, 85
Gaunt, Thomas 121
Gaylls See Gale
Gayte (Gaittes, Gaytes), Richard 380, 392;
    William 84
Gegges, John 224
Geldert (Geldard, Geldarde, Geldart, Gelder,
    Gelderd), Mr 468, 479, 485, 490, 495,
    499, 504, 519, 520; Anthony 432, 433, 434,
    440, 444, 448, 462, 475, 485; John 444, 584

Gell (Gel, Gelles, Gels) 428; John 457, 467,
    489, 651; William 478, 518, 532, 537, 540
Gerard, John 37, 38
Gibson (Gibsonne, Gibsons), Richard 180, 187,
    205; Thomas 451, 530, 544, 546, 562, 566
Gills (Gilli), Marmaduke 496; Paul 220, 224
Gillygate (Ielygatt) 247
Gilmyn (Gilmyne, Gilmyng), Mr 418; George
    654; William 101, 366
Gilping, Edward 653
Gilyoit, John 96
Girdler, John 567
Girdlergate 11, 28
Glasyn (Glason, Glasyng), widow 278; Thomas
    285, 330
Gledstones (Gledsone), Roland 518, 532, 533
Glewe, Richard 652
Gllot, William 219
Gloucester, Lord 67
Goddyrsswyke, William 92
Goodaike, John 426
Goodbarne, Thomas 238
Goodramgate (Goodromegate, Gotheremgate,
    Gotheromgate, Guderangaytt) 155, 247,
    264, 279, 298, 314, 406
Goodwyn, Mr 447
Goodyeare, John 654
Gotheromgate See Goodramgate
Gowland, John 437, 656
Goyme, John 438
Grab (Grubes), William 570
Grafton xvi, 405, 406, 420; Mr 414, 415;
    John xxii, 406, 423; Thomas 405
Granger, John 340, 436, 654, 656
Grantham (Granntham) 194
Graves (Graues, Grayves) 470; Hugh 332, 335,
    385, 406, 653; John 279, 394, 655; Ralph
    654; Richard 275, 276, 277, 318; Thomas
    435, 454, 460, 469, 470, 476, 482, 488,
    496, 499, 500, 501, 509
Gray, Lord 69; Alexander 231; Miles 372;
    Thomas 179
Grayson (Grason), Christopher 340; William
    Ierrett 223
Graystok (Grastoke), Baron 66, 71, 75; Lord
    69, 132

Greathead, George 433
Greges (Gregges), Hugh 540; Thomas 296-7
Grembez, Edward 313
Grenbury (Grenburie, Grenebery), Alderman 507; Mr 523; Edward 300, 302; Leonard 430, 656
Grenefeild, William 534
Grindal, Archbishop xl, 358-9
Grubes See Grab
Gryme (Grymees), Francis 502; John 390
Grymesby, John de 52
Gryndon, John 156
Gubbys, Robert 232
Guderangaytt See Goodramgate
Gybbon, Nicholas 160; Robert 160; William 160
Guest, Ellis 593
Gult, John 447
Gylde, John 105; William 651
Gylliot (Gylliat), Sir John 160, 191, 192, 195; John 651
Gyllyngton, William 54
Gylmyn (Gylmyng), William 130, 653
Gyseburn (de Gyseburne), John 11, 28

Haburne (Heburne), Mr 556, 558
Haliday, Nicholas 93, 100
Hall, George 653; Henry 381, 512, 513, 655; James 331, 654; John 249, 304; Leonard 343; Peter 364, 371, 373, 376, 380, 654; Ralph 652; Robert 339, 652; Thomas 490; William 283, 290
Halley (Hallay), William 406, 436, 513
Halton, Robert de 5
Halyfax, John 247
Halyland, Thomas 243
Hamleton, Marquis 587
Hancok (Hancock, Hancoke), Robert 118, 138; William 424, 656
Handlae, John 439
Harbart See Herbert
Hardy (Hardie, Hardye), Christopher 450, 461, 511, 529; Matthew 515
Hardyng 75

Hargyll, John 273
Harland (Harlandes), Christopher 535, 544, 559, 561; Cuthbert 544
Harper (Harpour, Herper), Christopher 66, 71, 75, 76, 77; John 129-30, 347; Simon 67, 68, 69, 70, 71, 75; Thomas 332; William 231
Harpham, Robert 11, 28; William 144
Harrison (Harisonn, Harisons, Harreson, Harresonnes, Harryson, Harysones, Herreson, Herressons, Herrison, Herryson, Heryson) 298, 313; Alderman 406; Searcher 503; Mr 485; John 112, 343, 434, 447, 455, 484, 502, 518, 532, 542, 566, 653; Robert 302, 398, 463, 480, 655; William 173-4, 273, 532, 534, 546, 548, 570, 572, 575
Harryngton (Harrington, Haryngeton, Haryngton, Herryngton, Heryngton), Lord 70, 71, 76; James 273, 277, 332, 653; John 69, 71, 73, 75; Thomas 70, 72, 76
Hart (Harte), Ralph 383, 416, 463, 655
Hartley (Hartlay), Mr 298; John 315; Matthew 236, 240, 242, 246, 247, 264, 278
Hastings (Haystynges), Lord 195
Hawkeshirst (Hawkeshyrsh), Richard 442, 656
Haxby (Haxeby), John 33; Robert 89
Haxope (Haxvp, Haxvpp, Haxvppe), Mr 438; Nicholas 315; 377; Thomas 455, 456, 465, 502
Hay, William 227, 672
Head, John 426
Hebbylthwait, Richard 319
Heburne See Haburne
Heckleton (Heckylton), Mr 272; Gilbert 653
Hedelay, Ralph 319
Helme, John 84
Helperby, John 27
Hemingbrough (Emmyngburgh) 221
Hemsworth, Alderman 575, 576, 583, 611, 614
Hemyngway, Abraham 582
Hendechild, Thomas 37-8
Henlickes, John 548
Henrietta Maria 590
Henrison (Henryson), Mr 356, 366; John 85
Henry IV (Bolingbroke) x, xlii
Henry VI xvii, xl, xli, 73-4, 94

Henry VII x, xvii, xviii, xl, xli, 137-43, 144, 145, 146-51, 153-6, 162-3, 271

Henry VIII ix, xvii, xviii, xxxii, xlii, 271-7

Herbert (Harbart, Harbarte, Harbert, Hurbart), Alderman 418, 506, 556, 589; Mr 486, 609; Christopher 366-8, 654; John 379, 384, 394, 655; Phillip 584; Richard 428, 656; Thomas 391, 463, 512-13, 655

Herbert House 356, 366, 414, 589

Hereford (Herefordensem, Herfordensis, Hertfordensis), Bishop of 74, 633, 634, 638

Heron 36

Herpar See Harper

Herrison See Harrison

Heslington Pits (Eslyngton Pyttes) 270

Hewetson (Hewetsons, Hewytson), Mr 278; John 653; Thomas 264; William 382

Hewit (Hewet, Hewite, Hewitt, Hewyt, Hewytt) 432; Robert 351, 374, 385, 397, 399, 416, 418; Thomas 654; William 130, 467

Hewley, Mr 611, 613

Hewnson, John 426

Heworth Moor 444

Hewyk (Hewike, Hewycke), Christopher 404, 655; Robert 87

Hexham, John 41

Heysbe, Lawrence 277

Hill (Hyl, Hyll), Henry 519; John 347; Robert 236; Thomas 653; William 316

Hirst (Hirste), Thomas 37-8

Hodgson (Hodgeson, Hodshon, Hogeson, Hogesyon, Hojeson), Doctor 556, 589; Mr 257; Arthur 346, 363, 381, 383, 389, 393, 397; James 265; John 263; Miles 652; Nicholas 436; Peter 412, 656; Thomas 93; William 105

Hogg, Robert 314

Holbeck (Holbek, Holbeke), William 55, 107, 201, 681

Holcrofte, William 486

Holgate, Nicholas 85

Holgate Lane 550

Holland, Earl of 604

Holme (Holemes, Holmes), Mr 327; Henry 227, 230, 231; John 434; Simon 573

Holy Trinity, Hospital of 27

Holy Trinity Church, Goodramgate xxxvii, 426, 439, 444, 478, 498, 503, 513, 518, 594, 612-13

Holy Trinity Gates 84, 93, 100, 105, 126, 263, 278, 313, 356, 366

Holy Trinity Priory, Micklegate 27, 28, 168, 278, 294

Hopperton (Hoppton), James 246, 247

Hopton, Robert 420

Horneby (Hornebe), Richard 265, 319

Horner, Mr 611

Horsley, Benedict 583

Hosier Lane (Hosyerlayn) 314, 556

Houeden, Robert de 621

Houghton, Baronet 539; Augustine 584

Howard, Katharine See Katharine, Queen

Howeolyff, William 277

Howes, Mr 594, 595

Howlley, Hugh 227, 677

Howson, William 655

Hoyle, Alderman 609

Hudson (Hudsone, Hudsonn), Adam 93, 100, 105, 143, 156; Henry 130, 138, 145; John 304; Robert 424, 656; Thomas 395, 511

Humes, Thomas 544

Hunsdon, Lord 397

Hunter (Huntees, Hunteres, Hunters), Edward 651; George 473, 494, 522, 525, 534, 537, 548, 558-9; John 576; Thomas 161, 178, 179, 182, 189; William 456, 465, 502

Huntington (Huntyngton), John 294, 295, 320

Hurbart See Herbert

Husthwait (Husthwate), Robert 324, 333, 346

Hutchinson (Hutchenson), Alderman 581, 582, 609; Mr 439; John 488, 489, 541; Thomas 654

Huthwayt, John 45

Hutton (Huton, Huttons) 356; Christopher 437, 656; Matthew 353, 354, 369; Richard 379, 384, 551, 554, 556, 655; Robert 265

Hyll See Hill

Hyndes, Edward 451

Iackson (Iacksons, Iakson, Jackson), Fr 422;
    Alderman 463; Mr 480; Christopher 655;
    George 597; James 279, 652; John 313,
    372, 375, 406, 410, 652, 655; Miles 652;
    Peter 653; Thomas 426; William 548, 653
Iacobs, Peter 354
Iake, Francis 340
Iameson, John 220, 652; William 652
Iamys, Robert 652
Iaques, Sir Roger 589, 601, 609, 613
Ielygatt See Gillygate
Ienkinson, William 436, 656
Ierrett See Grayson, William
Ileyes, Anthony 559, 575
Incecliff, William 152
Inglesbeye, Mr 514
Ingrams, Sir Arthur 611
Ingylby, Joan 635
Iohn, dumb 305
Iohnson, Edward 444; John 651, 652;
    William 156, 160, 204, 430, 435
Ioynour, Robert 82
Ipswich (Ipswiche) 405
Iunour, Thomas 621

James I xvii, xl, xli, 504-9, 513-15, 549-57,
    558, 559, 582
James IV of Scotland 193
Jubbergate (Iowbritgate, Iubretgate, Iubritgate)
    11, 28, 85

Katherine, Queen 274
Kempton, Robert 593
Kendale, Mr 130
Kendall (Kendale) 76, 166, 299, 680
Kent, Earl of 195; John 651, 652
Ketlandes, Mr 355, 372; Thomas 346, 364
Kexby, James 83, 84
Key (Cay), Richard 85, 93
Kidd, Ralph 568
Kiddall, John 521; Robert 477
Kilburn, Thomas 93, 100, 105

King (Kinge, Kynge), Robert 144; William 377,
    442
King Street 270
King's Manor 507, 508, 515, 555-6, 588, 590-
    1, 596, 599, 604-7
Kingston upon Hull 73
Kirke, George 189; William 652
Knapton, Thomas 232
Knaresborough (Knaresburgh) 67
Knavesmire (Knairsmire, Knaresmyer, Knares-
    myre, Knarsimyer, Knarsmyer, Knavesmyer,
    Knavesmyre, Knavsmyre) 444, 445, 452,
    458, 463, 480, 481, 491, 513
Knolles, William 85
Kydd, Christopher 652
Kylborn, Agnes 635
Kyme, Earl of 76
Kyrkeby, Robert 37; William 33, 41
Kyrkham, John 41
Kytchynman 314
Kyver, Edward de la 180

Lambe, Lady 153; Thomas 231; William 153
Lampton, Mr 264
Lancashire 382
Lancaster (Loncastre, Loncastrie), Duke of
    637; Nicholas 172, 175
Langley, Ralph 652
Langton (Langtons), Mr 286, 288; John xi,
    201; Nicholas xi; William 395, 442
Lassyter See Leicester
Lathom, Beatrice 630
Latimer, Lord 195
Laurence (Lowrans), Martin 493; William 242
Laverock, Thomas 547
Lawne, Thomas 549
Layton, Roger 155
Learmouth, Christopher 377
Leche, Robert 37, 94
Led, Martin 473
Ledall (Ledell), John 654; Thomas 432;
    William 426, 655
Lee, John 629
Leeds (Ledes) 87

Leicester (Laycestr') 69
Leicester (Lassyter), Lord 436
Lelomes, Vincent 347
Lennox (Lenox, Linox, Lynnox), Duke of 521, 524, 550
Lepington, James 654
Lescrope See Scrope
Lesenbye (Lusenby), James 477, 511
Leund, John 426
Lewte (Lewtie), William 201, 434
Lightlope (Leghtlop), John 95
Limerick (Lymrick), Bishop of 515
Lincoln (Lyncoln) 66
Lincoln (Lincolln, Llincoln'), Earl of 132, 151
Lincolnshire 535
Lionis (Lionssis, Lyonesses, Lyonis), Henry 456, 478, 525, 530; William 473
Liscrop' See Scrope
Little (Litle), Richard 471, 472, 511, 529, 541
Little Stonegate See Swinegate
Liuereidge, Alice 408
Loftus, John 612
Loksmyth, Piers 82; William 264
Loncastre See Lancaster
Londell, Thomas 395
London (Lonndon) 69, 75, 105, 120, 131, 256, 326, 365, 538, 549, 584, 594
Longes (Longs), William 518, 540, 542
Lonsdell (Lonsdaylle, Lonsdellelles, Lonstell), Stephen 431, 461, 484, 489, 502; Thomas 380
Lorde, Brian 236, 240
Louth (Lowth) 535
Louth, Richard 55
Lovell (Louell), Lord 132; George 130; Thomas 169, 593
Lowes, John 231
Lowrans See Laurence
Lowther, Anthony 654
Loyter See Luter
Lullay (Lulley), William 389, 653, 655
Lumley, Thomas 66; William 66
Lunde, Mr Chamberlain 498; John 443
Lusenby See Lesenbye
Luter (Loyter) 75; Hugh 66, 69, 71; Richard 75

Lutton, Adam 37
Lylle, Lord 132
Lyndeles, John 319
Lynnox See Lennox
Lynton, John 636
Lytster (Litster, Lyster), Mr 264; John 99, 100, 220, 224, 228, 230, 231, 234, 236, 240, 242, 246, 247; Tristram 279

Magdalen Chapel (Maudlan Chappell, Mawdleyn Chapell) 198, 505, 507, 612
Maghame, Ralph 439
Makblith, Robert 652
Mald, John 652
Malkerall, Richard 277
Malson, William 651
Maltbie, Mr 406
Malum 100
Mamond, Robert 653
Man, John 50, 223; Robert 236
Maners, Humphrey 198-9
Manhoue, John 651
Manor, Mannor, Manner, Mannour etc See King's Manor
Marche, John 46; Richard 37, 38
Margaret 121; Princess xvii, 193-8, 199, 215
Market, Henry 55
Marshall (Marschall, Marsshall), Agnes 636; Henry 200; John 86, 118, 228, 652; Lawrence 93; Martin 654; Richard 651, 654; William 73, 433-4, 436, 656
Marshrudder (Mashruther), George 520, 571
Marstons, William 314
Marygate 198, 464
Mashruther See Marshrudder
Maskewe, Alderman 378; Thomas 404, 655
Mason (Masons) 412; Mr 377; John 218, 228, 236, 242, 246; Thomas 420, 421
Masters, William 474
Mattis, Stephen 426
Maulyuerer (Malyuerer, Maulyuerere), William 70, 71, 75
Mawd, John 391, 655; Robert 655
Maxfeildes (Maxfeldes), Chamberlain 537;

Mr 544, 548; John 530, 532

Maxwell, Brian 413; John 478; Richard 489; William 439

Mayson, William 653

Mell, William 243

Melton, Friar William xix

Meltonby (Meltynby), John 304, 314

Menerous, Alexander 101

Merchant Taylors' Hall 466

Mertyn, Richard 258, 260

Meryman, Thomas 231

Metcalf (Metcalfes), Henry 416, 418, 460; John 652, 655; John, the younger 381, 655; Martin 278, 298, 314; Percival 652; Thomas 155

Metham, Sir Thomas 66, 588

Michell, John 112; Robert 82

Micklegate (Mekelgate, Mikellith, Mikillith, Mykilgate, Myklegate) xxii, 29, 30, 84, 85, 101, 143, 243, 263, 298, 313, 357, 414, 547, 609 See also Bridgemasters' Account Rolls

Micklegate Bar (Mickleth Barr, Micklithbarr, Miklithbar, Mykkylgate Barr, Myklithe Barr) xxii, 130, 154, 155, 193, 194, 195, 215, 271, 272, 273, 486, 507, 578, 582, 583, 596, 599, 600, 601, 604, 609, 614 See also Bridgemasters' Account Rolls

Micklegate Ward (Myklitheward) 232, 247, 265, 319, 330, 599, 607

Middilton (Middleton, Middlyton, Midilton, Myddleton, Mydleton), George 416; Geoffrey 75; Richard 71, 530, 531; Thomas 37, 76; William 651

Midylham, John 37

Mikillith See Micklegate

Milford Haven 148

Millington, Edward 545, 563, 580

Milner (Mylner), Christopher 277; John 471, 477

Misterton, John 79

Mitkyn, George 281

Miton, Richard 144

Monkhus, Christopher 426

Monkward (Munckwarde) 281, 491, 607

Monteagles, Lord 488

Moore (Mower), Thomas 333, 347, 381, 383, 389, 393, 397, 402

Moray (Murrey), Bishop of 194

Morden, Lord 455

Moresby, William 202

Moreton, John 30, 31

Morlay, William 37, 38

Morton, Richard 654

Mosley (Moselay, Moseleye, Mosleye), Mayor 512; Alderman 450, 455, 459, 463, 480, 485; Mr 481; Thomas 379, 416, 655

Mosse (Mosees), John 33, 41; Michael 534

Mowbray, John 202; Thomas xlii

Mower See Moore

Moxon (Moxand), John 655; Thomas 402

Mudd (Mud), Henry 428, 656; James 485

Mullans, William 242-3, 264

Multon, John 37; Walter 37, 38

Munckman, Dennis 542

Murrey See Moray

Musgrefe, Richard 67

Mycklethwate, Ralph 654

Mydleton See Middilton

Myers, John 228, 231; Robert 389, 655

Myklithe See Micklegate

Mylner See Milner

Myrni, John 224

Nalton, John 632

Nandyke (Nendyke), Cuthbert 653; Thomas 91

Nawton (Nauton), William 224, 233, 236, 652

Neleson, John 264; William 183, 184, 189

Nelstron, Wilfred 653

Nendyke See Nandyke

Neuland, Richard 49-50

Nevyll (Neuell, Neuyll), Alexander 75; Henry 655; John 71; Thomas 69, 75

Newall, John 223

Neweburgh 197

Newcastle upon Tyne 66, 69, 75, 156

Newsome, William 358

Newton (Neuton, Neweton), John 45, 111, 131; Miles 234, 236; Thomas 340; William de 629

Newtour, Richard 651

Nicholson (Nicholsonn, Nicholsonne, Nicolson, Nyccolson, Nycholson), George 651; John 180; Richard 421; Robert 384, 472; Thomas 240, 243, 246, 247, 345, 472; William 442, 456, 511

Noble, Richard 655

Norfolk, Duke of 66, 71; Lord 75

Norman, George 241, 652; John 652; Robert 239

North, John 402, 655; Richard 653

North Street 11, 28, 101, 140, 232, 633

Northampton 193, 194

Northumberland, Earl of x, 67, 69, 70, 72, 76, 132, 194; Countess of 195

Norton (Nortonnes, Nortons, Nortton), James 408; Miles 443, 451, 467, 472, 478

Norwich (Norwiche), Bishop of 194

Nottingham (Notingham, Notyngham) 72, 237

Novell, Henry 379

Nunnery Lane See Baggergate

Nyccolson, Nycholson See Nicholson

Oghtred, Robert 66

Ogle (Ogill), Lord 455; Robert 68, 71

Orgoner, William 621

Otley, Edward 520

Ouresby, William 34

Oureum, Thomas 633

Ouse Bridge (House Brigge, Owse Brige, Pontem Vse, Vuse Brigge) xii, xxii, 3, 34, 36, 51, 85, 88, 98, 111, 119, 124, 130, 140, 141, 148, 156, 182, 189, 190, 202, 204, 207, 209, 210, 213, 263, 278, 306, 308, 313, 320, 366, 549, 554, 558, 620, 639

Ouse River 91, 415, 549, 554, 586

Ousegate (Owsgate, Vsegate) 33-4, 119, 141, 272, 278, 356, 414

Outhwhate, William 654

Owen, Sir David 151

Owsherby, Anthony 654

Oxford (Oxinforde), Earl of 150, 151; Lord of 539

Pacock, Pacoke See Paycock

Page, John 531

Pageant Green See Toft Green

Paicock See Paycock

Palace of the Archbishop of York See York, Archbishop of, Palace of,

Pannall, John 84

Pantur See Paynter

Parke, Thomas 202

Parker (Parcour, Parkour), Thomas 205, 230-1, 366

Parkyn, Robert 231

Parot, Peter 93, 101, 144

Paton, Robert 9

Pavement (Pauimentum, Paveniement, Pavimentum) 11, 29, 85, 93, 106, 144, 184, 234, 243, 246, 356, 406, 414, 556, 589

Paycock (Pacock, Pacoke, Paicock, Paycocke, Paycok, Paycoke), Mr 356; Gregory 313, 653; Robert 371, 373, 375, 380, 407, 652, 655; Walter 573; William 463, 480, 654

Paynter (Pantur, Payntour), David 37-8, 58; Nicholas 319; Richard 96; Thomas 318; William 318

Pearson (Peareson, Peirson, Pereson, Person, Persson) 500, 508; Mr 425, 431, 437; George 567, 570; Nicholas 111, 118; Robert 651; William 111, 406, 410, 423, 453

Pease, Richard 306, 653

Peaseholme Green (Pesholme, Pyssome) 378, 449; Chapel 73

Peghan (Peighinge), John 653; Thomas 437, 656

Penbrook, Earl of, Chamberlain of England 550

Penpugh, Thomas 160

Penven, Mr 558

Penyngton (Pennyngton), John 67; William 343, 653

Pepper, Richard 428

Percelvels 292

Percy (Percey) x; Henry xlii, 70, 71, 76 See also Poynings; John, of Cleueland' 72; Thomas 67, 72

Pereson See Pearson

Perry (Perrie), Mr 580; William 593

Person, Persson See Pearson

Peter Lane Little 306, 308, 319

Peteres, William 456

Petergate (Pettergate) 11, 28, 184, 264, 279

Petty 317

Phillipa of Hainault xlii

Pierson See Pearson

Pinder, Robert 529

Piper, Joan 66

Plasket, Mr 280; Richard 653

Plomer, James 587, 603; William 105

Plompton (Plomipton, Plumpton), Richard
220, 224, 652; William 68, 72, 75

Pocklington (Pokelynaton) 69

Pontefract (Pomfrete) 120, 131, 156, 549, 584

Porter, Thomas 434

Portyngton 133

Potell, John 37

Potman 133

Pottowe, Robert 79

Powle, Richard 220, 224

Poynings (Poynynges, Puynynges), Lord 70,
76; Lord Henry 76 See also Percy

Prest See Prust

Preston (Prestons), Christopher 563; Henry 48;
John 34; William 34

Privy Seal, Lord 269

Proctor, Henry 426

Prussia (Pruys) 53

Prust (Prest), Anthony 419, 421

Prynce, Henry 319

Pudsay (Puddesay, Puddeszay, Puddezay,
Pudesay), Ralph 65, 66, 70, 71; Thomas 70;
William 75

Pullen, Mr 257; George 653; John 418; Peter
654

Pulley, Anthony 653, 655

Pulleyn (Pulleynes), Mrs 546; Henry 366

Pullinge, John 436

Puynynges See Poynings

Pycher, John 159

Quharton, Michael 651

Quonyenx Strete See Coney Street

Raby, Richard 58, 159

Raby Castle (Rabie Castle) 607

Race, Henry 653

Radclyf (Radclyff), John 34; Nicholas 73

Raines, Thomas 438

Ramston (Rampston'), Thomas 75, 76

Rasyn (Rasyng), John 651; Thomas 652

Raton Row (Ratanraw, Rattonrawe) 134
See also Bridgemasters' Account Rolls

Rawcliffe (Rocliff) 591

Rawlyn (Rawlyns) 506; Richard 159, 174

Rayncoke (Ranecock), Edward 314, 653

Redeman, Edward 227

Remyngton, John 653

Reveley (Reweley, Riveles), John 525, 541

Revetour, William xv, xvi, 78, 80, 88

Richard II x, xi, xvii, xxxiv, xlii, 590

Richard III ix, x, xvii, xxxv, 130-1, 132-3

Richardson (Rechardson, Richardsns,
Richardsones, Richerdson), Lady 460;
John 231; Ralph 372, 655; Thomas 167,
173-4, 434, 462; William 522, 548

Richmond, Duke of 240

Rigg, Thomas 426

Rilandes, Edward 518

Ripon (Rypon) 191

Riveles See Reveley

Roberto 75

Robinson (Robynson), Doctor 318; Alderman
416, 485; Mr 272, 514; John 58, 426;
Lawrence 654; Miles 220, 224; Peter 652;
Richard 391; William 133, 134, 179, 339,
391, 447, 655

Robson, Hugh 227; Roland 144

Rock (Rocke), John 401

Roger, Mr 306; Thomas 292

Rokeby, John 369

Rokesbie, Miles 542

Rooke, Thomas, the elder 160; the younger
160

Roos, Robert 66

Rose, George 430, 656

Ross (Rosse), Sheriff 480; Mr 486; George
473-4

Rothley, John 187

Rowes, William 76

Ruddestan, John de 5

Rusker, Anthony 426; John 426

Russell, Richard 37, 47, 53, 101; William 206, 651

Rutland, Earl of 539

Ruttre, Isabel 305

Ryche, John 380

Ryder, James 426; Nicholas 426

Ryuers, Earl of 151

Sadler, Thomas 222, 226, 230, 244

St Andrew Gate Corner 184

St Asaph (Assaphensis), Bishop of 132

St Crux Church (Croux Chyrch) 130

St David's, Bishop of 132

St George's Chapel 310

St George's Close 318

St Helen's Church 633

St Helen's in Stonegate (St Ellens in Staingate) 526

St James' Chapel 132, 139

St John's Church, Micklegate xxxviii, 85, 93, 313, 356, 429, 473-4, 478, 498, 604

St Martin's Church, Coney Street xxviii, 374, 413, 427, 429, 432-4, 437, 440, 444, 447-8, 451-2, 457-8, 462-3, 467-8, 474-5, 479, 485, 490-1, 495, 499, 504, 519-20

St Martin-cum-Gregory, Micklegate xxxviii, 427, 432, 439-40, 444-5, 448-9, 452, 458, 468, 474, 479, 485, 490, 495, 504, 513, 518-9, 608, 610, 613

St Mary ad Valvas 3

St Mary's Abbey x, xv, 215, 250

St Mary's Abbey, Abbot of 74, 146, 151, 169, 196

St Mary's Church, Bishophill 631

St Mary's, Manor of See King's Manor

St Michael's Church, Spurriergate xxxvii-xix, 219, 230, 238, 249, 266, 268, 270, 278, 281, 282-3, 285, 287, 485, 490, 495, 498-9, 504, 513-14, 519, 559

St Thomas' Hospital 154, 155

St William's Chapel, Ouse Bridge 51, 88, 124, 272

Salisbery, William 87

Salisbury (Sar', Sarem), Earl 69, 70, 71, 72, 73, 75; Lord 66, 68, 70, 75, 77; Bishop of 74

Sandwith, Anthony 656

Sauage (Sauadge, Savadg), James 654; John 66, 72, 75; William 653

Saunderson, Nicholas 101

Sawer (Saweres), Richard 93, 95, 101, 291; Roger 522

Say, Lord de 72

Saynell, John 77

Scalby, John 101, 105

Scatchley (Scatcley), Richard 515, 516

Scauceby (Scausby), Thomas 61, 79, 85, 93, 100; William 105

Schorthouse, Anthony 190-1

Sclater, William 187

Scoreburgh, William 49

Scotland 194, 504, 549, 556, 584, 600, 607, 612; a Scot 624

Scott (Scot, Skott, Skotte) 528, 539; Alderman 614; John 440, 475; Thomas 155; William 375, 583, 655

Scrafton, Mr 608, 610; Lancelot 579, 580

Scragge, John 37

Scrope (Lescrope, Liscrop', Scrop), Lord, of Bolton 67, 70, 75, 151; Archbishop Richard x, xlii, 637

Sedale See Siddall

Selby, Abbot of 74

Selby (Selbe, de Seleby), Percival 280; William xlii, 5-6, 26

Sell, William 428, 431

Seller (Sellerer), Richard 438, 502, 529

Semper, John 111

Setherthwaite, Mr 611

Setterwhites, Charles 573

Settle, Christopher 526

Sewell, Thomas 426

Shandos See Chandos

Sharp (Sherp), Robert 651; William 180

Shathelok, John 33

Shawe (Chaw, Shaw), Henry 652; John 189, 652; Peter 653; Richard 134; Thomas 304

Sheffield (Sheffeild), Lord Edmund 550

Sherman, John 651

Sherwod (Shirwod, Shrewodd) 87; Agnes 636; John 93

Sheyne, Robert 143

Shrewesbury, Earl of 151

Shypton (Shipton), James 233, 240, 242, 246, 247

Shyrley (Shirley), Robert 133-4

Siddall (Sedale, Siddelles, Sydall, Syddall), Lawrence 291; Richard 390, 392, 395, 461; William 529, 531

Siggeswik (Sigswicke), Adam 133; Thomas 495

Sigismund (Segismond, Sigismond), Emperor 586, 601

Simnell, Lambert x

Simpson See Symson

Sindwith, Anthony 412

Skarr, Ambrose 433, 434

Skayffees, Charles 364

Skeldergate (Skeldargate, Skeldrgate) 11, 28, 140, 318, 638

Skelton 591

Skelton (Skeltones), Mr 306; John 116; Robert 426; Steven 306

Skott, Skotte See Scott

Skotton, Thomas 92

Skrueton (Scrueton), Robert 37, 44

Skyrmer, Henry 34; John 34

Slater (Slaters), Thomas 881; William 304

Smalwod, Roger 200

Smarthwayte, Cuthbert 277

Smeght, Garnett 96

Smith (Smithe, Smithes, Smyth, Smythe, Smythes, Smyths), Mr 506; Christopher 453, 454, 460, 469; George 546; Gregory 372; Henry 272, 510; John 101, 105, 167, 168, 173-4, 243, 526; Marmaduke 284, 290; Peter 381, 655; Robert 313, 653; Thomas 167, 653; William 232, 426, 481

Smythies, John 402, 655

Snaudon, Thomas 48, 50

Snawes, John 530

Somers, Sir Charles of 151

Somersete 71, 76; John 77

Sotheby (Suddybie), Marmaduke 383, 655

Sowreby, Margaret 630

Spede, William 72

Spenser, John 651

Spicer, Thomas 187

Spofford, Church of 138

Spoford (Spoforde), Thomas 633, 638

Spon, John 154

Spurriergate (Sporyer gate) 264

Stafford (Staferd, Staffordes), Lord 382, 403, 430

Staith 313, 415

Stalby, John 93

Stamper, John 295, 319

Stanburne (Staynburn, Staynburne), John 49, 50; Robert 314, 653; William 421

Standish, Richard 130

Stanhope, Doctor 590

Stanley (Stanelay), Lord 132; Thomas 654

Staveley (Staueley, Stavelay), Mr 206; Agnes 228; Alan 187, 213, 224, 651; Thomas 651; William 651

Staynburn See Stanburne

Steresacre, Thomas 37

Sterop (Stirop'), Henry 77, 79

Stevenson (Stevynson), Mr 364; Humphrey 246, 247

Steyn Cowkes See Cowkes

Steynour, Thomas 78

Stirley See Styrlay

Stockdal (Stokdale), Christopher 653; John 189, 194

Stodderd, Robert 243

Stokton, Robert 87

Stone, John 581

Stonegate (Staingate, Stanegate, Stayngate) 28, 53, 85, 93, 101, 105, 130, 142, 247, 264, 298, 314, 526

Stosyn, Abraham 426

Strange (Straunge, Strawng'), Lord 132, 195

Strikland, William 369

Strins, John 213

Strynger, John 133-4

Stubbes, William 159

Studley (Studly), Richard 243, 247

Stultyng, John 631

Style, Simon del 34

Styllynton, Katherine 635

Styrlay (Stirley), Richard 224, 228
Suddybie See Sotheby
Suffolk (Sothfolk', Southff', Southfolch', Suffockes, Suthffolch), Duke of 76; Earl of 70, 269; Lord of 70, 72, 436
Surrey (Surre), Earl of 132, 194; Lord of 194 See also Arundell and Surrey
Sussex, Earl of 273; Lord of 396, 430, 435, 455
Sutton, John de 52
Swath, John 85
Swinbanke, Roland 529
Swinegate (Swynegale) 142
Sydall, Syddall See Siddall
Sylton, John 46
Symond, John 41
Symson, Mr xxxii, 348; Thomas 426, 653
Synowez, William, Abbot of St Mary's 169, 174

Tadcaster 146, 193, 611
Tadcaster Bridge 138, 139, 193, 195, 549, 584, 600, 609, 613
Tailboys (Tailbois), Walter 69, 70, 75, 76
Tailliour (Tayllour), Matthew 231; Thomas 651
Talbot, John 76
Talkan, Robert 28
Tanfeld, Thomas 44, 631
Tankdale, Richard 426
Tart (Tarte) 76; John 77
Tawnte, John 651
Tayllour See Tailliour
Tele (Thelle), William 95
Tempesse 155
Temple, Leonard 357, 653, 668
Tenant, Ralph 652, 653
Tenniswodd, James 408
Terre, George 444
Tesshe, Tristram 256
Thelle See Tele
Thomas the Master of Corpus Christi 238
Thomlynson, Christopher 101; Lawrence 279
Thomson (Thompson, Thomsom, Thomsonne,

Tompson), wife of 364; Brian 653; Christopher 496, 501, 509, 523, 526, 527, 536, 538; Cuthbert 453, 454, 460, 469, 470, 476, 482, 488, 496, 499; David 461, 473, 511; Henry 437, 463, 507, 583, 656; John 651, 652; Leonard 614; Martin 426; Richard 180; Robert 461; Thomas 437; William 112, 522
Thorne (Thoren, Thorn), James 652; Richard de 647; Robert 651
Thornell, John 653
Thorneton 353
Thornton (Thorneton), Mr 318; John 231; Richard 189; Thomas 652
Thorp, William de xvi, 3
Thowe, Peter 460, 461
Thowetson, Robert 265
Three Kings, The, Micklegate 313
Thuayter, wife of 180
Tirry, John 105
Titlowe, Walter 440
Todde, William 152, 155
Toft Green (Pagent Grene, Pagyant Garthe, Toftes) xxii, 5, 35, 192, 208, 209, 218, 219, 254, 345, 348, 350, 351, 354, 357, 362, 364, 371, 373, 375, 379, 382, 383, 390, 391, 394, 398, 402, 404, 412, 424, 428, 431, 436, 437, 442, 547 See also Bridgemasters' Account Rolls
Toller (Tollerer), wife of John 100, 105
Tollerton 5
Tong (Tonge), John 111, 112, 114, 115, 118, 129, 131
Topcliffe 514
Tournor See Turner
Townend, John 653
Trewe (Trew), Mr 485; Andrew 378, 416, 463, 512-3, 654
Trinity Priory See Holy Trinity Priory
Troubleveile See Turburvile
Troughton, John 384
Tubbar, Thomas 85
Tunstall, Richard 70, 162, 163
Turburvile (Troubleveile), Sir John 151, 155
Turner (Tournor, Turners), Christopher 485; Michael 439, 456, 457; Thomas 413, 484

Turton, George 654
Tyler, Robert 218
Tymanson, Lambert 144
Tyssone, William 449

Vaghain, John 363
Vale, William 652
Vance, William 209
Vaux, John 581, 582
Vavasour (Vavasor) 146; Mayor 506
Vicars, Simon 206
Vkkerbe, Thomas 421
Vnderwod, Joan 72
Vsclyff (Vsclyf), Thomas 64, 670
Vsflete, Nicholas 55

Wad, James 279
Wade See Waid
Wadsworth (Wadsworthe), Mr 463; John 430, 656
Wafferer (Waferer), John 66, 69, 71, 76; Robert 66, 68, 69, 70, 71, 73, 75, 76
Waghen, Robert de 5
Waid (Wade, Wayd), Francis 430, 656; Lawrence 442, 656
Waite (Wayte), wife of John 267; William 424
Wakefelde, Batildis 637
Wakefield 67, 521
Walker, Mr 609; Annes 277; Brian 502; John 462, 463; Richard 12; Robert 93; Roger 319
Waller, Lancelot 433
Walmgate Bar 243, 273
Walmgate Ward 247, 265, 319, 330, 407, 607
Walron (Walron'), Gilbert 220, 224
Walton, Robert 325
Wansforth, wife of Thomas 636
Warde (Ward), Anthony 474; Richard 541; Thomas 228, 263, 278; William 495
Wardell, Thomas 426
Wark, John 180
Warneby, William de 9
Warwick (Warrwick), Countess of 94

Warter, William 41
Warwyk, Edmund 651
Water Lane 392
Waterhouse, John 111
Waterton, Robert 69
Wath (Wathe), John 93, 652
Watkinson, George 436
Watman, Mr 611; John 446
Watson, Mr 313; Cuthbert 385; Henry 85, 119, 121, 144; John 402, 449, 454, 460, 469; 470, 476, 482, 488; 496; 499, 500, 501, 509, 517, 520, 523, 527, 528, 536, 538, 567, 637, 655; Richard 41, 637; Thomas 111; William 412, 653, 654, 656
Watter (Water), Christopher 447, 462, 468, 475, 479, 485, 491, 495, 499; Robert 176
Wawle, Percival 474
Wayd See Waid
Wayte See Waite
Weddall, Geoffrey 444
Weddrell (Wedderall), Mr 316; John 652
Wedowis, Edward 439
Weller, William 442
Wells (Wellas, Welles, Wels), Lord 66, 72; Richard 105; Thomas 144; William 118, 123, 128
Welton, Alice de 630
Welughby See Willoughby
Wentbridge 120
Westminster 549, 584, 600
Westmorland, County of 556
Westmorland (Westmorl'), Earl 66, 71, 72, 76; Lord 66, 75
Westrope, Mr 514
Wetelay See Whetley
Wetewad, John 111
Wharton, wife of 202; Mr Francis 549; Mr [Humphrey] 549-50, 554; William 583
Wharye, John 653
Whetley (Wetelay, Whetlay) 67, 69; Robert 199
White (Whyte, Whytes), Mr 289; George 313; John 205, 207, 213, 366; Michael 111
Whitehilles, Anthony 542, 575
Whittingeton, Richard 448
Whitwell, John 519

Wickham, Doctor 588

Widdrington, Thomas 601, 606

Wilberfesse, Alan 118

Wild See Wyld

Wildyng, John 105

Wilkok, Mr 333

Wilkynson (Wylkynson), John 101, 105, 240, 242, 278

Willand, Leonard 654

William, Abbot of St Mary's See Synowez

Williamson (Wylliamson), Bennett 33; Henry 92; James 381, 655; Geoffrey 273; John 372; William 412, 656

Willoughby (Welughby, Willobies, Willowbies, Willughbie, Willughby, Wiloghby, Wilowby) 333; Lord 70, 72, 464; Christopher 356; Hugo de 66

Willye (Wylly), Robert 653

Wilman, Thomas 240

Wilson (Willson, Wilsons, Wylson) 411; Edward 411; George 384; Gilbert 243, 247; John 306; Richard 431; Robert 544; Thomas 463, 480, 493, 494, 502, 547, 559; William 395

Wiltshire, Earl of 151

Winchester, Bishop of 606; Dean of 605

Wiseman (Wisemanees, Wysseman), Robert 446, 461; Nicholas 291

Wistow (Wistoe) 440

Woid See Wood

Wood (Wodde, Wode, Woid), Mr 514; Henry 241, 246, 247, 652, 653; John 654; William 394, 655

Wooller, William 656

Worcester (Worster, Worsters, Worsyter, Worsyters, Wygo(...)), Earl of 418, 442, 455, 464, 486, 488; Bishop of 132

Wormall (Wormemall), Mr 415, 420, 423; John 432

Wowar, Lancelot 330

Wrangle 82

Wrangwish (Wranghwys, Wrangwayssh, Wrangwishe, Wrangwysh, Wrangwyssh), Thomas xliii, 93, 107-8, 118, 125, 131, 134, 165

Wresill, Henry 27, 134

Wright (Wrighte), James 496, 497; Nicholas 329, 333, 338; Richard 373, 377; Thomas 93, 510; William 373, 521, 524, 529, 531, 534, 537, 539, 541, 542

Wrightman, John 366

Wyggen, Richard 281

Wylardby, George 632

Wyld (Wild, Wildes, Wyldes), Lady 264; Mr 241; Robert 231, 234, 246, 247, 325, 651, 652

Wylliamson See Williamson

Wylkynson See Wilkynson

Wylly See Willye

Wyllyson, Thomas 253

Wylson See Wilson

Wyman, Agnes 631, 637; Henry 11, 28, 637; John 37, 38

Wysseman See Wiseman

Wystow, Robert 634

W(.)ssen, John 293

Yhedyngham, Richard de xvi, 3

Yolton, Steven de 5

York, Archbishop of x, 51, 135, 138, 150, 151, 191, 196, 197, 368, 369, 378, 390, 550, 555, 637, 642, 647

York, Archbishop of, palace of 133, 150, 155, 196

York, Archdeacon of 133, 588

York, Duke of 66, 70, 72, 73, 85

York, Suffragan Bishop of 196

York (Yorke, 3ork), Bartholomew 241, 652; John 637; Richard 95, 128, 138, 155, 168, 172, 183

York Minster (St Peter's) xiii, xxxv, 46, 59, 79, 102, 122, 126, 132, 150, 155, 161, 168, 178, 179, 182, 196-7, 202, 204, 208, 209, 211, 213, 223, 239, 254, 256, 261, 278, 279, 326, 354, 515, 555-6, 588, 604, 606, 624, 630, 646-7

York Minster, Dean of 354, 390

York Minster Chapter House 152, 196, 279, 555, 588

York Minster Gates xxxv, 11, 28, 101, 132, 135, 197, 264, 279, 298, 314, 356, 366, 406, 414, 418

Yorkshire 514, 549, 600, 605
Yorkshire, Sheriff of 198, 554, 605
Young (Yong, Younge), Doctor 605; John
    167, 547; Robert 167
Yoworthe, Mr 444

Zouche (Souche), Lord le 72; Archbishop de
    xv, xl, 1-2

3arom, William 55
3ork See York